LONDON : HUMPHREY MILFORD
OXFORD UNIVERSITY PRESS

THE GLOBE PLAYHOUSE

THE GLOBE PLAYHOUSE
Detail from Visscher's "View of London," 1606–1614
From the unique original in the Folger Shakespeare Library

THE GLOBE PLAYHOUSE

LONDON : HUMPHREY MILFORD
OXFORD UNIVERSITY PRESS

THE GLOBE PLAYHOUSE

Its Design and Equipment

By JOHN CRANFORD ADAMS

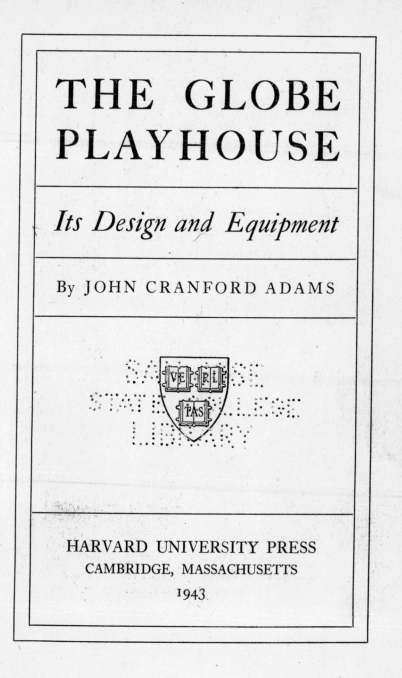

HARVARD UNIVERSITY PRESS
CAMBRIDGE, MASSACHUSETTS
1943

Second Printing

PRINTED AT THE HARVARD UNIVERSITY PRINTING OFFICE

CAMBRIDGE, MASS., U.S.A.

Preface

THE shape and the precise location of the Globe Playhouse have long been subjects of controversy. This is the more surprising because the panoramic views of London made in the first half of the seventeenth century contain clear representations of its exterior, and because a certified legal transcript of the original ground lease, minutely describing the Globe site and its boundaries in the Parish of St. Saviour's, Southwark, has been widely known for more than a generation.

Whether the Globe stood a few yards to the north or a few yards to the south of Maid Lane in no way affects an understanding of Shakespeare's plays. But it is important to the study of Shakespeare and his contemporary dramatists to understand the design of an Elizabethan playhouse and stage and the extent to which that stage was equipped with fixed or alterable scenery, with traps, machines, and properties — all helping to enlarge and sustain the scope and force of dramatic illusion.

It is important, for example, to know where the audience was placed in relation to any given unit of the multiple stage, and whether the inner stages (where such scenes as Othello's murder of Desdemona took place) were remote and dimly lighted or were in full view and well lighted. It revives some of the excitement Shakespearean audiences must have experienced to know that Lady Capulet came within an ace of finding Juliet pulling up the rope ladder by which Romeo had just descended, to learn how Antony was heaved aloft into Cleopatra's Monument, or to discover how the Vision of Jupiter appeared to the sleeping Posthumus. It is interesting to find that Shakespeare's method of staging the "Shew of Eight Kings" in *Macbeth* anticipated by sixty years a stage practice com-

monly regarded as originating in Restoration theatres; or
to discover that the warning delivered by Ariel to the enemies of Prospero was the occasion of a theatrical display
involving the first "free" flight from above in English
stage history. This scene from *The Tempest* also provides
the first instance of a visible actor (here Prospero) directing the alternating bursts of music and thunder which
guided (1) the dances of the "Shapes" on the outer stage
and (2) Ariel's sudden descent from and return into the
stage heavens. Unless the stage itself is known in its various details, Elizabethan theatrical technique cannot be
understood by modern readers.

The aim of this book is to reconstruct as fully as possible
the design and equipment of the Globe Playhouse. To
that end I have examined all available contemporary records bearing upon the subject — plays, dramatic enter-
tainments, playhouse documents, legal cases, letters, maps,
pamphlets, poems, and other material. And I have supple-
mented this examination by consulting stage historians for
the results of their specialized inquiries into the dating and
authorship of plays, the records of theatre ownership, the
organization of dramatic companies, and other matters
closely allied to the subject. I have then tried to examine
each problem in the light of all the pertinent evidence, proceeding systematically through the playhouse from part to
part, considering first the structure as a whole, next the
auditorium, and finally the multiple stage. The outcome
of this method of study, together with a fairly complete
citation of the evidence, is embodied in this book. The
total result, doubtless still subject in many ways to cor-
rection, constitutes, I believe, the first attempt at a complete and unified reconstruction of the Globe Playhouse.

The text and footnotes will show my indebtedness to
the many scholars who, through the years, have discovered and made accessible the great body of materials for a
study of the Elizabethan stage. Here I wish to express my
indebtedness: to the Trustees and Staff of the Folger

Shakespeare Library for a year of study in that matchless collection and for permission to reproduce a hitherto unpublished representation of the Globe from their unique copy of Visscher's View of London; to the authorities of the British Museum, the Harvard University Library, and the Cornell University Library for the opportunity to consult rare books and manuscripts; to the Cornell Trustee-Faculty Committee on Research for a contribution which lightened the task of preparing my manuscript for the press; and to my friends and colleagues, Professors A. M. Drummond, Morris Bishop, and R. C. Bald, and Professor John A. Hartell of the College of Architecture, for many helpful suggestions.

Above all I am indebted to Dr. Joseph Quincy Adams, Director of the Folger Shakespeare Library, for generous assistance during the progress of the work and for giving my manuscript the benefit of his expert and friendly criticism.

J. C. A.

Ithaca, New York
March, 1942

Contents

Illustrations

Key to Abbreviations

Throughout the notes I have used the short title entered in the left column when citing one of the texts named below:

Adams   Adams, Joseph Q. *Shakespearean Playhouses.* Boston and New York, 1917.

Chambers   Chambers, E. K. *The Elizabethan Stage.* 4 vols. Oxford, 1923.

Henslowe's Diary   *Henslowe's Diary.* Edited by W. W. Greg. 2 vols. London, 1904–1908.

Henslowe Papers *Henslowe Papers.* Edited by W. W. Greg. London, 1907.

Lawrence   Lawrence, W. J. *The Elizabethan Playhouse and Other Studies.* Stratford-upon-Avon, 1912. *Second Series,* 1913.

Outlines   Halliwell-Phillipps, J. O. *Outlines of the Life of Shakespeare.* 2 vols. The eleventh edition. London, 1907.

Variorum (1821) *The Plays and Poems of William Shakespeare.* 21 vols. London, 1821. (The *Variorum* edition edited by James Boswell.)

Wallace   Wallace, C. W. *The Children of the Chapel at Blackfriars, 1597–1603.* Lincoln [Nebraska], 1908.

THE GLOBE PLAYHOUSE

Chapter I

THE GLOBE PLAYHOUSE

1. The Shape of the Globe

THE shape, size, and interrelationships of the many parts of the Globe stage and auditorium were determined or at least strongly influenced by the shape, size, and structure of the playhouse as a whole. I shall begin, therefore, by presenting evidence from contemporary maps and views that the Globe was a three-story octagonal structure surrounding an unroofed, octagonal yard. Then, after a brief survey of the Globe site, I shall proceed to the builder's contracts which show that the playhouse measured 84 feet between outside walls, 34 feet high to the eaves-line, and 58 feet across the interior yard.

The Globe is represented as octagonal in all but one of those panoramic London views which illustrate the Bankside between 1599, when the first Globe was erected, and 1644, when the second Globe was demolished. (Since this essential agreement among the views has not hitherto been recognized — a fundamental error having long obscured the problem — the evidence is set forth in Appendix A.) These views are six [1] in number: the Delaram, undated (1603–1620?); the Visscher, undated (1606–1614); the Visscher-Hondius, dated 1616; the Merian, included in Gottfried's *Neuwe Archontologia Cosmica*, published at Frankfurt in 1638; the Hollar, dated 1647; and the anony-

---

[1] The most complete of the undated so-called "Ryther" maps (*ca.* 1636–1645) shows two unidentified polygonal amphitheatres on the Bankside, but the date and sources of the map are so uncertain and the drawing of the amphitheatres is so unskilled that the map merits less attention than the six under discussion. See also Appendix A.

mous view in Howell's *Londinopolis*, published in 1657. In their presentation of the London scene these six views differ in countless ways, but on two matters pertaining to the present discussion they coincide with some exactness: all but one contain a labeled representation of the Globe (the exception is Delaram's view, in which the Globe is unlabeled), and all but one represent the Globe as octagonal (the exception this time is Hollar's view of 1647, which represents both the Globe and the Hope playhouses as cylindrical).

The value of Hollar's 1647 representation of the Globe, however, is negligible. The view [2] — engraved on six plates, each about 18¾ inches high and 15½ inches wide — was made not only while the artist was living in Holland and unable to return to England, but also some three years after the Globe had been demolished and five years after a Parliamentary edict had closed all such places of amusement. Two characteristics of the view reveal Hollar's lack of first-hand data, particularly with respect to certain landmarks in Southwark. In the first place he selected an actual viewpoint atop the tower of St. Saviour's instead of the imaginary "bird's eye" viewpoint — higher in the air and considerably farther back from the Thames — as used by Visscher and others. By this means he places parts of Southwark behind him and reduces the angle of incidence with the horizon; in other words, he gains the effect of realism as a whole but at the same time escapes the necessity of having to exhibit cartographical or pictorial details. Except for the areas immediately before him (areas supplied imaginatively; all other records deny his extensive rows of houses lying between St. Saviour's and the Thames), he is able for the most part to limit his repre-

---

[2] Reproduced in exact facsimile by The London Topographical Society, 1907; and in photographic reduction by A. M. Hind in *Wenceslaus Hollar and his views of London and Windsor in the Seventeenth Century*, 1922. Hind's catalogue of Hollar's studies of London reveals the artist's inattention to buildings in Southwark. A biographical sketch of Hollar is given on pp. 1–8.

sentation to rooftops and to the outstanding landmarks of London. In the second place, he used the device of perspective from a fixed point in order to focus attention upon the middle plates of his view (containing the prominent buildings and spires of the City proper), with the result that he minimizes the size and importance of such suburbs north or south of the Thames as are included in the end plates. For these reasons his representation of the Globe, which is in the first full-sized plate counting from the left end of the view, appears at an exaggerated distance to the west of St. Saviour's and is but half as high and only slightly wider than a quite modest dwelling standing by the riverbank on the center line of the assembled sheets.

On examining the two playhouses included in the Hollar view, marked respectively "The Globe" and the "Beere bayting h[ouse]" or Hope, one finds that in almost every detail which can be tested by other sources of information its presentation is inaccurate. (1) Although the Globe is placed relative to the Thames much as in other maps, its neighbor, the Hope, which unquestionably lay between Maiden Lane and the Thames and to the west of the Globe, is here found at some distance south of the river and to the east of the Globe. (2) Hollar's Globe is drawn with a vague peak in the roof over one portion of the gallery frame, but without "huts" over its stage despite the fact that without them the actors could not have produced *deus ex machina* scenes. On the other hand, the Bear Garden or Hope is shown with large twin-gabled huts extending over fully one-half the open yard inside the building, although that amphitheatre, designed with a removable platform stage and used much of the time for those sports which are indicated by its more familiar name, had less need of full-sized "huts" than any other playhouse. (3) No animal pens appear in either playhouse lot, although they are specified in the contract for the Hope and are included in other views of that building. (4) The Globe is drawn with a flagpole rising high (but not upright) from the inner yard;

other maps and the drawing of the Swan interior indicate that playhouse flagpoles rose above the "hut" and at one side of the frame. The Hope, as represented by Hollar, is provided with a turret surmounted by an onion-shaped dome, but lacks a flagpole. (5) The flag on the Globe flagpole is marked conspicuously with a St. George's or Greek cross, yet no mention of the cross either for the Globe or for the Hope is found in any one of the numerous references to playhouse flags, nor is it shown in the larger representations of playhouse flags by Visscher and Visscher-Hondius.[3]

These particular errors — and there are others — show that Hollar's representation of the Globe is conventionalized and thoroughly untrustworthy. It does not follow, however, that Hollar has mistakenly interchanged the names of the Globe and the Hope;[4] neither representation meets the known requirements of either of those structures.

If, then, we exclude Hollar's view from the list of maps which reliably inform us as to the exterior of the Globe, we find that the remaining maps show without exception an octagonal building. And they are the more to be trusted for the reason that all but one were published while the first and the second Globe were still in existence. Such unanimity among these strictly contemporary maps verges on proof of the octagonal shape of the building. However short of finality that evidence may be, it is at least immeasurably more convincing than any other existing evidence to the contrary. Although three of the five maps are in varying degrees derived from Visscher's original, they do not on that account lack authority. The fact that Delaram, in making the chief landmarks of the prominent foreground of his view conform to the Bankside prospect in the coronation year 1603, represented an octagonal

---

[3] Crosses appear on the flags flying above the two pre-Globe amphitheatres included in the small Bankside view by Hondius published in Speed's *Theatre of the Empire of Great Britaine*, 1611.

[4] The suggestion advanced by W. W. Braines in *The Site of the Globe Playhouse Southwark*, 1924 (second edition), p. 60.

Globe is strong evidence that the original Visscher and its several derivatives are correct.

The original Visscher view (1606–1614), signed "*Visscher excudit*" in the lower left-hand corner, survives in a unique copy which I had the good fortune to discover in the Folger Shakespeare Library. The view was engraved on four plates, each plate producing an impression measuring 16⅛ inches high and 21⅝ inches wide (in the Folger copy the sides of the impressions from Plates II and III have at some time been slightly cropped). Prominent buildings and landmarks are named in English (with a few exceptions, for example Westminster Hall is labeled "Konigs Pallast"), among them the Swan, the "Bear Gardne," and the Globe, all conspicuous in the Bankside foreground. In beauty, in completeness of detail, and in skillful execution this original Visscher view easily surpasses any other seventeenth-century view of London.[5]

The first Visscher derivative, marked "Visscher delineavit: Hondius lusit" and dated 1616, was developed from the more artistic and painstaking original — so much is obvious at a glance; but no corresponding objects are identical in matters of detail, and certain large areas are entirely unlike Visscher's representation. Even the angle of view has been changed. The Hondius drawing of the Globe, however, is an almost line-for-line copy of the Visscher original, the only important differences appearing in the position of the "huts" relative to one another and in the pronounced taper which the engraver, without justification, chanced to impart to the outer walls as they rise towards the eaves. It may be recorded, therefore, that Hondius in 1616 made changes or corrections freely while

[5] The Folger copy has, mounted on the top, a large title, not a part of the original map, approximately 1½ inches high and bearing the inscription "LONDINUM FLORENTISSMA BRITANNIÆ URBS, EMPORIUMQUE TOTO ORBE CELEBERRIMUM" formed of white roman letters outlined in ink by a black ground. It was added by some early owner, who mounted the plates and had them glazed.

copying Visscher's map, but did not see fit in any important respect to depart from Visscher's representation of the Globe.

The second Visscher derivative is by Merian, dated 1638. Except that Merian works to a smaller scale, he copies the original "Visscher excudit" map with considerable fidelity so far as London north of the Thames is concerned, but in his Southwark foreground he appears to have followed the deeper foreground of the Visscher-Hondius map, with still other additions supplied either from his imagination or from some map as yet unidentified. While he was deliberately introducing these alterations in his view of Southwark Merian could readily have changed the shape of the Globe had Visscher's representation of that building been incorrect. Merian's Globe, however, is a fairly accurate reproduction of the Visscher-Hondius Globe.

The *Londinopolis* map of 1657 is an indifferent copy of Merian, and therefore has little independent authority. However slight its value, it does none the less continue the tradition of an octagonal Globe and supports the four more important maps made while that playhouse was actually in existence.

No more needs to be said to establish the importance of the original Visscher map in a study of the Globe exterior. It is clearly the most authoritative contemporary panorama of London in the first half of the seventeenth century, and as such its representation of the Globe (which I have reproduced for my frontispiece) is more valuable and trustworthy than any other. This relatively large drawing of the playhouse — it measures 2½ inches high (to the top of the flagpole), and slightly more than 1½ inches wide — records for us the following details of primary importance: the building was outwardly octagonal with a concentric octagonal court or yard inside; windows were inserted in the exterior walls at three levels, suggesting three stories; the eight sections of the gallery-frame forming the shell

of the playhouse were roofed; and on the southwest side
of the frame, apparently overhanging some portion of the
inner yard, rose a cluster of small buildings or "huts" with
a central turret surmounted by a flagpole and a large, unmarked, white flag.

2. THE NATURE OF THE GLOBE PROPERTY

Some notion of the composition and extent of the Globe
Playhouse property is given by the ground lease drawn up
on Christmas Day, 1598, and signed on February 21, 1598/
99, by Nicholas Brend (the owner, who also owned various
other parcels of land in Southwark) and by the syndicate
(composed of seven men: Richard and Cuthbert Burbage,
William Shakespeare, John Heminges, Augustine Phillips,
Thomas Pope, and William Kempe) planning the new
playhouse. No copy of the original lease has yet been
found, but a certified transcript, entered in the course of
litigation in 1616 between Thomasine Ostler and her
father, John Heminges, was discovered in 1909 by Dr.
C. W. Wallace in the *Coram Rege Roll*.[6] Since the entire
document has been reprinted more than once,[7] I cite here
merely those portions (as translated by Dr. Wallace [8])
which describe the property:

All that parcel of ground just recently before enclosed and made into
four separate garden plots, recently in the tenure and occupation of
Thomas Burt and Isbrand Morris, diers, and Lactantius Roper, salter,
citizen of London, containing in length from east to west two hundred
and twenty feet in assize or thereabouts, lying and adjoining upon a
way or lane there on one [the south] side, and abutting upon a piece of
land called The Park upon the north, and upon a garden then or recently
in tenure or occupation of one John Cornishe toward the west, and upon

[6] *Ostler v. Hemings, Coram Rege Roll* 1454, 13 Jac. I, Hilary Term, M. 692.
For an account of the proceedings see C. W. Wallace, *The* [London] *Times*,
Oct. 2 and 4, 1909; also April 30, 1914.

[7] It is given in full in the Shakespeare *Jahrbuch*, XLVI. 235 ff.; the portions
describing the Globe property are reprinted by Chambers, ii. 416–417.

[8] Cited from Adams, pp. 241–243. See also his sketch of the property according to the terms of the lease and other sources.

another garden plot then or recently in the tenure or occupation of one John Knowles toward the east, with all the houses, buildings, structures, ways, easements, commodities, and appurtenances thereunto belonging. . . And also all that parcel of land just recently before enclosed and made into three separate garden plots, whereof two of the same [were] recently in the tenure or occupation of John Roberts, carpenter, and another recently in the occupation of one Thomas Ditcher, citizen and merchant tailor of London . . . containing in length from east to west by estimation one hundred fifty and six feet of assize or thereabouts, and in breadth from the north to the south one hundred feet of assize by estimation or thereabouts, lying and adjoining upon the other side of the way or lane aforesaid, and abutting upon a garden plot there then or recently just before in the occcupation of William Sellers toward the east, and upon one other garden plot there, then or recently just before, in the tenure of John Burgram, sadler, toward the west, and upon a lane there called Maiden Lane towards the south, with all the houses. . .

A precise plotting of this Globe property together with the adjoining gardens and other boundaries mentioned in the lease is given by Mr. W. W. Braines in *The Site of the Globe Playhouse in Southwark* (1924).[9]

Because the land in that section of the Bankside where the Globe was built had formerly been a marsh, much of it was still undeveloped or had only recently been drained and divided into garden plots. There seems to have been a ditch between the Globe property and the Bishop of Winchester's Park on the one side, and unquestionably there was a ditch or sewer between the property and Maid Lane on the other. On February 14, 1605/6, the owners of the Globe were ordered by the Surrey Sewers Commission —

before the xxth day of Aprill next well and sufficientlye [to] pyle boorde and fill vp viij poles more or lesse of theire warfe [i.e. ditch embank-

[9] Frontispiece, and pp. 39 and 44. Despite the terms of the ground lease, the evidence of all contemporary Bankside views, and the implications of the Surrey sewer records, Mr. Braines contends that the Globe lay to the *south* of Maid Lane. Since the appearance of the second edition of his book this contention has prevailed. (*On the Site of the Globe Playhouse of Shakespeare*, by George Hubbard, published in 1923, presents the arguments of those maintaining that the Globe lay to the *north* of Maid Lane.)

ment] against theire said Play house vpon pain to forfeit for every pole
then left vndone xx*s*.[10]

A second order from the Sewers Commission dated the
same day reads:

that Burbidge and Heminges and others, the owners of the Playhouse
called the Globe in Maid-Lane shall before the xxth day of Aprill next
pull vp and take cleane out of the Sewar the props or postẹs which stand
vnder their bridge on the north side of Mayd-lane vpon paine to forfeit xx*s*.[11]

Despite these orders of the commissioners, however, the
ditch between the playhouse property and Maid Lane was
eventually filled in.   According to a record of July 6, 1653:

The Jurie of the Sewers for the East parte of Surrey vpon their Oathes
Saie That vpon a viewe made of the Sewer in Maide Lane nere the place
where the Globe Playhouse lately stood Doe present that there is 80.[tie]
yards or thereaboute at the head of the said Sewer Stopt and filled
vp and fortie yards or thereabouts built vpon by S.[r] Mathew Brand Kn.[t]
And further Saie that in their Judgem.[te] the same Sewer is better to bee
Stopt vp then laied open again (being the head of a fowle Sewer

And at a Session of Sewers holden in Southwark
the 13th day of October then following/

The Said Jurie did present that vpon theire Viewe taken with the
Com.[es] of Sewers in Maide Lane they doe finde that 80.[tie] yardes thereof
is stopt vp And 40.[tie] yardes thereof built vpon by S.[r] Mathew Brand
Kn.[t] And further Said that they are informed It was stopt vp by virtue
of a former Comission of Sewers And therefore saie and present that
the Same as now it is is more Convenient for the neighborhood and for
Passengers than to be laied open again as formerly it was for that then
Jt was a noysome filthy place adioyning vpon the Churchway.[12]

Two records from other sources are worth reprinting
here. Ben Jonson, lamenting the destruction of the first
Globe in his poem *An Execration upon Vulcan*,[13] briefly

[10] C. C. Stopes, *Notes and Queries* (Series xi), XI. 448.

[11] C. W. Wallace in *The* [London] *Times*, April 30, 1914.

[12] Preserved by Halliwell-Phillipps (see his *Calendar of Shakespeare Rarities*,
p. 81) and now in the Folger Shakespeare Library. Cf. Chambers, ii. 433, note 4.

[13] Written after the burning of his own library in 1625. The passage cited
appears in *Under-Woods*, 1640, p. 212.

describes the nature of the property and also provides
unique reference to the piles upon which the foundations
of the building rested:

> The *Globe*, the Glory of the *Banke*,
> Which, though it were the Fort of the whole Parish,
> Flanck'd with a Ditch, and forc'd out of a Marish,
> I saw with two poore Chambers taken in
> And raz'd, e're thought could urge, this might have beene!
> See the worlds Ruines! nothing but the piles
> Left! and wit since to cover it with Tiles.

And a general description of the Globe neighborhood is
given somewhat later in Strype's edition of Stow's *Survey
of London*:

Maiden Lane, a long straggling place, with ditches on each side, the
passages to the houses being over little bridges, with little garden plots
before them, especially on the north side, which is best both for houses
and inhabitants.[14]

[14] Cited by Adams, p. 243.

Chapter II

THE PLAYHOUSE FRAME

ALL contemporary views of London misrepresent the proportions of the Globe. Visscher exhibits a building approximately as high (to the ridge of the gallery roofs) as it is wide. Other cartographers even more seriously exaggerate the height, notably Delaram, whose Globe dwarfs all near-by buildings and is overlooked only by the tower of St. Saviour's. Needless to say such exaggeration is the result of pictorial emphasis.

But by means of the extant builder's contracts for two other playhouses erected early in the seventeenth century it is possible to discover the dimensions of the Globe frame with some degree of accuracy and completeness. A knowledge of these dimensions is necessary before we can intelligently weigh the mass of evidence bearing on the minor details of the building — the stairs, doors, partitions, seats, and so forth, and the many complex features of the stage and tiring-house — evidence which for the most part is found not in the contracts themselves but in other sources of information, notably in the plays written for the Globe Company or for other companies possessing playhouses closely resembling the Globe. The two extant builder's contracts, for reasons soon to be taken up, give little more than directions for constructing the frame of the Fortune or the Hope (as the case may be) on the lines of some other playhouse, and for including or altering certain standard appointments; but I believe that by a close study of the two contracts we can discover the exact size of the Globe and obtain a reasonably complete knowledge of how its component parts were designed. With these facts as a guide, the work of later chapters dealing with the auditorium and the stage will be greatly facilitated.

For our purposes the more important of the two contracts is that for the Fortune, a playhouse built one year later than the Globe and by workmen under the direction of the same master builder, Peter Streete. Streete was instructed by Philip Henslowe and Edward Alleyn to produce in the Fortune a replica of the Globe in every important respect except one: the new structure was to be built about a square instead of an octagonal yard. In three places in the comparatively short contract (reprinted in Appendix B) strict adherence to the design of the Globe is insisted upon. The second of these clauses reads:

And the saide howse and other thinges beforemencioned to be made & doen To be in all other Contrivitions Conveyances fashions thinge and thinges effected finished and doen accordinge to the manner and fashion of the saide howse Called the Globe.

It is such general statements as this that hide details of both houses which one would gladly know. But obviously the contract was so drawn because Peter Streete had just completed the Globe, and, of course, if he needed to do so, could at any time refresh his memory by a visit there.

The other contract (reprinted in Appendix C), drawn up in August, 1613, for replacing the out-moded Bear Garden with a new building in which both animal baiting and plays could be presented, is less useful in a study of the Globe because, in addition to being even shorter than the Fortune contract, it calls for a house of "suche large compasse, fforme, widenes, and height as the Plaie house Called the Swan." The document does provide, however, certain details of construction not included in the Fortune contract. Further, with two distinct contracts, we are in a better position to determine which elements were peculiar to one house and which were common to all.

While studying these two contracts, we must not lose sight of the fact that all playhouses were structurally simple. They were built in the manner which until a generation or two ago had prevailed from time immemorial for all sizable wooden buildings. The Theater, of 1576, the prototype of the Globe and of all its rivals, was designed and built by James Burbage. Having been by trade a carpenter, Burbage planned the first playhouse according to the well-defined rules of his craft. Those rules have changed little since his time; and a person today can more readily visualize the problems facing a builder of an Elizabethan playhouse if he will acquaint himself with the way in which all old-time wooden buildings were made. An hour's scrutiny of the framework of an old English or American barn is perhaps the best introduction to a study of the Fortune and the Hope playhouse contracts.

Like the Fortune and the Hope, the Globe stood on marshy ground.[1] Like them, therefore, it must have had a "good suer [sure] and stronge foundacion of Piles, brick, lyme, and sand both without & within [i.e. for both outer and inner walls] to be wrought one foote of assize att the leiste above the grounde."[2] The use of piles in the Globe foundation is attested by Jonson's *An Execration upon Vulcan*, already quoted.[3]

Once the pile and brick foundations were ready — the Fortune foundations were completed exactly four months after the builder's contract was signed[4] — carpenters could begin their task of erecting the frame. Into the Globe, as also into the Fortune and the Hope, went a certain amount of used material. At the Globe the proportion of used material was exceptionally high, for the Burbages tried to salvage as much as possible of their original playhouse, the Theater. Threatened in 1598 by the reversion of their property to Gyles Alleyn, the owner of the land, under the terms of an expired ground lease which they had sought in vain to renew,[5] Cuthbert and Richard Burbage

---

[1] See above, Chapter I, sec. 2.
[2] The Hope contract calls for a foundation 13 inches high above ground level.
[3] See above p. 12.
[4] *Henslowe Papers*, pp. 4 and 10.   [5] For a full account see Adams, pp. 52 ff.

availed themselves of a recovery clause in the lease and caused the playhouse to be dismantled during the last days of December while Alleyn was absent from the city. They then carried "all the wood and timber thereof unto the Banckside in the parishe of St. Marye Overyes, and there erected a newe playehowse with the sayd timber and woode." [6] Dekker alludes to the episode in the following terms: [7]

How wonderfully is the world altered! and no marvel, for it has lyein sick almost five thousand years: so that it is no more like the old *Theater du munde*, than old Paris Garden is like the King's garden at Paris. What an excellent workman therefore were he, that could cast the *Globe* of it into a new mould.

It would be a mistake, however, as Dr. Joseph Q. Adams points out, [8] to assume that the Globe was merely the old Theater newly set up on the Bankside — at least £400 [9] was spent by the syndicate for new materials and workmanship, — but I am inclined to believe that the *frame* of the new building was substantially if not piece for piece the frame of the Theater. It is difficult otherwise to justify the dismantling of the old playhouse with the risk of the inevitable litigation by the outraged Alleyn, or to understand why it cost but £400 or even £500 [10] to complete the Globe whereas the Theater itself had cost nearly £700 [11] and the second Globe, a building of the same size as the first and spared the expense of new foundations, cost approximately £1400. [12]

[6] *Allen v. Burbadge* (1602), quoted by C. W. Wallace, *Nebraska University Studies*, xiii. 279.

[7] Cited by Adams, p. 244, from *The Guls Hornbook*, published in 1609 but written a few years earlier.

[8] Adams, p. 244.

[9] See Wallace, *The* [London] *Times*, Oct. 2, 1909, and also his *Children of the Chapel at Blackfriars*, p. 29, note 4.

[10] Adams, p. 249, believes that the sum of £400 is too small.

[11] Wallace, *The First London Theatre*, p. 277.

[12] *Outlines*, i. 316; cf. Adams, p. 258, note 1.

Manifestly it was the valuable heavy oak framework of the Theater that the Burbages were endeavoring to recover. Under the circumstances, little else could be salvaged. The foundations had to be abandoned. Once disturbed, the thatch and plaster work would crumble into rubbish. Many of the interior fittings — partitions, railings, stage fixtures, and so forth — being of light timber, were not likely to survive the wrecker's festinate crow-bar; and those that emerged unscathed were of doubtful value, for during the first twenty years of practical experience with playhouses so many improvements in stage design, together with a few minor modifications in gallery divisions, had come about that by 1599 the old Theater fittings must have been in large measure obsolete. In the same period, however, no corresponding advance had been made in the design and construction of the frame. Based on centuries of general building experience as well as on fifty years of trial and error in temporary "scaffolds" and permanent arenas for animal baiting, the frame was subject to little change so long as the amphitheatre type of playhouse persisted.

In 1598 the frame of the twenty-two-year-old Theater was no doubt sound and sturdy — compare the long life of such other wooden playhouses as were spared by fire or by the animosity of a Puritan parliament. The Curtain, built in 1577, was in active use up to the reign of Charles I and appears to have been in existence many years later.[13] The Hope, built in part of timbers from the much older Bear Garden which it replaced in 1613, was still standing after seventy years. Unquestionably, therefore, the Theater frame, probably of sturdy oak, had many years of life remaining in it. There is no reason why its timbers could not have been unpegged, taken apart, and reassembled — provided that the frame was of the right shape and size for the new theatre.

[13] Leslie Hotson (*Commonwealth and Restoration Stage*, p. 92) has discovered a reference which seems to show that the Curtain was still standing in 1660.

With regard to these last considerations we are on uncertain ground. Almost nothing has survived to indicate the exact size and shape of the Theater. Its cost (£700), almost twice that of the rebuilt Hope (£360),[14] and considerably more than that of the great Fortune (£520),[15] shows that it was large. During its last years, when several other playhouses furnished a basis of comparison, writers described it as "vast," [16] or referred to it as "the great house called the Theatre." [17] In the absence of specific data there is no good reason to suppose that it was smaller than the Globe or that its shape was other than octagonal.[18]

Had the frame of the Theater been unsuitable as a frame for the Globe, its timbers would, of course, still have been of some value. Yet that value would hardly have warranted the legal risks and expense of salvaging the old playhouse, much less have reduced the outlay for the new playhouse to the sum stated. Working used lumber into a new building of different size or design is a time-consuming, wasteful task more frequently undertaken by well-to-do antiquarians than by practical theatre-owners. Where safety is important, structural members cannot be spliced; where beauty is desired, exposed beams cannot be disfigured by old mortises, sockets, and pegholes. Since the Burbages and their associates were attempting to save what they could of the Theater, they probably were willing to concede a few minor departures from an ideal size or design in order to make use of the old frame. For if the old frame could be reassembled on new foundations, the syndicate could expect to save approximately half the total cost of a new structure.[19] In this fact, I believe, lies the key to

[14] *Henslowe Papers*, p. 21.
[15] *Henslowe Papers*, p. 7. The cost of painting and "rendering" (i.e. plastering) the playhouse is not included in the contract figure of £440.
[16] *Skialethea*, 1598.
[17] Cited by Adams, p. 46.
[18] Cf. Adams, p. 46 and note 2; and Chambers, ii. 393.
[19] *Henslowe Papers*, p. 7.

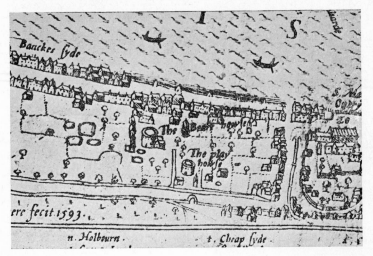

THE BEAR GARDEN AND THE ROSE IN 1593

From the ground plan by Keere in Norden's *Speculum Britanniae*, 1593

THE BEAR GARDEN, THE ROSE, AND THE FIRST GLOBE

From an equestrian portrait of King James I, by Delaram, representing
the Bankside as it appeared in 1603

the entire proceeding — (1) the swift decision to dismantle
the Theater wherein the frame was recoverable even if the
rest of the building was regarded as for the most part obsolete or subject to destruction in the process; (2) the securing of an expert, Peter Streete (who later was to build the
Globe and subsequently the Fortune), to superintend the
dismantling, when any unskilled group of laborers could
have razed the structure merely for its materials; and,
above all, (3) the low final cost of the Globe in comparison
with the cost of other playhouses of comparable size.

Let us now try to follow the operations of Streete and
his helpers in erecting the Globe. First, on the two concentric octagonal "rings" of brick foundation were placed
heavy oak sills into which were then mortised the floor
joists of the first gallery. The depth of this gallery in the
Fortune was 12½ feet, a depth presumably obtaining also
in the Globe. At every corner of both inner and outer sills,
and also at every mid-point between the corners, were set
upright posts not much less than a foot square in cross
section and tall enough to support the second level of galleries 12 feet above the first. In the Fortune these posts
on the inside of the building, and also the corresponding
posts of the second and third galleries, were carefully designed to harmonize with the square outline of the building. The contract reads:

All the princypall and maine postes of the saide fframe and Stadge
forwarde [i.e. facing on the yard] shalbe square and wroughte palasterwise with carved proporcions Called Satiers to be placed & sett on the
Topp of every of the same postes.

In the Hope these inner posts were artistically less
elaborate:

The Jnner principall postes of the first storie to be Twelve footes in
height and Tenn ynches square.

In the stage or tiring-house section of the inner façade at
the Hope "Turned Collumes" were to be substituted for
the square posts used elsewhere throughout the building.

The contract gives detailed structural specifications as to the timber to be used:

Make the Principalls and fore front [i.e. frame and inner façade] of the saide Plaie house of good and sufficient oken Tymber, And no furr tymber to be putt or vsed in the lower most, or midell stories, excepte the vpright postes on the backparte [i.e. outer wall] of the saide stories (All the Byndinge Joystes [i.e. main cross members of the frame] to be of oken tymber).

Because the description of the Fortune posts as "wroughte palasterwise with carved Satiers" is thus particularized, we may reasonably suppose that the Globe posts were of a different order. They may have been round, and probably they were less ornate. Jonson likens one of his characters to a post at the Globe: "A well-timberd fellow, he would ha' made a good columne and he had beene thought on, when the house was a building." [20]

In an effort to reduce the cost of the Hope (which, together with outbuildings, stables, and kennels, cost but £360 when rebuilt) Henslowe and Meade permitted the use of "prick-postes" eight inches square in the middle of the first gallery sections in place of ten-inch "principall postes" as used at the corners. This particular economy may have been prompted by a supply of eight-inch posts taken from the Bear Garden frame which Henslowe had turned over to Katherens the builder. There is no need to assume a similar practice at the Globe, a playhouse of much greater splendor than the Hope, for there was no such disparity in years and type between the Globe and the Theater as existed between the Hope and the old Bear Garden.

The distance between the vertical posts of the inner wall is specified in neither contract, but it can be determined at the Fortune from other given factors. Since that playhouse was to have galleries 12½ feet deep constructed in the form of a hollow square, the corner bays necessarily were square and measured 12½ feet on a side. Put an-

[20] *Every Man out of his Humour*, Prologue (cited by Adams, pp. 246–247).

other way, the corner posts which formed these particular bays must have been spaced exactly 12 feet between centers in both directions (if there was to be a six-inch allowance for the outer wall of studs, lath, and plaster). Now a large wood-frame building is constructed whenever possible in a series of units of the same size; I suggest, therefore, that the other bays likewise were square and of the same very convenient unit of measure. If a ground plan is developed to scale (1) with square bays (six on each side) measuring 12 feet in both directions between the centers of foot-square posts, and (2) with a half bay added to each of the four sides of the building (one for the spectator entrance to the yard and galleries, and the other three to make possible a tiring-house shaped as at the Globe), it will be found that the plan measures precisely 80 feet across — the given dimension of the Fortune exterior.[21]

In the octagonal frame of the Globe the corresponding bays obviously were not square, but one can determine the shape and dimensions of a bay if he knows the spacing of the inner posts and the depth of the gallery. If, then, for these two dimensions we adopt the implied 12-foot spacing of the Fortune posts and the given 12½-foot depth of the Fortune gallery, and work out a ground plan accordingly, the result is an octagonal building 84 feet across surrounding an octagonal yard 58 feet across. These figures are remarkably close to those given for the over-all dimensions of the Fortune — 80 and 55 feet respectively — and the differences are what one would expect in changing from an octagonal to a square ground plan, namely, that the dimensions of the square would be slightly reduced to offset the added space created by deeper corners.

Some indication of the size of the beams used in the Globe as "breastsummers" and "binding-joists" spanning

[21] This conjecture, with certain modifications, is adopted by Mr. Walter H. Godfrey in drawing his well-known reconstruction of the Fortune Playhouse. His drawings were most recently reprinted in full in *A Companion to Shakespeare Studies* (edited by Granville-Barker and Harrison), 1934, pp. 24–29.

the gallery bays is given by the specifications for corresponding beams in the Hope. There:

the Brest sommers in the lower moste storie [are] to be nyne ynches depe, and seaven ynches in thicknes and in the midell storie to be eight ynches depe and six ynches in thicknes. The Byndinge Jostes of the firste storie to be nyne and Eight ynches in depthe and thicknes and in the midell storie to be viij and vij ynches in depthe and thicknes.

The Fortune contract merely specifies that the frame is to be "in every poynte for Scantlynges [22] larger and bigger in assize Then the Scantlinges of the Timber of the saide new erected howse Called the Globe." This increase in the thickness and depth of beams did not, of course, affect the size of the frame; it was designed to strengthen the building, partly for reasons of greater safety [23] and partly, one conjectures, to compensate for the inherently less rigid shape of a square building.

At this point one can most readily indicate the structural difficulties which stand in the way of framing a cylindrical playhouse (a type many scholars have proposed) out of wood. A circular seating plan wholly or partially surrounding the platform stage is, of course, ideal; but a literally cylindrical wooden playhouse would be difficult to make and decidedly more expensive than a polygonal playhouse of equivalent size. Wood does not lend itself readily to curved lines. The heavy beams required in the main frame of so large a structure — unlike the relatively slender ribs of a boat — cannot be bent to a curve, however flat. Yet at every level of the playhouse, beginning with the sills and

[22] "*Scantling. techn.* with reference to the measurement of timber ... the word denotes the sectional dimensions (thickness and breadth) of a beam, etc., in contradistinction to its length." *N. E. D.* This sense is exactly sustained by the Hope builder's contract which specifies that the builder is to make the playhouse "of such large compasse, fforme, widenes and height as the Plaie house Called the Swan" and also to abide by the specified "scantling of timbers ... as is aforesaide without fraude or coven."

[23] The smaller size in the Globe may be still another indication that its timbers came from the older Theater.

ending with the roof plates and ridgepole, all horizontal beams in the frame forming the inner and outer walls (the "breastsummers" of the contracts) would have to be cut by hand to the requisite curve out of bulks of timber far heavier than the finished members. If placed end to end, these curved beams in a playhouse the size of the Globe would approach a total length of 1900 feet, so that the labor involved in shaping them would add greatly to the cost.

Yet even when these specially hand-shaped beams were prepared, the difficulties of fabricating a circular playhouse would have only begun. In a polygonal playhouse all beams would, of course, be straight lengths of timber; each breastsummer could therefore carry up to the limit of its breaking strength all the weight placed upon it without twisting or moving from place, for the thrust of the load would descend in the plane of the posts which supported it at both ends. If, on the other hand, the structure were circular, each breastsummer would have to conform to the curve of the wall and would be incapable of carrying as much weight as a straight beam, for the thrust of the load would descend not in the plane of the supporting posts but at the mid-point of the curve (well outside that plane), thus tending to twist the breastsummer loose. Long before the breaking point of the timber was reached, its pegged joints would tend to give way, thereby endangering the spectators in that section of the playhouse. Needless to say, those concerned in theatrical affairs were eager to avoid a repetition of the Paris Garden accident of 1583 in which eight persons were killed and several others injured by the collapse of the galleries.

To offset the weakness caused by a load resting on a curved beam it would be necessary to reduce the length of the span, either by shoring up the breastsummer in the middle of every gallery bay or by constructing a frame with much narrower bays. Both plans would considerably increase the number of posts standing between the gallery spectators and the stage, thus nullifying the advantages possessed in theory by the circular design.

One could compromise, of course, and achieve the effect of a circle by setting up curved banks of seats and curved balustrades inside a polygonal frame, but such a plan would be structurally illogical and would materially reduce the capacity of the house.

Rejecting, therefore, the hypothesis that the Globe was cylindrical, let us return to a consideration of its erection as an octagonal structure. Whereas the breastsummers of the inner façade of the Globe spanned posts 12 feet apart, those of the outer wall were necessarily longer, for they spanned posts 17½ feet apart; on the other hand, they were supported at intervals by studs or "prick-posts" [24] spaced conveniently for the oak laths later nailed in place to form a basis for the coat of plaster which sheathed the exterior.

Once the inner and outer ring of breastsummers, the heavy binding-joists, and the lighter floor beams were in place, the framework of the second story could be undertaken. In the main, the second and third galleries were structurally similar to the first gallery: posts rose over posts, unit over unit. There were, however, slight differences of width and height. The outer wall rose vertically from the sills to the plate, but in the case of the inner wall each upper story extended forward of the story below it, a "juttey forwardes" less for appearance than to conform to the almost universal rule in wooden buildings not wholly encased in a protective coat of plaster. By this means drip courses were provided which kept rain from driving or seeping into the joints of the frame and rotting them. In the Fortune a 10-inch overhang was specified, probably reflecting a similar overhang at the Globe. Since the outside wall was vertical, this means that the second gallery was 10 inches deeper than the first, and the third or top

[24] "*Prick-post.* The posts in a wooden building between the principal posts at the corner. Also the posts framed into the breastsummers between the principal posts for strengthening the carcase of a building." *N. E. D.*

gallery 10 inches deeper yet. It may be doubted if this added space was of particular value in the two upper galleries unless to provide wider corridors or standing room behind the rows of benches. The higher a spectator went in the galleries the more needful it was for him to find a place near the front in order to command a good view of the stage.

Although slightly wider, the upper galleries were less high. The Fortune contract provides that "the second Storie [is to contain] Eleaven foote of lawfull assize in height And the Third or vpper Storie to conteine Nyne foote of lawfull assize in height." The Globe unquestionably possessed the same number of stories,[25] each of which probably had the height that is specified by the Fortune contract. The height of the first gallery in the Hope was the same as in the Fortune, and although the heights of the upper galleries are not given, the fact that the posts and beams of those galleries were to be made progressively lighter implies a comparable lowering of the headroom.

Some years ago it was pointed out as strange that no contemporary view of any playhouse showed the "black-and-white" outer walls one might expect to find in an Elizabethan timber-framed playhouse;[26] but the two contracts we possess do not warrant an exterior finish other than a uniform coat of plaster. The Fortune contract reads:

All the saide fframe and Staircases thereof to be sufficyently enclosed withoute with lathe lyme & haire.

The Hope contract likewise includes lime, hair, and sand in a section treating with exterior details "necessarie for the full finishinge of the saide Plaie house." The evidence of

---

[25] In this respect the public playhouses were alike from the beginning — witness the descriptions by visitors (cf. Rye, *England as seen by Foreigners*, p. 88), the De Witt sketch of the Swan playhouse interior, the two builder's contracts, the three levels of windows in the Visscher and derivative views, the allusions in the plays, Wright's *Historia Histrionica*, 1699, etc.

[26] Wallace, pp. 31–32.

the maps on this point would have more weight were it not that they show an entire disregard of accuracy when representing wall surfaces. Visscher's panorama in this respect is unreliable; all his London buildings, whether church or playhouse, palace or hut, appear to be made of stone and plaster, with windows and doorways framed accordingly. In his Globe (and therefore in all the Globe pictures which derive from it) there are traces of stone-work over the windows and at the cornice. Needless to say, in a wooden building such a trim is entirely out of place.

With regard to windows in the outer wall behind the gallery sections of the Globe the maps are again misleading. The Fortune contract provides for "convenient windowes and lightes glazed to the saide Tyreinge howse," but makes no mention of windows in the galleries. Indeed windows there would be wholly superfluous, for the galleries, being unenclosed on the side facing the unroofed yard, were adequately lighted. On the other hand the tiring-house, being enclosed with opaque walls of one sort or another on both sides, needed glazed apertures suitably placed in its exterior walls to admit light and air into the back-stage rooms and passages. A representation of this distinction between the two parts of the playhouse would not be in accordance with the practice of Visscher and his successors, who supply all their buildings with a uniform and conventional exterior.

The Globe had a roof of thatch (as did the Hope, Swan, and probably all other sixteenth-century playhouses). This economy, however, proved to be unfortunate, for it brought about the total destruction of the building by a fire during a performance of *Henry VIII* on the afternoon of June 29, 1613. The disaster, the first of its kind in Elizabethan playhouse history,[27] is described in several con-

---

[27] The second playhouse to burn to the ground was the Fortune (on December 9, 1621) despite the fact that it had, according to its builder's contract, a roof of tiles. It is remarkable that playhouse fires were not more frequent. Private theatres were lit by candles for all performances, and in both private and public theatres torches, fireworks, and other dangerous devices were used daily.

temporary accounts, two of which may be cited for the light they throw on the materials used in the playhouse and the way in which the fire spread. Howe, in his continuation of Stow's *Annals*, wrote:

Upon St. Peter's Day last, the playhouse or theatre called the Globe, upon the Bankside, near London, by negligent discharge of a peal of ordnance, close to the south side thereof, the thatch took fire, and the wind suddenly dispersed the flames round about, and in a very short space the whole building was quite consumed; and no man hurt: the house being filled with people to behold the play, *viz.* of Henry the Eight.[28]

And Sir Henry Wotton, in a letter to a friend, adds the following details:

Now King Henry, making a masque at the Cardinal Wolsey's house, and certain cannons being shot off at his entry, some of the paper or other stuff wherewith one of them was stopped, did light on the thatch, where being thought at first but an idle smoke, and their eyes more attentive to the show, it kindled inwardly, and ran round like a train, consuming within less than an hour the whole house to the very ground. This was the fatal period of that virtuous fabrick; wherein yet nothing did perish but wood and straw, and a few forsaken cloaks.[29]

Playhouse design evidently made no provision for the rainwater dripping from the inner slope of the gallery roof into the yard. Gutters of lead were provided at the Fortune and at the Hope — and presumably at the Globe as well — to carry off the water falling on the stage-cover over the platform stage; but beyond this the contracts are silent. Perhaps for the rest of the building it mattered little. Fortunately (for eaves-troughs are seldom feasible with thatched roofs) thatch absorbs such rain as falls on it during a passing shower; and of course no play was given when the windows of heaven were opened.

No indication of the shape of the roof is contained in the contracts, but Visscher draws all his Bankside playhouses

---

[28] *Annals* (ed. 1631), p. 1003.
[29] *Reliquiæ Wottonianæ* (ed. 1672), p. 425.

with a series of gable-type units, each one having a ridge parallel to its section of the polygonal frame. His drawing of the Globe is too small to show much of the inner slope,[30] nor perhaps is any early seventeenth-century cartographer to be relied upon for so minute a detail; but other considerations support the gable type. Such roofs, whether covered with thatch or with tiles, were standard in the period. The gable type conserved materials and space, and resulted in a strong roof even when constructed with light rafters, for the spans were short and the design was rigid. One cannot accept the conjecture advanced in certain recent reconstructions of the Globe [31] that the roof sections pitched in one plane from a ridge over the inner façade to eaves at the outer wall. Since a thatched roof must incline at an angle approaching 45 degrees from the horizontal, the style of roof proposed would add at least 12 feet to the height of the inner wall (already 35 feet high) surrounding the yard. Such an addition would be structurally abnormal, ungainly, and costly. Even on bright days it would materially reduce the illumination of the outer and inner stages and, throughout the playhouse, would substitute shadows for sunlight an hour or two earlier in the afternoon than would a roof of the gable type.

Apart from the interest inherent in any aspect of a building so intimately associated with Shakespeare's career as the Globe, the facts about the frame which have been brought together in these pages — particularly the exact size and shape of the building as a whole, and the location of vertical posts which determined the bays or units of interior space — will be of great assistance in subsequent chapters when problems of seating and of stage design and equipment are raised.

[30] An early but undated drawing of the Globe, deriving from Visscher and preserved in a copy of Pennant's *London* now in the British Museum, shows the inner portions of the gable roof in more detail.

[31] See, for example, the models by Mr. H. E. Conklin deposited in the Folger Shakespeare Library and in the Widener Library, Cambridge, Mass.

Chapter III

THE AUDITORIUM

1. THE SIGN

OF THE octagonal frame of the Globe three-quarters was converted into spectator-galleries encircling a corresponding portion of the playhouse yard, and the remaining quarter into a highly complex acting area (known as the "tiring-house") fronted by a large platform stage projecting into the yard. These two portions of the building were as distinct in appearance as they were in function, and I shall discuss them in turn.

In common with other playhouses of the same type,[1] the Globe had a sign prominently displayed over the main entrance. Johannes de Witt, a Dutch priest visiting London in 1596, reported that signs were affixed to the four public playhouses then standing:

The two more magnificent of these are situated to the southward beyond the Thames, and from the signs suspended before them are called the Rose and the Swan.[2]

The rebuilt Fortune, and doubtless the original Fortune likewise, had a sign over the entrance door:

> I'le rather stand here,
> Like a statue in the fore-front of your house,
> For ever, like the picture of Dame Fortune
> Before the Fortune Playhouse.[3]

---

[1] I have found no record of a sign affixed to any private playhouse.

[2] Cited from the translation quoted by Adams, p. 167.

[3] Thomas Heywood, *The English Traveller* (1633), ed. Pearson, iv. 84, cited by Adams, p. 277. Dr. Adams adds: "Heywood generally used 'picture' in the sense of 'statue'."

On the basis of notes by William Oldys (1696–1761) Malone recorded that the Globe sign had "a figure of Hercules supporting the Globe, under which was written *Totus mundus agit histrionem.*" [4] Malone's further suggestion [5] that the sign was painted on the wall over the door in the manner of signs denominating the stews in the Liberty of the Clink seems unlikely in view of the projecting signs of other playhouses. Whatever the details, it is surprising to find in all the literature of the period no clear reference to the Globe sign and only a very few passages which can be construed as alluding to it. There is a bit of dialogue in *Hamlet*, II. ii:

Hamlet. Do the Boyes [i.e. boy actors] carry it away?
Rosencrantz. I that they do my Lord, *Hercules* & his load too.

In a contemporary copy of the anonymous *Funerall Elegye on ye Death of the famous Actor Richard Burbedg who dyed on Saturday in Lent the 13 of March 1618* occur the lines:

And you his sad Compannions to whome Lent
Becomes more Lenton by this Accident,
Hence forth your wauing flagg, no more hang out
Play now no more att all, when round aboute
Wee looke and miss the *Atlas* of your spheare.[6]

And just possibly there is a glance at the sign in the well-known lines in *As You Like It*, II. vii:

All the world's a stage,
And all the men and women meerely Players.

[4] *Variorum* (1821), iii. 67, and *As You Like It*, ed. G. L. Kittredge, pp. xvii–xviii. Mrs. C. C. Stopes (*Burbage and Shakespeare's Stage*, p. 77) suggests that Hercules carrying the Globe points to the herculean task of carrying the Theater over to the Bankside and there re-erecting it.

[5] *Variorum* (1921), iii. 67, note 9.

[6] Cited from Ingleby, "The Elegy on Burbadge," in *Shakespeare, the Man and the Book*, ii. 180.

2. THE MAIN ENTRANCE

In pre-playhouse days Londoners attending a performance at an inn-theatre entered by way of the inn-yard gate-
way and found themselves at the opposite end of the inn-
yard from the wall against which the stage was set up.[7] It
is supposed that the earlier playhouses copied this design;
and such evidence as has come down to us suggests that
the Globe, in turn, was similarly designed. If we can trust
the pictorial views of London in the first half of the seventeenth century, particularly Visscher's, the Globe tiring-
house had its back to the afternoon sun, which means that
the main entrance to the playhouses was in the opposite
side of the building. The great majority of spectators entered the playhouse through this main door, but by 1599 a
well-established custom permitted a few patrons, on payment of sixpence (the normal entrance fee was a penny)
to enter through the stage door at the rear and find a place
either on the stage or in the adjoining boxes. The accommodations for this limited group will be considered
later.

The main entrance of the playhouse was narrow —
deliberately made so, one conjectures, for the purpose of
restricting the influx of spectators to a single file. John
Chamberlain, in a letter to Sir Ralph Winwood describing
the burning of the Globe, wrote that "yt was a great
marvayle and fayre grace of God, that the people had so
litle harme, having but two narrow doores to get out." [8]
He refers, of course, to the main door and to the door of
the tiring-house.

At the main doorway stood an attendant known as the
doorkeeper who held a box into which every person entering dropped a penny (or two pennies on the occasion of a
new play). Since these details are well known,[9] a few quo-

---

[7] Cf. Lawrence, *Pre-Restoration Stage Studies*, p. 11.
[8] *Letters of John Chamberlain*, ed. McClure, i. 467.
[9] Several illustrative references are cited by Chambers, ii. 531–533.

tations will suffice to illustrate them. From *Every Woman in her Humour* (1609), IV. i:

Tis even as common to see a Bason at a Church doore as a Box at a Playhouse.

In the dedication of *If It be not Good, the Devil is in It* (1612), Dekker hopes that his friends, the Queen's Players, will have "a full audience and one honest doorkeeper." (Note the implication of a single entering door.)

From *The Cuck-queanes and Cuckolds errants* (written 1601), I. ii:

Nim. What now the newes in London, Shift.
Shift. These. Thames is as broade as it was ever, Poules steeple stands in the place it did before, And Twopence is the price for the going in, to a newe Play there.

A later passage found in Flecknoe's *Miscellania*, 1653, compares the scene before a then closed theatre with that of former days:

Passing on to Black-fryers, [one sees] never a Play-bil on the Gate, no Coaches on the place, nor Doorkeeper at the Play-house door, with his Boxe like a church-warden, desiring you to remember the poor Players.

3. THE YARD

Once the playgoer had dropped his penny into the box, he passed through a corridor leading into the benchless and unroofed yard of the playhouse. If he chose he could remain in the yard without further payment, standing with his fellow "groundlings" throughout the performance. Apart from many uncomplimentary references to the judgment, behavior, and cleanliness of its frequenters, we are told surprisingly little about the yard and even less about its physical characteristics — its size and shape; whether its floor was level or sloping, paved or earthen; the height of the platform stage projecting into it; and so forth. Yet these details, though they seem to have occasioned no comment from contemporary writers, can be determined with a fair degree of confidence.

Despite a number of epithets which imply that the auditorium was circular, the yard of the Globe, framed by the gallery tiers, was octagonal. The misleading epithets can be accounted for partly by Renaissance enthusiasm for the past and partly by poetic necessity. Elizabethan dramatists were fond of likening their wooden playhouses to the stone amphitheatres of Greece and Rome, and hence they might apply to the one descriptive phrases more suitable to the other. The phrases were wholly conventionalized. Among the twenty or more passages to be found in plays and poems of the period which specifically refer to the auditorium as round, several occur in plays written for private theatres [10] every one of which we know was rectangular.

Certain lines in the prologue to *Henry V* (a play which may have opened elsewhere but which undoubtedly was performed at the Globe prior to its publication in 1600) —

> May we cramme
> Within this Woodden O, the very Caskes
> That did affright the Ayre at Agincourt? —

are frequently advanced to support the notion of a circular playhouse. It should be remembered, however, that the image suggested by the letter "O" might be the familiar polygonal black letter "𝕺" of the hornbook and popular literature rather than the elliptical roman style "O." Moreover, "this wooden O" referred more to the *name* of the playhouse, I believe, than to its exact shape. "The Globe" meant a wooden world (whether spherical or discoid) in miniature. These considerations indicate that the passage from *Henry V* need not be regarded as proof of a circular auditorium. One might quite as reasonably take it as suggesting an octagon.

Usually no other consideration than the ease with which

[10] See, for example, the Prologue to *Wily Beguiled*, 1606, and the Epilogue to *The Family of Love*, 1608 (both Whitefriars plays); the Prologue to *A Fine Companion*, 1633 (Salisbury Court); the Epilogue to *The Muses Looking Glass*, 1638 (Blackfriars); and the Prologue to *The Lady Errant*, 1635 (academic).

a descriptive word or phrase — "ring," "orb," "circled orbe," "sphere," "wooden O," "circumference," and even "round circumference" — could be incorporated in a blank verse line determined its selection,[11] hence an absolutely exact description of the playhouse cannot be inferred. In two Fortune plays the auditorium was appropriately labeled "square."[12] One would be surprised that "square" was employed so infrequently did he not realize that there was good reason for the author to be vague. Many playwrights were unattached to any particular company and sold their plays where they could. After 1609, moreover, one company might regularly present its stock of plays in two different theatres. It follows, therefore, that, much as today, a play would be written without such passages as would limit its performance to a given theatre.

The paramount objections to a circular yard and auditorium at the Globe lie, as we have seen in an earlier section, in the practical limitations of wooden construction and in the evidence of the pictorial views. Further, in that section evidence was cited to show that the Globe yard was octagonal in shape and measured 58 feet across between sides uniformly 24 feet long.

Although, so far as I can discover, the problem has not been thoroughly investigated, scholars apparently have assumed that the yard was level,[13] possibly because (1) the inn-theatre yard was level, (2) the De Witt sketch of the Swan appears to show a level yard, and (3) the designs by

[11] In addition to being metrically unsuitable to iambic verse the word "octagon" is unrecorded in English literature until the Restoration, and then in a mathematical work.

[12] Only twice so far as I can discover (*The Whore of Babylon*, Prologue, and *The Roaring Girl*, I. i) is the Fortune Playhouse referred to as square despite the obviousness of the term and the ease with which it can be entered in a metrical line.

[13] E.g., A. H. Thorndike, *Shakespeare's Theater*, p. 93, and presumably those others, as Archer, Lawrence, and Sisson, who reproduce Mr. Godfrey's Fortune Playhouse reconstruction.

Inigo Jones for the little Cockpit-in-Court,[14] a roofed
building of stone erected 1632–33, show a level floor, with
rows of benches placed at an angle to the middle aisle,
reached by steps leading down from an elevated platform
or dais at the back of the hall. But at best such reasoning
is inconclusive, whereas it can be demonstrated, I believe,
that the Fortune yard — and hence presumably the Globe
yard also — was excavated in such a way as to form a slope
from the rear and also the sides towards the platform.

The first step in the demonstration is to consider the
height of the platform stage above the yard. Modern
scholars estimate this height to have been approximately
5 feet.[15] Serlio, in 1545, had recommended that the stage
floor be built at eye level;[16] Platter wrote in 1599: "The
places [theatres] are so built, that they play on a raised
platform, and every one can well see it all." [17] Contemporary representations of the stage bear out these observations. Although only one of them gives evidence of being drawn to scale, the presence of human figures in three
views enables us to form some notion of dimensions. The
height of the actor standing on the forefront of the Swan
platform as sketched by De Witt is found to be less than
twice the height of the (removable) platform.[18] In the
little *Roxana* engraving (1632) the heads and shoulders of
five spectators are shown in the foreground in front of the
platform. Because of their presence one cannot distinguish
the height of the palings which enclosed the platform below; but the artist, evidently looking down on the scene
from some elevation (such as the second gallery), makes it

[14] First identified by J. Q. Adams and reproduced by him in his *Shakespearean
Playhouses*, facing p. 396.

[15] Cf. Lawrence, *Physical Conditions of the Elizabethan Public Playhouse*,
pp. 5–6.

[16] L. B. Campbell, *Scenes and Machines on the English Stage during the
Renaissance*, p. 33.

[17] Cited by Chambers, ii. 365.

[18] Chambers, ii. 528, writes: "The stage may be some 3 or 4 feet above the
ground."

appear that their eyes are about on a level with the low wooden railings of the stage.[19] Of the recently discovered plans by Inigo Jones for the Carolinian Cockpit-in-Court theatre, Mr. Hamilton Bell writes: "If one may trust an elevation of the stage, drawn . . . to twice the scale of the general plan, the stage was four feet six inches above the [level] floor of the pit." [20] (It may be worth adding here that modern theatre design normally raises the stage 3 feet 4 inches above the floor at row A, i.e. 6 to 10 inches below eye level.[21])

Even if the platform was merely 4 feet above the level of the yard, it follows that the yard must have been excavated 18 inches or more, for the playhouse contracts show that the floor of the platform (co-extensive with the floor of the first gallery) was only 30 inches above the outside ground level. At the Fortune, the brick foundation walls were to be made "one foot of assize at the least above the ground," and at the Hope "thirteen inches." The height thus indicated for foundations appears, therefore, to be standard. Following normal Elizabethan building practice,[22] the construction then proceeded as follows: on these

[19] The *Messallina* engraving (1640) is of no help in estimating the height of the platform, for there the palings are curtailed by the lower margin, and no persons are anywhere represented. In the foreground of *The Wits* frontispiece (1662), which illustrates a type of stage improvised during the Commonwealth, appears a row of seven heads barely higher than the shield to the footlights. Here, as in the *Roxana* vignette, the angle is confusing, and were no other spectators shown, one would conclude that the top of the footlight shield was at eye level. On the right side of the platform, however, sit four clearly drawn figures, and of these the farthest and most completely displayed is drawn with his waist on a level with the floor of the stage.

[20] Quoted from Adams, p. 397.

[21] None of these views and plans shows a stage-gallant sitting on his low three-legged stool or reclining on the outskirts of the platform; but it seems at least possible that stages intended to accommodate gallants must have been lower (by at least one foot?) than those not so intended, otherwise the obstruction caused by the fringe of gallants would have been intolerable.

[22] Cf. C. F. Innocent, *The Development of English Building Construction,* pp. 160 ff.

foundation walls the sills of the frame were laid. (The size of the sills is not specified in either contract, but they would necessarily be at least as large in cross section as the vertical posts and first-floor "binding-joists" of the frame, i.e. between 10 and 12 inches square.) Into these sills, and spanning the 12-foot space between them at intervals corresponding to the width of the bays, would then be mortised the "binding-joists" or main cross beams. After that, smaller beams or floor-joists, parallel to the "binding-joists" and placed at frequent intervals in between, would also be mortised into the sills. Finally, on top of all, the flooring of the first gallery would be laid. The flooring itself, made of "good & sufficyent newe deale bourdes of the whole thicknes wheare need shalbe," was doubtless well over one inch in thickness, but was not likely to have exceeded two inches. Adding to the height of the foundation above ground the thickness of the superimposed sills, joists, and floor-boards gives a minimum of 24 inches (assuming that the foundation walls were the mean specified height and that the sills were only 10 inches deep) and a probable maximum of 30 inches (assuming that the foundations were an inch or two over specification, the sills 14–15 inches deep, and so on) as the height of the first gallery floor above the ground.

Support for this interpretation of the structural implications of the contracts is found in the well-known conjectural reconstructions of two architects, Mr. W. H. Godfrey and Mr. G. T. Forrest,[23] working independently. Faced with the problem created by a stage platform approximately 2½ feet high relative to the outside ground level but at the same time 4 to 5 feet high relative to the yard into which it projected, both architects concluded that the entire yard must have been excavated uniformly to a depth of some 2 feet below ground level, and that the

[23] Mr. Godfrey's reconstructions of the Fortune are reproduced in *A Companion to Shakespeare Studies*, pp. 26–27; Mr. Forrest's of the Globe in *The Site of the Globe Playhouse Southwark* (1924), p. 107.

corridor leading from the main playhouse door sloped from the outside ground level downwards until it reached the yard. Their conclusion is of further interest: it indicates that to architects with professional experience in such matters the risk of rain and other surface water collecting in the unroofed yard was negligible, or at least not insurmountable. If the water did not seep into the ground as fast as it collected, presumably it could be carried off by drains leading to the open sewers near the playhouse. It is unlikely that the problem of drainage was overlooked by both these architects while preparing their conjectural plans, or that it continued to escape the notice of other experts in subsequent years during which those conjectural reconstructions have been subjected to close scrutiny.

Needless to say, the actors found in the inn-theatre no precedent for a yard sunk below ground or street level, but in the playhouse they had no reasonable alternative. It would have been possible, of course, to set the entire building on foundations constructed 3 feet instead of 1 foot above ground; but the contracts read otherwise, and in an age of cheap labor and expensive bricks it was far more economical to excavate the yard a foot or two rather than to heighten the surrounding foundation walls by that amount. Again, it would have been possible to raise the platform stage relative to the rest of the building, but that was the last thing the actors or the spectators desired, since, for the reasons cited below, it would have entailed raising the level of the entire floor of the tiring-house also, thus reducing the height of the inner stage where every available inch of headroom was needed. Obviously the floor of the inner stage could not be lower than the floor of the outer stage. Nor could the ceiling of the inner stage be raised, for its ceiling level was conditioned by the frame of the building, — a frame which was, all records imply, uniform in height throughout the building. The loss of a foot or two in the height of the inner stage would have imposed a serious handicap in the staging of spectacular scenes, for such scenes often called for trees to form an arbor, a royal state arched over with a canopy, and the like. Moreover, a reduction in the height of the inner-stage opening would have interfered with a view of the interior scenes, particularly for spectators in the second and third galleries. I suggest that the primary reason for a first and second gallery 12 and 11 feet high respectively (compared with a third gallery only 9 feet high) was to ensure adequate height for the first- and second-level inner stages. If ever spectator headroom was needed, it was needed in the third gallery where the presumption of rows of seats placed in sharply rising tiers is strongest; yet that gallery was markedly lower than the two below.

In short, the practical solution of the problem brought about by the need of a platform stage between 4 and 5 feet high in a building where that platform stage was only 2½ feet high (relative to the ground level) was to excavate the yard.

We come now to the second step in the demonstration. A close examination of the Fortune contract provision for palings to enclose the yard shows that the yard was not level, but was excavated in such a way as to slope from the rear and sides toward the platform. The contract reads:

The same [platform] Stadge to be paled in belowe with good strong and sufficyent newe oken bourdes And likewise the lower Storie of the saide fframe withinside, and the same lower storie to be alsoe laide over and fenced with stronge yron pykes.[24]

[24] The brief line in the Fortune contract is the only known contemporary reference to the iron pikes, but the fact that the contract contains it suggests either a similar provision at the Globe or a recognized deficiency there. A wall of palings, breast high and "laide over and fenced with strong yron pikes," is shown in a later picture entitled "The Days before the Queene" which W. J. Lawrence reproduced as the frontispiece to his *Old Theatre Days and Ways* and identified with the pit door at Drury Lane in 1784. For a survival of this type of barrier in place between the pit and the orchestra in 1823, see the Cruikshank drawing reproduced by Montague Summers in *The Restoration Theatre*, facing p. 128.

The need for paling the lower portions of the platform is obvious, for its sides had to be enclosed in order to make trap scenes possible. The palings of the platform rose no higher than the floor of the stage; but the palings on "the lower Storie [i.e. the first gallery] of the saide fframe" extended higher than the floor of the first gallery in order to provide the low wall or guard-rail fronting the first-gallery rooms (as shown in the De Witt sketch of the Swan). Solid paling above the first-gallery floor rather than open balustrades (such as are shown in certain post-Restoration interior views) best conformed to Elizabethan needs and traditions. In amphitheatres used in whole or in part for animal baiting, the solid wall created by stout paling would be essential as a protection against the animals. In playhouses admitting spectators to the yard at low prices the close-set paling would be a wise precaution against fraudulent climbing from the yard into the more expensive gallery rooms. Inasmuch as spectators in the front rows of all gallery rooms were seated, one estimates that the upper portion of the palings, that is, the portion which extended above the gallery floor, could hardly have exceeded a height of 3 feet, and probably approximated the modern standard of 32 inches.

Now the provision for iron pikes affixed to the palings surrounding the yard shows that the paling by itself was not sufficient — which can only mean not high enough — to keep those in the yard from climbing over either to avoid payment of the proper fees or to seek shelter during a shower.[25] Yet had the yard been excavated uniformly to a depth of 18 inches or more, the total distance from the yard floor to the top of the gallery paling would have exceeded 6½ feet — a height which of itself would have sufficed to keep the groundlings in their place. The addition

---

[25] The latter contingency is implied in a prediction for April in *Vox Graculi*, 1623: "If, at this time, about the houres of foure and five it waxe cloudy, and then raine downeright, they shall sit dryer in the galleries than those who are the understanding men in the yard."

VIGNETTE FROM THE TITLE–PAGE OF *ROXANA*, 1632

The original measures 7/8 by 1-1/4 inches

of pikes therefore presupposes a paling that otherwise could readily be scaled, that is to say, not more than 5 or 5 ½ feet high. But a paling of precisely this height would result if the rear portions of the yard were everywhere level with the ground outside the playhouse, for the floor of the first gallery would then be 24–30 inches above the yard (just as it was above the outside ground level), and the guard rail would add 32–36 inches, making a total height of 56–66 inches. (A height of less than 5 feet is inadmissible, since the heads and hats of groundlings with their backs to the palings would then be interposed between the stage and the eyes of those sitting in the first rows of the lowest gallery. This conclusion eliminates the possibility that the floor of the yard might have been raised *above* outside ground level at its outskirts.)

It will thus be seen that we are given two different measurements relative to the depth of the yard. Where the yard adjoined the platform, its floor had to be at least 18 inches below ground level in order to make the platform 4 feet high, the lowest figure we are justified in assuming. Where the yard met the surrounding first gallery, its floor must have been at ground level, otherwise it would not have been necessary to go to the considerable cost of supplementing the palings with iron pikes. One can reconcile these two measurements only by assuming that the floor of the yard was not level, but that it pitched from all sides towards the platform. (If one could be sure that the pikes were affixed to the palings only at the side of the yard opposite to the tiring-house, one might conceive of a floor inclining in one plane only; but the sense of the contract seems to point away from this conclusion.) The incline toward the platform would be slight — a drop of 18 inches in 28 feet would be hardly appreciable underfoot — but would be sufficient to improve in no small degree a view of the stage from every part of the yard. In no other way was it possible to have a platform low enough to meet the requirements of those standing close at hand and at the same time not impair the view of those standing farther away. Evidently somewhere between the days of the inn-theatres and the Fortune (perhaps at the Globe?) the mind of some-one connected with the playhouses saw the advantages to be gained by having the yard slope from rear and sides toward the stage. The innovation could have been intro-duced at any time in the public playhouses with their earthen yards (it was not feasible, except at great expense, in the private houses built in halls already framed and floored); but in planning a new playhouse the idea would be well-nigh inescapable. It meant removing half as much dirt as when excavating the yard to a uniform depth. If the reader is unaware that inclined groundstands were used in pre-Commonwealth days, let him turn to Hollar's en-graving entitled "The True Maner of the Execution of Thomas Earle of Strafford Lord Lieutenant of Ireland vpon Towerhill the 12th of May 1641." [26]

The Globe yard doubtless was paved — but whether with brick or some other hard surface one cannot be sure — otherwise, following a rain, the soil which formerly had been a marsh would have become a mire. We are given what appears to be a clue to the type of paving used at the Fortune in a list of Henslowe's personal disbursements at various times for materials delivered in the builder's ab-sence during the construction of that playhouse. Under the date May 30, 1600, we read: "pd mr william for ix thowsand of brickes." [27] Now, study of the list as a whole shows (1) that Henslowe's payments were made either in earnest of future delivery or in settlement of a delivery made that day; (2) that the items enumerated in the list do not constitute a complete bill of materials even for the period covered by the list (for a general bill and for the agreement concerning payments see the contract itself); and (3) that the brick foundations of the playhouse had

[26] Reproduced by A. M. Hind, *Wenceslaus Hollar and his Views of London*, plate xxxi.
[27] *Henslowe Papers*, p. 11.

been completed on May 8, three weeks before the payment in question. These considerations, together with the fact that a wooden building designed without chimneys has little or no need for bricks above the foundation line, suggest that the bricks bought on May 30 were intended for paving the yard. The quantity stated closely approximates a modern estimate of the number required for paving an area the size of the Fortune yard; it represents less than a quarter of the number required for the Fortune foundation walls, assuming that they extended only 30 inches below ground level. If this reasoning is correct with regard to the Fortune, one is probably justified in assuming that the yard at the Globe Playhouse likewise was paved with brick.

Slightly more than one-third of the Globe yard was occupied by the platform stage which, 41 feet wide at the rear where it met the scenic wall, extended forward "to the middle of the yarde." In the remaining area, measuring 1780 square feet, one estimates that approximately 600 spectators (allowing 3 square feet for a person) could stand without undue crowding. At popular plays and on certain holidays, as the records of the period show, the groundlings packed themselves into the yard until there was not an inch to spare. The inset view on the title-page of *Roxana* (1632) and the frontispiece of *The Wits, or Sport upon Sport* (1662) illustrate how pre-Restoration spectators crowded about the sides of the stage.

One other function of the yard, namely to provide light for the stages and the auditorium, may well be considered here. It is too often forgotten that the Globe playhouse was twice as wide as it was high and similarly that the width of the unroofed yard was almost twice the height of the encircling galleries, measured to the eaves. Such a yard and all that faces on it will not be appreciably darker than a wholly unenclosed area. In mid-winter, particularly after several days of rain, a playhouse interior doubtless seemed black and cheerless, and one is not surprised to learn that at such a time audiences were likely to be small. So much, at least, we learn from Webster's explanation of the poor reception accorded his *White Devil* (1612) when it opened at the Red Bull: "It was acted in so dull a time of Winter, presented in so open and *blacke* [i.e. "bleak" [28]] a Theater, that it wanted (that which is the onely grace and setting out of a Tragedy) a full and understanding Auditory." A wide difference, however, exists between Webster's phrase "open and black" and the statement recently made that "The visibility inside the tall unroofed public theatres must often have been very bad, especially on dull winter days." [29] Inevitably there are dull days in winter or in any other season, but the playhouse was not tall, nor did its yard have the proportions of a well. In order to make the best of the situation, actors began their plays at two o'clock and finished them at four or shortly thereafter.[30]

Whatever our modern disinclination to submit to the rigors of open-air spectacles given in mid-winter and whatever our opinion as to the effect of grey skies upon the full enjoyment of a play, the fact remains that Elizabethan dramatic companies ran up their flags in winter almost as regularly as they did in summer. And what is more, the spectators came. Henslowe's record of theatrical receipts for January and May (months equal in length but preeminently unequal in climate) in the years 1592–3, 1594, and 1596 [31] shows an average of 25 performances in January and of 27 in May — less difference than one might expect. And as to attendance during those same months, the records show an average receipt for January of £37/11/0 and for May of £44/19/0. Further, it is revealed that during

---

[28] Cf. *The Works of John Webster*, ed. F. L. Lucas, i. 274.

[29] A. Hart, "The Time Allotted for Representation of Elizabethan and Jacobean Plays," *R. E. S.*, VIII (Oct., 1932), 408.

[30] The evidence on this point has been definitively presented by Mr. Hart in the article referred to in the preceding note.

[31] *Henslowe's Diary*, pp. 14, 15, 17, 21, 22, 24, 50, 52, and 53.

this period the difference between winter and summer attendance grew less pronounced; Henslowe's receipts for January, 1596, were only £2/17/0 less than his receipts for the following May.

Until the opening of the Blackfriars roofed theatre in 1608 by the great professional company of which Shakespeare was a member, I doubt if the average theatre-goer thought much of the discomforts of the unroofed type of playhouse, though, of course, in all seasons and for all spectacles clear skies and a warm sun would have been welcome.

4. THE GALLERY ENTRANCES

Much of the evidence relating to the spectator galleries in the Elizabethan playhouse has long been known, with the result that a superficial notion of the general plan and of the location of certain "rooms" is fairly widespread; but, so far as I am aware, a thorough investigation has never been attempted. No available verbal description or conjectural plan is sufficiently accurate or complete to enable a scholar readily to visualize the whole, or in imagination to find his way, say, to a "two-penny room," or to a seat in the second or third gallery. Certain minor details will continue to remain obscure unless fuller evidence is discovered, but the evidence in hand is adequate, I believe, to establish with reasonable certainty not only the number, size, and location of the gallery subdivisions but also the nature and disposition of entrances, passageways, and stairs connecting them.

In all three levels of the Globe frame, twelve of the sixteen bays (there being two in each section of the octagon) were made available for theatre-goers willing to pay for better accommodation than standing-room in the yard. For these more substantial or extravagant patrons the penny surrendered at the main door was merely the first of a series of payments demanded of them. To enter into the roofed gallery section of the building cost a second penny, collected by a "gatherer" stationed at one of two gallery entrances. Having paid this general gallery fee, the patron was entitled to mount without further charge to the rather undesirable third gallery and take his place there, or with a further supplement to secure a still better place in one of the lower galleries. No tickets of any kind were used.

It is not to be supposed, however, that this system was clumsy in operation. From a spectator's point of view the major shortcoming — one not unknown today — was that in order to secure a good seat one had to arrive early:

And up came our dinner, at which each man sate downe without re-specting of persons, for he that first comes is first seated, like those that come to see playes.[32]

Elizabethans appear to have accepted the rule of first come first served with equanimity. I find no allusions in pre-Restoration literature to the various stratagems employed in later times to evade it.

Moreover, from the actors' and also the housekeepers' point of view the system was effective. Apart from servants to do the cleaning, the only staff required consisted of a doorkeeper and a number of "gatherers" to collect the supplementary fees imposed at the barriers marking off rooms of higher price. Pennies taken at the main door for admission to the performance went to the actors; money taken for admission to the galleries went to the housekeepers who owned the building and the theatrical stock (later, some time before 1635, the gallery takings also were divided with the actors [33]).

In an earlier section it was shown that all patrons (with the exception of a relatively small number of nobles and gentry whose privileges will be reviewed later in this chapter) entered the playhouse through one "narrow door"

[32] William Fennor, *Compters Common-Wealth*, 1617, p. 8.

[33] *Outlines*, i. 317. For discussion see T. W. Baldwin, *The Organization and Personnel of the Shakespearian Company*, pp. 16–20.

guarded by a doorkeeper. This fact must not be over-looked, for it indicates that all spectators reached the various parts of the auditorium from *inside* the building and not, as in certain Restoration and later theatres, from outside (by means of a number of doors, each with its own doorkeeper — one for the pit, another for the first gallery, and so forth).

At first glance the problem of locating the entrances to the galleries would appear to be solved by the De Witt sketch of the Swan Playhouse interior in 1596. There two short flights of steps (marked, on the left side of the drawing, "ingressus") are shown leading up from the yard into the first gallery. But no other evidence supports this location; and the more one studies the problem — even without reference to evidence pointing quite another way — the more one suspects that Van Buchell, who drew the sketch from information supplied by De Witt,[34] either placed the steps considerably nearer the tiring-house than they actually were or, failing to understand precisely where they were, supplied them from his own imagination. The Swan sketch, as scholars who have studied it know, must always be approached with reservations, for it abounds in so many contradictions, omissions, and obvious errors that no reliance can be placed upon any detail unless that detail is sustained by evidence from other sources.

The objections to gallery entrances placed as in the De Witt sketch are formidable. If other entrances existed elsewhere, these forward entrances would be a nuisance, a standing invitation to the groundlings in the yard to slip into the galleries or to sit down and obstruct the passage of those mounting there. If no other entrances to the gallery existed, these, located so far from the main door of the playhouse,[35] would be as awkwardly placed as it is

[34] For discussion see J. Q. Adams, "The Four Pictorial Representations of the Elizabethan Stage," in *J. E. G. P.*, X (April, 1911), No. 2.

[35] In the best-known reconstruction of an Elizabethan playhouse, that of the Fortune drawn up by Mr. Godfrey in 1907, the entrances are placed still farther

possible to conceive. To provide no means for a large and highly diversified audience to separate into its various classes until all have crossed the yard where the ground-lings were accustomed to be "glewed together" in a compact mass, and then to place the steps in the most restricted part of that area, is, putting it mildly, to invite difficulty and delay. And on those inevitable occasions when gallery patrons entered after the play had begun, or left before the play was over, the distraction and inconvenience to one and all would have been intolerable. Further, steps placed so far from the main entrance would compel most of those mounting to the galleries to return inside the gallery (regardless of the level selected) towards the point at which they entered the building. Yet another complication would arise from the tendency of those first entering the galleries to seat themselves or remain standing in bays near the steps (for sections near the stage were highly prized), thus impeding the flow of patrons to seats elsewhere.

In short, with gallery entrances placed as De Witt indicates, the groundlings either would have been forced to wait until the last gallery patron had passed through the yard before taking their final places — a supposition which, to one who knows something of the temper of the groundlings, is little short of fantastic; or the gallery patrons would have been put to no little trouble and delay in reaching their places. Such a system, the reverse of all that a modicum of experience and common sense prescribes in planning the entrances and exits of any auditorium, would at all times operate clumsily. When the yard was filled with groundlings coming early to a popular play, it would not work at all.

But were the steps placed in the corridor which led from the outer door through the frame to the inner yard the

from the main door, at the ends of the tiring-house. Such a position is open to the objections advanced in the text to a degree yet more pronounced than the position indicated by De Witt.

objections set out above would wholly disappear. The corridor would then serve as a vestibule for all the spectators, with the groundlings hurrying on to take up places as near to the stage as possible, and with the other patrons mounting right and left by steps into the galleries. Several advantages would result from such a plan: (1) the crowd would of its own accord tend to break up into three divergent streams as soon as it had passed the doorkeeper and entered the building; (2) the gallery patrons would tend to move away from the points at which they entered the lowermost gallery in an attempt to secure places in or as near as possible the rooms of greatest desirability or they would mount the stairs which led to galleries above; (3) the time and effort required to reach any point in the three galleries would be reduced to a minimum; and (4) since the routes leading in and out of the galleries lay behind the assembled audience, the disturbance caused by untimely arrivals and departures would be reduced to a minimum.

The alternative to placing the gallery entrances in the entrance corridor would be to place them in sections at the rear of the yard; but such an arrangement would be less satisfactory, and a passage in Stephen Gosson's *Plays Confuted in fiue Actions*, 1582, seems to imply that though it was possible it was not necessary to enter the yard before mounting to the galleries:

In the playhouses at London, it is the fashion of youthes to go first into the yarde, and to carry their eye through euery gallery, then like vnto rauens where they spye the carion thither they flye, and presse as nere to ye fairest as they can.[36]

5. GALLERY PASSAGEWAYS AND STAIRS

The design of the passageways, stairs, and rooms of the playhouse galleries was probably taken over — with certain modifications to permit the addition of a third gallery

---

[36] Cited from Chambers, iv. 218.

and a greater variety of rooms — from long experience in animal-baiting arenas and inn-theatres. The De Witt sketch, it is true, does not indicate what lay beyond the top of the steps leading into the first gallery, nor does it show any of the partitions implied in the Fortune and stipulated in the Hope contracts separating the gallery rooms, and yet, with the aid of other sources, one can piece out with some completeness the nature and position of those features in the Globe and other playhouses.

As stated, a spectator, after paying a penny at the main door, entered a vestibule from which he could pass without further payment into the yard. If, however, he desired better accommodation, he turned to the right or to the left inside the vestibule, paid a second penny at a second "door," mounted two or three steps, and found himself at the foot of one of the two stairways leading to the upper gallery sections of the auditorium. At this point he had a choice of mounting to the second or third gallery, or of paying a third admission fee at a third "door" opening to the first gallery. These stairways to the upper galleries were affixed to the outside of the frame and could not well be constructed except against a flat section of exterior wall. It was illogical to place them side by side, and there was not room enough against one section of exterior wall for them to flank the vestibule. The stairways were therefore constructed beyond the first subsequent corners of the frame on either side, and a pair of short passageways connected them with the vestibule. It was obviously desirable, if only to minimize the disturbance caused by late-comers, to locate all these units outside the building.[37]

Let me review the evidence leading to these various conclusions.

At the entrance to each passageway stood a gatherer, in the employ not of the actors but of the housekeepers, whose duty it was to collect a penny from everyone desir-

[37] I am particularly indebted throughout this section to Dr. Joseph Q. Adams for suggestions and criticism.

ing to enter the galleries, no matter what his final destination might be. Evidence establishing the payment of this

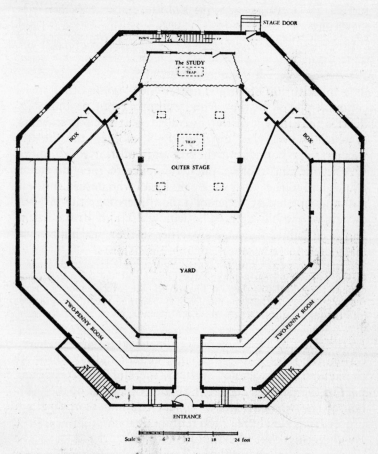

RECONSTRUCTED PLAN OF THE GLOBE: FIRST LEVEL

second fee — and the fact that it was paid before proceeding farther than the entrance to the galleries must not be overlooked — is found in three independent sources. In William Lambard's *Perambulation of Kent*, published in

1576, the year in which the Theater was being erected, the author illustrates a point by noting that no spectators

suche as goe to Parisgardein, the Bell Sauage, or some other suche common place, to beholde Beare bayting, Enterludes, or Fence playe, can account of any pleasant spectacle, unlesse they first paye one penny at the gate, another at the entrie of the Scaffolde, and the thirde for a quiet standing.[38]

The substitution of "the Theater" for "some other suche common place" in the second edition (1596) probably indicates that in regard to fees collected at various stations, of which one was the "entrie of the Scaffolde," the Theater was patterned on its inn-theatre and bull-ring forerunners.

A second and more explicit reference to the gallery entrance and to the gallery fee paid by all who passed through is found in a court order of 1590 directed at the *de facto* owners of the Theater. The widow of John Brayne, who had been James Burbage's partner in that playhouse, was instructed to go with one or more assistants

to the Theater uppon a playe daye to stand at the door that goeth uppe to the gallaries of the said Theater to take & receive for the use of the same Margarett half the money that should be gyven to come uppe into the said Gallaries at the door.[39]

As the relict of a part-owner of the Theater her rights concerned the income due the householders and not that due the actors. She was not entitled, therefore, to attach any part of the pennies collected at the outer door of the playhouse; she was entitled to collect one-half of the gallery proceeds, as her share of the rental due to the housekeepers. By directing that she should "stand at the door which goeth uppe to the gallaries" and "take & receive" for her own use "half the money that should be gyven to comme uppe into the said Gallaries" the court order shows that all patrons entering the galleries had to pass through

[38] *Perambulation*, 1576, pp. 187–188.
[39] Quoted from Wallace, *The First London Theatre*, p. 114.

a "door" or control point in order to gain access to any part thereof.

A third reference, relating this time to the Globe and showing that the system of entrances to the gallery and to the gallery rooms there was similar to that at the Theater, is given by Thomas Platter following his visit to the playhouse in 1599. On the matter in question he writes:

Anyone who remains on the level standing [i.e. the yard] pays only one English penny: but if he wants to sit, he is let in at a further door, and there he gives another penny. If he desires to sit on a cushion in the most comfortable place of all, where he not only sees everything well, but can also be seen, then he gives yet another English penny at another door.[40]

Platter's description, one should note, makes it quite clear that two sets of gallery "doors" existed, the first at the entrance to the galleries and the second at the entrance to a room — in his case a so-called "two-penny room." Thus to reach "the most comfortable place of all"[41] one had to pass progressively through a series of three control points: (1) the main entrance to the playhouse, (2) a "further door," i.e. the general entrance to the galleries, and (3) the door to the room itself.

Familiarity with the foregoing quotations and their import will give added point to the following quotation from John Field's *Godly Exhortation*, 1583. Inveighing against those who spent their substance in "Dicing house, Bowling alley, Cock pit, or Theater," Field wrote that "Pounds and hundreds can be well ynough afforded, in following these least pleasures, though euery dore hath a payment, & euery gallerie maketh a yearely stipend."[42]

The Fortune contract provides for the installation of gallery passageways, partitions, and stairs, but does not

[40] Cited by Chambers, ii. 365. For the entire account see *Thomas Platter's Travels in England 1599* (ed. Clare Williams, London, 1937). The passage in question appears on p. 167. Minor errors abound in the *Travels*.

[41] See below, p. 61.

[42] Quoted from Chambers, iv. 219.

tell us much more than that the stairs and "Conveyances" (passageways) were outside the building and that in all these details the Fortune was to be made similar to the Globe. When brought together these specifications read:

Wth suchelike steares Conveyances & divisions wthoute & wthin as are made & Contryved in and to the late erected Plaiehowse . . . Called the Globe . . . [the stage] shalbe placed & sett As alsoe the stearecases of the saide fframe in suche sorte as is p^{r}figured in a Plott thereof drawen [the plan is lost] . . . And the saide fframe Stadge and Stearecases to be covered wth Tyle . . . And also all the saide fframe and the Staircases thereof to be sufficyently enclosed wthoute wth lathe lyme & haire . . . And the saide howse and other thinges beforemenc̄oed to be made & doen To be in all other Contrivitions Conveyances fashions thinge and thinges effected finished and doen accordinge to the manner and fashion of the saide howse Called the Globe.

The Hope contract is rather more explicit with regard to the number and the placing of the stairways outside the building:

Builde two stearecasses wthout and adioyninge to the saide Playe house in suche convenient places as shalbe most fitt and convenient for the same to stande vppon, and of such largnes and height as the stearecasses of . . . the Swan nowe are or bee;

but with regard to passageways the Hope contract contains nothing specific; it does, however, call for "p[ar]ti-cōns betwne the Rommes as they are at the saide Plaie house called the Swan."

The wording of these two contracts is of further interest in showing (as does other evidence) that there was little change from first to last in the basic plan of an Elizabethan playhouse structure: the Fortune (1600) sedulously copied the Globe (1599), and the Hope (1613) sedulously copied the Swan (1595).

If only to conserve space and to expedite the movement of patrons, the main door, the vestibule, the passageway leading from it on each side, the entrance to the first gallery and the stair-landing of the stairway on that side of the building formed, we may be sure, one closely related unit. From this it follows that if the gallery entrances opened from the vestibule and passageways inside the main playhouse door, the gallery stairs must have flanked the playhouse door at no great distance from it. In an octagonal building the first "convenient place" for the outside stairs leading to the upper galleries would be beyond the first corner of the frame, against the flat wall of the section beginning there. If, as seems probable, the Globe entrance vestibule was placed in the middle of the section opposite the platform stage, only 10 or 12 feet would have remained between the side of the vestibule and the first subsequent corner post of the frame — space adequate for the "door" or control point, the steps up from the vestibule to the first gallery level (which was between 24 and 30 inches above the ground level), and the door into the first gallery, but inadequate for those three units in addition to the flight of steps to the second gallery 12 feet above.

Staircases large enough to serve the several hundred spectators mounting to the two upper galleries must have formed a conspicuous feature of the exterior walls of the playhouse, a fact which suggests a scrutiny of the larger and more detailed Bankside views. But apparently the Swan, the Hope, and the Globe were all three so placed that the stage faced the south, and hence that half of the building containing the main door and the outside gallery stairs faced the north, which meant that artists sketching London from the south were unable to represent that side of the playhouses. Whatever the reason, no trace of outside stairs or of playhouse doors appears in any Bankside view executed while playhouses were in use. However, in Hollar's 1647 representation of the Globe and the Hope there is a projection, enclosed and roofed and unquestionably a staircase, jutting out from the wall of each building towards the northeast (i.e. on the side visible from the viewpoint Hollar assumes in the tower of St. Saviour's; the roof of a second staircase is indicated on the northwest side of the Hope). So placed, that staircase in the Globe (and also the staircase presumably paired with it on the other side of the entrance door) could not have been seen by Visscher, who established his viewpoint south of the Bankside. Hollar's staircases so exactly bear out the building-contract terms that one is inclined to except this detail from the suspicion that in general attaches to his representation of the two buildings. For what it is worth, moreover, his drawing confirms the position of the Globe staircases relative to the main entrance which has been postulated in the foregoing pages.

In the absence of evidence to the contrary, it seems reasonable to suppose that the two stairways at the Globe were placed symmetrically, and were uniform in plan, size, and height. Little would be gained by having one to serve only the second gallery and the other to serve only the top gallery, for such a limitation would not reduce crowding, and, unless signs were prominently displayed and all patrons could read, would succeed only in confusing those not wholly familiar with the building. From the size and shape of the staircase represented in the Hollar view and from considerations of convenience and safety for those using the stairs, we may further assume that the stairs were designed in straight flights extending from one level to the next. Such a design, which presupposes on the second level a passageway inside the frame connecting the *up* stair-landing with the *down* (and enclosed to prevent third-gallery patrons from slipping into the second gallery without paying the gatherer stationed at the door leading to the second gallery), would be stronger, more economical of materials, and easier to build than either a spiral stairway (and one constructed with "returns" to bring each stair-landing directly over the one below) or a stairway extending in one flight from the lowest gallery to the highest.

6. GALLERY SUBDIVISIONS

The Fortune contract, dated January 8, 1599/1600, presumably gives us an exact definition of the *types* of subdivisions available in the Globe, then but a few months old, and of the interior finish given to the rooms of higher price. Its specifications call for:

ffower convenient divisions for gentlemens roomes and other sufficient and convenient divisions for Twoe pennie roomes wth necessarie Seates to be placed and sett Aswell in those roomes as througheoute all the rest of the galleries of the saide howse . . . the gentlemens roomes and Twoe pennie roomes to be seeled wth lathe lyme & haire . . . the said Peeter Streete shall not be chardged wth anie manner of pay[ntin]ge in or aboute the saide fframe howse or Stadge or anie p[ar]te thereof nor Rendringe the walls w^thin Nor seeling anie more or other roomes then the gentlemens roomes Twoe pennie roomes and Stadge before remembred.

These clauses show that in the galleries three types of spectator accommodation were provided, namely, "gentlemens roomes," "Twoe pennie roomes," and "the rest of the galleries." Thus, in all, the Globe and Fortune made available five classes of spectator accommodation (for the moment let us disregard the question of sitting and standing): in the unroofed yard, in three types of gallery subdivisions graded according to price, and — as will later be shown — on the platform stage. This five-fold range of accommodation needs to be stressed, for an approach to the problem by way of records of admission fees and of supplementary fees collected in the galleries seems to imply a far greater number of classes. In the years 1576–1644 the range of charges extends, with many gradations, from a penny to a half-crown, a range that led Sir Edmund Chambers to remark: "The whole question of seating and prices is rather difficult, and it is further complicated by obscurely discerned changes of fashion." [43] Four qualifications at least must be taken into account when consider-

---

[43] Chambers, ii. 531.

ing the evidence of prices: (1) the date of the reference, (2) the distinction between prices at public and private houses, (3) the practice of charging double prices on the occasion of a new play, and (4) the habit of referring to a gallery subdivision in terms either of the total cost of admission or of the room-supplement only.

Without attempting to study the problem throughout the entire period, I shall try to determine the relationship between prices and accommodations at the Globe during the first ten years of its existence. Between 1599 and 1609 the range of prices is by no means as extensive as in the period as a whole. Apart from references to double charges for new plays, there exist numerous references (1) to the penny entrance fee to the yard; (2) to "penny galleries," "two-penny galleries," "Twoe pennie roomes," "gentlemens roomes," and "twelve-penny rooms"; and (3) to fees of sixpence and one shilling paid either for a place on the outer stage or in some room near the stage. (Many of these references will be cited in the pages to follow.) The names "penny gallery" and "two-penny gallery" apparently relate to the same subdivision, namely the top or third gallery, of the playhouse; and an Elizabethan called this subdivision the "penny gallery" if he had in mind merely the gallery supplement, or the "two-penny gallery" if he had in mind the total cost of admission there, that is, one penny at the outer door of the playhouse and one penny additional at the entrance to the gallery stairs.

As the Fortune contract shows, the "two-penny *rooms*" were distinct from the "rest of the galleries." Inasmuch as they are not called "three-penny rooms" (nor is there any mention of a "three-penny gallery" — at least not before 1635, by which time several shifts in prices had come about), one is perhaps justified in assuming that the fee charged at the door of a "two-penny room" was twopence, and that the total cost of admission to one of these gallery subdivisions was fourpence, that is, one penny at the door of the playhouse, one penny more at the entrance to the galleries, and a final twopence at the door of the "room" itself.

It is less easy to determine the supplementary charges for the "gentlemen's rooms." Pertinent on the one hand is Platter's very explicit account, relating to the Globe in 1599, of paying a total of threepence "to sit on a cushion in the most comfortable place of all, where he not only sees everything well but can also be seen," and, on the other hand, the implication of the Fortune contract executed a few months later that the two-penny *rooms* (to which, as I have tried to show, admission in 1600 actually cost a total of fourpence) were not the best. Nor can one reconcile Platter's account with a series of references beginning two or three years later to a "twelve-penny room" [44] at the Globe, and to a "twelve-penny room next the stage" [45] there and also at the Blackfriars playhouse. Perhaps Platter as a visiting tourist disregarded the few "private rooms" reserved by custom and by high fees for the use of the nobility and gentry; but however that may be, the evidence leads us to conclude that at the time of or not long after Platter's visit the total price of admission to the gentlemen's rooms at the Globe was one shilling. From this analysis it will be seen that a primary distinction between a "room" and a "gallery" was this: admittance to a "room" entailed a supplementary charge (i.e. a charge in addition to the main entrance plus the gallery entrance fees) paid to a gatherer at the door of the room; whereas admittance to the "gallery" (i.e. the top gallery) entailed no supplementary fee, and hence involved no gatherer and required no "door" beyond those at the entrances to the gallery staircases.

So much, then, for the types of gallery subdivisions and the prices normally paid for admission to each in the first decade of the Globe's existence. What can be determined about their size and location? To make headway with this

[44] Induction to *The Malcontent*, 1604, a Globe play.
[45] *The Guls Hornbook*, ed. R. B. McKerrow, p. 9.

aspect of the problem one must keep in mind the fact that Elizabethan public playhouses derived from democratic inn-yard theatres and animal arenas, and not from aristocratic or academic great halls. In particular one must be wary of confusing the "rooms" of the public playhouse with the small "boxes" of Restoration and subsequent theatres, or of being misled by the custom, begun in Jacobean private playhouses (but never, it appears, adopted in public playhouses), of reserving a box for the exclusive use of one person and his guests. The Elizabethan term "room" seemingly bore no implication of size; it denoted simply some gallery subdivision — large or small — into which, so long as all "places" there were not already pre-empted, anyone might enter on payment of the required supplement.

7. THE TWO-PENNY GALLERY

In an Elizabethan public playhouse the "two-penny rooms" and the "two-penny gallery" were as different as the first and top balconies today. They differed in location, comfort, price of admission, and, consequently, in class of patron. In accordance with the logical rule of the theatre, "the higher the cheaper," we are justified in assuming that in the Globe, as in Restoration theatres of a generation later,[46] the "gallery commoners" congregated in the top gallery of the playhouse. A passage of sustained theatrical metaphor in Dekker's *Ravens Almanacke* (1609) bears out this assumption:

Suffer me to carry vp your thoughts vpon nimbler winges where (as if you sat in the moste perspicuous place of the two-pennie gallerie in a Play House) you shall clearly and with an open eye beholde all the partes, which I (your new Astrologer) act among the stars.

The passage leads, moreover, to the inference that there was only one two-penny (or top) gallery; and this inference is confirmed elsewhere in Dekker's writings, for example:

---

[46] Summers, *The Restoration Theatre*, p. 35. See also Lawrence, i. 38.

"The player loues a poet so long as the sicknesse lyes in the two-pennie gallery when none will come into it"; [47] and "Pay thy twopence to a Player, in his gallerie maist thou sitte by a Harlot." [48] And again: "One of them is a nip; I tooke him once i' the twopenny gallery at the Fortune." [49]

Evidence bearing on the physical details of the two-penny gallery is for the most part incomplete or inferential. (1) At the Fortune only the gentlemen's rooms and two-penny rooms were to be given plaster side-walls and ceilings. The omission of a plaster ceiling in the third gallery (a gallery only 9 feet high) was probably dictated by motives of economy, but the need for headroom might also have been taken into consideration, for without the additional space available under the gable roof it would have been impossible to elevate the "standings" more than 2 or 3 feet, an elevation hardly adequate to enable those at the rear of the gallery to see the near-half of the outer stage 23 feet below. (2) The third gallery at the Fortune, and presumably at the Globe, was 20 inches deeper than the first by virtue of the "Juttey forwardes in either [i.e. both] of the saide Twoe vpper Stories of Tenne ynches of lawfull assize." (3) There is no reason to suppose that any

[47] *Knights Conjuring*, 1607.

[48] *Lanthorn and Candlelight*, 1608.

[49] *The Roaring Girl*, 1611, V. i. Although the great majority of references point to only one "two-penny gallery" in each playhouse, there are at least two which seem to imply more than one such gallery. Dekker writes in his *Seven Deadly Sins* (1606):

> Tis given out that Sloth himselfe will come and sit in the two-pennie galleries amongst the gentlemen, and see their [the players'] knaveries and their pastimes.

Middleton writes in his *Father Hubburds Tales* (1604) of a "dull audience of Stinkards sitting in the pennie-galleries of a theatre and yawning upon the players." In these passages Dekker and Middleton are probably thinking of the auditorium in general terms (one can hardly expect precise language in all parts of the hastily written pamphlets of the age). But it is also possible that they were thinking of less fashionable theatres where, to secure an audience, the number of two-penny galleries probably was greater than in theatres of the class of the Globe and Fortune.

gallery or room was subdivided by partitions into small units. (4) Persons emerging from the stairs into the third gallery were entitled to proceed to any vacant place. (5) It may be that the third-story bays immediately adjoining the tiring-house on both sides were closed off by partitions and incorporated in the tiring-house for use as storage rooms. Such bays were too close to the scenic wall and too high above the platform stage to be desirable to spectators. (6) The Fortune contract, as we have seen, calls for "necessarie Seates to be placed and Sett" in the top as in other galleries; but since the seating and standing arrangements of the various galleries and rooms constitute a unified problem, I shall take up the evidence relating thereto in a later part of this chapter.

Common sense as well as the De Witt view of the Swan and Restoration practice suggest that some sort of railing was provided at the forward edge of the two upper galleries, comparable to the palings of the first gallery, particularly since spectators aloft were inclined to crowd towards the front in order to see well. A different reason for crowding to the front of the galleries is suggested by a puritanical writer (Anthony Munday?):

Whosoeuer shal visit the chappel of Satan, I meane the Theater, shal finde there no want of yong ruffins, nor lacke of harlots, vtterlie past al shame: who presse to the fore-frunt of the scaffoldes, to the end to showe their impudencie, and to be as an obiect to al mens eies.[50]

Admission to the third gallery cost, as we have seen, a total of twopence, of which one penny was surrendered at the outer door of the playhouse, and a second at the entrance to the gallery stairs. This system of gallery supplements gave rise to Dekker's statement in *The Guls Hornbook* (1609): "Your groundling and gallery commoner buys his sport by the penny"; and to the opprobrious phrase "penny-bench theatres."

The quotations cited above give some indication of the

[50] *A second and third blast of retrait from plaies and Theatres*, 1580, p. 139.

nature of the spectators patronizing the two-penny gallery. Their numbers are suggested by a passage in *Work for Armourers* (1609), wherein Dekker writes of "terme times, when the Twopenny Clients and Peny Stinkards swarme together to heere the Stagerites." The Prologue to *The Woman-Hater* warns:

If there be any amongst you, that come to hear lascivious Scenes, let them depart: for I do pronounce this, to the utter discomfort of all two-penny Gallery men, you shall have no bawdery in it.

The Epilogue to *Satiromastix* thus bids them farewell:

Are you pleas'd? . . . if you be not, by th' Lord Ile see you all — heere for your two pence a piece agen, before Ile loose your company. . . Good night my two penny Tenants, Good night.[51]

8. THE TWO-PENNY ROOMS

The general terms of the Fortune contract conceal from us the location and size of the two-penny rooms, indicating that in these details, as in so many others, the Fortune was closely modeled upon the Globe. But that there were two or more two-penny rooms in both playhouses seems clear. One of the two clauses of the Fortune contract relating to subdivisions in the galleries calls for "sufficient and convenient divisions for Twoe pennie *roomes.*" The other releases the builder from having to install plaster ceilings in "anie more or other roomes then the gentlemens roomes, Twoe pennie *roomes* and Stadge before remembred."

Of course it does not follow that all playhouses were alike in the extent of their provision for well-to-do patrons. When the Hope was erected in 1613, for example, only two "boxes" were contracted for, in contrast to the four at the Fortune. It seems probable, therefore, that the size or the number of two-penny rooms in theatres smaller, older, or less fashionable than the Globe and the Fortune was re-

[51] See also Chambers, ii. 532–533, where several of the quotations given here are cited; *Dekker's Works*, ed. Grosart, iv. 55; *Middleton's Works*, ed. Bullen, ii. 94; and *The Fliere*, II. i.

duced also. Differences of this sort are reflected in contemporary literature; writers sometimes referred to the two-penny "rooms" of a theatre, and sometimes to the two-penny "room."

The two-penny rooms were designed for theatre-goers of average means, those for whose approval playwrights and actors put forth their best efforts. The Prologue to *Every Man out of his Humour*, when told to proceed with his interrupted speech, retorts, "And I doe, let me die poyson'd with some venemous hisse, and neuer liue to looke as high as the two-penny roome againe" (i.e. let me never lift my head again). In the Epistle Dedicatory to *The Hospitall of Incurable Fooles* (1600) Blount writes, "I beg it with as forced a looke, as a Player that in speaking an Epilogue makes loue to the two-pennie roume for a plaudite."

For the most part writers mention the two-penny rooms only as a setting for certain types of spectators. Dekker remarks of Satan that "You may take him . . . in the afternoones, in the twopenny roomes of a Play-House, like a Puny, seated Cheeke by Iowle with a Punke"; [52] and elsewhere makes a jest at the expense of "a Wench hauing a good face, a good body, and good clothes on, but of bad conditions, sitting one day in a two-penny roome of a play-house, & a number of young Gentlemen about her, against whom she maintained talke." [53] Middleton speaks of courtesans sitting there, and of actors on the stage who "took such a good conceit of their [the courtesans'] parts into th' two-penny room, that the actors have been found i' th' morning in a less compass than their stage." [54] Richard Brathwaite, in *Whimzies: or a New Cast of Characters* (1631), illustrates the way ruffians forced their way into one of the two-penny rooms:

To a play they wil hazard to go, though with never a rag of money: where after the *second Act*, when the [main playhouse entrance] *Doore*

[52] *News from Hell*, 1600 (*Works*, ed. Grosart, ii. 96).
[53] *Jests to Make You Merry*, 1607 (*Works*, ed. Grosart, ii. 292).
[54] *A Mad World, my Masters*, 1608, V. ii.

is weakly guarded, they will make *forcible entrie*; a knock with a Cudgell is the worst; whereat though they grumble, they rest pacified upon their admittance. Forthwith, by violent assault and assent [i.e. ascent] they aspire to the two-pennie roome; where being furnished with Tinder, Match, and a portion of decayed *Barmoodas*, they smoake it most terribly, applaude a prophane jeast unmeasurably, and in the end grow distastefully rude to all the Companie. At the Conclusion of all, they single out their *dainty Doxes*, to cloze up a fruitlesse day with a sinnefull evening.[55]

Quotations such as these from satirical writers give a one-sided view of the first and second gallery audience, which, needless to say, contained its share of respectable men and women about whom there is never much to remark.

The location of the two-penny rooms at the Globe can be determined by a process of elimination. As we have seen, the playhouse made provision for three classes of patrons: the poorest flocked to the yard, or mounted to the "two-penny gallery" in the third level; the wealthiest (as we shall learn) either sat on the stage, or in the gentlemen's rooms which occupied the bays immediately adjoining the tiring-house in the first and second galleries; the middle-class spectators, therefore, occupied the remaining bays in the first and second galleries.

The contract specifications concerning rooms at the Fortune are of no help in determining the location of the partitions set up between rooms of different price in the same gallery. The Hope contract, however, illuminates the problem somewhat by stipulating that the builder

shall make Two Boxes in the lowermost storie fitt and decent for gentlemen to sitt in And shall make the p[ar]ticōns betwne the Rommes as they are at the saide Plaie house called the Swan.

Since at the Fortune (and presumably at the Globe) there were to be *four* gentlemen's rooms, in those two playhouses the arrangement of both the first and the second galleries

55 *Whimzies*, 1631, G5 verso.

probably corresponded to the arrangement of the "lower-most" gallery at the Hope. Thus there was a "box" or gentlemen's room flanking the tiring-house at the ends of each of those two galleries where they abutted on the stage, and a two-penny room, separated from the gentlemen's rooms by partitions, occupying the remainder. The lower-most gallery was divided in the middle by the corridor giving access to the yard. Each half was entered through a door, guarded by a gatherer, placed in the passageway leading from the vestibule to the gallery stairs. The two-penny room on the second gallery extended without a break from the partition marking the end of the gentle-men's room on one side of the auditorium to the corre-sponding partition on the other. Entrance to this upper two-penny room was gained through a door, guarded by a gatherer, in each of the second-story stair-landings forming a part of the two outside staircases. I agree with Sir Ed-mund Chambers [56] in finding no valid reason for subdivid-ing any of the gallery rooms. Dekker specifically refers to them as "vast":

> Giue me *That Man*,
> Who when the *Plague* of an Impostumd *Braynes*
> (*Breaking* out) infects a *Theater*, and hotly raignes,
> Killing the *Hearers* hearts, that the vast roomes
> Stand empty, like so many Dead-mens toombes,
> Can call the *Banishd* Auditor home.[57]

The Fortune contract provides that the two-penny rooms (and the gentlemen's rooms) were to be ceiled with lath and plaster, and it may be that they had plastered and painted walls also. Streete was specifically not to be held responsible for painting any part of the Fortune Playhouse, nor for "Rendringe [i.e. plastering] the walls within." Since, in addition to the £440 paid to Streete upon com-pletion of the structure, Henslowe subsequently disbursed £80 in making the playhouse ready for use,[58] the reference

---

[56] Chambers, ii. 531.
[57] *If It be not Good*, 1602, Prologue.   [58] *Henslowe Papers*, p. 108.

to "rendering" the inside walls may mean that Henslowe intended, in addition to the paintwork, to supervise the interior wall plasterwork himself. Some finish, at least in the best rooms, is implied in the phrasing of the Hope contract relative to its gentlemen's rooms — "fitt and decent for gentlemen to sitt in" — for the inner surface of the lath-and-plaster exterior wall would be both rough and unsightly.

A verbal picture of an Elizabethan auditorium during a performance, with the galleries and the yard full of spectators intent upon the play, is given in the opening scene of Middleton and Dekker's *Roaring Girl*, acted at the Fortune. Except for a reference to the square shape of the building, the description was no doubt equally applicable to the Globe. Sir Alexander, leading his friends forward on the outer stage and pointing to the auditorium as if it were the missing half of his house, asks them how they like the magnificent tapestried room:

Laxton.   See how tis furnisht.

Sir Davy.   A very faire sweete roome.

Sir Alex.   Sir *Davy Dapper*,
    The furniture that doth adorne this roome,
    Cost many a faire grey groat ere it came here,
    But good things are most cheape, when th'are most deere,
    Nay, when you looke into my galleries,
    How brauely they are trimm'd vp, you all shall sweare
    Yare highly pleasd to see what's set downe there:
    Stories of men and women (mixt together
    Faire ones with foule, like sun-shine in wet wether)
    Within one square a thousand heads are laid,
    So close, that all of heads, the roome seeemes made,
    As many faces there (fil'd with blith lookes)
    Shew like the promising titles of new bookes,
    (Writ merily) the Readers being their owne eyes,
    Which seeme to moue and to giue plaudities,
    And here and there (whilst with obsequious eares,
    Throng'd heapes do listen) a cut-purse thrusts and leeres
    With hawkes eyes for his prey: I need not shew him,
    By a hanging villanous looke, your selues may know him,

The face is drawne so rarely, Then sir below,
The very flowre (as twere) waues to and fro,
And like a floating Iland, seemes to moue
Vpon a sea bound in with shores aboue,
Omnes. These sights are excellent.[59]

9. THE GENTLEMEN'S ROOMS

The first public playhouses seem to have made no provision for spectators belonging to the world of fashion. How soon men of wealth and rank began to attend performances at the "penny-bench" theatres has not yet been determined, but before 1590 their presence — not, to be sure, in the spectator-galleries but in some box or balcony fronting the second level of the tiring-house — had been reflected in plays (e.g. *The Taming of a Shrew* and *The Spanish Tragedy*); and not long after, in 1592, they were attending in sufficient numbers and with sufficient regularity to warrant, at least in Henslowe's "little Rose," the setting aside and decorating of two rooms for their private use. From that time on their presence in the tiring-house balcony, later in the "private rooms" or boxes immediately adjoining the tiring-house, and eventually even on the stage itself, gave rise to a stream of comment on the part of contemporary playwrights, poets, and pamphlet writers, who found abundant material, especially in the more foppish element of this privileged group, for satire. Their satirical comments, together with other records, make it possible to trace the origins of the Globe and Fortune gentlemen's rooms with some completeness, to locate those rooms with precision, and to discover a number of details distinguishing them from other gallery rooms.

The Fortune contract informs us that there were four "gentlemens roomes" at that playhouse, and hence by implication at the Globe, but it gives no hint either as to their size or their location. The Hope contract provides

[59] *The Roaring Girl*, 1611, I. i. First cited by M. W. Sampson, *Modern Language Notes*, XXX (June, 1915), No. 6.

for "Two Boxes in the lowermost storie fitt and decent for gentlemen to sitt in" and for "p[ar]ticōns betwne the Rommes as they are at the saide Plaie house called the Swan." The two boxes in the first gallery at the Hope no doubt corresponded to the two lowermost of the four "gentlemens roomes" at the Globe and Fortune, playhouses larger than the Hope and designed for a greater number of well-to-do patrons. De Witt's sketch of the Swan interior in 1596 illustrates precisely where in "the lowermost storie" of that playhouse the two boxes were located, and in addition disposes of the notion that gentlemen's rooms (come by 1613 to be known as "boxes") were an innovation at the Globe and Fortune. Across the low wall of palings below a section of the first gallery immediately to the left of the tiring-house (and implying that a similar designation would have appeared to the right had the sketch been developed on that side) the word "orchestra" is written; and "orchestra," according to a definition given by the playwright Thomas Heywood,[60] meant "a place in the Theatre onely for the Nobilitie." In Cotgrave's *Dictionary*, 1611, "*orchestre*" is defined as "the senators' or noblemen's places in a theatre, between the stage and the common seats." [61]

Dekker refers to the location of the gentlemen's rooms ("twelve-penny rooms") in the *Proœmium* to his *Guls Hornbook* (published in 1609 but written somewhat earlier):

I conjure you (as you come of the right *goose-caps*) staine not your house; but when at a new play you take vp the twelve-penny roome next the stage; (because the Lords and you may seeme to be haile fellow wel-met) there draw forth this booke, read alowd, laugh alowd, and play the *Antickes*, that all the garlike mouthd stinkards may cry out, *Away with the fool.*[62]

---

[60] *History of Women*, 1624, p. 449.

[61] Cited by Lawrence, i. 39, where other quotations are given showing this to be the standard meaning during the first half of the seventeenth century.

[62] Dekker is using the normal name for the room without regard to the double prices usually charged on the occasion of a new play.

This passage, one observes, indicates a location for the twelve-penny rooms which coincides precisely with the location shown by De Witt and defined by Cotgrave. The passage is also notable in that it mentions the presence of Lords in the twelve-penny rooms; as W. J. Lawrence observed,[63] "the witling could not give the impression of being hail fellow well met with the nobility without sitting in their midst." Since, as we have just seen, the "twelve-penny room" was merely another name for the "gentlemens roome" of the Fortune contract, 1600, or for the "box fitt and decent for gentlemen to sitt in" of the Hope contract, 1613, we are thus provided with a link connecting the twelve-penny room with the "orchestra" ("a place in the Theatre onely for the Nobility") of the Swan sketch, 1596, and the "Lords rooms" at the Rose in which Henslowe in 1592 installed plaster ceilings. One thing is clear: the terms, to cite them in the chronological order of their occurrence, "Lords room," "orchestra," "gentlemens roome," "twelve-penny room," and "box" are merely different names given at different periods or by different writers to the same thing, to wit, the best accommodations in the playhouse.

As we have seen, Dekker in *The Guls Hornbook* speaks of "the twelve-penny rooms next the stage" at the Globe and the Blackfriars. Elsewhere in the same pamphlet he speaks of "the Lords roome (which is now but the Stages Suburbs)." Despite efforts which have been made to read a sinister meaning into Dekker's use of the word "suburbs," he is manifestly referring to the final phase in the evolution of the gentlemen's rooms, rooms originating (as we shall see in the pages to follow) in the upper level of the tiring-house in early playhouses, established for a time over the stage doors, and finally removed to the galleries adjoining the tiring-house — the position we are familiar with today.

It may be that one or two Jacobean private playhouses

[63] *Elizabethan Playhouse*, i, 37.

perpetuated the lords' rooms of the tiring-house, after their original position was no longer available, by creating two or more small boxes (possibly screened with lattice to afford some privacy) located either in the second level of the tiring-house and just beyond the two window-stages or in the first level just beyond the stage doors. Private playhouses, notably in Carolinian times, were called upon to provide special boxes for nobles of high degree [64] who could hardly be expected to occupy the twelve-penny rooms along with Inns-of-Court students and persons of the middle class. Jacobean evidence, although too meagre to tell much about these boxes, does prepare us for the appearance after 1660 of small and sometimes partially curtained or latticed boxes (distinct from the "side-boxes" of the auditorium) on the stage itself adjoining, and occa-sionally over, the proscenium doors. In the first half of the eighteenth century a "stage-box" was occasionally used by royalty.[65]

But that the Globe had such latticed boxes appears highly improbable. Royalty never crossed its threshold. If the king or a member of his family wished to see a Globe play he commanded the services of the company at a special performance given at Court or in the house of some great nobleman. The presence of noblemen in the twelve-penny rooms at the Globe, on the other hand, is mentioned by Dekker as if it were a matter of course. Had there been special boxes for them better than the twelve-penny gen-tlemen's rooms, a hint, presumably, would have appeared in the Fortune contract or in some contemporary record, as a play, pamphlet, letter, or sketch. But the Fortune contract implies that the gentlemen's rooms were the best boxes in either that playhouse or the Globe, an implication confirmed by Overbury, who, in describing a Proud Man,

[64] For the details of a quarrel about a box between the Duke of Lenox and the Lord Chamberlain see Adams, p. 232.

[65] See Lawrence, *Old Theatre Days and Ways*, pp. 148, 149, and the illustration facing p. 148.

writes, "If he have but twelve-pence in's purse, he will give it for the best roome in a playhouse." [66]

Some years ago, in an article which went far towards clearing a path through the problems with which we are now concerned, W. J. Lawrence stated that all four gentlemen's rooms at the Globe and Fortune playhouses were located in the lowermost gallery. In support of this view he remarked that "in the English theatre the rule has invariably held good (beginning with the first tier of boxes, not with the basement) the higher you go, the less you pay." [67] And in the succeeding paragraph he added, "In the Fortune contract we read of 'fower convenient divisions for gentlemen's roomes' in one of the galleries, the particular locality, however, remaining unspecified." Both these statements need some qualification. According to Lawrence's own findings, the lords' rooms of earlier playhouses were "situated aloft in the tiring-house"; and admission there was undoubtedly more costly than admission to any part of the first gallery of the auditorium one floor below. The Fortune contract, moreover, does not say or imply that all four gentlemen's rooms were located in *one* of the galleries — that is an unwarrantable assumption on Lawrence's part, an assumption, furthermore, which fails to take into account the practical objection to partitions dividing rooms internally. Elsewhere in the galleries, one has reason to believe, rooms were not subdivided. The Hope contract calls for "partitions *between* the rooms," between the rooms, that is to say, of different price. Such partitions were essential to the Elizabethan system of collecting admission, and to be effective the partitions had to extend at least higher than a man's head. The recurrence of the word "door" in records relating to a gallery *room* suggests that these partitions probably extended to the ceiling and contained an opening at the rear of the gallery narrow enough to be guarded by one gatherer. The con-

[66] *Characters*, 1622: "Character of a Proud Man."
[67] Lawrence, i. 38.

tract does not, however, call for partitions *inside* the rooms. Nor were internal partitions feasible, for, as a moment's study of a ground plan of a playhouse gallery will show, partitions would gravely interfere with a view of the stage. The posts of the frame were bad enough —

> Let their [i.e. playwrights'] desarts be crowned with mewes and hisses.
> Behinde each post and at the gallery corners
> Sit empty guls, slight fooles, and false informers [68] —

but by moving his head a spectator seated behind a post could command all parts of the stage and tiring-house. Partitions, on the other hand, would create unavoidable blind spots increasing at the sides of the building to one-half the area of a gallery bay (roughly 12 feet square).

It will perhaps be urged that in addition to a high partition separating rooms of different price there were low partitions or barriers marking off small boxes inside the larger unit. But low partitions seem not to have been introduced into English theatres until well into the eighteenth century. Elizabethan theatre designers evidently saw no more need to separate from each other the spectators, say, in a two-penny room than to separate from each other the spectators standing in the yard. The plans by Inigo Jones for the Cockpit-in-Court, a royal theatre built as a part of Whitehall Palace in 1632, show an open gallery "ten feet deep, with, it would seem, two rows of benches on four of its sides; the fifth side in the centre, directly opposite the stage, being partitioned off into a room or box, in the middle of which is indicated a platform about five feet by seven, presumably for the Royal State." [69] One should note that four-fifths of this gallery is

---

[68] *Isle of Guls*, 1606, IV. iii.

[69] From the description by Hamilton Bell in *The Architectural Record*, New York, March, 1913. These designs (reproduced by Adams, facing p. 396) reveal blind corners in the galleries flanking the stage. Blind corners were unavoidable in the Globe rooms near the stage.

free of partitions. So in 1632. When, however, in 1660 the Cockpit-in-Court was renovated for the return of Charles II, the gallery was divided into "five large boxes with several degrees . . . and doores in them." [70] The five boxes corresponded to the five sections indicated in Jones's plans; and inasmuch as the gallery for the most part was framed by the outer wall of the building, it follows that the "doores" could not have admitted to the boxes from the back, but must have been placed in partitions separating one box from another. The use of the term "doores" again suggests that the partitions extended to the ceiling over the gallery, or at least higher than a man's head. These "large boxes" in the Cockpit of 1660 call to mind the "vast rooms" in an Elizabethan playhouse gallery, but in fact, because the Cockpit was small (its dimensions were exactly those of the Globe Playhouse yard, an octagon 58 feet across), they more closely resembled the small enclosed boxes standard in theatres built shortly after 1660, boxes illustrated in many Restoration theatre views and described by not a few visitors to London. [71] A vital difference in depth, however, distinguished the Elizabethan and the Restoration theatre gallery. As in Continental theatres of the post-1660 period, [72] Restoration side-galleries were only deep enough for three or four rows of spectators (witness the views referred to a moment ago and also a passage in Shadwell's *Bury-Fair*, III. i, acted at the Theatre Royal in 1689, in which Wildish is rallied for his promise to sit daily in the side-boxes "where the Beaux draw up three Ranks deep every day"). In so shallow a gallery, partitions between boxes would cause little interference with a view of the stage; but in the far deeper Elizabethan gallery designed as the structural frame of the building (rather than an appendage to an outer wall) and intended for more

[70] E. Boswell, *The Restoration Court Stage*, p. 239.

[71] Accounts are given by Summers, *The Restoration Theatre*, pp. 32–35.

[72] See, for example, Blondel's ground plan of the *Théâtre Français*, built in 1689, reproduced by Lawrence, *Old Theatre Days and Ways*, facing p. 28.

than twice as many rows of spectators, partitions, especially at the sides of the auditorium, would have cut off all
view of the stage from those not seated in one of the first
two rows.

This reasoning applies with particular force to the gentlemen's rooms because of their position "next the stage,"
that is to say, in sections of the frame adjoining the tiring-
house, sections which in an octagonal building actually
faced *away* from the scenic wall. The notion of internal
partitions dividing into two rooms or boxes each of the
two areas set aside for the use of the nobility and gentry
(and how otherwise could there be *four* gentlemen's rooms
in *one* gallery?) is quite untenable, for, however placed,
partitions would have rendered useless a large portion of
one of each pair of rooms.

That two of the gentlemen's rooms were located in the
lowermost gallery, one on each side adjoining the tiring-
house, the evidence of the De Witt sketch, of the Hope
contract, and of other records is conclusive; the other two
rooms, therefore, were in all probability located in the
middle gallery and directly over the lower two. A review
of the antecedents of the gentlemen's rooms and of the
privileges pertaining to them shows that this must have
been so.

Before the Theater and Curtain Playhouses were many
years old, their housekeepers appear to have allowed a few
spectators of superior rank or wealth to enter by the stage
door (on payment, no doubt, of a sizable fee) and to view
the performance from the second level of the tiring-house.
There, either on the balcony which overlooked the platform stage from the back or from windows at each side of
the balcony, these favored spectators could observe the
proceedings well enough, could come and go without dis-
turbing others, could be reasonably inconspicuous, and
could avoid all contact with the common patrons of the
theatre. That gallants in the tiring-house balcony and
windows had to watch the performance from the rear mat-

tered little in the years 1576–1590 in a playhouse where spectators already faced three sides of the stage and where the majority of scenes were acted on the platform projecting deeply into the yard. In the Elizabethan theatre there was no equivalent of the modern rule of acting, "Face front!"

But by 1590 the tiring-house balcony could no longer regularly be spared for spectators, however great their rank. With the rise in popularity of historical plays it was constantly needed (as time and again in *King John*, *Edward the Third*, *Henry the Sixth*, *Soliman and Perseda*, and many other plays) for scenes involving a castle or a city wall, when kings and burghers appeared above to parley with armed forces below, or to battle with those who scaled the walls with the aid of ladders. Once spectators had been ousted from the tiring-house balcony, playwrights could devise scenes (as in *The Taming of a Shrew* and *The Spanish Tragedy*) having "presenters" sitting aloft to watch a procession, a masque, or a play-in-a-play acted on the platform below.

Actors made increasing demands upon the second level of the tiring-house in the years after 1590. Notwithstanding the De Witt sketch of 1596 of the Swan interior with its six little boxes in the second gallery at the back of the stage, each with a spectator or two, the conclusion is inescapable that after 1595 the balcony (together with the windows flanking it and the inside stage behind it) was frequently reserved for theatrical use, and accordingly that gallants could not be permitted to sit there. Not that the more serious-minded among them were reluctant to be ousted; for by that time it was no longer possible to witness an entire performance from a place in the scenic wall. After the introduction of inner-stage scenes it was only a question of time before all those interested in the drama would of their own accord refuse to sit where only the outer-stage parts of the action could be seen.

After 1595, finding it increasingly difficult to permit

gallants to sit in any part of the tiring-house, housekeepers were faced with the problem of providing other accommodations elsewhere or of foregoing a sizable profit. (Not until several years had passed were the actors allowed to share in this source of income.[73]) By 1596, as the De Witt sketch (supported by other evidence) attests, boxes immediately adjoining the tiring-house in the lowermost gallery were made available in public playhouses, probably by opening a doorway into that gallery through each end wall of the tiring-house.

At about the same time, and possibly for the same reason, the Blackfriars company began to allow gallants to sit on the two sides of the outer stage,[74] where, with their backs to the side walls of the theatre, they occupied much the same position relative to the rest of the stage and to the auditorium as they did when sitting in the new type of box created for their use in public theatres. From the Blackfriars, where it interfered with no one's view of the stage, the custom of sitting on the stage platform spread to public playhouses, where it was a thorough-going nuisance. None the less, references to sitting on the stage of the Globe appear soon after 1599.

It is hardly necessary to point out that accommodations for spectators in the original lords' rooms in the second level of the tiring-house, on the side fringes of the outer stage, and in the gentlemen's boxes "next the stage" in the first and second galleries shared one particular advantage quite apart from their proximity to the sphere of dramatic action. All were accessible through the tiring-house, thus enabling the gallant to reach his seat without first having to elbow his way through groundlings and "gallery commoners" in the crowded vestibule, and then

[73] See the articles of agreement between Robert Dawes, an actor, and Philip Henslowe and Jacob Meade, dated April 7, 1614 (*Henslowe Papers*, p. 124), and also *Outlines*, i. 312, 317.

[74] Wallace, pp. 130 ff., and C. R. Baskerville, "The Custom of Sitting on the Elizabethan Stage," *M. P.*, VIII (April, 1911), No. 4.

thread his way through the galleries. Normally a gallant, after entering the playhouse through the tiring-house door, proceeded first to the front of the outer stage and from that point of vantage displayed to the audience his expensive suit while he sought out an acquaintance either there or in one of the boxes. If he elected to remain on the stage, he seated himself on the rushes or (at a private theatre) on a low stool. If he elected to sit in a box, he withdrew into the tiring-house and passed back stage to his chosen destination. These details are reflected in a number of plays. In the Induction to *The Malcontent* (1604), a Globe play, one of the actors asks a "gallant" on the outer stage, "Good sir, will you leave the stage? I'll help you to a private room." Again, in *The Careless Shepherdess*, a Salisbury Court play acted *circa* 1631, the Induction closes with:

Spruce [who has been sitting on the stage]. Perhaps our presence
        daunteth them; let us
    Retire into some private room, for fear
    The third man [i.e. the third Prologue] should be out.
Spark. A match.
                                                    Exeunt.
Landlord. I'le follow them, though't be into a Box.
    Though they did sit thus open on the Stage
    To show their cloak and Sute, yet I did think
    At last they would take sanctuary 'mongst
    The Ladies, lest some Creditor should spy them.
    'Tis better looking o're a Ladies head,
    Or through a Lettice-window, then a grate [i.e. in prison].
                                                Exit Landl.

Ben Jonson's habit of emerging from the Blackfriars tiring-house upon the outer stage when a play of his was ended in order "to exchange courtesies and compliments with the gallants in the Lords rooms, to make all the house rise up in arms and to cry 'that's Horace, that's he! that's he!'" is recorded in *Satiromastix*, 1601.

I know of no evidence bearing directly on the size of the gentlemen's rooms, but several indirect hints, taken together, suggest that those rooms were small. Each one occupied perhaps not more than one bay of the gallery frame. I refer to (1) the history of the rooms, (2) the presumed need for the Globe Company to provide for an increase in the number of aristocratic patrons and the probability that the number would be twice but hardly four times as great as in earlier theatres, (3) the conjecture that in 1599–1609 the proportion of these box patrons to the rest of the gallery audience might have approximated 10 per cent but is not likely to have reached 20 per cent, and (4) the assumption that, as in the 1660 division of the Cockpit-in-Court gallery, partitions separating the gentlemen's rooms from the two-penny rooms were placed with intelligent relation to the octagonal form of the building, that is, in the corners of the frame and not in the middle of the sections between corners. This latter assumption is supported by the passage cited on page 75 which tells of spectators sitting "behinde each post and at the gallery corners," and also by a passage in *The Second Maiden's Tragedy*, a Globe Company play written in 1611:

> Thou knows't this gallery? well, tis at thy use now...
> Thou may'st sit
> Like a most private gallant in your corner
> For all the play, and ne'er be seen thyself.[75]

Wherever placed, the partitions separating the gentlemen's rooms from the two-penny rooms necessarily caused some interference with a view of the stage. Since it would be to the interests of the householders to sacrifice space in the less expensive rather than in the more expensive rooms, it may be conjectured that the partitions crossed the galleries at right angles (more nearly the line of vision), and not in a plane connecting the inner post and corresponding outer post of the frame.

[75] Ed. Hazlitt, *Dodsley's Old Plays*, x. 454.

10. Gallery Seats and Standing-Room

From the beginning Elizabethan playhouse galleries provided benches for at least a part of the audience. Describing the behavior of a playhouse audience in 1579 — destined to mend but little in the following sixty years — Stephen Gosson wrote:

In our assemblies at playes in *London*, you shall see suche heauing, and shoouing, suche ytching and shouldring, too sitte by women; Suche care for their garments, that they bee not trode on: Such eyes to their lappes, that no chippes light in them: Such pillowes to ther backes, that they take no hurte: Such masking in their eares, I knowe not what: Such giuing them Pippins to passe the time: Suche playing at foote Saunt without Cardes: Such ticking, such toying, such smiling, such winking, and such manning them home, when the sportes are ended, that it is a right Comedie, to marke their behauiour.[76]

De Witt's sketch of the Swan Playhouse interior shows in each gallery three rows of benches arranged in concentric rising tiers; but his evidence as to the total number of rows in the Swan galleries is necessarily inconclusive, if only that owing to the scale of his sketch and the limitations of perspective he was unable to represent more than the forward half of any gallery. The evidence of the Fortune and Hope contracts is vague. The first merely stipulates that the builder, Streete, was to provide the "necessarie Seates to be placed and sett Aswell in those roomes [the gentlemen's and two-penny rooms] as througheoute all the rest of the galleries." The second does not mention seats, but by making available to Katherens, the builder, the "tymber, benches, seates" of the old Bear Garden it implies their inclusion among the "other thinges needfull and necessarie for the full finishinge of the saide Plaie house."

The truth of the matter appears to be that throughout the reign of Elizabeth and for some years thereafter playhouse galleries were not solidly filled with benches, and that for possibly the majority of gallery spectators, prior

[76] *The School of Abuse*, 1579, sig. C1.

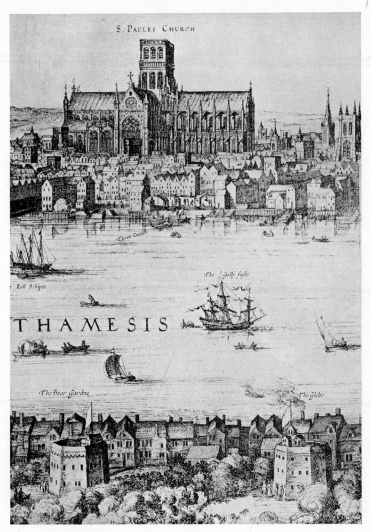

THE BEAR GARDEN AND THE SECOND GLOBE

From the Visscher-Hondius "View of London," 1616

at least to 1600, sitting was rather the exception than the rule. Lambard's description of the Paris Garden, the Bell Savage inn-theatre, and "some other suche common place" in which one paid "one penny at the gate, another at the entrie of the Scaffolde, and the thirde for a quiet standing," indicates that in 1576 (and again in 1596, when for the second edition "the Theatre" was substituted for "some other suche common place") the best accommodation normally available in animal arenas and inn-yard theatres consisted of standing room in some part of the scaffold where one could see well and escape the elbows and the garlic breath of the baser commonality.

Whether or not seats were to be had in inn-theatre galleries prior to 1576 I do not know, but in the amphitheatres designed for animal baiting, seats were apparently not available in the lowermost gallery, usually called the "stand" or "ground-stand" (evidently this latter term may be taken literally), and possibly not even elsewhere — witness John Field's *Godly exhortation . . . shewed at Parris-garden* (1583):

Beeing thus vngodly assembled, to so vnholy a spectacle and especially considering the time; the yeard, standings, and Galleries being ful fraught, being now amidest their iolity, when the dogs and Bear were in the chiefest Battel, Lo the mighty hand of God vppon them. This gallery that was double [i.e. of two tiers over and above the earthen-floored "standings"?], and compassed the yeard round about, was so shaken at the foundation, that it fell (as it were in a moment) flat to the ground, without post or peere, that was left standing, so high as the stake wheruunto the Beare was tied. . . . But it shoulde appere that they were most hurt and in danger, which stoode vnder the Galleries on the grounde, vpon whom both the waight of Timbre and people fel. And sure it was a miraculous worke of God, that any one of those should haue escaped.[77]

Stow writes to the same effect in his *Survey of London*:

As for the bayting of Bulles and Bears, they are till this day much frequented, namely in Beare-gardens, on the Banks side, wherein be prepared Scaffolds for beholders to stand upon.[78]

[77] Cited from Chambers, iv. 220–221.
[78] Edition of 1603, page 96; cf. p. 407.

But in playhouses benches were to some extent available from the very beginning, and no doubt the proportion of patrons thus provided for increased from year to year. When in 1585 the ground lease for the Theater was renewed, Gyles Alleyn, the landlord, entered (or perhaps renewed) a condition:

> & further that yt shall or may be lawfull for the sayde Gyles & for hys wyfe & familie vpon lawfull request therfore made to the sayde Jeames Burbage his exec[utors] or assignes to enter or come into the premisses & their in some one of the vpper romes to have such convenient place to sett or stande to se such playes as shalbe ther played freely without any thinge therefore payeinge soe that the sayde Gyles hys wyfe and familie doe come & take ther places before they shalbe taken vpp by any others. [79]

This clause not only indicates the means by which one could secure a place — namely, by coming early — but also implies willingness on the part of spectators to stand throughout the performance if all seats were taken. Other writers indicate that standing was not unusual. In *King John*, II. i, produced in 1596, the Bastard exclaims:

> By heaven, these scroyles of Angiers flout you kings
> And stand securely on their battelments
> As in a Theater, whence they gape and point
> At your industrious Scenes and acts of death.

That standing in the galleries was still common in 1597 is shown by the wording of an edict which followed the performance in late July of Nashe's scandalous *Isle of Dogs* at the Swan. The Privy Council directed the Justices of Middlesex and Surrey "to send for the owners of the Curtayne, Theatre, or anie other common playhouse, and injoyne them by vertue hereof forth with to plucke down quite the stages galleries and roomes that are made for people to stand in." [80]

Thomas Platter specifically mentions standing in the

---

[79] Quoted from Wallace, *The First London Theatre*, pp. 177–178.

[80] J. R. Dasent, *Acts of the Privy Council of England*, xxvii. 313, cited in *Outlines*, i. 356.

galleries at the Globe in the autumn of 1599. "There are," he writes, "separate galleries, and there one stands more comfortably and moreover can sit, but one pays more for it [i.e. for a place in the galleries whether to stand or sit]."[81] The Epilogue to *Satiromastix* (1601) contains the request: "beare witnes all you Gentle-folkes (that walk i' th Galleries)." In the accounts of the Board of Works for February and March, 1602, are entered the charges incurred at Westminster in "making ready the Haull and great chamber with seates or standinges and particions in sundrye places . . . for the plaies at Shrovetide."

In the tense moments of a performance those who were seated rose to their feet also. Gosson alludes to this fact "in publike theaters" in his *Triumph of Warre* (1598):

When any notable shew passeth on the stage, the people arise out of their seates, and stand upright with delight and eagerness to view it well.

Benches presumably were introduced into playhouse galleries primarily as a concession to comfort, but their use benefited those standing at the back of the gallery by giving them a less obstructed view of the stage. A clear view of the stage was not easy for spectators standing in the rear of upper galleries as deep as those specified in the Fortune contract. For various reasons the ceilings of playhouse galleries were made as low as possible, but even so the angle of view from a point in the two upper galleries was fairly steep; and there is no disputing the fact that, without the provision of "degrees" or steps in the gallery flooring, patrons in the rear third of the middle gallery and in the rear two-thirds of the top gallery would have had an imperfect view of the outer stage. To demonstrate this fact one has only to lay a ruler across a sectional plan of a playhouse drawn to scale.[82] Elizabethan playhouse build-

---

[81] Quoted from Chambers, ii. 365.

[82] Mr. Godfrey's sectional plans for the Fortune Playhouse are reproduced in *A Companion to Shakespeare Studies*, pp. 26, 27.

ers must have been perfectly familiar with degrees; the arrangement of seats in rising tiers is as old as the Greeks; degrees at the Swan in 1596 are pictured by De Witt, and are proposed for the gallery of the Cockpit-in-Court in 1642 by Inigo Jones.

The number of rows of benches in a gallery can be rather closely approximated. The Fortune contract specifies 12½ feet as the (inside) depth of the first gallery. The space the average spectator occupies when seated is a relatively unchanging factor. In modern theatres the usual space allowance for one person is 30 inches of depth and 18 inches of breadth in the gallery and 30 by 20 or 22 inches in the orchestra stalls. In an out-of-door grandstand used the year round, however, where thicker clothing is the rule — a standard of comparison more akin to Elizabethan galleries open to the weather — the minimum allowance, I am told, is 30 by 22 inches. Assuming, then, that the rows of benches in the lowermost gallery at the Globe were spaced 30 inches apart, two rows would occupy 5 feet, leaving a space 7½ feet wide for standing room behind; three rows would occupy 7½ feet, leaving a space 5 feet wide for standing room; and four rows would occupy 10 feet, leaving a space only 2½ feet wide between the rear bench and the outer wall of the building. I am inclined to believe that the Globe had three rows of benches, for the following reasons. One or two rows alone would hardly suffice in the foremost playhouse of a fairly luxurious age. The demand for comfort in London playhouses is thus emphasized by Dr. C. W. Wallace:

From the many thousands of contemporary documents I have examined, directly bearing upon the life of the times, I am more and more convinced that the people of the time of Elizabeth and James were as solicitous for means of comfort as we are today. Quite contrary to the ill-founded notion commonly circulated by writers on stage-history that audiences put up with woeful discomforts simply to see a great play well enacted, it would seem that reasonable consideration was given the tastes of different classes of patrons, and that those in the choicer parts of the house were charged the higher prices on account of the better accommodations as well as the better view... The best boxes or rooms were patronized by lords, nobles, and other gentlemen used to the best at home and in society, and it is unlikely that they should have gone in such numbers if discomforts had been so great as to cause them to do penance while watching the play.[83]

Moreover, the Swan sketch happens to show three rows, a number retained, as we have seen, in the galleries of Restoration theatres. Four rows would leave so little standing room, even in the deeper second and third galleries, as to render meaningless the constant allusions throughout the era to that considerable proportion of gallery patrons who stood during the performance.

11. THE CAPACITY OF THE GLOBE

Assuming (1) that the width of the average seated spectator was 22 inches, (2) that there were three rows of benches spaced 30 inches apart in all three galleries, and (3) that a standing-room allowance of 4 square feet for each gallery patron was ample, I have compiled Table A to show the probable capacity of the Globe galleries.[84]

TABLE A

Gallery		Seated	Standing	Totals
I	Gentlemen's rooms (two)..........	40	20	60
	Two-penny rooms (two)...........	208	170	378
II	Gentlemen's rooms (two)..........	40	20	60
	Two-penny room..................	220	186	406
III	Two-penny gallery................	270	254	524
	Totals........................	778	650	1428

[83] *Children of the Chapel*, pp. 50–51.

[84] In preparing this table I have made suitable deductions for the corridor which bisected the first gallery, for the passageways in the second gallery connecting the up and down landings of the external staircases, and for the two end bays in the third gallery, which, because of their location adjoining the top floor of the tiring-house, were of little value to spectators.

In a previous chapter the capacity of the yard was estimated at 600. By including this figure in a second table
(B), we can show the probable capacity of the entire playhouse and the capacity of one part relative to another and
to the whole.

TABLE B

Types of Accommodation		Percentage of the Whole
1. On the stage	20?	1
2. Gentlemen's rooms	120	6
3. Two-penny rooms	784	37
4. The penny gallery	524	26
5. The yard	600	30
Grand total	2048	

So far as I am aware we have no contemporary estimate
of the exact capacity of any Elizabethan playhouse, but it
will be interesting to note certain round-number estimates.
De Witt reported in 1596 that the Swan could accommodate 3000. Fynes Moryson recorded in 1617 that "the
Theaters at *London* in *England* for stageplaies, are more
remarkeable for the number and for the capacity then for
the building," but added that their combined accommodations were "capable of many thousands." [85] In his petition
on behalf of the Thames watermen in 1614 John Taylor
submitted that the opening of the Fortune and Red Bull
theatres in Middlesex withdrew "three or foure thousand
people, that were vsed [daily] to spend their monies by
water" crossing to the Bankside theatres. [86]

Modern estimates vary even more widely. On the basis
of his conjectural seating plan for the Fortune, Dr. C. W.
Wallace gives 1320 as the capacity of that theatre. [87] On
the basis of a somewhat similar conjectural plan, but al-

[85] *Harrison's Description of England*, ed. F. J. Furnivall, Pt. IV, Supp. 2,
p. 254.
[86] *Works*, 1630, p. 172.
[87] Wallace, following p. 50.

lowing 18 by 30 inches for each gallery seat (and ignoring the question of standing in the galleries) and 18 by 18 inches for each groundling, John Corbin gave 2138 as the maximum at the Fortune.[88] Working from Henslowe's records of gallery takings at the Fortune, Dr. W. W. Greg estimates that the normal attendance in the Fortune galleries averaged 700, and that the capacity of the entire playhouse, when full, may have approximated 3000.[89] In a recent review of the evidence Professor Alfred Harbage gives the Fortune Playhouse a capacity of 2344 spectators.[90]

[88] *Atlantic Monthly*, XCVII (1906), 369.

[89] *Henslowe's Diary*, ii. 134, note 1.

[90] Professor Harbage writes (in *Shakespeare's Audience*, 1941, pp. 22–23): "The Fortune is the one Elizabethan theatre of which we have the exact dimensions, and knowledge of its capacity and distribution of space will prove of use. The building contract of January 8, 1600, and an exercise of elementary arithmetic reveal that there were 1,842.5 square feet of space in the yard unoccupied by the stage. All of this space would be available for standing spectators, and, allowing 2.25 square feet of space per person, 818 persons could be accommodated in this section of the house. The galleries contained 7,156.65 square feet of floor space. Not much more than 80 percent of this would be available for seats, the remainder being consumed by staircases, aisles, and railing space. The available 5,725.32 square feet divided by a 3.75 square foot allowance per sitting spectator gives us a 1,526 person capacity for the galleries of the Fortune."

Chapter IV

THE PLATFORM STAGE

1. Size and Shape

THE width of the Globe platform stage (hereafter to be called "the platform") has already been considered in an earlier chapter. It was there pointed out that, in an octagonal building designed with 12-foot bays (measured on the inside of the frame) arranged two to each section of the octagon, the distance from the middle post of one section to the corresponding middle post of the next section but one would measure 41 feet.*

The depth of the Globe platform is nowhere specifically referred to; but if, like the Fortune platform, it extended to "the middle of the yard," it was 29 feet deep. At the Fortune, where the yard was square and of slightly smaller dimensions, the platform was 27½ feet deep.[1] This difference in depth, though immaterial, is in keeping with the subsequent tendency of the platform to shrink to an "apron stage" as the inner stages (from which our modern proscenium-type stage developed) grew in size, flexibility, and importance.[2]

The dimensions given in the Fortune contract for the platform — "And which Stadge shall conteine in length [i.e. width] ffortie and Three foote of lawfull assize and in

---

* On pages 22, 45, 90, 92, 95, 97, 98, and 173 of the first printing of this book I stated that the Globe platform measured, not 41, but 43 feet in width. This error, arising from an incorrect reading of my own scale drawings, was first called to my attention by Dr. Charles H. Shattuck.

[1] Cf. Chambers, ii. 528.

[2] According to Summers, *The Restoration Theatre*, p. 95, the apron of the Theatre Royal, opened in 1674, projected only 17 feet into the pit.

breadth [i.e. depth] to extende to the middle of the yarde"
— seem at first glance to imply a rectangle; and it is generally assumed that the Globe platform likewise was rectangular (except, of course, for the rear corners lost to the
oblique side-walls of the tiring-house).

The front of the platform unquestionably was straight,
and parallel to the middle section of the scenic wall. All
platform stages are so depicted in every contemporary
stage view.[3] Less clear, however, is the disposition of the
two sides of the platform, for the evidence relating to them
is conflicting, part of it indicating that the sides were
parallel to each other and part indicating that they were
not parallel, but tapering toward the front.

The notion of a rectangular platform is supported by the
wording of the Fortune contract just quoted, by the sketch
of the Swan platform drawn in 1596 from information supplied by De Witt, by the frontispiece of *The Wits, or Sport
upon Sport*, 1662 (which shows a stage improvised for
drolls during the Commonwealth), by conjectures as to the
amount of space required for the stage-sitting gallants,
and by certain Jacobean stage-directions which call for
traps in all four "corners" of the platform.[4] Taken together, these indications of a rectangular platform have
seemed convincing to the majority of scholars.[5]

But upon a closer examination the validity of this case
for a rectangular platform is seen to be doubtful. The
wording of the Fortune contract is not so explicit as to pre-
clude the possibility of a tapering platform, especially
since a "plott" or diagram was originally attached to the
contract for the express purpose of showing precisely how

[3] E.g., the De Witt sketch of the Swan, 1596; the title-pages of *Roxana*,
1632, and *Messallina*, 1640; the plans for the Cockpit-in-Court, 1662; and the
frontispiece of *The Wits*, 1662. Mr. G. T. Forrest has no authority for the
curved front shown in his reconstruction of the Globe.

[4] *The Golden Age*, final scene. Cf. *The Witches of Lancashire*, II: "*Enter 4.
Witches: (severally)*"; and *If This be not Good*, V; *The Rival Friends*, V. ii; etc.

[5] E.g., Adams, Archer, Baker, Chambers, Lawrence, Thorndike, Tucker
Brooke.

the platform, the tiring-house, and the gallery stairs were to be "placed & sett." These three elements of the Fortune, since they were modeled on corresponding elements in an octagonal building where to a large extent the interrelationship of parts was determined by the shape of the building, necessarily acquired a somewhat arbitrary relationship when installed in a square building; and the inclusion of a diagram to supplement the text of the contract suggests that the phrasing of that text was not sufficiently detailed to be clear and complete on the various adjustments needed. Moreover, although in the remodeling of the old Theater into the Globe the rear of the platform had to be widened to 41 feet in order to equal the width of the expanded tiring-house, the front of the platform could have retained its former width of 24 feet. Had the custom of sitting on the platform not arisen, one would be put to it to explain the need of a platform having so large an area as that created by a rectangle 41 by 29 feet (an area greater than that of most large stages today). But even the need to provide space for stage-sitting gallants would hardly seem to warrant an increase of 70 per cent over the area of the Theater platform, particularly in view of the tendency, increasingly manifest after 1595, to place a good part of the action in the inner stages and to relate much of the outer-stage action to the scenic wall, — to doors, posts, "corners," bulks, and shop-fronts below, and to windows, balconies, "penthouses," and walls above. With the growth of this tendency, well marked by 1599, width at the *rear* of the platform (and movement *across* the stage close to the scenic wall) rather than width at the *front* of the platform (and movement perpendicular to the scenic wall) was desirable.

The De Witt sketch of the Swan was made, I believe, before the tiring-house in any theatre had absorbed the adjoining bays and thus had doubled in size with a radical alteration of the rear proportions of the platform and of its relation to the yard. The improvised stage shown in *The*

Wits probably as little resembled the stage of a Jacobean public theatre as the Commonwealth drolls themselves resembled the plays from which they were abstracted. Of more direct bearing on the shape which I believe the Globe platform assumed are two views contemporary with the second Globe, one on the title-page of *The Tragedy of Roxana*, 1632, and the other on the title-page of *The Tragedy of Messallina*, 1640. Both show platforms tapering in a marked degree toward the front. The engravings are small, but in each the shape of the platform is unmistakable; and the only reason for not at once relating the evidence of the two views to the Globe is one's inability to determine the type of playhouse represented — whether public, private, or academic.

In both vignettes the limitations of size (the size is approximately that of an ordinary postage stamp) forced the engraver to reduce the scope of his representation to a minimum. In each, as a result, the upper margin cuts across the second level of the tiring-house; the right and left margins cut into the sides of both the platform and the tiring-house (so deeply that if there were stage doors they would lie outside the drawing); and the lower margin cuts away the foregound a little below the front edge of the platform. The *Roxana* view exhibits the heads and shoulders of half a dozen spectators standing or sitting (it is impossible to determine which) in front of the platform, and persons who appear to be spectators, two in each of two small boxes over the back of the stage (much as in the Swan sketch). It shows also three actors standing well forward on the platform. By supplying the corners of the platform cut off at the sides, and by using as a scale the actors down stage and the spectators in the gallery at the back, we can estimate that the front of the platform was approximately half as wide as the rear, with dimensions (though in so small a view the scale cannot be worth much) of roughly 8 and 15 feet respectively. *The Tragedy of Roxana* was produced at Trinity College, Cambridge, *circa*

1592,[6] and printed for a London publisher in 1632. Written throughout in Latin and academic in character, the play was never performed on a London public stage, but it does not follow that the engraver secured by the London publisher would take that fact into account. Too many years had elapsed between performance of the play at Cambridge and its publication in London to make probable much direct connection between the original stage and the decorative vignette. On the other hand, if the engraver sought a model for his sketch, the chances are that he took for that purpose some London playhouse; Salisbury Court was then new and popular, and might have served his turn better than one of the larger public playhouses.

The *Messallina* view is devoid of figures, but except for certain minor details (notably the curtained aperture substituted for the upper spectator-boxes of the *Roxana* view) it is substantially like the earlier view. Not only do both appear to represent the same type of theatre, but, as Dr. Joseph Q. Adams has pointed out,[7] it is quite possible that the later of the two engravings was based upon the earlier. *Messallina* was written in 1637, was produced at Salisbury Court by a professional London troupe (the Revels company), and was published in 1640.

In the absence of clear evidence to the contrary, and from observing (1) that the spectators in front of the *Roxana* stage seem to be standing rather than sitting, (2) that no apparatus for lighting the stage by artificial means is visible — compare the conspicuous, low-hanging chandeliers and the footlights of the *Wits* view — and (3) that the shadows represented suggest daylight, one is led to suspect that the two vignettes were in their general features intended to represent the public, unroofed type of stage. If one could be sure of this, or even that the playhouses represented were of the late private type, there would be good reason for inferring that the Globe platform

---

[6] Chambers, iii. 208.

[7] J. Q. Adams, *J.E.G.P.*, X (1911), 329 ff.

tapered also. When all is said, the most valid basis for a conjecture as to the shape of a Jacobean platform stage is that of the actual playhouse views, and the only views — whatever their source or accuracy — contemporary with either the first or the second Globe show a tapering stage.

A telling objection to the theory of a rectangular platform is the greatly reduced capacity for groundlings that would result from the introduction into the yard of a platform 29 feet deep and 41 feet wide throughout. In the Theater, the areas on either side of its 24-feet wide platform had provided space for approximately 230 groundlings, or one-third of the total capacity of the yard (estimated at 693). But in the Globe with a rectangular platform 41 feet wide, the corresponding areas would be almost eliminated. The narrow strips remaining between the sides of that platform and the walls of the galleries (strips 9½ feet wide at the Globe and only 6 feet at the Fortune) would provide space for only 45 groundlings to a side, or one-sixth of the total capacity (estimated at 537). And the capacity of the Globe yard, despite the fact that its outside dimensions were identical with those of the Theater yard, would drop to three-fourths that of its forerunner. Neither of these results would seem warranted.

On the other hand, a tapering platform 41 feet wide at the scenic wall and only 24 feet wide at the front would provide sizable flanking areas of the yard commanding a good view of the stage. And with a tapering platform the capacity of the Globe yard would slightly exceed 600.

The argument that a considerable space was required to accommodate seated gallants on the Globe platform is of doubtful validity. It fails to take into account the relationship of the platform to the playhouse as a whole and the effect that a group of bodies at the front and sides of the platform would have upon the visibility of the stage from the yard and the lowermost gallery. At the Blackfriars private theatre, where the custom of sitting on the stage originated a year or two before the Globe was built, the

platform extended in width from one side-wall of the hall
to the other, and the audience sat in front of its forward
edge.[8] In a theatre so planned gallants perched on stools
even three or four rows deep at the sides of the stage
blocked no-one's view. But the Globe had an entirely
different ground plan. Gallants sitting on stools placed
on the sides of its platform would have formed a serious
obstacle to a good view of the stage by those of the audience who stood in the yard immediately behind them and
those who sat in the first-gallery gentlemen's rooms. Before gallants could be allowed on the stage, some means had
to be devised of ensuring that they would be as little as
possible in the way of other spectators. To that end —
if my interpretation is correct — stools were discouraged
and in their place rushes were provided upon which gallants were permitted to recline. The presence of gallants
on the stage at the Globe and the Blackfriars is thus sati-
rized by Dekker in his *Guls Hornbook*: [9]

Let our Gallant [having entered through the tiring-house door] . . .
presently advance himself up to the throne of the stage; I mean not
into the lords' room . . . But on the very rushes where the comedy is
to dance [i.e. the most conspicuous place in the building, the stage] . . .
Salute all your gentle acquaintance, that are spread either on the
rushes, or on stools about you . . . [or] turn plain ape: take up a rush,
and tickle the earnest ears of your fellow gallants, to make other fools
fall a laughing.

The income from stage-sitting gallants probably never
compensated for the nuisance they occasioned. At Salisbury Court in 1639 the housekeepers were allowed merely
"one dayes p'ffit wholly to themselves in consideration of
their want of stooles on the stage," an adjustment in income brought about by the royal edict of that year pro-
hibiting gallants from henceforth sitting on the stage of
that playhouse.[10] As early as 1603 dramatists began to

---

[8] See the plat of the Blackfriars in Wallace, following p. 50.

[9] Ed. McKerrow, pp. 50, 54, and 55.

[10] *Shakespeare Society Papers*, iv (1849), 99–100.

gird at the custom, and in subsequent years they rarely ceased to do so. It cannot therefore have been desirable or profitable to set aside very much space on the Globe platform for the limited number of fops who might prefer to display themselves to the audience rather than to sit comfortably in one of the four gentlemen's rooms. But for those who demanded a place on the stage itself, the increase in platform area caused by widening the rear to 41 feet would, I believe, have been adequate. In short, the custom of sitting on the stage at the Globe would indicate a platform of some size, but not necessarily one as wide as that at the Blackfriars, nor one requiring a rectangular shape.

The objections to a tapering platform which have been advanced by modern scholars [11] are directed, to judge from their content, not so much against the notion of the shape itself as against the particular proposal advanced in 1909 by V. E. Albright,[12] namely that the front of the Globe platform was merely 15 feet wide. This narrow front, reflecting a too literal acceptance of the *Roxana* and *Messallina* views, would fail to allow for seated gallants or for traps in the "corners" of the platform (details of which Albright apparently was unaware), and hence was rejected by a succession of workers in the field. A platform of the proportions I have suggested, however, would have had ample space for these rarely-used corner traps.

To sum up. The over-all dimensions of the Globe platform are almost certainly reflected in the terms of the Fortune contract, hence its width was 41 feet and its depth 29 feet. In shape it may have been rectangular, with an area of 1133 square feet. On the other hand — and for myself I incline to this alternative hypothesis — when the Theater was rebuilt as the Globe and the rear of the plat-

[11] E.g., C. F. Tucker Brooke, *The Nation* (New York, 1910), XCI, No. 2372; J. Q. Adams, *J.E.G.P.*, X (1911), 329 ff.; Lawrence, *Physical Conditions*, p. 4; Chambers, ii. 528.

[12] *The Shaksperian Stage*, frontispiece, plate 8, and p. 77.

form was widened to 41 feet to match the enlarged tiring-house, the front may have been kept as before (equal in width to a 24-foot section of the octagonal frame), with sides tapering between the front and the rear. Such a platform would have an area of 958 square feet. Even with a fringe of gallants its acting area would have been the largest in London. More accurately than a rectangle with deep, down-stage corners, its shape would conform to the space most often used after 1595 by actors entering upon the platform to strut and fret their hour upon the stage.

2. The Platform Paling and Rails

While discussing the nature of the playhouse yard I noted that the three sides of the platform not connected with the tiring-house were "paled in belowe with good stronge and sufficyent newe oken bourdes." [13] This paling screened from the audience the varied activities which took place in the cellar beneath the platform (the substage area was usually referred to as "the Hell") — the preparation for trap-scenes, the production of smoke, mists, "hell-ish music," and other emanations proper to an infernal region. "Mar[r]y, the question is, in which of the Playhouses he [the Devil] would have performed his prize . . . Hell being vnder euerie one of their Stages." [14] Playhouses intended for occasional animal baiting, as the Hope and perhaps also the Swan, had perforce to have removable platforms. That meant dispensing with an excavated "hell" and, consequently, confining trap-scenes and other substage business to the rear stage. Permanent platforms walled in with paling, on the other hand, made it possible to install the chief trap down stage where there was plenty of room for the actors and stage-mechanics above and below, and where the displays could more readily be seen from all parts of the auditorium.

[13] Fortune Contract, in *Henslowe Papers*, p. 5.
[14] Dekker, *News from Hell*, 1606 (ed. Grosart, *Works*, ii. 92).

In playhouses such as the Globe, the Fortune, and the Red Bull we may be fairly sure that the paling on the sides of the platform was unadorned and smooth, not only because the Fortune contract and the *Messallina* view so indicate, but also because a mild precaution had to be taken against the chance of groundlings trying to clamber upon the stage during some exciting moment of a play. Gayton records, in his *Pleasant Notes on Don Quixot*,[15] that on one occasion a butcher, swept away by sympathy for Hector in his unequal struggle with the Myrmidons, leaped from the yard upon the stage to prevent the hero from being overpowered.

He [the butcher] strooke moreover such an especial acquaintance with Hector, that for a long time Hector could not obtaine leave of him to be kill'd, that the play might go on; and the cudgelled Mirmydons durst not enter againe, till Hector, having prevailed upon his unexpected second, returned him over the Stage againe into the yard from whence he came.

Recessed panels and moldings,[16] which would have made climbing easier, were avoided.

Surmounting the outer edges of the Globe platform, and augmenting the palings which ended flush with the stage floor, was a low balustrade formed of turned spindles spaced well apart, and supporting a top rail. This balustrade probably served in part as a precaution against invasion by groundlings [17] and in part as a back-rest and guard-rail to keep the gallants from tumbling into the yard. The first mention of a railing connected with a London playhouse [18] occurs in Middleton's *Black Book*, 1604, in which Lucifer remarks:

[15] 1654, p. 3.

[16] As shown in the Harvard Elizabethan stage erected under the supervision of G. F. Baker (illustrated in his *Development of Shakespeare as a Dramatist*, facing pp. 250 and 260); or by Albright, *The Shaksperian Stage*, frontispiece.

[17] The reason advanced by Lawrence, *Physical Conditions*, p. 6.

[18] A "stage & Railes" is mentioned in the Trinity College accounts for 1562–1563 (cited in the Malone Society *Collections*, II. part 2, p. 163) but one cannot be sure where the rail was placed.

> And now that I have vaulted up so high
> Above the stage rails of this earthen globe
> I must turn actor and join companies,
> To share my comic sleek-ey'd villainies.

As W. J. Lawrence pointed out, this passage shows that the balustrade was in position in the first Globe early in its history.[19]

Stage rails are clearly illustrated in the *Roxana* and *Messallina* views, and also in the Inigo Jones plans for the Cockpit-in-Court, where they appear to be about 18 inches high.[20] Rails are again included by Jones in his designs for a production in 1640 of Habington's *Queen of Aragon*.[21]

As with all other physical features of the stage within reach of an actor, the platform rails were occasionally pressed into service. Shakespeare provides the first of two known dramatic references to the balustrade in *Henry VIII*, 1613...In Act V, scene iv, a Porter is required to clear a path for a procession. In his efforts to restrain the crowd of citizens congregated about one of the stage doors he calls out:

> You i' th Chamblet, get up o' th' raile,
> Ile pecke you o're the pales else.

The second reference occurs in *The Hector of Germany*, acted at the Red Bull and the Curtain and published in 1615. In Act V, scene v, a "Frenchman, and Englishman druncke" enter on the platform as to a hall in the palace and pretend that a play is in progress:

Frenchm. Players, by this light players: Oh I love a play with all my heart.

English. Begin, begin, we are set. ([They] *sit on the Railes*.[22]

---

[19] *Physical Conditions*, p. 7.

[20] Hamilton Bell, *The Architectural Record*, New York, 1913.

[21] Reproduced by Allardyce Nicoll, *British Drama*, p. 106.

[22] This reference was cited in *TLS* (Feb. 16, 1933) by G. F. Reynolds, believing that it had not previously been noted. It can be found, however (together with certain others which I have quoted), in Lawrence, *Physical Condi-*

The passage in Middleton's *Black Book* in which Lucifer vaults the Globe rails and proposes to turn actor probably indicates that such behavior was not unknown to London audiences, as does also the story recorded by Gayton of the butcher who came to the rescue of Hector. A somewhat parallel situation is found in Beaumont's *Knight of the Burning Pestle* in which three actors reach the platform from the yard. Before the Prologue has begun his fourth line, a Citizen climbs up from the yard and shouts out, "Hold your peace, goodman Boy!" After some bickering they are both interrupted by the Citizen's Wife, who asks, "Husband! shall I come up, husband?" He replies, "Ay cony.—Ralph, help your mistress this way.—Pray, gentlemen, make her a little room. — I pray you, sir, lend me your hand to help up my wife. I thank you, sir. — So." Such stage business as is revealed in this and in other scenes [23] dispels the notion sometimes advanced that there were steps leading up from the yard to the platform.[24]

A balustrade that will withstand the rough and tumble treatment indicated in the passages cited above must have been solidly built and was probably of oak. It was of course painted, like the rest of the stage,[25] for otherwise the turned spindles, exposed to the weather, would not last long.

The presence of the balustrade accords with (and tends to confirm) our earlier conclusion as to the height of the platform in playhouses erected or extensively modernized after 1599 (that is, a height of not more than 4 feet above the yard floor), for had the balustrade been added to a platform built at eye-level, as in early playhouses, the

---

tions, 1927, pp. 7–10, where a study is made showing that stage rails were standard equipment on Jacobean and later stages into the early years of the Restoration. See also E. Boswell, *The Restoration Court Stage*, pp. 239 and 242.

[23] E.g., *Gratiae Ludentes*, 1638, pp. 15–16; Gayton's *Pleasant Notes on Don Quixot*, 1654, p. 271; *The Careless Shepherdess*, 1656, Induction.

[24] E.g., Chambers, iii. 107.

[25] Cf. Malone Society *Collections*, II. part 2, pp. 172 and 176.

groundlings would have been forced to witness the performance through the openings below the rail — a hardship not to be endured.[26] Only by postulating that the rail was below the eye-level of groundlings standing close to the platform is it possible to reconcile the presence of a balustrade with the right of the groundlings to enjoy a fair view of the stage.

3. RUSHES ON THE PLATFORM

Inside the rails lay the outer-stage platform, co-extensive with the ground floor of the tiring-house immediately behind it and of the first gallery. This platform probably was not, as many have supposed, everywhere covered an inch or two deep with rushes, but normally presented a hard surface of painted boards. It is noteworthy that the four contemporary stage views show no trace of rushes, and that the title-page of *The Roaring Girl* (1611) depicts an actor standing on a platform, presumably a stage, where wide boards are emphasized by heavy lines. A bare stage is certainly implied in *Troilus and Cressida*, I. iii, when Ulysses speaks of

> A Strutting Player, whose conceit
> Lies in his Ham-string, and doth thinke it rich
> To hear the woodden Dialogue and sound
> 'Twixt his stretcht footing, and the Scaffolage.

A moment's reflection will show that a blanket of rushes over the entire platform would have been useless, troublesome, and expensive: useless because rushes were needed only where it was planned to have actors sit or fall; and

---

[26] Faced with the problem of supplying rails on a stage supposedly 5 feet high and at the same time recognizing the need of a clear view of the stage from the yard, the late William Archer was led first to postulate a wide central gap in the balustrade (see the Godfrey reconstruction of the Fortune dated 1907, reproduced in *A Companion to Shakespeare Studies*, p. 24) and later to abandon efforts to include it (see his article in *The Quarterly Review*, April, 1908; the plate there reproduced appears again in his joint article with Lawrence for *Shakespeare's England*, ii. 306).

troublesome because rushes would conceal the trapdoors from an actor called upon to take his correct position without hesitation or error, would obstruct the opening and closing of traps, and would for every performance involve first the strewing and later the removal and storage of more than 100 cubic feet of rushes — no slight or inexpensive chore in a theatre giving daily performances. Many Globe scenes, moreover, demand a prompt and spectacular use of hell-fire and smoke, and it is hard to conceive how such displays could have been produced effectively and safely through a matted cover of rushes.

That at least some part of the stage was bare is indicated by situations in a number of plays. In *Titus Andronicus* (1594), sig. F4 verso, the mutilated Marcus and Lavinia try to communicate with each other. Marcus *"writes his name with his staffe and guides it with feet and mouth,"* adding orally:

> This sandie plot is plaine, guide if thou canst
> This [staff] after me, I have writ my name.

When Lavinia attempts to reply, *"Shee takes the staffe in her mouth, and guides it with her stumps and writes."* For this grim writing upon the "sands" bare boards would serve better than rushes.

Again, how could Viola have been sure of recovering the ring which Malvolio threw at her feet (*Twelfth Night*, II. ii) had loose rushes paved the street where he caught up with her? There are several outer-stage scenes where jewels or coins are dropped and immediately picked up (see, for example, *The Court Secret*, I. i, and *The Knave in Grain*, V). On the other hand, the difficulty in homes of finding small objects once they had fallen into the rushes was notorious, witness the proverb "seeke a needle 'mongst the rushes" recited in *The Partial Law*, III. iii, and the explanation offered (but not acted out) in *Sir Thomas More*, IV: "Your lordship sent eight angells by your man, and I have lost two of them in the rushes."

In keeping with the other exposed woodwork of the playhouse, the outer stage was painted. Henslowe's *Diary* [27] contains the entry: "Itm pd for payntinge my stage . . . . xj*s*." Eleven shillings seems a reasonable cost for this particular work since £6 was paid for painting the tiring-house, and at Trinity College two shillings and sixpence was paid "for paynting the Rayles on the Stage."

Some twelve contemporary references to the painted woodwork of Elizabethan playhouses were collected by T. S. Graves,[28] but although many of them draw attention to the "beautie of the houses and the Stages" or deplore their "gorgeous" decoration, none gives any notion of the colors used. De Witt described the wooden columns of the Swan in 1596 as "painted in such excellent imitation of marble that it is able to deceive even the most cunning"; [29] but it may be well to recall that De Witt mistook the plastered exterior walls of the Swan for "a mass of flint stones."

The Induction to *Bartholomew Fair*, acted at the Hope in 1614, corroborates what one might assume, namely, that the outer stage was swept shortly before the play began.

Bookholder [to stage-keeper who is making ready the stage]. Your Judgment, Rascal? for what? sweeping the Stage? or gathering up the broken Apples for the Bears within?

But on a relatively unroofed platform and in an age of costumes so costly [30] as to excite widespread comment and the strongest Puritan disapproval, sweeping the stage was not enough; more thorough steps had to be taken to ensure that certain areas of the stage would be clean and dry during the hours of performance. Two Elizabethan methods of solving the problem — one sensible and the other ludi-

[27] Ed. W. W. Greg, p. 8.
[28] *The Court and the London Theatres during the Reign of Elizabeth*, pp. 68–69.
[29] Quoted by Adams, p. 168.
[30] See, for example, Gosson, *The School of Abuse*, 1579, p. 39; Pryne, *Histriomastix*, 1633, p. 216; *Henslowe's Diary*, i. 179–180; *Henslowe Papers*, pp. 113 ff.

crous — are referred to in *Summers Last Will and Testament* (1592). In the course of Nashe's satire Will Summer says to Summer: [31]

You might haue writ in the margent of your play-booke, Let there be a fewe rushes laide in the place where *Back-winter* shall tumble, for feare of raying his cloathes: or set downe, Enter *Back-winter*, with his boy bringing a brush after him, to take off the dust if need require. But you will ne'er haue any ward-robe wit while you liue.

These remarks help us to understand precisely why plays wherein actors sit, recline, fall, wrestle, or lie upon the floor — in short, every Elizabethan play — had need of some outer-stage area carpeted with freshly strewn rushes. In other words the chief function of strewn rushes was identical with that of the green cloth stage-cover used in Jacobean Court masques [32] and in Restoration theatres, [33] and of the absurd "tragic carpet" rushed on by eighteenth-century stage-hands for the hero to collapse and die upon, [34] namely, the protection of valuable costumes. However incongruous for out-of-door scenes a layer of rushes obviously similar to that used in domestic interiors might be, professional companies evidently found no preferable substitute until the Restoration. Then, quite understandably (and with the usual contempt for the ways of an earlier generation), writers could afford to be scornful of rushes. On page 280 of his *Discourse of the English Stage*, 1664, Flecknoe writes:

Now for the difference betwixt our Theatres and those of former times, they were but plain and simple, with no Scenes, nor Decorations of the Stage, but onely old Tapestry, and the Stage strew'd with Rushes, (with their Habits accordingly). [35]

[31] *The Works of Nashe*, ed. McKerrow, iii. 290.
[32] E. Welsford, *The Court Masque*, p. 206.
[33] Boswell, *Restoration Court Stage*, p. 146.
[34] Lawrence, *Those Nut-Cracking Elizabethans*, pp. 106–111.
[35] Flecknoe's comment is sometimes cited as evidence that the *entire* Elizabethan stage was strewn with rushes. Such an inference, however, seems to me unwarranted.

The area to be strewn with rushes probably varied with the play, but the position of permanent doors and traps, and the position of the rush-strewn inner stage, which not infrequently was merged with the outer stage to form a large interior, suggest that the usual practice was to strew the rear half of the outer stage midway between the stage doors. This location, together with the contrast afforded by unstrewn areas elsewhere on the platform, is implied in several plays, for example, *King John*, II. i, where, during the parley before the wall (i.e. the stage balcony directly over the inner stage) of Angers, France speaks of treading "In warlike march, these greenes before your town." Again, in *A Midsummer-Night's Dream*, III. i:

Bottom. Are we all met?

Quince. Pat, pat; and here's a marvailous convenient place for our rehearsall. This greene plot shall be our stage, this hauthorne brake our tyring house.

The two quotations last given are of further interest, for they illustrate the way in which Elizabethan dramatists habitually pressed theatrical details into the service of dramatic illusion, a process which furnishes us with the greater part of the numerous references to rushes on the stage. A few examples of this sort may be worth adding here. From *Love's Labours Lost* (1598), V. ii:

King [to Boyet]. Say to her we have measur'd many miles
To tread a Measure with her on this grasse.

From *Antony and Cleopatra*, III. v:

Enobarbus.   Where's Antony?
Eros. He's walking in the garden — thus; and spurns
The rush that lies before him.

Rushes and flowers strewn beforehand or during the progress of a play were early turned to dramatic account. In Part One of *The Contention . . . of York and Lancaster* (1594), sig. G4, is found the stage-direction "*Enter Jacke Cade at one doore . . .* [he] *lies downe picking of herbes and eating them."* Similar quotations illustrating the uses to which rushes were put for the enhancement of realism and illusion could be multiplied indefinitely.[36]

The same reason that had originally led to the strewing of rushes on parts of the platform where actors were destined to sit or fall led also (as stated in a previous chapter) to the strewing of rushes on the outskirts of the Globe platform when gallants succeeded in introducing there the Blackfriars custom of sitting directly on the stage. This was particularly necessary on public stages because the little half-roof or "shadow" designed to shield the up-stage half of the platform and protect it and the tiring-house façade from rain did not extend over the areas released to gallants. Even with rushes provided, we may imagine that many a fop followed the example of Brachiano in *The White Devil*, III. ii, who, before sitting on the rushes, *"Laies a rich gowne under him."*

By the end of Queen Elizabeth's reign households of the well-to-do generally used plaited-rush matting in place of strewn rushes.[37] A letter by Sir Henry Wotton describing the burning of the Globe in June, 1613, shows that the Globe Company followed suit: "The King's players had a new play called *All is True*, representing some principal pieces of the reign of Henry the Eighth, which was set forth with many extraordinary circumstances of pomp and majesty, even to the matting of the stage." [38] Whether or not this occasion marked the first appearance of matting on a public stage, it certainly was not the last, for in subsequent plays there are several situations and terms which

[36] For outer-stage scenes see *The Alchemist*, IV. iii; *The Bloody Brother*, II. i; *Blurt Master Constable*, I. i; *Covent Garden*, I. i; *The Dumb Knight*, IV. i; *1 Henry IV*, III. i; *The Tragedy of Hoffman*, H1 verso; *Satiromastix*, I. i; *Your Five Gallants*, V. ii; etc.

[37] Percy Macquoid, "The Home," in *Shakespeare's England*, ii. 128.

[38] Quoted in full in *Variorum* (1821), iii. 67. Dr. Adams has suggested to me that in the quotation from Wotton "matting" may be a verb, and thus that some floor covering more appropriate to "pomp and majesty" than rush matting was used.

distinguish matting from the older and humbler form of strewn rushes.[39]

Whether loose or woven, rushes were a not inconsiderable item of expense. The Revels Accounts of 1576 [40] itemize a payment to "Wydow Lease for two dozen [bundles?] of rushes, with vi*d*. for the cariadge . . . . v*s*. x*d*."; and in the same year coarsely plaited rush matting cost five shillings a square yard.[41] As late as 1639 the cost of rushes was great enough to warrant inclusion in the agreement reached between the proprietors and actors of the Salisbury Court Theatre. Each group was to pay half: "for lights, both waxe and tallow, which halfe all winter is neare 5*s*. a day; halfe for coles to [heat] all the roomes; half for rushes, flowers and strewings on the stage." [42]

4. THE STAGE POSTS

The most conspicuous permanent objects on the outer stage were two tall posts which rose vertically to support the weight of the "stage-cover" and the "huts" — a superstructure known in Elizabethan times as the "heavens."

> We are now like
> The two poles propping heaven, on which heaven moves,
> And they are fixed and quiet,

boasts Pompey, in Chapman's *Caesar and Pompey*, V. i.[43] I cannot agree with the scholars [44] who find a reference

---

[39] For examples, see *The Atheist's Tragedy*, I. iv, and IV. v; *The Broken Heart*, IV. i; *The Fair Favorite* (written *ca.* 1638), III. ii; *A Mad World, my Masters*, IV. iii; *No Wit, no Help*, III. i; *Orestes* (an academic play), IV. vi; *The Scornful Lady*, II. i; *The Siege*, II. i.

[40] Cited in *Variorum* (1821), iii. 388.

[41] Macquoid, "The Home," in *Shakespeare's England*, ii. 124.

[42] *Shakespeare Society Papers*, iv (1849), 99.

[43] Cf. *The Fool would be a Favorite* (written 1638), F2 verso:

> "No, Madam, they are as firm as the Poles,
> That prop up heaven."

[44] E.g., Chambers, ii. 545.

to this pair of stage posts in a passage of the Fortune contract which reads:

All the princypall and maine postes of the saide fframe and Stadge forwarde shalbe square and wroughte palasterwise with carved proporcõns Called Satiers to be placed & sett on the Topp of every of the same postes.

Henslowe is here instructing Streete in a detail which is to give a distinctive finish to his playhouse. He wishes all the posts facing the audience on the inside of the building to be uniformly square, pilastered, and carved. His order refers not only to the posts of the tiring-house but also to the posts of the galleries. His particularized instructions regarding these inner or "forwarde" posts seem to indicate, first, that the corresponding posts of the Globe frame were shaped and decorated in some other fashion (square posts were of course architecturally appropriate in the square Fortune; we may suspect that in the octagonal forerunner of the Fortune all "forwarde" posts had mitred corners or were round [45]) and, secondly, that the posts in the tiring-house sections of the Globe frame differed from the posts in the gallery sections. If this is the true meaning of the Fortune contract, as prolonged study has led me to believe, then no part of the phrase, "postes of the saide fframe and Stadge forwarde," relates to the free-standing pillars rising from the platform to support the stage superstructure.

This reading of the Fortune contract is supported by a comparison with the corresponding provisions of the Hope contract. At the Hope Jacob Meade, the builder, was instructed

to make Turned Cullumes vppon and over the stage And to . . . make the Principalls and fore fronte of the saide Plaie house of good and sufficient oken Tymber, And no furr tymber to be putt or vsed in the lower most, or midell stories, excepte the vpright postes on the backparte of the saide stories . . . the Jnner principall postes of the first storie to be Twelve footes in height and Tenn ynches square . . .

[45] See Chap. II. pp. 19–20.

The Hope contract also calls for a stage heavens to be "borne or carryed without any postes or supporters to be fixed or sett vppon the saide [removable platform] stage." At the Hope, therefore, the "Turned Cullumes vppon and over the stage" (corresponding to the "postes of the . . . Stadge forwarde" at the Fortune) are parts of the frame; furthermore, they differed in shape from all other posts on the inside (the "fore fronte") of the building.

Except, then, for the design of the "forwarde" posts of the tiring-house, and for certain other minor differences called for in the contract (i.e. the depth of the platform, the use of oak paling on the sides of the platform, etc.), the Fortune stage and tiring-house were to be "in all pro-porcōns Contryved and fashioned like vnto the Stadge of the . . . Globe." [46] It seems probable, therefore, that the Fortune stage posts were not square but round. An additional reason for suspecting that they were round is that so tall a timber is easier to obtain and far cheaper in the round than in the square; and for a theatre built within a mile of the great fleet of ships anchored below London Bridge, a pair of masts — either new or old — would have served admirably. [47]

At the same time it must not be overlooked that the Swan drawing shows round pillars with square, carved bases, or more exactly pedestals, extending at least three feet above the level of the stage floor. So many contradic-

[46] *Henslowe Papers*, p. 5.

[47] On February 19, 1599, some 30 days after beginning work on the Fortune, Henslowe (*Papers*, p. 9) paid 25 shillings "in part payment . . . for a mast." Mr. Greg conjectures that this "mast" was used as the flagstaff of the playhouse, but I am inclined to doubt this. If a new flagstaff at the Rose in 1592 cost Henslowe 12 shillings (*Diary*, p. 7), then a part payment of 25 shillings (imply-ing that the full sum was considerably greater — i.e. twice as great or more?) seems too much for a flagstaff at the Fortune. The cost of "ij lode & hallfe of tymber" was but 35 shillings. Again, the date on which the part payment was made is close to the period of construction when stage posts were needed. It was months earlier than the period when a flagpole, the highest part of the build-ing — hence one of the last pieces to be set in place — was needed.

tions are inherent in the De Witt sketch, and particularly
in the detail of massive pillars resting on a lightly constructed, temporary stage, that its evidence is of doubtful
importance. Some sort of base, however, would seem to be
demanded by the stage business of many a play in which
an actor climbs a tree. (Except for easily recognized exceptions, the word "tree" in stage-directions means
"post.") In Jonson's *The Case is Altered*, IV. vii, Jaques
hears noises and enters (the outer stage) to discover who
is in his garden. To avoid being found, *"Onion gets up into
a tree"* and remains there during 81 lines of dialogue. In
the anonymous *Thracian Wonder*, written *circa* 1600 (but
not printed until 1661), II. ii:

Clown. I go, I go, I go . . . *The Clown climbs up a tree.*
Pallemon. Puff, they'r blown away with a Whirlewinde:
    Thanks gentle Eolus, th'ast left my Love upon a lofty Pine.
Clown. Yes, I shall pine . . . I come, I come down to thee.
    He'l break my neck, if he get up once.   *Comes downe.*

In *The Miseries of Enforced Marriage*, sig. F2, three thieves
come running in with the money bags they have just
taken. Pursued, one of them cries, "Squat hart squat,
creepe mee into these Bushes, and lye me as close to the
ground as you would to a wench . . . in the meane time
[having another plan of escape for himself] . . . off with
my skin [coat], so you on the ground, and I to this tree to
escape the Gallows." He climbs up, but is soon discovered,
and is unable to convince his captors that he is "gathering
of Nuts, that such fools as you are may cracke the shels,
and I eat the kernels." [48]

After the first three or four feet of ascent have been accomplished with the aid of a molding or two, the illusion of
climbing a tree (and I have run across no play demanding
that one climb very high) can be satisfied with a few feet
more. Without initial help afforded by a pedestal or sim-

[48] For other examples of tree-climbing, see *The Honest Lawyer* (1616), I2;
Sicelides (1631), IV. vi; and *The Rival Friends* (1632), III. iv.

ilar projections, it is difficult to see how an actor could ascend the large stage posts at all.

One wishes that the frequent references in plays to the stage posts made clear their position on the platform; but, although indicating their use in a great variety of ways (for example, as trees; [49] as a means of hiding from others on the platform; [50] as posts to which notices of various sorts are affixed, [51] or to which rogues or victims are bound; [52] as a seeming may-pole, [53] or road-side cross, [54] or the gates of a bridge [55]), these allusions afford no clear evidence as to the exact location of the pillars.

A close reading of the plays reveals that there were sections of the platform where the posts could not have been placed, but no situation has come to my notice which establishes their exact position. One is prone to believe them at some distance from the scenic wall, for the greater the distance the less they would obscure or interfere with action taking place at doors and other vital points there. They could not be in the very middle of the stage or even close to it, partly because of their structural function, and partly because the main trapdoor was located there and its operation and visibility were not to be impaired. On the other hand, that they were perhaps nearer to the main trap than to any other part of the platform is implied in two trap scenes. In Dekker's undivided Red Bull play of

[49] *The Bashful Lover*, III. iii; *The Beggar's Bush*, IV. iv; *The Distresses*, III. iv; *Gallathea*, I. i; *The Guardian*, I. i; *The Hog hath lost his Pearl*, IV. i; *The Witch of Edmonton*, III. i; etc.

[50] *The Devil's Charter*, F3 verso; *The Guardian*, I. i; *The Partial Law*, II. ii; *The Siege*, V. vii; *Two Angry Women*, line 1949; etc.

[51] *As You Like It*, III. ii; *The Devil's Charter*, A4 verso; *The Hog hath lost his Pearl*, IV. i; *James IV*, C1; *Orlando Furioso*, line 572; etc.

[52] *A Larum for London*, line 1491; *The Bashful Lover*, III. iii; *Cymbeline*, V. iv; *The Distresses*, III. iv; *Greene's Tu Quoque*, final scene; *The Pilgrim*, IV. ii; *The Rebellion*, IV; *Soliman and Perseda*, V; *Three Lords and Three Ladies of London*, I3 verso; *The White Devil*, V. ii; etc.

[53] *Englishmen for my Money*, lines 1603 and 1654.

[54] *Old Wives Tale*, line 368.

[55] *Thomas Lord Cromwell*, C2 verso.

circa 1610, *If It be not Good*,[56] Scumbroth has climbed "high" into a "blacke" tree in search of gold. At that point: "*Rayne, Thunder and lightning: Enter* [in this scene the direction "*enter*" clearly means "rise"] *Lucifer and Diuels*."

Omn. Oooh.
Luc. This is the tree . . . *Sits vnder the tree all* [others] *about him.*

The later Phoenix play, *The Arcadia*, also contains a scene (sig. D2) implying that the trap was at no great distance from the posts. Wherever set on the outer stage, the posts caused some hindrance to vision, and no location down stage is appreciably better in this regard than another. Clearly a thorough understanding of the "heavens" which the posts helped to support is required before their position can be determined with anything like certainty, and since a consideration of this feature more appropriately falls in Chapter X, I shall set the problem aside until later.

5. THE PLATFORM TRAPS

Mention has previously been made of traps and other devices operated from below the stage.[57] As seen by the audience, the trapdoors probably were noticeable only when in use, and the rest of the time fitted closely, solidly, and of course level with the surface of the floor.

In the plays of 1576–1642 there are to be found upwards of two hundred instances of the use of outer-stage traps. With so much data, consisting of specific stage-directions, properties employed, and indications of technique, it is not

---

[56] *If It be not Good*, H4 verso and I1.

[57] No discussion of traps elsewhere is sufficiently accurate or detailed for our present need. Contributions to the subject have been made by Reynolds, Wegener, Graves, Creizenach, Chambers, and Campbell during the last thirty years, but the only presentation which really clears the ground is that by Lawrence, *Pre-Restoration Stage Studies*, pp. 145–175. To his chapter the reader is referred, particularly for historical and histrionic details which lie outside the scope of the present discussion.

difficult to establish the location, number, and even the size
and mechanical efficiency of these traps.

Let us begin with the most important trap of the entire
playhouse. That it was located in or near the middle of the
platform the following quotations show. From the first
Prologue to *Poetaster* (in the 1616 folio of Jonson's *Works*):
"*Envie. Arising in the midst of the stage.*" From a MS.
play *The Aphrodisial*, written in 1602, folio 120, verso:
"*A Trap door in middle of the Stage.*" And from the Globe
play *The Devil's Charter*, sig. A2 verso:

> *Roderigo . . . whome the Monke draweth to a chaire in midst of the Stage*
> *which hee circleth, and before it an other Circle, into which . . . appeare*
> *exhalations of lightning and sulphurous smoke in midst whereof a divil in*
> *most ugly shape* [rises] *. . . hee beeing conjured downe after more thunder*
> *and fire, ascends another divill like a Sargeant with a mace under his*
> *girdle: . . . Hee discendeth: after more thunder and fearfull fire, ascend in*
> *robes pontificall* [a devil] *with a triple Crowne on his head, and Crosse*
> *keyes in his hand.*

This middle trap was also the largest in the entire theatre, which explains why Pope Alexander (the Roderigo
Borgia of *The Devil's Charter*) always advances from the
inner stage (which also was provided with a trap) to the
middle of the outer stage when conjuring up large, spectacular apparitions; for example (sig. G1 and G1 verso):

> *Alex*[ander] *commeth upon the Stage out of his study with a booke in his*
> *hand . . . Fiery exhalations lightning thunder ascend a King, with a red*
> *face crowned imperiall riding upon a Lyon or dragon.*

Another reason for the actor's coming down stage to use
the large platform trap was, of course, to furnish the audience in all parts of the house with an unhampered view of
elaborate spectacles. But this, needless to say, is merely
another way of explaining why the platform center trap
was made the largest and was provided with the most
effective apparatus for raising and lowering objects.

Some idea of the size and mechanical possibilities of this
trap will be found in the following stage-directions. From

VIGNETTE FROM THE TITLE–PAGE OF *MESSALLINA*, 1640

The original measures 1 by 1-3/16 inches

Chapman's Globe and Blackfriars play, *Caesar and Pompey*, II. i:

Thunder, and the gulf opens, flames issuing, and Ophioneus ascending, with the face, wings, and tail of a dragon; a skin coat all speckled on the throat.

From *The Arraignment of Paris*, line 488:

Hereuppon did rise a Tree of gold laden with Diadems & Crownes of golde . . . The Tree sinketh.

Again from the same play, line 902:

Pluto ascēdeth from below in his chaire. Neptune entreth at another way.

From *Tancred and Gismund*, line 855:

Before the Act Megæra riseth out of hell, with the other Furies, Alecto and Tysyphone, dauncing an hellish round; which done she saith.

> Sisters be gone, bequeath the rest to me,
> That yet belongs unto this Tragaedie.
> *The two Furies depart down.*

From *The Birth of Merlin*, sig. F3:

Merlin strikes his wand. Thunder and Lightning, two Dragons appear, a White and a Red, they fight a while and pause.

From *A Looking Glass for London and England*, line 522:

The Magi with their rods beate the ground, and from under the same riseth a brave Arbour, the King returneth in another sute while the Trumpettes sounde.

(Sir Edmund Chambers points out that the title-page of the 1615 *Spanish Tragedy* shows the arbor of that play as a small trellised pergola with an arched top, not too large, he thinks, to come up and down through a commodious trap.[58])

Trap signals were given by stamping or rapping upon the floor so that actors and stage-hands below could know when to spring the trap. The last two quotations cited

---

[58] *Elizabethan Stage*, iii. 89n.

incorporate the signal in action called for by the stage-direction. The following quotation from *The Silver Age*, III. iv, tells the audience what the signal will be (namely, a decisive stamping of the foot), but does not happen to include it in the final stage-direction:

Pluto. Cleave earth, and when I stampe upon thy breast
Sinke me, my brasse-shod wagon, and my selfe,
My Coach-steeds [i.e. devils], and their traces altogether
Ore head and eares in Styx.

Proserpine. You Gods, you men.

Pluto. Eternall darkenesse claspe me where I dwell
Saving these eyes, wee'le have no light in hell.
               Exit [i.e. he stamps, and all six descend].

Again, from *Women Beware Women*, V. i:

Guardiano.   Look you Sir,
This is the trap-door to't.

Ward. I know't of old Uncle, since the last triumph: here rose up a Devil with one eye I remember, with a company of fire-works at's tail.

Guard. Prethee leave squibbing now, mark me, and fail not; but when thou hear'st me give a stamp, down with't: The villain's caught then.

Still again, from *The Silver Age*, the last scene:

Exeunt three wayes Ceres, Theseus, Philoctetes, and Hercules dragging Cerberus one way [i.e. through an exit at the rear]: *Pluto, hels Judges, the Fates and Furies downe to hell* [i.e. through a trap]: *Jupiter, the Gods and Planets ascend to heaven.*

A trap at least 4 feet by 8 feet would probably be required to accommodate the large group here mentioned.

There is still another means of estimating its size. The term "grave trap" is sometimes used by scholars to denote the smaller trap located in the inner stage. To merit the name (which, as we shall later see, is warranted by evidence in a number of plays), that trap must have been large enough to receive a full-sized coffin, and so must have been at least 2½ by 6 feet. Now the comparative sizes of the bulkiest objects associated with the platform trap and the inner-stage trap suggests that the former was at least a foot larger in both dimensions. That the main trap was rectangular in shape is suggested by the stage-directions calling for a pair of dragons, a chariot with four devils harnessed to its pole, and various groups of actors, sometimes numbering as high as eight [59] to descend together, for these displays would show to far better advantage on a rising or falling rectangular trap-cover than on a square or a circular cover of equal area. Moreover, in the middle of the platform in the *Messallina* view there is marked by unmistakable lines a rectangular area, presumably the trap-cover. This fact, together with the cited quotations and considerations of a practical nature, wholly outweighs the implications contained in an obscure play of about 1640, *The Unfortunate Usurper* (belatedly printed in 1663), V. iii:

He makes a Circle, and mutters something to himself, at which, out of a trap-door in the Stage of the same bigness and Figure as the Circle rises a Daemon in black.

We may also assume, for the reasons given above, that the long axis of the trap was parallel to the front edge of the stage, and so faced the greater part of the audience.

In addition to this main, centrally-located trap there were other traps on the platform. In *Alphonsus, King of Aragon*, a pre-Globe play, at line 951, appears the direction, "*Rise Calchas up in a white Cirples,*" and nineteen lines later, "*Calchas sinke downe where you came up.*" This implies that there were two or more traps on the stage.[60] More convincing evidence is found in the final scene of *If It be not Good, the Devil is in It*: "*From under the ground in several places rise up spirits*"; and still clearer evidence in *No Wit, no Help, like a Woman's*, IV. ii:

From under the stage, on different sides, at the farther end, rise Overdone as Water and Petterton as Earth.

[59] See, for example, *Grim, the Collier*, last scene, and *If It be not Good*, L4.

[60] Lawrence, *Pre-Restoration Stage Studies*, p. 167n, takes another view, but see the quotation from *The Silver Age* on the next page.

Here two traps, each capable of lifting a single person, are located for us. By implication, the phrase "at the farther end" suggests that there were other traps at the "nearer end" of the stage, or in all four traps in addition to the large middle one. And this conjecture is made certain by three unmistakable stage-directions. The first occurs in a dumb show in the undivided Fortune play, *The Whore of Babylon*: [61]

A caue [at rear] *suddenly breakes open, and out of it comes Falshood, (attir'd as Truth is) her face spotted, shee stickes vp her banner on the top of the Caue; then with her foot in seuerall places strikes the earth, and vp riseth Campeius a Frier with a boxe: a gentleman with a drawn sword, another with rich gloues in a boxe, another with a bridle. Time-Truth with her banner, and Plain-dealing enter & stand aloofe beholding all.*

The second occurs at the end of Heywood's *Golden Age*:

Sound, Thunder and Tempest. Enter at 4 seuerall corners the 4 winds: Neptune riseth [i.e. from the middle trap] *disturb'd: the Fates bring the 4 winds in a chaine, & present them to Æolus, as their King.*

The third occurs near the end of Heywood's equally spectacular *Silver Age*:

Hercules sinkes himselfe [through the middle trap] *Flashes of fire; the Diuels appeare* [i.e. rise] *at every corner of the stage with seuerall fireworkes. The Judges of hell, and the three sisters run over the stage, Hercules after them: fire-works all over the house.*

The quotations just given merit close study. [62] In no detail bearing on the four small traps are they contradictory. Apparently only one person emerges from a single trap on a given occasion. It would appear, therefore, that these traps, four in number, were located in the corners of the platform and were small affairs of the simplest type. They are not used frequently enough to warrant anything very elaborate. Possibly steps or a ladder was available under each up which when the cue was given an actor

[61] Quarto 1607, G2 verso.
[62] For other examples of the corner traps in use, see *The Witches of Lancashire*, II; and the academic *Rival Friends*, V. ii.

could climb unassisted, open the hinged trap-cover, and scramble out upon the stage. I have encountered no instance of an actor's descending through a corner trap.

If the corner traps were elementary in type, the main trap, as abundant evidence shows, must have been equipped with an elaborate machine, the result of many years of experience and development. The heavy loads it was called upon to bear proves that it was sturdily constructed and, what is quite as important, sure in its operation. The great number of trap scenes used in plays of the age surely testifies to competent design and control. Notice the following amazing display in Heywood's *Brazen Age*, I. i:

> *Alarme. Achelous is beaten in, and immediately* [re-]*enters* [through a door?] *in the shape of a Dragon.*
>
> *Hercules.* Bee'st thou a God or hell-hound thus transhap't,
> Thy terrour frights not me, serpent or divell
> Il'e pash thee.
> *Alarme. He beats away the dragon. Enter* [through a trap] *a Fury all fire-workes.*
>
> *Herc.* Fright us with fire? our Club shall quench thy flame,
> And beat it downe to hell, from whence it came.
> *When the Fury sinkes, a Buls head appeares.*
>
> *Herc.* What, yet more monsters? Serpent, Bull, and Fire,
> Shall all alike taste great *Alcides* ire.
> *He tugs with the Bull, and pluckes off one of his horns. Enter from the same place Achelous with his fore-head all bloudy.*

Here the trap has been down and up two or perhaps three times in as many minutes.

In a dumb show in *A Warning for Fair Women*, sig. E2 verso, we are shown that the main trap could rise swiftly:

> *They offering cheerefully to meete and embrace, suddenly riseth up a great tree betweene them, whereat amazedly they step backe.*

It could also be raised slowly. From *Edward I*, line 2527:

> *Potters wife.* Would it please you to walke and leaue of your knauerie, but staie *Iohn*, whats that riseth out of the ground, Iesus blesse vs *Iohn*, look how it riseth higher and higher.

Iohn. Be my troth mistres tis a woman, good Lord do women grow
I neuer saw none grow before.

Still other plays show that it could sink slowly. For example, in *The Virgin Martyr*, V. i, Theophilus holds a cross
of flowers before the fiend Harpax. Then:

Harp. Keep from me.   *sinks a little.*
Theop. Art posting to thy centre? down, hell-hound, down!

Again, in *Messallina*, sig. E8 verso, Saufellus, Hem, and
Stitch enter to the outer stage bearing lights.

Hem. The ground shakes, I sinke,
    *Thunder and lightning, Earth gapes and swallowes the three mur-
    der*[er]*s by degrees.*
  Hems hem'd to the earth
  I cannot stirre.
Stitch. Nor I I sinke, *Stitch* sinkes
  Had we our names for this, a vengeance of
  All false *Stitches*, they have stitcht me, O horror.
Saufellus. How's this
Hem. Hell and confusion ⎱
                  ⎰ *Sinke both.*
Stitch. Divells and Furies ⎰
Saufellus. Horror of darkenesse, what dread sight is this
  What black Red-raw-eyed witch hath charm'd this ground.
  Sink'st thou my limbes supporter . . . sinke
  Me O — earth; *Pindus* and *Ossa* cover
  Me with Snow . . . My Eye sight failes . . .
  Farewell *Romes* Emp'resse
               Shot with a Tunderbolt
  To all ambitious vermine,
  Puncks, Pimpes, and Panders, Whores and Bawdes farewell.
  Confound the world, the worst of death is hell.
                    Sinkes.

Here, I take it, the trap has made two trips, the first time
lowering Hem and Stitch, and the second, even more
slowly and dramatically, Saufellus (he speaks twenty-four
lines between the time the trap begins to descend with him
and the time the thunderbolt falls).

A variety of startling and prolonged sounds commonly

attended the ascent and descent of lower-world creatures. Thunder and Lightning were usual; [63] "hellish musick," [64] "charges" or other trumpet calls,[65] Alarums,[66] or a falling chain [67] were variants. Friendly river gods and beneficent apparitions rose to music slowly breathed.[68] Underlying the histrionic value of such sounds was the practical purpose of concealing the noise made by the trap mechanism. Awareness of this fact helps one to reconstruct the staging of many Elizabethan scenes. Whenever creatures associated with the lower world — as devils, furies, ghosts, and so on — "enter" to the accompaniment of "thunder and lightning," "loud musick," or the like, the presumption is that they rise through a trap. This in turn suggests that they may leave by the same means, a possibility which the all-inclusive term *"exeunt"* in no way contradicts. Even when (as not infrequently happens) a stage-direction fails to record disguise sounds as accompanying the entrance or departure of such creatures and merely reads "Enter ————," one is justified in suspecting that a trap was used and that sounds were made in order to conceal its motion.

In order further to heighten the spectacle and to disguise visual aspects of trap scenes harmful to the dramatic effect, flames and sulphurous smoke were occasionally produced as the trap opened either to lift or to lower its burden. The following quotations illustrating this point will supplement those already given in recent pages. From *A Looking Glass for London and England*, line 1230: "*A flame of fire appeareth from beneath, and Radagon is swal-*

---

[63] *The Birth of Merlin*, E1; *Bussy D'Ambois*, IV. ii; *The Contention of York and Lancaster*, C1; *The Devil's Charter*, A2 verso; *Dr. Faustus*, F3; *1 Henry VI*, V. iii; *John of Bordeaux*, line 1134; *Locrine*, Prol.; *Old Wives Tale*, line 748; *The Seven Champions*, lines 412 ff.; *The Valiant Welshman*, F1 and F1 verso; *The Virgin Martyr*, V. ii; etc.

[64] *If It be not Good*, I. i; *The Valiant Welshman*, A4 verso.

[65] *The Jew of Malta*, V. iv; *A Looking Glass for London*, line 521.

[66] *Caesar's Revenge*, line 1.

[67] *The Jew of Malta*, V. iv.

[68] *The Prophetess*, V. iii; *A Shoemaker a Gentleman*, I. iii.

lowed." From the last scene of *If It be not Good, the Devil is in It*; *"Sinck downe, above flames."* And from *Caesar's Revenge*, line 1: *"Sound alarum then flames of fire —"* in the midst of which Discord ascends.

Once stage-hands had learned to produce a cloud of smoke upon demand, dramatists called upon them for smoke effects in scenes not involving Hell. The twelfth scene of *The Cobler's Prophecy*, acted in 1580, begins:

Enter the Duke, his Daughter, Priest, and Scholler: then compasse the stage, from one part let a smoke arise: at which place they all stay.

In Beaumont and Fletcher's long stage pageant, *Four Plays in One,*[69] occurs the direction, *"A Mist ariseth, the rocks remove."* Fletcher again had recourse to smoke — *"Delphia raises a mist"* — in an outer-stage dumb show preceding Act IV of *The Prophetess*. The explanation later added by the Chorus gives us a clearer idea of the volume and density of this mist:

> Then too weak
> Had been all opposition and resistance
> The Persians could have made against their fury,
> If Delphia by her Cunning had not rais'd
> A foggy Mist, which, as a Cloud, conceal'd them,
> Deceiving their Pursuers.

This timely mist obscuring a not small group of persons in *The Prophetess* perhaps gives a clue to the otherwise puzzling stage business in Jonson's *Catiline*, I. i, acted at the Globe in 1611.

> *A darknesse comes ouer the place.*
> *Longinus.* A strange vn-wonted horror doth inuade me,
> I know not what it is. *Lecca.* The day goes back,
> Or else my senses! *Cvr.* As at Atreus feast!
> *Ful.* Darkenesse growes more, and more! *Len.* The *vestall* flame,
> I thinke, be out.

A scornful opinion of hell smoke, together with a hint as to how it was produced, is given by Comedy during her de-

---

[69] *Works*, ed. Glover and Waller, x. 307.

bate with Tragedy in the Induction to *A Warning for Fair Women*:

> With that a little Rosen flasheth forth,
> Like smoke out of a Tabacco pipe, or a boyes squib.[70]

6. THE "HELL"

Underneath the platform and the inner stage behind it was excavated a large cellar called "hell." The Prologue to *All Fools*, first acted at the Rose, remarks:

> The fortune of a stage (like Fortune's self)
> Amazeth greatest judgments; and none knows
> The hidden causes of those strange effects,
> That rise from this hell, or fall from this heaven.

Dekker, in *News from Hell*, 1606, wrote: [71]

> Mar[r]y the question is, in which of the Playhouses he [the Devil] would have performed his prize . . . Hell being vnder euerie one of their Stages, the Players (if they had owed him a spight) might with a false Trappe doore haue slipt him downe, and there kept him, as a laughing stocke to al their yawning spectators.

"Hell" probably had an area equal to the two stages which formed its ceiling (recall the four traps "in the corners" and the "grave trap" in the inner stage), and it must have had a height sufficient to make possible the ready operation of trap mechanisms. Lacking windows, it was almost totally dark, except where, at the rear, a little indirect light may have entered through the tiring-house stairway.

The use of a substage, and of the term "hell" applied to it, goes back to the medieval plays. The early sixteenth-century Digby mystery *Mary Magdalene* contains the direction: "*Here xal entyr the prynse of dylls in a stage, and Helle ondyr-neth that stage.*" [72] Later in the same play the

---

[70] For additional examples see *Love's Changelings Change*, MS. Egerton, p. 294; *Old Wives Tale*, line 670; *Histriomastix*, III. i. For further discussion, see Lawrence, ii. 5.

[71] *Dekker's Works*, ed. Grosart, ii. 92.

[72] Ed. J. Q. Adams, *Chief Pre-Shakespearean Dramas*, p. 232.

bad angel enters "*into hell with Thondyr.*" *Gorboduc*, produced early in 1562 at Whitehall, opened Act IV with:

*First the musick of howboies began to plaie, during which there came from
vnder the stage, as though out of hell three Furies, Alecto, Megera, and
Ctesiphone, clad in black garmentes sprinkled with bloud and flames.*

The term "hell" was standard in Shakespearean times
for the cellar under the stage. In this technical sense it has
already been used once or twice in quotations appearing on
recent pages. Homer, who apparently rises from below to
be Epilogist to *The Silver Age*, plays upon it before sinking
out of sight:

> Here I haue done: if ill, too much: if well,
> Pray with your hands guide *Homer* out of hell.

The Hope playhouse, designed "bothe for players to
playe in, And for the game of Beares and Bulls to be
bayted in," had a removable stage which, according to the
contract,[73] was made "to be carryed or taken awaie, and
to stande vppon tressells good, substantiall, and sufficient
for the carryinge and bearinge of suche a stage." At the
Hope, therefore, only a cellar at the rear under the tiring-
house could be used, for between the pit floor and the removable platform there would be no space for a large and
deep excavation.

In all the other playhouses of the period [74] the platform
was not set on removable trestles, but was built as a permanent feature, with a cellar below having a paling of
"good, strong, and sufficient new oaken boards" to form
its walls, and with posts, rising from the cellar floor, to
support the stage above. The Globe platform was of
necessity strongly made, for it had to withstand the activities of a large number of actors — some plays enumerate

---

[73] *Henslowe Papers*, p. 20.

[74] Unless perhaps the Swan, which also appears to have been used for bear-
baiting. See Adams, pp. 165–166.

as many as thirty characters in one scene [75] — to say nothing of the two stage posts rising from the platform to support the "heavens." A glance at the many posts in the cellar needed to support the weight above is provided by a passage in *The Custom of the Country*, III. iii:

Rutilio. Cannot a man fall into one of your drunken cellars,
  And venture the breaking on's neck, your trapdoors open . . .
  I fell into it by chance, I broke my shins for't:
  Your worships feel not that: I knockt my head
  Against a hundred posts.

The Roaring Girl, sig. C2 verso, hints at the fears others beside Rutilio may have experienced, namely that of stepping on a "false" or unsecured trap and thus falling into "hell":

Alexander [to Trapdore, a character in the play]. *Trapdore*, be like thy
    name, a dangerous step
  For her to venture on, but unto me.
Trap. As fast as your sole to your boote or shooe sir.

In *The Staple of News*, III. i, we hear of

                    a trick
        To open us a gap by a trap-door,
        When they least dream on't.

Some such mechanism as "the large plate spring boults for a trap doare on ye stage," which cost five shillings a pair in 1673,[76] must have been employed to ensure that traps would stay closed when not in use.

Some type of flooring for the cellar was surely needed as underfooting for the often elaborately dressed actors, and to provide support for the heavy platform floor upon which, in turn, rested the weight of the stage pillars and a part of the stage superstructure. It will be remembered

[75] See, for example, *Edward I*, line 683; *The Fatal Dowry*, II. i; and *The Fatal Contract*, III.
[76] Boswell, *Restoration Court Stage*, p. 252.

that the Globe was erected in "a long straggling place, with ditches on each side," and that Ben Jonson described it as "Flanck'd with a Ditch, and forc'd out of a Marish." [77] Such ground must have made any deep excavation troublesome, and probably the Globe's "hell" was not remarkable for dryness.

Yet a survey of the activities that there took place points to it as on occasion a busy place. The Ghost of Hamlet's father moved about "in the cellarage," calling upon his son, above, to "Sweare!" Manifestly, voices emanating thence would sound well muffled and appropriately ghostly, as is indicated when the Ghost of Andrugio in *Antonio's Revenge*, line 1186, cries from below:

> *From vnder the stage a groane.*
> *Antonio.* Howle not thou puny mould, groan not ye graves.

In addition to being used as Hell, the cellar was sometimes used to represent other places. Occasionally it was a wine cellar, as in *Rule a Wife, and Have a Wife*, V:

> *Duke.* Are there none here?
> Let me look around; we cannot be too wary. . .
> > *Noise below.*
> What's that you tumble?
> > *Cacafogo makes a noise below.*
> I have heard a noise this half hour under me.
> A fearfull noise.
> *Margarita.* The fat thing's mad i' th' cellar,
> And stumbles from one hogs-head to another.

Or an underground cave, as in *The Queen's Exchange*, V. i; or a dungeon, whence the prisoners groan, call out, or talk with their jailors above, as in *Believe As Ye List*, line 1930, or in *The Renegado*, IV. iii. In this last instance, Francisco, having come to the jail to extricate his friend Vitelli, puts some gold coins into the hand of the Gaoler:

[77] See above, Chapter I, section 2.

Gaol. 'Tis the best oratory. I will hazard
  A check for your content — Below there!
Vit. Welcome!   *Vitelli vnder the Stage.*
  Art thou the happy messenger that brings me
  News of my death?
Gaol. Your hand.   *Vitelli pluck'd vp.*
Fran. [to Gaoler] Now, if you please,
  A little privacy.

In *Antonio's Revenge*, line 1858, Sir Geoffrey Balurdo, a
prisoner confined below, breaks his chains and crawls out
unaided as from a dungeon upon the platform, probably
by means of one of the corner traps.

> *Balurdo from under the stage.*

Bal. Hoe, who's above there, hoe? a murren on all Proverbes. . .
  [he climbs out] O, now sir *Gefferey*, shewe thy valour, breake prison,
  and be hangd.

The "hell" was also useful when distant or confused off-
stage cries were called for. In *Catiline*, I. i, "*A grone of
many people is heard vnder ground*"; and a few minutes
later there is "*a second groan.*" In *A Shoemaker a Gentleman*, I. i, the stage-direction, "*Follow, within (and below)
follow,*" shows how the savage cries of those pursuing the
royal party were produced with unusual vividness. In
The Duchess of Malfi, V. iii, is heard an "*Eccho (from the
Dutchesse Grave).*" A similarly eerie effect is produced in
Antonio's Revenge, at line 1110, when the voices of three
ghosts dispersed above and below the inner stage solemnly
echo the last word of Antonio's soliloquy:

> — Contempt of heauen, vntam'd arrogance,
>   Lust, state, pride, murder.

And. Murder. ⎫
Fel. Murder. ⎬ *From aboue and beneath.*
Pa. Murder. ⎭
Ant. I, I will murder: graues and ghosts
  Fright me no more, Ile suck red vengeance
  Out of *Pieros* wounds. [The three ghosts echo in unison:]
                    Piero's wounds.

Antony and Cleopatra, IV. iii, provides a clear example of the occasional presence of musicians in the cellar, and attests to the illusive quality imparted to sounds produced there.

> *Musicke of the Hoboyes is under the Stage.*
>
> 2. [Soldier]. Peace, what noise?
> *1.* List, list.
> 2. Hearke.
> *1.* Musicke i' th' Ayre.
> *3.* Under the earth.[78]

The operation of the traps has already been described. We can readily imagine the bustle in "hell" while certain scenes were in progress. A glimpse at timely preparation is afforded by a prompter's marginal note in *Believe As Ye List*, line 1825, which runs: "*Gascoine: & Hubert below: ready to open the Trap doore for Mr. Taylor*"; not until a hundred lines later is the command given for the trap to be opened. The signals to workers below were in almost all cases given from above, either by stamping on the floor (as in *The Silver Age* and *The Whore of Babylon* cited on pages 116 and 118),[79] or by striking the stage floor with a wand,[80] a dagger,[81] a crosier,[82] a grave shovel,[83] or some solid object actually used in the scene.

The trap mechanism gives us our chief clue to the depth of "hell." W. J. Lawrence was of the opinion that the depth cannot have been less than ten feet; but his figure was based partly on conjecture and partly on a woodcut of

---

[78] For other examples of cellar music see *If It be not Good*, I. i; *Cymbeline*, V. iv; *The Prophetess*, V. iii; *A Shoemaker a Gentleman*, I. iii.

[79] See also *Four Plays in One* (Beaumont and Fletcher, ed. Glover and Waller, x. 362). The illustrations now cited, and those immediately to follow, have been chosen both for their clarity and to supplement the list given by Lawrence, *Pre-Restoration Stage Studies*, pp. 162–163.

[80] *The Birth of Merlin*, quoted above, p. 115; *Orlando Furioso*, line 1257; *The Rare Triumphs of Love and Fortune*, I.

[81] *Antonio's Revenge*, line 1780.

[82] *Two Noble Ladies*, line 1855.

[83] *Old Wives Tale*, line 712.

a modern French stage in which the floor is cut away, the trap is shown in use, and three figures in the cellar give some idea of scale.[84] My own conjecture is that the Globe "hell" was not more than eight feet in depth, for the marsh on which the building was erected probably would not permit a very deep cellar. An eight-foot-deep cellar would provide a full seven-foot-high ceiling, after allowing for the beams supporting the platform floor. Anything less than headroom would be a constant and irritating barrier to comfort and efficient work; more than seven feet would be agreeable perhaps, but not necessary.[85] The eight-foot cellar postulated for the Globe would have required an excavation of not more than five feet, for a two-and-a-half or three-foot space already existed between the ground level and the stage floor. With a water-filled sub-soil, a deeper cellar, I believe, would have been unwise.

Another guide in estimating the height of "hell" is to be found in the list of stage properties used in trap scenes. Obviously no property taller than the height of the cellar could be employed. In any calculation, however, we must make some allowance for the space occupied by the machinery used in lowering and raising objects, for the trap's cover could not sink to the absolute level of the cellar floor unless there was a pit to receive it (this, to be sure, is not outside the realm of possibility). Now Lawrence's demand for a ten-foot "hell" is based on the clumsy trap depicted in the French woodcut which he reproduces. That trap is so built that its cover at the lowest part of its descent is still waist high above the cellar floor. As a result, even in a ten-foot cellar the height of usable properties would be limited to not more than six feet. With a

[84] Reproduced by him, *Pre-Restoration Stage Studies*, facing p. 169.

[85] Scale drawings by Inigo Jones for erecting the stage in the great hall at Whitehall in 1640 for the masque *Salmacida Spolia* (reproduced by P. Reyher, *Les Masques Anglais*, facing p. 370) show headroom of 7 feet in front and 8 feet in back. The windlasses employed to raise and lower clouds are located under the stage, thus creating the same problems faced by designers of a public stage.

trap of better design, or with a sunken pit beneath it, properties seven feet high could easily be handled even in a cellar only eight feet in depth. I venture to suggest that some one or two minds among the scores, even hundreds, of actors, managers, ingenious property-makers, and stage-hands — to say nothing of the master-builder Peter Streete — would have bettered a trap design so obviously wasteful of space and effort as that shown in the French woodcut of 1897.

It has perhaps been noticed in the stage-directions re-produced on recent pages that only two objects mentioned in trap scenes could in themselves have been taller than six feet. Through the whole range of the period most trap scenes have to do with devils, ghosts, underworld gods and furies, kings standing or enthroned, bulls, dragons, and the like. All these average about the same height — none appears to be more than six feet. So great is their number and so uniform is their maximum height that one becomes suspicious of any apparent exception that at first thought seems to be taller. Every stage imposes certain limitations; the Elizabethan stage, elastic to a degree rarely encountered today, was no exception to the rule. When one singles out objects like the "Tree of Gold laden with diadems and crowns," "a great tree riseth," or an "arbour," he may play with the notion that those objects were controlled in point of size only by the whim of the property maker; but the physical limitations of the stage must not be forgotten. Whatever was lifted through the trap had to be stored in the cellar, at least for a time, and had to be placed upright on the trap mechanism. It is simpler to be content with a tree or arbor six or seven feet high than to insist upon a foot or two more — the absolute maximum — and be forced to conjecture a cellar excavated deep into a marsh.

Undoubtedly a good many of the properties for trap scenes were kept ready for use in some corner of "hell." There, too, other rarely used, bulky objects probably found storage space and were brought up to some more

accessible location before the morning rehearsal. Somewhere in the Globe's dark cellar might have been found
altars, idols, statues, a box of graveyard bones and relics,
the well-head with its windlass and bucket, the "two moss
banks," a crocodile, dragons and a bull or two, the flaming
rock, and even the whale's mouth which cast out Jonah
upon the dry land.

Chapter V

THE TIRING–HOUSE: EXTERIOR

1. Introduction

RISING from the rear line of the Globe platform, and forming a permanent scenic wall, stood the "tiring-house."

Prologus.   Or, with three rustie swords,
And helpe of some few foot-and-halfe-foote words,
Fight ouer *Yorke*, and *Lancasters* long iarres:
And in the tyring-house bring wounds, to scarres.
             — *Every Man in his Humour*, 1616.

The name was derived from the curtained alcove (or "tyre-house") used as a dressing room on platforms antedating inn-yard theatres; before 1599 it had come to refer not merely to the dressing rooms but to a three-story section of the playhouse frame containing several small stages, dressing and property rooms, a music gallery, connecting passageways, and stairs. All these were constructed in the space, 12½ feet deep, which lay between the outer and inner walls of the frame. The tiring-house was closed off from the spectator galleries by partitions on all floors. In the Globe it occupied one-quarter of the octagonal frame, and thus bore approximately the same proportion to the spectator's share of the playhouse that a modern stage-house (including wings, backstage, dressing and property rooms) bears to its auditorium.

When Burbage's Theater was built in 1576, probably only one of the eight sections which made up the frame was devoted to actors' use, but this space represented a marked increase in size and convenience over the accommodations previously available. A single section of the frame, terminating at heavy posts in the corners, would suggest an obvious point of division. The De Witt drawing of the Swan in 1596 illustrates with some accuracy this relationship of early tiring-house to auditorium.

But in the last decade of the sixteenth century, while the drama and the playhouse together grew in importance and splendor, the actors' need for a larger and more resourceful stage out-paced in any one theatre the need for a larger auditorium. The growing popularity of the drama was met by increasing the number of playhouses; a stage could be enlarged only by increasing the width of the tiring-house, which meant encroaching upon the galleries; or by deepening the platform, which meant encroaching upon the yard; or by both. After about the year 1595 width and greater inside space were more essential in a tiring-house than depth.

The tiring-house of the Globe could, of course, have been made wider by enlarging the frame of the building. But to increase by 2 feet the inside length of each section of an octagonal frame 12½ feet deep would require an increase of 7 feet in the diameter of the building; and in order to have a flat or straight-fronted tiring-house 40 feet wide, an octagonal playhouse would have to measure 135 feet across. But so large a dimension for the Globe is inadmissible. Unquestionably Henslowe's Fortune (1600) was considerably larger than his "little Rose" (1586). The Red Bull (1605) may have been slightly larger than the Swan (1595). But, as we have noted, the builders of the Globe removed and reassembled the frame of the "vast" Theater; hence the size and shape of the Globe was probably the same as the size and shape of the building it replaced and any enlargement of the tiring-house would have to be accomplished by encroaching upon space in the frame formerly available to spectators.

When the Globe was erected in 1599 the decision evidently was taken (I suspect it may have been borrowed from Henslowe's Rose, which was extensively remodeled in 1592 and again in 1595 [1]) to make all three levels of the tiring-house wider by one bay (i.e. half a section) on both sides (and, of course, to widen the platform correspondingly). The added bays, each 12 feet wide on the inside of the frame and 17½ feet wide on the outside, gave the new tiring-house twice the area of the old and a far better design from the point of view of acting, acoustics, and appearance. The scenic wall no longer formed a flat plane — as represented in the De Witt view of the Swan — but comprised a middle section 24 feet wide (in which two levels of inner stages topped by a music gallery were installed), flanked on either side by sections 12 feet wide (in which the stage doors topped by bay-windows were installed). Because the playhouse frame was octagonal, the flanking sections formed a wide angle with the middle section, a fact that contributed — as the following pages will attempt to show — a new range of flexibility and realism to the staging of plays.

As seen by the audience, the Globe tiring-house contrasted strongly with the rest of the playhouse interior. It was enclosed, instead of open. It had a superstructure of "huts" which rose above it, as well as a platform which extended forward from its base. Finally, it was to some extent shaded by a stage-cover which extended, on a level with the ceiling of the top spectator-gallery, part way over the outer stage.

Altogether the Globe tiring-house was five stories high, for in addition to the three main levels (matching the three galleries) there was the "hell" below and the "huts" above. These two last-named divisions, however, were more closely associated with the outer stage than with the tiring-house. A description of "hell" was therefore included in the last chapter, and a description of the superstructure will be reserved for a later chapter.

Thus, ignoring the "hell" and the "huts," the tiring-house proper consisted of only three stories. The floor of

[1] See *Henslowe's Diary*, pp. 4 and 7; and Adams, pp. 148 and 154.

the first story was level with that of the platform (not, as Wegener, Neuendorff, Bond, and Reynolds would have us believe, one or more steps higher [2]) and hence was also level with the floor of the lowest spectator-gallery. The floor of the second story was 12 feet higher, level with the floor of the middle spectator-gallery; [3] and the floor of the third was 11 feet higher yet, level with the floor of the top spectator-gallery. [4] To those in the auditorium the entire stage section of the building appeared as a unit. The façade of the tiring-house was the permanent back-drop of the platform, and in action all parts could be related to one another.

2. The Stage Curtains

The façade of the tiring-house differed from its model, a short row of London houses, mainly in having upper and lower curtains suspended in the middle. Each of these large curtains [5] was made in two sections which, when closed, overlapped so as to leave no gap. Unlike the modern theatre-curtain, the Elizabethan playhouse curtain was suspended from a fixed rod upon which the sections were caused to move laterally.

Evidence concerning the mechanical details of this suspension is meagre. Certain records dating nearly three-quarters of a century earlier [6] mention "ironwork to hang the curtains with, 2s; 4 doz. curtain rings, 4d; a whole piece of cord to draw the curtains, 14d." In the *Revels Accounts* for January 1, 1574/5, [7] we find the entry:

[2] Cf. Chambers, iii. 85.

[3] *Henslowe Papers*, pp. 5 and 20.

[4] *Henslowe Papers*, p. 5.

[5] Various cloth hangings were used in the tiring-house: arras on the walls, window- and bed-curtains, etc. To avoid confusion in this work the word "curtains" standing alone will always refer to the stage curtains hanging before an inner stage.

[6] J. S. Brewer, *Letters and Papers of Henry VIII*, iv (for the year 1527), 1391, 1604.

[7] *Variorum* (1821), iii. 383–384.

To John Rosse (property maker) . . . xij*d*. for sowing the curtyns and setting on the frenge for the same; iij*s*. Wyer to hang the Curtyns; vj*d*. vyces for the Pulleyes, etc., iiij*s*.

In the *Accounts* for the following year:

For a line to draw a curteyne, 4*d*.[8]

These items, hinting at the means of supporting and handling the curtain, are all that the *Revels Accounts* yield.[9]

The four contemporary pictures of the stage are of greater assistance, but even their evidence is contradictory. The Swan drawing shows no curtains whatever, an omission that is perhaps the most conspicuous error of the many in the drawing. The case for stage curtains is not weakened by this omission; the accuracy of the drawing is.

The *Roxana* title-page shows a pair of curtains extending across as much of the rear of the outer stage as the tiny engraving exhibits. They appear to be of light-weight, unfigured cloth and to be supported by rings. The rings probably move on a rod (although no rod is visible in the engraving) located immediately below the front edge of the upper stage. The upper stage shows two openings with a pillar between, but no curtains.

The *Messallina* title-page, in much the same way,[10] shows a pair of curtains across the rear of the outer stage; but these curtains are adorned with figures, and because the rings are closer together they hang less badly. In the wall of the upper stage is an unglazed opening curtained by two pieces of plain material which also appear to be suspended on a rod by means of rings.

The *Wits* frontispiece shows in much larger scale two sets of narrow double curtains, one set on the lower, the

[8] *Variorum* (1821), iii. 390.

[9] These slender hints may not be referring to stage curtains but to curtains of other sorts. Their value is still less when it is remembered that a rising, not a drawn, curtain was occasionally used in Court performances. Cf. Graves, *The Court and London Theatres*, p. 8.

[10] Cf. Adams, "The Four Pictorial Representations of the Elizabethan Stage," in *J.E.G.P.*, X (1911), 331–332.

other on the upper level. The lower set conceals a rear doorway or opening which gives access to the improvised platform; the upper set, directly above the first, conceals a section of the stage balcony. Both curtains appear to open, not by sliding back, but in the manner of tent-flaps. Three points are worth noting, however: the generous overlapping of the lower curtain, the heavy tapestry of which that pair seemingly is made; and the boldly striped, and apparently thin, cloth of the upper pair.

A woodcut on the title-page of *The Bloody Almanack*, 1643, by John Booker, shows an inner stage filled with a medley of figures. In the upper right-hand corner appears a curtain hanging from rings and drawn well back below.

Much the best contemporary illustration of a stage curtain with its rod and rings appears in a Cavalier cartoon of 1649 entitled: "The Curtain's drawne, all may perceive the plot." [11] The rod, which is slender, crosses from side to side just below the top edge of the engraving. The rings, fastened to the top of the curtain, are small and close together; the curtain hangs in narrow, regular folds. No cord or pulleys can be seen, but a hand is shown grasping the edge of the curtain, implying that some stage-employee behind is in the act of "discovering" the scene.

The material reviewed so far is chiefly valuable for the light it throws on mechanical details — the rod and the rings by which the curtain was suspended, and the cord and pulleys by which they sometimes were operated. It is to the plays, however, that one must turn for most of the information about curtains.

Drawing aside the curtains of either the lower or the upper stage made visible to the audience prepared settings: a king's tent, a scholar's study, a tomb, a bed- or sitting-room, and so on. The element of surprise was no small part of the effect. The curtains, therefore, must have been of opaque material, and have met closely when drawn.

[11] Reproduced by Hotson, *The Commonwealth and Restoration Stage*, facing p. 30.

Few things are more destructive of theatrical illusion than glimpses or sounds of the stage-hands at work; this was especially true in Shakespeare's time, for interior scenes were being prepared while the action continued on some other stage. The admonition in *Lady Alimony*, I. ii, is apropos:

Be your stage-curtains artificially [i.e. skillfully] drawn, and so covertly shrouded as the squint-eyed groundling may not peep into your discovery.

Curtains had been used in the performances of mystery plays in England and in France.[12] A pair of striped curtains of "green and yellow sarcenet" is heard of in 1530,[13] which Steevens may have had in mind when he wrote: "A striped curtain was the sign hung out at [the Curtain] theatre, and corresponded with the curtain drawn before the stage on the inside." [14] (The striped upper curtain shown in *The Wits* may just possibly be a distant echo of some earlier theatrical tradition.)

That designs were worked upon playhouse tapestries is evident from a number of sources.[15] For example, in Beaumont's *Knight of the Burning Pestle* (first acted at Whitefriars in 1607), II. v, the Citizen and his Wife are watching the play from seats on the platform facing the stage curtains:

Wife. Now sweet Lamb, what story is that painted [really woven] upon the cloth? the confutation of Saint Paul?
Cit. No Lamb, that's *Ralph* and *Lucrece*.

[12] "Coventry Plays," in *Publications of the Shakespeare Society*, ii. 261, 303; and Graves, *The Court and London Theatres*, p. 8.

[13] Graves, *The Court and London Theatres*, p. 10.

[14] J. P. Collier, *The History of English Dramatic Poetry*, iii. 86. But see Adams, p. 78.

[15] For inner-stage tapestries, see Chapter VI, pp. 177-181. Lawrence has written at some length upon the subject of curtains in his *Physical Conditions of the Elizabethan Public Playhouse* (pp. 29–46). Readers will observe that my review includes several of the quotations he has cited, but that I arrive at different conclusions.

THE BEAR GARDEN AND THE SECOND GLOBE
From the Hollar "View of London," 1647

(It is possible that each theatre had its own distinctive tapestry-subject woven in the curtains.[16])

The advent of figured silk curtains at the Blackfriars is called attention to in the Induction to *Cynthia's Revels*, acted in 1600:

'Slid, the boy takes me for . . . some silke cortaine, come to hang the stage here! sir cracke, I am none of your fresh pictures, that vse to beautifie the decaied dead arras, in a publicke theatre.

And a reference to silk curtains in a public playhouse is provided in *Fancies Theatre*, 1640:[17]

> Only we would request you to forbear
> Your wonted custom, banding tile and pear
> Against our curtains, to allure us forth: —
> I pray, take notice, these are of more worth;
> Pure Naples silk, not worsted.[18]

The hundreds of references to "discovering" an inner-stage scene are about evenly divided (before 1603) between those naming a visible actor who himself draws back the curtain and those giving no clue to the agent or means. The following examples of the first group, drawn from plays produced between 1590 and 1612 (together with one later example), are typical of a host of others. From *A Looking Glass for London and England*, line 510:

They draw the Curtaines, and Musicke plaies.

From *Friar Bacon and Friar Bungay*, line 1561:

Enter Frier Bacon drawing the cortaines with a white sticke.

From *The Spanish Tragedy*, IV. iii:

Enter Hieronimo; he knocks up the curtaine.

---

[16] See "To the Reader" prefixed to Jonson's *New Inn*, 1629; the figures drawn upon the lower stage curtain included in the *Messallina* view; *The Bird in a Cage* (1633), IV. ii; etc.

[17] "A Prologue upon the removing of the late Fortune Players to the Bull," by J. Tatham. For the entire prologue, see *Variorum* (1821), iii. 79.

[18] The curtain depicted in the Cavalier cartoon of 1649 (see above, note 11) appears to be made of silk. See also Middleton's civic masque *The Triumph of Truth*, 1613.

From *Edward I*, line 1867:

The Nurse closeth the Tent.

From *The Tragedy of Hoffman*, sig. B1:

Strikes ope a curtaine where appeares a body.

From *The Woman-Hater*, V. i:

Secretary draws the Curtain.

From *Claudius Tiberius Nero*, line 2494:

They draw aside the Arras, and banquet on the stage, Spado tasteth to Tiberius, and after infuseth the poyson.

From *The Devil's Charter*, sig. L3 verso:

Alexander draweth the Curtaine of his studie where hee discouereth the diuill sitting in his pontificals, Alexander crosseth himselfe starting at the sight.

From *The Tempest*, V. i:

Here Prospero discovers Ferdinand and Miranda playing at chess.

From *The White Devil*, V. iv:

Flamineo.   I will see them
  They are behind the travers.   Ile discover
  Their superstitious howling.

  Cornelia, the Moore, and 3. other Ladies discovered, winding Marcello's Coarse.

From *The Jovial Crew*, II:

Randal opens the Scene. The Beggars discovered at their Feast.

The second group of directions, in which no agent is indicated as drawing the curtain, is yet more numerous, notably after 1603. It contains three types which it may be well to consider separately. In the first the stage curtains are mentioned. (The examples represent the years 1588 to 1637.) From *2 Tamburlaine*, II. iv:

The arras is drawen and Zenocrate lies in her bed of State, Tam. sitting by her: three Phisitians about her bed tempering potions.

From *Sir Thomas More*, line 104:

An Arras is drawne, and behinde it (as in Sessions) sit the L. Maior, Iustice Suresbie, and other Iustices, Sheriffe Moore and the other Sherife sitting by, Smart is the Plaintife, Lister the prisoner at the barre.

From *Dido, Queen of Carthage*, I. i:

Here the curtains draw: there is discovered Jupiter dandling Ganymede upon his knee, and Mercury lying asleep.

From *Lust's Dominion*, I. iii:

The Curtain being drawn, there appears in his bed King Philip, with his Lords; the Princess Isabella at the feet.

From *The Faithful Shepherdess*, V. i:

The Curtayne is drawne. Clorin appeares sitting in the Cabin, Amoret sitting on the one side of her, Alexis and Cloe on the other, the Satyr standing by.

And from Cartwright's *Siege*, V. viii:

They being all set, a Curtain being drawn discovers five valiant Generals, standing in Severall Postures, with fix'd Eyes like Statues.

For the lists just given I have purposely chosen examples to illustrate (1) unchanging technique during a long period, and (2) different terms — "curtain," "curtains," "arras," and more rarely "traverse" — for the same thing, to wit curtains to the inner stage. Other directions, increasingly numerous after 1603, ignore the opening of the curtains when indicating a discovery. From *The Case is Altered*, I. i:

Iuniper a Cobbler is discouered, sitting at worke in his shoppe and singing.

From *The Fawn*, V. i:

Tiberio and Dulcimel above, are discovered hand in hand.

From *The Atheist's Tragedy*, V. i:

A Closet discover'd. A Servant sleeping with lights and money before him.

From *The Brazen Age*, III. ii:

Two fiery Buls are discovered, the Fleece hanging over them, and the Dragon sleeping beneath them.

From *The Game at Chess*, V. i:

An Altar is discovered with tapers and Images standing on each side.

And from *The Traitor*, V. iii.

The body of Amidea discovered on a bed, prepared by two Gentlewomen.

Still other directions, common to every year in the period 1590 to 1642, merely indicate the nature of the scene discovered. From *The Jew of Malta*, I. i:

Enter [i.e. discover] *Barabas in his counting-house, with heapes of gold before him.*

From *Edward I*, line 2668 (following the "*Exeunt Omnes*" of scene 24):

Elinor in child-bed with her daughter Ione, and other Ladies.

From *The Shoemaker's Holiday*, IV. i:

Enter Jane in a Semsters shop working.

From *The Devil's Charter*, I. iv:

Alexander in his study with bookes, coffers, his triple Crowne vpon a cushion before him.

From *The Fair Maid of the Inn*, IV. i:

Enter Forobosco as in his Study.

And from '*Tis Pity She's a Whore*, III. vi:

Enter the fryar sitting in a chayre; Anabella kneeling and whispering to him; a table before them and wax lights.

The directions relating to discoveries on the second level of the tiring-house follow precisely the pattern of those relating to discoveries below (except that for obvious reasons the curtains were never opened from in front). Four examples will suffice at this time. From *Titus Andronicus*, I. i:

Enter the Tribunes and Senators aloft.

From *The Dumb Knight*, IV:

Enter aloft to cards the Queen and Philocles.

From *The Double Marriage*, V. i:

Enter Ferrand and Ronvere above [to a supper].

And from *The Maid of Honor*, II. iv:

Ferdinand, Drusio, Livio above.

Instances of actors visibly closing the curtains are rare, but they can be found. Examples follow from the period 1590 to 1619. From *Edward I*, line 1675 (see also above, p. 140):

They close the Tent.

From *The Widow's Tears*, IV. ii:

She shuts up the Tomb.

And from *The Faithful Shepherdess*, V. i:

Clorin [on the outer stage, having placed the wounded Alexis in her
cave].
  Soon again he ease shall find
  If I can but still his mind:
  This Curtain thus I do display [i.e. close],
  To keep the piercing air away.

There are a few directions for a rapid opening of the stage curtains. From *Grim, the Collier of Croyden*, I. i [an outer-stage scene]:

He layeth him down to sleep; lightning and thunder; the curtains drawn on a sudden: Pluto, Minos, Æacus, Rhadamanthus [are discovered] *set in counsel; before them Malbecco his Ghost guarded with Furies.*

From *The Unnatural Combat*, V. ii:

Montreville above[,] the curtaine [below] *suddenly drawn.*

And from Cartwright's *Siege*, V. viii:

The Statues by the stealth of a slow Motion do by little and little as it were assume life; and descending from their Pedestals walk about the [outer] *Stage in a grave sad March to Trumpets . . . the Curtain in the mean time shutting: But making at the last toward their former stations, the Curtain flies aside, and they find five Ladies on their Pedestalls, in the posture of Amorous Statues.*

There are, of course, situations which call for a peering between the curtains, or through a partial opening, or a lifting of the lower border. Examples will be found in *The Unfortunate Lovers*, V. iv; *The Princess*, II. i; *The Fatal Union*, I. v; and *The Wits*, I. i.

A study of the representative examples given on these last pages yields the following conclusions:

(1) In many scenes where the curtains are opened by no specified agent the outer stage is clear, hence in all scenes it was possible to open and close the curtains by invisible means.

(2) The terms "curtain," "curtains," "arras," and "traverse" refer to the same thing, namely the curtains concealing the lower or upper inner stage. It does not follow, however, that these terms were used only with reference to the stage curtains; we shall elsewhere encounter them applied to other types of cloth hangings.[19]

(3) During the entire period 1576–1642, the technique of "discovering" an inner stage (on either level) underwent no appreciable change. In some scenes the curtains were opened by visible agents concerned in the action; in

[19] Lawrence wrote (*Physical Conditions*, p. 29): "The terms curtain, curtains, hangings, arras, traverse, and canopy all had precisely the same significance [i.e. designating a curtain before the inner stage, and that curtain only]." Nothing could be more misleading. Only five of the terms apply to the stage curtains, and all are frequently used with reference to hangings employed elsewhere in the playhouse. See Chapters VI and VIII.

the majority (including all discoveries above) they were opened by invisible agents.

(4) The curtains were rarely closed by a visible agent.

(5) Directions beginning "Enter ——" do not necessarily imply motion of any sort. (This point is vital to a proper understanding of Elizabethan dramatic texts; it must constantly be borne in mind.[20])

For a time during the reign of Queen Elizabeth, it seems that when a tragedy was to be enacted the usual gay tapestries were replaced by black stage curtains. Malone,[21] Sir Edmund Chambers,[22] and W. J. Lawrence [23] each list a number of quotations illustrating this custom.

The curtains drawn across the stage on the third level of the tiring-house differed in function and in kind from those of the levels below. I shall return to them in the chapter describing the playhouse music gallery.

3. THE OUTER-STAGE DOORS

Flanking the lower-stage curtains, and placed in the two oblique walls of the tiring-house, was a pair of large doors. References to them occur in such abundance that it is needless to supply examples here. The usual formula when

[20] Unless the full range of directions relating to a discovery is kept in mind, modern readers of Elizabethan plays are likely to assign a given scene to the outer stage, whereas it was originally enacted on one of the inner stages. An error of this sort is basic, for it influences and often confuses all that follows. Conclusions based upon a series of such errors have long obscured the importance of the curtained units of an Elizabethan multiple stage and have contributed to a mistaken view of the principles and trends of Elizabethan staging. Sir Edmund Chambers, for example, writes (*Elizabethan Stage*, iii. 116): "I do not find extensive chamber scenes 'above' in any King's play later than 1609." Again (*idem*. p. 121): "The tendency of the seventeenth century was towards a decreased and not an increased reliance upon the curtained space." I incline to the contrary opinion. For evidence, see below, particularly Chapters VI and VIII.

[21] *Variorum* (1821), iii. 107.

[22] Chambers, iii. 79.

[23] *Physical Conditions*, pp. 30–33. A stage-direction in *The Just General* (1652), V, reads: "*Enter upon a black stage . . .*"

both doors are used at the same time reads, "*Enter, at two doors, A and B.*" This formula has a number of variants, as, "*Enter at one door A, at the other B,*" "*Enter severally A and B*"; in plays written after 1600 one finds "*Enter A and B at opposite ends*" or "*at opposite sides*"; and in plays written after 1620 "*Enter A and B at opposite doors.*" These directions show that two entering doors located at the sides or opposite "ends" of the platform (which after 1599 can only mean in the oblique side-walls of the tiring-house) formed part of the standard equipment of the stage.[24]

A somewhat smaller group of directions makes it evident that there was a third entrance, the usual formula reading, "*Enter severally A, B, and C.*" Variants commonly met are: "*Enter at three several doors A, B, and C,*" "*Enter A and B at several doors, C at the middle door,*" and "*Enter severally A and B, C in the midst.*" At first glance this seems to imply a permanent door located in the middle of the stage and in the plane of the curtains. But such a door is out of the question; for, when the curtains are opened, the inner stage must be fully exposed to the audience. A door and frame so placed would be wholly in the way.

What is meant by the "middle door" directions is an actor's entrance either through the closed curtains where they overlap in the middle, or, if the curtains are opened for a discovery, through an actual door in the rear wall of the inner stage. Entrance through the curtains dates from days when the tiring-house was little more than a curtained alcove behind the platform. It is illustrated in *The Wits* frontispiece and is called for in plays from every year of the period.[25]

These three ways of entering the outer stage from the

[24] The problem of oblique doors has been carefully studied by Lawrence (*Physical Conditions*, pp. 22–28), who by means of an historical approach reaches conclusions identical with mine.

[25] For further discussion see G. F. Reynolds, *Some Principles of Elizabethan Staging*, p. 7; Chambers, iii. 132; and Lawrence, *Physical Conditions*, pp. 16 ff.

tiring-house are at once apparent in any study of Elizabethan and Jacobean plays. In the course of such study one is tempted at first to postulate in the Globe the survival from earlier theatres of a supplementary pair of doors on either side of the stage curtains to facilitate an actor's passing from the platform to the inner stage. But on closer examination one discovers that there was no need for such doors, and that the objections to them are insurmountable. The first objection is the absence of evidence, which not only reduces the problem to rather pointless speculation, but is tantamount to proof that supplementary doors never existed since every other known feature of the scenic wall within reach of an actor gave rise to scenes in which stage business involved the use of that feature. Secondly, such doors, even if made as narrow as possible, would still occupy a space hardly less than 3½ feet wide each, reducing the width of the inner-stage opening from 23 to 16 feet. Discoveries which demand space for elaborate dumb shows, rooms of state, courts of justice, and scenes crowded with bulky properties and as many as a dozen actors are frequently found after 1595. At no time are these scenes more numerous or more spectacular than in the period served by the first Globe. It seems illogical, therefore, to assume that in the very age of striving to provide elaborate discoveries in the inner stage one-third of the opening was eliminated by fixed doors.

Nor is this all. Without such doors, the curtains could be drawn back out of sight behind the large corner posts of the frame. On the other hand, with doors standing between the curtains and the corner posts, the curtains must either be stopped at the outer edges of the door-casings or be drawn back entirely beyond the doors. Neither conclusion is tenable. When drawn aside the heavy curtains necessarily took up some space; and even if drawn close to the postulated door-casings the folded portions must still have projected a foot or more into the opening, and thus have reduced the opening to less than 14 feet, or to only three-fifths of the otherwise available space. But this was precisely what the Globe designers would seek to avoid, for greater width to ensure full visibility and more elaborate spectacles in the inner stage was the primary reason for enlarging the tiring-house. Alternatively, to draw the curtains beyond the doors into the corners would have been distinctly clumsy, for while the doors were in use the curtains could be neither opened nor closed.

The only other parts of the scenic wall where any doors could have been placed were the flanking bays added when the tiring-house was enlarged. Sir Edmund Chambers suggests the possibility of there having been not one, as I have suggested, but two doors in each flanking wall.[26] But before considering whether there was room for two doors — one at least of which had to be not a little wider than a normal house door — in a section of scenic wall only 12 feet wide, we demand fairly clear evidence of the existence of twin doors in some play. But no such evidence exists, so far as I know, nor does any scene in the period make use of the many situations that would inevitably arise out of the presence of two closely adjoining doors.

Some idea of the size of the stage doors is given by the many scenes in which processions "pass over the stage," where crowds collect swiftly, and where armies surge on and off the field of battle. Even more revealing are the properties which must pass through the doors. Funeral marches sound at the close of many a tragedy as the dead are carried off, shoulder high, on shields; occasionally a coffin or an elaborate hearse is carried on, and, after some ceremony, is carried off through the other door; sedan chairs, newly fashionable after the turn of the century, appear; but perhaps largest of all single objects are the chariots which are drawn in during a stately procession. From *The Silver Age*, III:

Enter Pluto, his Chariot drawne in by Divels.

[26] Chambers, iii. 84, 85, and 100.

From *The Bashful Lover*, IV. iii:

Loud music. Enter Soldiers unarmed, bearing olive branches, Captains, Lorenzo, Matilda crowned with a wreath of laurel, and seated in a chariot drawn by Soldiers.

From *The Wounds of Civil War*, line 1070:

Enter Scilla in triumph in his chare triumphant of gold, drawn by foure Moores, before the chariot: his colours, his crest, his captaines, his prisoners: Arcathius Mithridates son, Aristion, Archelaus, bearing crownes of gold, and manacled. After the chariot his souldiers bands, Basillus, Lucretius, Lucullus: besides prisoners of divers Nations, and sundry disguises.[27]

Because even a stage chariot has to be almost 4 feet wide, one is led to believe that the doorways through which they were drawn from the tiring-house were at least 5 feet wide.

Similar considerations point to stage doors of more than the average height. Soldiers with colors, pikes, scaling ladders, and cressets on poles, and conquerors standing upright in chariots could come on and go off with more assurance if the doorways were lofty. So far as the space available is concerned, there is no reason why the stage doors could not have been 8 or even 9 feet high.

Stage business of many sorts, including violent assaults, indicates that the doors were solidly made. Probably they were not unlike those doors of the years 1600 to 1650 which have lasted until modern times, that is, of oak, heavily framed, with simple panels and molding. One must reject the round top or arched doors shown in the De Witt drawing of the Swan in favor of the rectangular, flat-topped doors which alone appear to have been normal in the wooden-frame houses of Shakespeare's age.[28] Moreover,

[27] See also *The Battle of Alcazar*, line 212; *The Contention between Liberality and Prodigality*, line 341; *The Roman Actor*, I. iv; *Captain Thomas Stukely*, K1 verso; and *2 Tamburlaine*, IV. iii.

[28] For illustrations of standard Elizabethan doors see Nathaniel Lloyd, *History of the English House*, 1931, pp. 307–310. For an arched doorway of stone with a wooden door to fit, see *The Belman of London*, 4to, 1608, frontispiece.

they were made in one piece, and not divided either vertically, as in the De Witt drawing (and derivatively by Albright and Quennell), or horizontally. The vertical division into narrow half-doors is abnormal in English domestic architecture until the advent of stone and stone-trimmed palaces of a later time.[29] The horizontal division into "Dutch," or, to use the Elizabethan term, "heck" (i.e. hatch), doors is not alluded to in the plays and would be a needless elaboration.

The stage doors were hinged to the side of the door-frame nearest the corner post and the curtains and swung inwards. This was dictated by the wish to screen the interior of the tiring-house from the audience while the door was open. The doors swung into the tiring-house, both from dramatic custom [30] and from the effort of playhouse designers to simulate the London scene. Architectural tradition is well-nigh absolute in the matter of hanging an outer door; [31] from motives of prudence and defense, street doors in the humble dwelling as well as in the great palace open inwards.

To each stage door was fastened a knocker, probably mounted as today, breast high and in the middle of the door. *The Puritan*, sig. E2 verso, contains a good illustration:

Exeunt with him, passing in they knock at the doore with a knocker.

From *The English Traveller*, II. ii:

Old Lionel. What strange and unexpected greetings this,
That thus a man may knocke at his owne gates . . .

Note the ring knocker and large keyhole depicted, also the doorpost below the steps.

[29] Innocent, *The Development of English Building Construction*, pp. 230 ff.

[30] See, for example, *The Phoenix*, IV. iii.

[31] In addition to the works by Lloyd and Innocent referred to above, see W. Briggs, *The Homes of the Pilgrim Fathers in England and America, 1620–1682*; Joseph Nash, *The Mansions of England in the Olden Times*; and M. C. Salaman, *London Past and Present* (a Special Number of *The Studio*, 1916).

Reignald. Said you Sir;
Did your hand touch that hammer?

It appears that in certain theatres the knockers were of the usual kind, namely a solid ring about six to eight inches in diameter, supported at the top by a loop or "eye bolt" backed by a round, flat shield, often decorated. The lower rim of the ring rested against the head or "boss" of a second bolt.[32] Two Paul's plays and one Whitefriars play imply such a knocker. From *Blurt Master Constable*, II. ii:

Imperia. Keep the door.
Frisco. That's my office: indeed I have been your doorkeeper so long that all the hinges, the spring locks, and the ring, are worn to pieces.

From *Epicoene*, II. i:

Morose. . . . speake not, though I question you. You have taken the ring, off from the street dore, as I bad you? answere me not, by speech but by silence; unless, it be   *at the breaches* otherwise (- - -) very good.   *still the fellow makes legs: or signes*

The ring could be made to spin inside the "eye bolt" without knocking on the boss. A situation arising out of this fact is developed in *The Phoenix*, III. ii:

Jeweller's wife. And do but whirl the ring a' th' door once about; my maid-servant shall be taught to understand the language.

(Later in the play, Phoenix, the wrong gallant, of course, accidentally "jars" the ring and is drawn into the darkened house by the maid.) Whether or not the Globe doorknockers were of this ring type I do not know.

The passage from *Blurt Master Constable* just quoted is representative of several other scenes [33] which suggest that

---

[32] A ring knocker of ornate design is shown in the last plate of Nash's *Mansions of England*; less ornate examples appear in C. Holme, *Old English Country Cottages*, p. 159. See note 28 above.

[33] See *The Case is Altered*, II. i; *Monsieur Thomas*, III. iii; and *The Woman's Prize*, III. v.

the outer-stage doors were provided also with locks; but since the inside of these doors was never visible to the audience, and since a pretense at locking the door from the outside would be as convincing as actually locking it, I suspect that real locks were not provided. And this conclusion is supported by a series of directions [34] relating to the outer-stage doors in which the words "seems to lock the door" occur during situations where the effect of locking is called for. A noisy bolt on the inside of the door, however (which is not subject to the risk — ever present with a key — of being mislaid), would be useful in plays where an assault is made upon the door, and is demanded in certain scenes; for example, in *John a Kent*, line 848: "*Exit* [John a Cumber] *into the Castell, & makes fast the dore*." [35]

The "middle" door at the rear of the inner stage, on the other hand, was equipped with a conspicuous lock having a removable key, for the business of locking that door was fully in view of the audience. The following examples, drawn from a great number,[36] occur in well-defined inner-stage scenes. From *Lust's Dominion*, III. ii:

King. Begin, I'le lock all doors, begin Spains Queen,
   Loves banquet is most Sweet   *Locks the*
   When 'tis least seen.   *doors.*

From the Paul's and Globe (?) play, *Bussy D'Ambois*, V. i:

Montsurry turns a key.

From the Blackfriars play, *The Two Maids of More-clacke*, sig. E1 verso:

Sir William. Locke fast that dore and leaue me. Giue me your light, Sonne Humil?

---

[34] See, for example, *The Case is Altered*, II. i; *The Death of Robert, Earl of Huntington*, H1 verso; *Orgula*, III. iv; *The Platonic Lovers*, III. i; *The Puritan*, G2 verso.

[35] See also *The Coxcomb*, II. i.

[36] See, for example, *Captain Underwit*, V. i; *The Devil's Law Case*, V. iv; *The Duke of Milan*, V. ii; *The Fair Favorite*, III. iii; *Hamlet*, V. ii; *The Hollander*, V;

From *The Island Princess*, III. iii:

Enter Armusia, locks the door.

From *Match Me in London*, undivided: [37]

Enter Queene and Tormiella

Qu. Make fast the Closet — so — give me the key
I meane to kill thee.

And from *The Changeling*, IV. i:

Beatrice.   Here's his closet;
The key left in't, and he abroad i' th' park?
Sure 'twas forgot; I'll be so bold as to look in't.
            [She opens the door.]
Bless me! a right physicians closet 'tis.

A later Salisbury Court play, *The Twins*, V. i, mentions a
bolt instead of a lock:

*Enter Charmia in her night gown, with a prayer Book and a Taper, boults
the door and sits down.*

After 1595, scenes involving locks on inner-stage doors
outnumber by at least ten to one scenes involving locks on
outer-stage doors, a useful fact to remember when trying
to discover on which one of the six playhouse stages some
particular scene was originally presented.

4. THE PROMPTER'S WICKET

In addition to a knocker, keyhole, and inner bolt, at
least one of the outer-stage doors was provided with a
wicket, or small barred opening, in its upper half. The
presence of this wicket is attested by many plays, among
which *The Comedy of Errors* is an early example. In Act
III, scene i, Antipholus leads his friends to the street door
of his house, but finds it locked. His servant, Dromio of

The Man's the Master, V. i and iii; *Money is an Ass* (Q1, 1668), p. 30; *Richard
III*, V. iii; *The White Devil*, V. vi; *A Woman is a Weathercock*, V. i.

   37 *Dekker's Dramatic Works*, ed. Pearson, iv. 184.

Ephesus, calls to those within to unlock the door. At once he is answered by Dromio of Syracuse, standing "within," that is, on the other side of the door, which remains closed and locked throughout the scene. Questions, puns, insults, and even blows with a staff are exchanged through the wicket by the two Dromios, until at last the angered Antipholus leads his friends elsewhere.

Before analyzing this stage business, we will do well to examine at some length several other scenes which seem to imply a wicket, partly because evidence for wickets has not been brought together before, and partly because one or two situations, considered without reference to the evidence as a whole, have proved misleading to some scholars.[38]

The following two scenes show that persons speaking behind a closed and locked oak door could readily be *heard* by persons on the outer stage and by the entire audience. From the revised (1594?) *1 Henry VI*, I. iii (an outer-stage scene):

> *Enter Gloster, with his Serving-men.*
>
> *Glost.* I am come to survey the Tower this day;
>   Since *Henries* death, I feare there is Conveyance:
>   Where be these Warders, that they wait not here?
>   Open the Gates, 'tis *Gloster* that calls.
>
> *1. Warder* [within]. Who's there, that knocks so imperiously?
>
> *Glost. 1. Man.* It is the Noble Duke of Gloster.
>
> *2. Warder* [within]. Who ere he be, you may not be let in.
>
> *1. Man.* Villaines, answer you so the Lord Protector?
>
> *1. Warder* [within]. The Lord protect him, so we answer him,
>   We doe no otherwise then wee are will'd.

---

[38] Four situations are examined by Lawrence (*Physical Conditions*, pp. 67–69) in support of his "discovery . . . of a grated opening . . . between the rear-stage curtains and one of the entering doors." Two of these scenes have no bearing upon the subject: in *Antonio's Revenge*, II. iii, the "grate" appears to be part of a trap; in *Eastward Ho*, V. ii, the "grate" is almost certainly part of the bay-window above. *The Humorous Lieutenant*, IV. v, could take place before an inner-stage door. For further discussion, see Chambers, *William Shakespeare*, i. 106–107 and note 3 on p. 107.

Glost. Who willed you? or whose will stands but mine?
There's none Protector of the Realme, but I:
Breake up the Gates, Ile be your warrantize;
Shall I be flowted thus by dunghill Groomes?

   Glosters men rush at the Tower Gates, and Woodvile the Lieutenant speakes within.

Woodvile. What noyse is this? what Traytors have wee here?

Glost. Lieutenant, is it you whose voyce I heare?
Open the Gates, here's *Gloster* that would enter.

Woodvile [within]. Have patience Noble Duke, I may not open,
The Cardinall of Winchester forbids.

For nine more lines the argument continues, and then the outer stage finally clears without the "Tower" door having been opened.

From Jonson's Globe play *Catiline*, III. v: the scene is a street before Cicero's house at night; Cicero and his friends, expecting a visit, have drawn back from the window above. Vargunteius, Cornelius, and other armed men enter upon the outer stage.

Var. The dore's not open, yet. *Cor.* You'were best to knocke.

Var. Let them stand close, then: And, when we are in,
Rush after vs. *Cor.* But where's Cethegvs? *Var.* He
Has left it, since he might not do't his way.

Porter [behind the door]. Who's there? *Var.* A friend, or more. *Port.* I
may not let
Any man in, till day. *Var.* No? why? *Cor.* Thy reason?

Por. I am commanded so. *Var.* By whom? *Cor.* I hope
We are not discouer'd. *Var.* Yes, by reuelation.
Pray thee, good slaue, who has commanded thee?

Por. He that may best, the Consul. *Var.* We are his friends.

Por. All's one. *Cor.* Best giue your name. *Var.* Do'st thou heare,
fellow?
I haue some instant businesse with the Consul.

The next quotation shows not only that persons behind the closed stage doors could be *heard* outside, but that objects could be thrust through an opening in the door. In Fletcher's *Woman's Prize*, III. v (perhaps originally written for some other company but later owned and produced by the Globe Company), Petruchio feigns sickness to "make a Rascal" of his wife, Maria. She promptly assumes that he is dying of the plague, orders her servants and her household goods into the street, sends for "a Physitian and a whole peck of Pothecaries," nurses, a parson, and the Watch. The scene is the outer stage with Petruchio storming about inside the house.

Petronius. How long is't
  Since it first took him?
Mar. But within this three hours.
                    Enter Watch.
  I am frighted from my wits: — O here's the Watch;
  Pray doe your Office, lock the doors up Friends,
  And patience be his Angel.   *they lock the [outer-stage] dore.*[39]
Tranio. This comes unlook'd for:
Mar. I'll to the lodge; some that are kind and love me,
  I know will visit me.   *Petruchio within.*
Petru. Doe you hear my Masters: ho, you that lock the doors up.
Petron. 'Tis his voice.
Tra. Hold, and let's hear him.
Petru. Will ye starve me here: am I a Traytor, or an Heretick.
  Or am I grown infectious?
Petron. Pray sir, pray.
Petru. I am as well as you are, goodman puppy.
Mar. Pray have patience.
  You shall want nothing Sir.
Petru. I want a cudgel,
  And thee, thou wickedness.
Petron. He speaks well enough.
Mar. 'Had ever a strong heart Sir.
Petru. Will ye hear me?
  First be pleas'd
  To think I know ye all, and can distinguish
  Ev'ry Mans several voice: you that spoke first,
  I know my father in law; the other Tranio,
  And I heard Sophocles; the last, pray mark me,

[39] This direction, implicit in the dialogue, is supplied by the *Lambarde* MS. transcript (i.e. the earliest extant version) of the play.

Is my dam'd Wife Maria;
If any Man misdoubt me for infected,
There is mine Arme, let any Man look on't.
Enter Doctor and Pothecary.
Doct. Save ye Gentlemen.
Petron. O welcome Doctor,
Ye come in happy time; pray your opinion,
What think you of his pulse?
Doct. It beats with busiest,
And shews a general inflammation,
Which is the symptome of a pestilent Feaver,
Take twenty ounces from him.
Petru. Take a Fool;
Take an ounce from mine arme, and Doctor Deuz-ace,
I'll make a close-stoole of your Velvet Costard.

Maria, Petronius, Tranio, Doctor, and Pothecary go away. Petruchio is unable to persuade the Watch to unlock the door until he threatens to go for a gun loaded with chain shot. At that they unlock the door and run away; Petruchio returns, finds the door unlocked, and emerges on the outer stage with gun in hand. The similarity between this stage business and that in *A Comedy of Errors*, III. i, is at once apparent.[40]

I have deliberately chosen examples (1) from two plays produced before, and two plays produced after the Globe was erected, and (2) from plays written for Shakespeare's company of actors. The object of the first basis of selection is to show that the wicket was a stage feature in use before 1595; of the second, to show that the Globe stage — the model for most professional public stages erected after 1599 — had a wicket. From a study of these four examples of wicket scenes, several facts emerge.

(1) Each scene takes place at one of the outer-stage doors.

(2) Prolonged conversations were possible between a person or persons "within," that is, behind the door, and

---

[40] For still other examples of wicket scenes see *The English Traveller*, IV. i; *Monsieur Thomas*, III. iii; and *The Novella*, IV. i; see also note 47 below.

persons on the platform, the door remaining firmly closed the while. The "within" half of such dialogues would be inaudible more than a few feet from the thick stage door were there not some aperture for the "within" person to speak through.

(3) There obviously was an aperture, for such relatively slender objects as a staff or an arm were thrust through the locked door into the full view of the audience.

(4) Two of the scenes date from a period in stage history when the tiring-house was limited to merely one section of the playhouse frame, and when every available inch of the façade was taken up by the two stage doors and by an inner stage made as wide as possible. In this period there could be no thought of reducing the width of any one of these three vital elements in order to make room for a separate wicket or window. After 1599 there presumably was room for a wicket in the Globe scenic wall, but as the passage from *The Woman's Prize* demonstrates, the wicket remained in its former place, that is, in one of the stage doors. I find no play which demands two wickets on the lower stage, but I am inclined to believe that there were two, for similarity in the equipment of the doors would be desirable.

Other plays and other sources of evidence indicate how the wicket was designed, where it was placed, how it was used, and by what various names it was called. No contemporary English view of the stage, it is true, shows a wicket, but that is not surprising. The De Witt view is known to be inaccurate in most details; the small *Roxana* and *Messallina* views do not include the entering doors at the sides of the tiring-house; and the *Wits* frontispiece shows an improvised stage having a curtained entrance instead of a door. On the other hand, a view of the Amsterdam *Schouburgh* in 1638, by Nicholaes van Kampen,[41] exhibits a wicket in the stage door on the so-called

---

[41] Reproduced by S. Cheney, *The Theatre*, 1936, p. 306.

"prompter's side" of the stage. The wicket is centered in the upper half of the door (which also has a ring knocker and latch), is barred or latticed, and is approximately one foot square.

A hand and arm could be extended through either a grating or vertical bars, but one finds that windows screened by inch-square oaken bars, set vertically and spaced three to four inches apart, were in widespread use in place of glass in English buildings from the fourteenth to the eighteenth century,[42] and that in the same period iron gratings were by comparison rare. Door wickets were not uncommon in Shakespeare's time. Alleyn contracted with Peter Streete for "proportionable" wickets to be constructed in both doors of a Paris Garden tenement that he was remodeling in 1606.[43] That wickets were sometimes hinged and could be opened is shown by a passage in Davenant's Globe and Blackfriars play *The Wits*, IV. i: Lucy *"Opens a wicket at the end of the chest"* in which the Elder Pallatine is enclosed, in order to let him breathe and talk.[44]

A wicket in the upper half of a stage door helps to make clear many situations or allusions in the Elizabethan drama hitherto obscure; for example, *The Wit of a Woman*, line 1187 (a street scene):

Ludovica. Content: but look where an old Fox is peering out of his hoole: we will be gone.

From *The Puritan*, sig. B2 verso:

Skirmish. I would eyther some of vs were employde, or might pitch our Tents at Usurers doores, to kill the slaues as they peepe out at the Wicket.

Later in the same play (at sig. E2 verso) Pyeboord, arrested in the street for debt, persuades his captors to go

---

[42] Lloyd, *History of the English House*, p. 333.

[43] *Memoirs of Edward Alleyn*, ed. Collier, 1841, p. 80.

[44] Cf. a Restoration theatre charge for alterations (Boswell, *Restoration Court Stage*, p. 254): "cutting a hole in ye upper dore & battening ye hole with a flapp to it."

with him to call upon a Gentleman. They find the house door open, pass through into a "gallery" (the inner stage), and while a servant goes to notify his master, Pyeboord reflects on his chances of borrowing money from a total stranger:

> *Pyb.* Wee will attend his worship, — worship I thinke, for so much the Posts at his doore should signifie, and the faire comming in, and the wicket, else I neither knew him or his worship, but 'tis happinesse he is within doores, what so ere he bee, if he be not too much a formall Citizen, hee may doe me good.

From *The Golden Age*, IV: Jupiter, having rung a bell,[45] stands at the stage door:

> *1. Beldam* [on an inner stage]. To the gate, to the gate, and know who 'tis ere you open.

The Blackfriars (?) play of 1611, *Amends for Ladies*, V. ii, illustrates the use of a wicket as a means whereby persons on the outer stage can seemingly observe what takes place "within" when the doors and stage curtains are closed. The scene begins on the outer stage with a wedding procession about to leave the house for the church. The bride suddenly swoons and is carried within to her bed; a doctor is sent for. Her father's choice of a bridegroom, the elderly Count, sits down in a chair and falls asleep. The girl's lover, Ingen, then arrives in haste, disguised as a doctor, and accompanied by his brother and a parson. After ordering all others to forbear the house (that is, remain on the outer stage), Ingen and the Parson go in. "*Parson shuts the door.*" After a few minutes Proudly, the bride's brother, leaves the group of guests and crosses to the wicket (called "window") in the closed door, peers through (as if into some room within the house)

---

[45] For other examples of outer-stage scenes requiring a bell-rope see *The Bloody Brother*, IV. ii; *Histriomastix*, B4 verso; and *Women Pleased*, II. iii. Instances are so rare, however, that one is justified in assuming that the rope was not normally a part of the visible stage equipment. For discussion touching upon this topic see Lawrence, *Those Nut-Cracking Elizabethans*, pp. 93 ff.

and asks, "How fares she, master doctor? Zounds! what's here?" The others on the outer stage, with the exception of the Count, immediately join him, exclaiming "Heyday! How now?" One of them, Feesimple, evidently elbows Proudly aside and himself peers through the window. The text then reads:

Looking in at the window.[46]

Fee. Look, look! the parson joins the doctor's hand and hers: now the doctor kisses her, by this light!

Omnes whoop.

Now goes his gown off. Heyday! he has red breeches on. Zounds! the physician is got o' th' top of her: belike it is the mother she has. Hark! the bed creaks.

Proudly. 'Sheart, the door's fast! break 'em open! We are betrayed.

Brother. No breaking open doors: he that stirs first,

Draws and holds out a pistol.

I'll pop a leaden pill into his guts,
Shall purge him quite away. No haste, good friends:
When they have done what's fit, you shall not need
To break the door; they'll open it themselves.

A curtain drawn, a bed discovered: Ingen with his sword in his hand and a pistol: the lady in her petticoat: the Parson.

Other examples of stage business involving a wicket are listed in the notes.[47]

This is not the place to digress very far into the subject of the prompter (or "book-holder") and prompting, but the knowledge of a few facts is essential to an understanding of the primary purpose of the wicket. It will at once be obvious that, in presenting a different play each day, Elizabethan actors had at least as much need of a prompter as the actors of any other age; and further, that stage design

[46] For the contemporary meaning of "window" see the definition of *sportello* given on p. 162, and see the *N.E.D.*

[47] See *All Fools*, I. ii; *Elvira* (1667), II; *The Law Against Lovers* (1661), III. iii; *The Lover's Progress*, I. i; *Lust's Dominion*, I. i; *Match Me in London*, undivided (*Dekker's Dramatic Works*, ed. Pearson, iv. 136); *The Novella*, I. ii; *Ram Alley*, E4 verso; *The Spiteful Sister*, II; *The Widow's Tears*, IV. ii, and V. i; and *Your Five Gallants*, II. i. See also note 40 above.

had to take prompting into account. The first essential was some means by which the book-holder, himself unseen by the audience, could see and hear all that took place on the platform, and also be heard there if need arose.[48] The second was that during outer-stage scenes he take a position at or near one of the entrance doors, for another of his duties was to repeat to an actor about to come on the first few words of his speech.[49] The third was that he be placed where he could readily superintend the numerous back-stage activities accompanying every play.[50] Now, as I have pointed out, it is highly improbable that the façade of a late sixteenth-century tiring-house had space for a permanent aperture of adequate size, at eye-level above the platform, except in the entering doors. But just there, it will be observed, the prompter's window best met every requirement outlined above.

In tiring-house doors, furthermore, an unglazed, barred opening intended primarily for the book-holder's use would pass muster with all Elizabethans as merely the usual appurtenance of a London dwelling-house door. A contemporary English definition of the Italian word *Sportello* reads: "any little outbutting porche, window, shed, stall, or penthouse; also a wicket or little window, as tavern doores use to have, to sell wine uppon Sundays or Holy days."[51] The presence of a wicket in the stage door helps to explain, therefore, the frequency with which tavern and tavern-lattice allusions occur in the plays of the period.[52]

---

[48] Cf. *Romeo and Juliet* (Q1), I. iv; and *The Antipodes*, III. viii.

[49] Cf. *The City Night Cap*, IV; *Hyde Park*, III. iii; and *No Wit, no Help*, IV. ii.

[50] For admirable discussion and textual illustration see the MS. *Believe As Ye List*, edited by C. J. Sisson for the Malone Society, 1928; see also Chambers, *William Shakespeare*, i. 106–122.

[51] Quoted from J. O. Halliwell-Phillipps, *Scrapbooks* (now in the Folger Shakespeare Library), No. 52.

[52] Examples: *All Fools*, V. i; *Antonio and Mellida*, V. i; *The City Match*, I. ii; *2 Henry IV*, II. ii; *May Day*, I. i; *The Merry Wives of Windsor*, II. ii; and *The Miseries of Enforced Marriage*, D4.

FRONTISPIECE OF *THE WITS, OR SPORT UPON SPORT*, 1662

An improvised stage used for Drolls after the closing of the playhouses
in 1642

5. THE DOOR POSTS

The passage from *The Puritan* reproduced on page 160 is but one of many (occurring chiefly in plays written after 1599) which direct attention to the presence of posts flanking the stage doors. A second such passage is found in Fletcher's *Maid in the Mill* (acted in 1623), I. iii. The scene opens at night with Ismena and Aminta on the inner stage awaiting the visit of Antonio. Aminta at last hears footsteps (off stage), and hurries with Ismena up to the second-floor window. Antonio and his friend Martine then appear on the platform as in the street, and grope their way without lights up to the housefronts, which they recognize by one means or another. They come to the last house:

Ant. What place is this?

Mar. Speak softer: 'may be spies;
   If any, this, a goodly window too,
   Carv'd far above, that I perceive: 'tis dark,
   But she has such a lustre.

         Enter Ismena and Aminta above with a Taper.

Ant. Yes Martine,
   So radiant she appears.

Mar. Else we may miss, Sir:
   The night grows vengeance black, pray heaven she shine clear:
   Hark, hark, a window, and a candle too.

Ant. Step close, 'tis she: I see the cloud disperse,
   And now the beauteous Planet.

Mar. Ha, 'tis indeed,
   Now by the soul of love a Divine Creature.

Ism. Sir, Sir.

Ant. Most blessed Lady.

Ism. 'Pray ye stand out [i.e. not under the bay-window].

Am. You need not fear, there's no body now stirring. . .

         [The two men move out from the wall into view.]

Ism. 'Tis the right Gentleman:
   But what to say to him, Sir.

Am. Speak.

Ant. I wait still,
   And will do so till I grow another Pillar,
   To prop this house, so it please you.
Ism. Speak softly.

Again, from *The English Traveller*, IV. i, a scene in which many parts of one side-bay of the scenic wall are singled out by Reignald in his effort to induce Old Lionell to buy Ricot's house:

Reig. See what a goodly Gate?
Old Lio. It likes me well.
Reig. What braue caru'd poasts; Who knowes but heere,
   In time Sir, you may keepe your Shreualtie;
   And I be one oth' Seriants.
Old Lio. They are well Caru'd.
Ric. And cost me a good price Sir; Take your pleasure,
   I haue businesse in the Towne.   *Exit.*
Reig. Poore man, I pittie him;
   H'ath not the heart to stay and see you come,
   As 'twere, to take Possession; Looke that way Sir,
   What goodly faire Baye windowes?
Old Lio. Wondrous stately.
Reig. And what a Gallerie, How costly Seeled;
   What painting round about?
Old Lio. Euery fresh object to good, adds betternesse.
Reig. Tarrast aboue, and how below supported; doe they please you?

These three passages indicate that the posts existed in fact and were not merely figments of dramatic illusion. Now in Shakespeare's time posts of some sort stood before many a London doorway to support a door-hood [53] or a bay-window,[54] or, detached from the building, to identify the house of a city official.[55] As part of a tiring-house

[53] Illustrated in a contemporary engraving reproduced by W. Besant, *London South of the Thames*, p. 110. See also Lloyd, *History of the English House*, p. 474.
[54] For contemporary illustration see *Shakespeare's England*, i. 64, and the "Shakespeare's London" series of prints published by the Folger Shakespeare Library.
[55] See the title-page of *The Belman of London*, 1608.

façade posts were, therefore, wholly appropriate; and it was perhaps the wish to copy a familiar London architectural detail as much as the need to shore up the large bay-window over each entering door which led to their incorporation in the scenic wall.

The presence of posts placed a little out from the wall on either side of the platform doorways at once afforded a realistic means by which an actor could stand concealed at that oft-used point, a situation seized upon by many dramatists. One example has already been given in the passage from Jonson's *Catiline*, III. v, quoted on page 155. When Vargunteius, Cornelius, and their ruffians approached Cicero's door, Vargunteius directed the others, it will be recalled, to "stand close," that is, to stand out of sight against the wall beyond the door posts where they could not be seen by the Porter who came to the door.

Another example occurs in *Othello*, V. i, when Iago directs Roderigo to stand concealed by the door of Bianca's house and await Cassio's departure from supper there:

Iago. Here, stand behind this bulk [56]; straight will he come.
Wear thy good rapier bare, and put it home.

A third example occurs in *Monsieur D'Olive*, V. i. Vaumont and Vandome enter at night to the street door of Vaumont's house. Vandome orders Vaumont to "stand close" under the projecting bay-window so as to be unseen when he calls his sisters Eurione and Marcellina (Vaumont's estranged wife) to the window. They appear above and he persuades them to descend for a private talk with him; while they are on the way down, accompanied by a man-servant, Dicque, bearing a light, he again urges Vaumont to "stand close." This second time he means that Vaumont is to stand behind a door post so as to be unseen by those standing in the doorway. Dicque opens the door and the ladies stand there for several minutes talking with Vandome. Vaumont listens but remains un-

[56] Cf. *N.E.D.* under *Bulk, Balk, Baulk*, and *Beam*.

seen. At last the ladies depart, following the servant with the light to another house.

Other examples are listed in the notes.[57]

The door posts, like the wicket, gave rise to a series of allusions [58] and occasionally to minor stage business of some special sort.[59]

I do not find sufficient evidence to warrant any additional curtains, doors, windows, grates, posts, or other fixed appurtenances on the first-floor portion of the tiring-house façade. Pairs of objects, such as locality boards, inn-signs, and the like, were sometimes called for in certain periods or in certain plays, but I believe that they never formed a permanent part of the scenic wall at the Globe.

[57] See *All's Well that Ends Well*, IV; *Antonio and Mellida*, line 1390; *The Cunning Lovers* (Q1, 1654), p. 12; *The Humorous Lieutenant*, I. i; *The Novella*, I. i; *The Obstinate Lady*, III. ii; *The Phoenix*, III. ii; *The Spiteful Sister*, B4 verso; and *Wit Without Money*, I. i.

[58] Examples: *The City Match*, I. i; *Eastward Ho*, II. i; *Every Woman in her Humour*, G2; *Holland's Leaguer*, I. v; *The Puritan*, E3; and *Satiromastix*, V. i.

[59] See, for example, *Humour out of Breath*, IV. iii; and *1 Thomaso*, II. i and iii.

Chapter VI

THE TIRING–HOUSE: FIRST LEVEL

1. INTRODUCTION

ONCE those in charge of designing the Globe tiring-house broke with the past and installed stage doors in the flanking bays of the scenic wall, they were free to expand the opening of the inner stage up to 23 feet in width — the distance between the fixed corner posts of the playhouse frame. The effects of this expansion were revolutionary. What in earlier playhouses had been essentially an appendage to the outer platform became an entity. What had been an alcove became a full stage. In all playhouses before 1599 action in the inner stages had been limited by reasons of size, shape, and sight-lines to such effects as a handful of actors could achieve who were constrained to avoid up-stage corners and to keep as much as possible in the middle fore-front of the alcove. In so small a recess only the middle portions of the rear wall could be seen by the majority of the audience; thus there was little incentive to develop interior settings or to explore the opportunities for realistic stage business at interior doors, windows, and hangings. Prior to 1599 the inner-stage setting — as: a "tent" for a king, a "study" for Friar Bacon or for Doctor Faustus, a "tomb" for Juliet, a "bower" for Titania, and so forth — was in effect hardly more than a habitation and a name; the setting itself played little or no part in the action. A property or two and dialogue would set the stage.

The need to enlarge so cramped an inner stage and to multiply its usefulness was uppermost, I believe, in the minds of those who saw in the transformation of the Theater into the Globe a chance to design a new and much better stage. How successful they were in improving their stage is attested in many ways. After 1599 the range of inner-stage settings began to expand and the proportion of inner- to outer-stage scenes to rise. Now interior scenes could compete in effectiveness with exterior scenes, and hence the tendency of the drama to move indoors was accelerated. The greater visibility of all parts of the enlarged rear stage gave rise to dramatic activity involving interior doors, windows, and other fittings comparable to activity on the outer stage. Furthermore, the way was opened for variable, realistic scenery comparable to that used in later theatres having a proscenium-type stage.

So immediate were the advantages of the Globe's new inner stage that the design was copied detail for detail in the great Fortune Playhouse erected the following year, and copied yet again (to judge by available evidence) in the Red Bull Playhouse erected in 1605. Indeed, the Globe stage design gave final form to the only major unit of the Elizabethan stage which was destined to expand during the Restoration and to survive into modern times. The "picture stage" of today is not the offspring solely of the Continental proscenium-type stage; one of its parents assuredly is the Elizabethan inner stage, with its curtained opening, its three flexible interior walls, its side and rear entrances, and its traps above and below.

Experience as well as vision went into the new design. Rudimentary in the inn-yard, experimental but increasingly useful in the late sixteenth-century playhouse, the inner stage as developed in the Globe rose to a position of usefulness rivaling that of the outer stage. An analysis of plays written between 1599 and 1609 shows that nearly half as many scenes were acted on the rear stage as on the platform; and, furthermore, that the tendency to place scenes of dramatic importance on the rear stage, and scenes of climax on the combined stage (the platform and the rear stage), was growing every year.

It will be convenient from now on to follow modern practice and refer to the curtained inner stage at the rear of the platform as "the study," thereby distinguishing it from a second curtained stage on the second level of the tiring-house which I shall call "the chamber." Special names for these two stages were not needed by Elizabethan dramatists, who, of course, took their own stage for granted. By resorting occasionally to the guide-words "above" and "below" in their stage-directions, they were able to devise plays suitable for performance on any multiple stage merely by composing in terms of action which flowed logically from unit to unit.

The first scene of *Doctor Faustus* opens in the lower inner stage; the direction reads, "*Enter Faustus in his Study.*" This famous scene led to a number of imitations in the years to follow [1] and may be said to have inaugurated the practice of standardized inner-stage settings. Prior to *Dr. Faustus* the inner stage had occasionally been called "the place behind the curtains." [2] After 1620 it is sometimes identified as "the scene," [3] a term earlier employed either for the curtain suspended before a prepared setting, or, loosely, in the sense of *locale* for the entire stage. As a rule, however, Elizabethan dramatists appear to have thought in terms of action and of stage-settings. In time those settings for the inner stage which followed Marlowe's study came to be numerous and varied: a tent, tomb, cave,

[1] The term is used in the following plays: *Barnavelt*, IV. ii; *The Devil's Charter*, I. iv, and IV. i; *Hamlet*, Q1, scene vi; *Histriomastix*, I; *Law Tricks*, IV. ii; *The Massacre at Paris*, line 438; *The Novella*, I. ii; *Satiromastix*, I. ii; *The Staple of News*, II. i; *Sforza*, V. iii; *Thomas Lord Cromwell*, III. i; *Titus Andronicus*, V. ii; *Two Noble Ladies*, line 82; *The Woman-Hater*, V. i; etc.

[2] Cf. *Thersites, ca.* 1537: "Mulciber must have a shop made in the place and Thersites comethe before it"; *Goodly Queen Hester*, 1561, at line 896: "Here must bee prepared a banket in yᵉ place"; and Greene's *Alphonsus*, 1589, line 1246: "in the middle of the place behind the stage." Cf. the *loca* of the church drama.

[3] Examples: *The Merry Beggars*, I. i; *The Jovial Crew*, I. i; *Monsieur Thomas*, III. i; *The Pilgrim*, IV. i; and see the quotation from Davenant on p. 171.

grove, or glade; a prison, cell, shop, gallery, hall, or ante-
room; a tavern, hall of state, church, and so forth. None
of those settings, however, provides us with a better term
for the lower inner stage than Marlowe's "study"; other
terms are, for one reason or another, less satisfactory.

2. THE SIZE AND SHAPE OF THE STUDY

The alcove that was contrived by means of curtains under an inn-yard balcony could have been no deeper than
the projection of the balcony, a matter, presumably, of
4 or 5 feet. The curtains may have extended across the
entire rear line of the platform (as shown in contemporary
views of stages set up for strolling players on early sixteenth-century market places) or, like the lower curtain in
The Wits view, may have merely concealed a wide doorway behind which lay a dressing room. Because inn-yard
play texts demanded little of this rear alcove appendage to
the platform, our knowledge of its details is vague.

In early permanent playhouses the rear stage was limited in size by three structural factors: the height of the
first gallery, the depth of that gallery (less a reserve for
the passageway behind the rear stage), and the width of the
span between corner posts of the frame (less a reserve for
the two large stage doors). In the Theater (1576), and
perhaps also in the Curtain (1577), these limitations allowed a study of not more than 12 feet in height, 7 or 8 feet
in depth, and 15 or 16 feet in width. The results of a careful scrutiny of the seventy-four plays "which may reasonably be taken to have been presented upon common stages
between the establishment of the Queen's men in 1583 and
the building of the Globe for the Chamberlain's men in
1599 and of the Fortune for the Admiral's men in 1600"
and of the limited resources of the inner stage indicated by
those plays have been set forth by Sir Edmund Chambers
in the twentieth chapter of his Elizabethan Stage.

The inner stage of the Globe, contrived within the re-

assembled frame of the dismantled Theater, was necessarily subject to the physical limitations of the older frame.
Therefore, as in the Theater, its height was determined by
that of the first gallery (12 feet). Its depth also was determined by the space (12½ feet) available between the
scenic wall and the exterior wall of the building; but, as
before, not all this space could be allocated to the inner
stage, for as in the Theater a passageway behind the rear
stage had to be provided to make back-stage circulation
possible during the course of a rear-stage scene. This need
was basic. It had been pointed out as early as 1545 by
Serlio in his treatise on the staging of plays in a great hall.[4]
The use of a door at the back of the rear stage presupposes
the existence of such a passage in all Elizabethan playhouses, public and private. Passageways were still standard
when, near the end of the pre-Restoration era, Davenant
wrote in his Preface to *The Siege of Rhodes* (1656):

It has often been wished that our scenes . . . had not been confined to
about eleven feet in height and about fifteen in depth, including the
places of passage reserved for the musick.

(Davenant's dimensions apparently refer to private playhouses, but one observes a close similarity between them
and the corresponding dimensions for the Theater and the
Globe.)

But the Globe inner stage differed radically from that of
the Theater in the width of its opening. With the stage
doors now transferred to the flanking bays, the inner stage
could be 23 feet in width. The diagrams on page 172
will show more clearly than words can how this fifty per
cent increase in the actual width of its opening more than
doubled the effective visibility of the rear stage and
thereby multiplied its usefulness many times over.

To sum up, the dimensions of the Globe inner stage were:
height 12 feet (the height of the first gallery); depth (allowing for a passageway approximately 5 feet wide) 7 to

---

[4] Campbell, *Scenes and Machines*, p. 33.

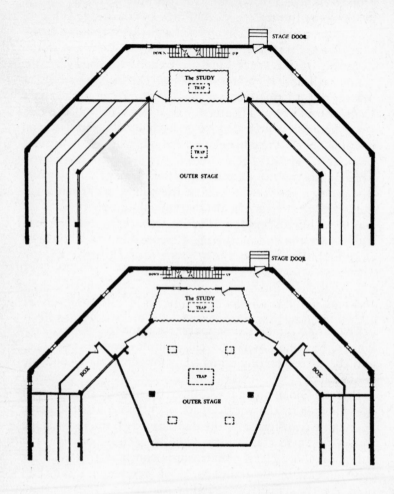

EVOLUTION OF THE PLATFORM AND OF THE
TIRING–HOUSE: FIRST LEVEL

Theater (1576) and Globe (1599) plans compared

8 feet;[5] and width 23 feet (the distance between corner posts of the frame).

It will be seen that the rear stage was now three times as wide as it was deep. This was not the awkward shape that may at first sight appear. Experience showed that, having a large outer stage, Elizabethan actors needed a supplementary, shallow rear stage suitable for use (1) as a three-dimensional back-drop when the two stages were merged into one large interior (examples: the Capulet ball-room, a court of justice in Venice or in Sicily, a throne room at Elsinore); (2) as an interior logically connected with a larger exterior (examples: the Capulet burial vault in a Verona graveyard, a royal tent near a battlefield, a cave near a lime-grove in Bermuda, a row of shops or booths facing a street), and (3) as in itself an interior (examples: Friar Laurence's cell, a room in Olivia's house or at the Boar's Head Tavern, a tent near Dover). Except when used as (3), depth in the rear stage (beyond what was needed for such large properties as a judicial bench and bar, a throne under a canopy, and the like) was of little advantage, for the outer stage alone was 29 feet deep and the two stages together measured 37 by 41 feet — a size rarely equaled today except for metropolitan opera companies. Nor, on closer inspection, was greater depth needed in (3) scenes, for, in keeping with the more domestic nature of such scenes, the properties employed were smaller, and the actors present at any one time rarely numbered more than six or seven (in static scenes where a council deliberates or a group sits down to eat and drink the number rises to ten or twelve [6]). I assume, moreover, that the actors could advance 3 or 4 feet in front of the curtain line and still remain under the projecting balcony overhead, much as a modern actor is free to advance on

[5] Cf. Chambers, iii. 82–83.

[6] See, for example, *The Bloody Banquet*, D4 verso; *Henry VIII*, I. ii; *King John*, III. i; *Richard III*, III. iv; *Satiromastix*, G1 verso; *Sir Thomas More*, I. ii; *A Warning for Fair Women*, D1 and G3.

the "apron" in front of the proscenium arch. This means that in practice the study when used alone had an acting area measuring 11 by 23 feet — an area deep enough (and of course wide enough) to ensure reasonable freedom of movement in any direction. Actors were not compelled, as some have supposed, to move forward from the study to the outer stage in order to be seen well and to achieve acting space.

3. The Visibility of Study Scenes

On looking at a ground plan of the Globe one observes that the widening of the lower and upper rear stages (without increasing their depth) greatly improved their visibility. Spectators in all parts of the auditorium could now see the rear wall and one or more of the side walls of the study, whereas formerly only those sitting directly opposite the tiring-house enjoyed so complete a view. Patrons of the Globe sitting even in the spectator-galleries at right angles to the stage had an adequate view by reason of the octagonal shape of the building. Only those seated in the gentlemen's rooms adjoining the ends of the tiring-house were hampered in this respect. As part of the price they paid for sitting "where they could be seen as well as see," gallants in the boxes could not command the nearer corner of the study (for the same reason that today a box-holder cannot command the nearer corner of the stage behind the proscenium opening).

A section plan of the Globe is equally enlightening. It reveals that spectators in the first gallery could see the floor, walls, and ceiling of the study. Those in the second gallery could see all but the study ceiling (coextensive with the gallery floor on which they sat). And, since the sight-lines from the third gallery pass under the fore-edge of the balcony (12 feet above the platform) and meet the rear wall of the study at a point some 8 feet above the floor, top-gallery spectators could command a good view of an actor standing even at the very back of the study.

Another advantage of widening the study was the increase of the amount of light entering through the study opening. Torches, lanterns, and candles were, of course, used in public theatres solely to enhance illusion and to indicate night scenes.[7] All the real illumination of the stage came from the daylight flooding the open yard. On this subject a few writers have been led astray. Thirty-odd years ago, at the dawn of modern interest in the design of the Elizabethan playhouse, the late Professor George P. Baker endeavored to defend the theory that curtains were strung between the forward stage posts to form the "inner" stage. He insisted that the inner stage as otherwise conceived was "so far back that it must have been out of sight for many of the audience and inaudible to many more."[8] The so-called "alternation theory of staging" to which he was giving support has since been modified or abandoned, but his mistaken concept of the inner stage has persisted, leading subsequent writers to suggest that it was "none too good for sight and hearing,"[9] and (more recently) "dark,"[10] "obscure,"[11] and "on dull days . . . almost invisible."[12] The facts are patently otherwise. The distance between the back of the Globe inner stage and the spectator at farthest remove in the top gallery was not more than 85 feet. In the matter of illumination the unroofed Elizabethan playhouse evidently suffered from too much

---

[7] It remained for the private playhouse, always dependent upon artificial lighting, to show the way to the deep "picture stage" of Restoration and later days.

[8] Baker, *Development of Shakespeare*, p. 88.

[9] Lawrence, *Those Nut-Cracking Elizabethans*, p. 118. Cf. H. Granville-Barker, *Prefaces to Shakespeare*, ii. 252.

[10] Chambers, iii. 120.

[11] Chambers, iii. 120: "the tendency of the seventeenth century was to confine its use [i.e. the study] to action which could be kept narrow, or for which obscurity was appropriate. It could still serve for a prison, or an 'unsunned lodge,' or a chamber of horrors."

[12] G. H. Cowling, *Shakespeare and the Elizabethan Stage*, published in 1927 by the Shakespeare Association.

light rather than too little. From inn-yard theatres to the last public playhouse for which we have details of construction — the Hope, erected in 1613 — the trend was increasingly toward extending the roof over the stage; at the Hope the roof covered the entire platform [13] (and this, too, in a playhouse so oriented that the inner-stage openings faced away from the afternoon sun [14]). I call attention, furthermore, to a contemporary term for this stage-cover, namely "the shadow," [15] the significance of which is obvious.

With the platform and the tiring-house façade deliberately shaded in the Globe by a stage-cover extending over approximately two-thirds of the platform and projecting from the playhouse roof-line 32 feet above, the lower and upper inner stages were illuminated by both direct and reflected natural light. Though this illumination was subdued — providing a condition artistically appropriate to interior scenes—there is no reason to suppose that it was inadequate even at the back of the study, for the height of the opening (12 feet) was almost twice the depth of the study (7–8 feet). Countless scenes of great importance both as regards acting (examples: Romeo in the Capulet tomb, Hamlet with his mother in her bedroom, Othello steeling himself to murder Desdemona and later discovering his hideous error) and elaboration of setting, properties, and costumes (examples: Portia and the caskets, Imogen's bedroom, Cleopatra's death scene, Paulina's unveiling of Hermione's statue) were inner-stage scenes enacted either above or below. Increasingly after 1599 such scenes tended to be the rule rather than the exception. They were imitated at the Fortune and the Red Bull — playhouses of the same type — with all the resources the two rival companies could muster. In short, to suggest that inner stages were too distant, too obscure, and too dark for use in important scenes is to disregard both logic and facts.

[13] *Henslowe Papers*, p. 20.
[14] See above, p. 33.
[15] See the Fortune Contract, in *Henslowe Papers*, p. 5.

4. THE USE OF HANGINGS IN THE STUDY

Unlike the outer stage with its unalterable scenic background of doors, bay-windows, balcony, and other fixed elements employed or disregarded according to dramatic need, the inner stages of the Globe had flexible "walls" at the sides and rear which, like the "wings," "flats," and "back-drops" of a picture-stage setting, could be modified or changed to harmonize with the needs of a given scene. The evolution of interior "walls" formed of nondescript hangings into realistic scenery was by no means complete at the close of the era, but it had made considerable progress toward the degree of completeness realized in Restoration theatres. Space in which to trace this evolution in detail from 1576 to 1642 is lacking here, but certain portions of the evidence are relevant to our present investigation. I shall begin by showing that the Globe inner stages were enclosed on the two sides or "ends" by cloth hangings, and at the rear by a rigid partition having in the middle a curtained aperture flanked by a window and a practicable door.

First as to the hangings at the sides of the inner stage and in the middle of the rear wall. Theatrical use of cloth hangings suspended from the ceiling and extending to the floor was entirely appropriate for the reason that wall coverings of tapestry (for the rich) and of woven and sometimes painted cloth (for the poor) were extensively used in Elizabethan palaces and homes. These domestic hangings did not, as today, serve merely for decoration; in the main their use was functional — to conserve heat, eliminate drafts, and conceal a rough, unfinished wall. They were usually supported at the top by brackets, or a rod, or a wooden ledge built out from the wall;[16] they hung at a distance of several inches from the wall; and they extended

[16] *Shakespeare's England*, ii. 129, and plate 129, facing page 186. Cf. also Boswell, *Restoration Court Stage*, p. 242: "Putting up 182 ft. of ledges for hangings in the great hall . . ."

clear to the floor. Thus, in the playhouse, inner-stage "walls" formed in part of hangings resembled closely what spectators were familiar with at home. Actors entering between a pair of hangings at the side of the study emerged as from an adjoining room beyond. Arras from floor to ceiling left no gaps to reveal back-stage activity. And if a Polonius wished to overhear a conversation about to take place, he had only to step behind one of the sets of hangings to enact a situation familiar in real life.

The following quotations, representative of many, testify to the employment of hangings as part of the visible walls of lower and upper inner-stage scenes (I draw examples from study and chamber scenes because in respect to hangings the two inner stages were identical). In *Law Tricks* (a Blackfriars play of 1604), sig. D4 verso, Julio and Polymetes enter the study and exchange comments on the room with Emilia who is already there:

Pol. A rare vault by this light . . . fore God a prettie lodging.
Jul. And verie faire hangings.
Pol. Passing good workman-ship, what storie is this Tris?
Emil. Why my Lord? the Poeticall fiction of *Venus* kissing *Adonis* in the Violet bed.
Jul. Fore-God tis true, and marke where the Cuckoldy knave *Vulcan* stands sneaking behinde the brake bush to watch a'm. . .
Pol. Hart, has the Arras an ague, it trembles so?

(Pulling back the hangings, they discover Lurdo, trembling with fright, behind.) Again, in *The Custom of the Country* (a Globe play of *circa* 1620), II. iv, Rutilio, escaping pursuers, has darted into a stranger's house:

Rut. Whither have my fears brought me?
I am got into a house, the doors all open
This by the largeness of the room, the hangings,
And other side adornments, glistring through
The sable masque of night, sayes it belongs
To one of means and rank.

And in *The Cunning Lovers* (written in 1638), Quarto 1, page 34, the Duke of Mantua and his Lords are searching the house from which Montecelso and Prince Verona have just fled:

Mantua. Soft, make no noise, the Chamber's whist and still . . .
   Search round the Chamber.
Florence. I find no man here.
Ferrero. Here's naught but walls and Arras.

In *The City Match* (a Globe and Blackfriars play of 1631), II. iii, the dialogue turns on the figures appearing in the hangings:

Aurelia. Why sir, I took you for a mute i' th' hangings
   I'll tell the faces.
Timothy. Gentlemen, do I
   Look like one of them Trojans?
Aur. 'Tis so; your face
   Is missing here, sir; pray step back again,
   And fill the number. You, I hope, have more
   Truth in you than to filch yourself away
   And leave my room unfurnished.[17]

In houses of the well-to-do the hangings were frequently changed, e.g. to honor a guest. In the theatre changes were possible also, though not during the course of a scene. Such a change is implied in *The Woman's Prize*, III. iii; Maria, while inspecting her new bedroom, gives the order:

                    For those hangings
   Let 'em be carried where I gave appointment,
   They are too base for my use, and bespeak
   New Pieces of the Civil Wars of France,
   Let 'em be large and lively, and all silk work,
   The borders Gold.

In III. v, Maria gives a second order:

             Sirha, up to th' Chamber,
   And take the Hangings down, and see the Linnen
   Packt up, and sent away within this half hour . . .
   Alass, we are undone else.

[17] See also *The Traitor*, III. i.

From Shirley's *Lady of Pleasure*, I. ii:

Celestina. What hangings have we here!
Steward. They are arras, madam.
Cel. Impudence! I know't.
   I will have fresher, and more rich; not wrought
   With faces that may scandalize a Christian,
   With Jewish stories stuffed with corn and camels . . .
   I say I will have other,
   Good master Steward, of a finer loom;
   Some silk and silver . . . I'll have
   Stories to fit the seasons of the year,
   And change as often as I please.

In Shirley's *Grateful Servant*, II, Jacomo examines the condition of his room:

> Tis well, here should have been a fresh suite
> Of Arras, but no matter, these beare the age
> Well, let 'em hang.[18]

And in *Love's Cure*, I. ii, Eugenia, on hearing that her exiled husband is returning after many years, gives immediate orders to her servants:

> Haste, and take down those Blacks with which my chamber
> Hath like a widow, her sad Mistriss mourn'd,
> And hang up for it, the rich *Persian* Arras,
> Us'd on my wedding night.

This last quotation helps to make clear the stage business in *The Custom of the Country*, I. ii, where a bride's bedroom is being made ready for a husband whom she and her family have cause to hate:

> *Enter Charino, and servants in blacks. Covering*
> *the place with blacks.*

Char. Strew all your withered flowers, your Autumn sweets
   By the hot Sun ravisht of bud and beauty
   Thus round about her Bride-bed, hang those blacks there

[18] See also *The City Madam*, IV. iv; *Holland's Leaguer*, V. iii; and *The Night Walker*, I. i.

The emblemes of her honour lost . . .
This is no masque of mirth, but murdered honour.[19]

The directions given in certain of these quotations were not, of course, carried out before the eyes of the spectators, since changes in those inner-stage hangings which formed a screen between the audience and the "wings" had to be effected while the outer-stage curtains were closed; but the passages as a whole reflect a normal and familiar custom both in the home and in the theatre. The point I wish to emphasize is that changes in the rear-stage hangings *could* be effected between scenes, and from its supply of arras the company could lay out sets appropriate to each play.

5. The Hangings in the Rear Wall of the Study

In the first years of permanent playhouses the three inner-stage walls probably were formed entirely by cloth hangings, those at the rear being suspended some 4 or 5 feet forward of the exterior wall of the tiring-house in order to leave space for the passageway essential to back-stage circulation. Some time elapsed after 1576 before stage-directions clearly denote the presence of a practicable door and fixed door-frame in the rear wall, and in that period, one assumes, entrance to the study from the sides and the rear was effected through openings made in pairs of curtains. Scrutiny of scenes from 1590 to 1642 reveals, however, that sections of permanent wall eventually replaced some of the hangings at the rear of the study, but that the middle section, perhaps 6 or 7 feet wide, continued as before to be formed by hangings. The hundred or more instances of eavesdropping, hiding, sitting, and even sleeping behind the rear hangings indicates that an actor who "slipp'd in here betwixt the hangings" found himself actually in the passageway beyond, and not in a space

---

[19] This and the preceding quotation were included for the additional purpose of showing that black hangings used in tragedies need not have been restricted to the black stage curtains referred to at the close of the last chapter.

some few inches deep between the hangings and a wall (as in a real room). Elsewhere at the rear a rigid wall was required, if only to frame the door (and later the window balancing the door on the opposite side); but the middle portion had to be kept flexible. Freedom to approach unseen to the back of some property set up in the study against the rear hangings is implied in many a direction before and after 1600; for example, in *Friar Bacon and Friar Bungay*, at line 1635:

Heere the Head speakes and a lightning flasheth forth, and a hand appeares that breaketh down the Head with a hammer.

Again, from *Alphonsus of Aragon*, at line 1246:

Let there be a brazen Head set in the middle of the place behind the Stage, out of the which, cast flames of fire, drums rumble within. . . Cast flames of fire forth of the brazen Head. . . Speake out of the brazen Head.

And again, from *St. Patrick for Ireland*, II:

An Altar discovered, two Idolls upon it, Archimagus and Priests, lights and incense prepar'd by Rhodomant. . . A flame behinde the Altar . . . The Song being ended, the Idol that presented Jupiter Moveth.[20]

The following passages illustrate concealment and eavesdropping behind the hangings at the rear of the inner stage. Perhaps the best known occurs in *1 Henry IV*, II. iv. Hearing that the sheriff is at the tavern door seeking the Gadshill robbers, Prince Hal orders Falstaff to hide "behind the arras." He sends the others to "walk up above." After the sheriff has been persuaded to leave, the Prince exclaims:

This oyly Rascall is knowne as well as Poules: Goe call him forth.
Peto. Falstaffe? fast asleepe behinde the Arras, and snorting like a Horse.
Prince. Harke, how hard he fetches breath: search his Pockets.
He [Peto] *searcheth his Pockets, and findeth certain Papers.*

[20] See also *Two Noble Kinsmen*, V. i.

Prince. What hast thou found?
Peto. Nothing but Papers, my Lord.

Needless to say, the entire audience must be given the opportunity of witnessing the unveiling and searching of Falstaff, which means that Falstaff lay behind the midpoint of the rear hangings. Falstaff was all too familiar with the usefulness of arras as a place of concealment. In *The Merry Wives of Windsor*, III. iii:

Robin. Mistris *Ford*, Mistris *Ford*: heere's Mistris *Page* at the doore, sweating, and blowing, and looking wildely, and would needs speake with you presently.
Fal. She shall not see me, I will ensconce mee behinde the Arras.
M. Ford. Pray you do so, she's a very tatling woman.

No stage business in our early drama was more common than this of hiding behind the arras. To illustrate various details of the business let me cite a few more examples. In *A Wife for a Month*, I. i, Valerio does not leave the royal apartments with his fellow nobles when the king dismisses them, but slips behind an arras hoping to learn the King's intentions regarding Evanthe, the girl Valerio loves: "I'le not be far off, because I doubt the cause." His suspicions are well founded. Evanthe's brother, King Frederick's "wicked instrument," lures the innocent Evanthe to the King's rooms and joins his threats to the King's solicitations. All this (a matter of some 200 lines), together with Evanthe's unshakable refusals, Valerio hears. Seizing an opportunity to get away unnoticed, Valerio emerges from his place of concealment behind the arras, comments briefly —

> Tongue of an Angel, and the truth of Heaven,
> How I am blest! —

and leaves the room.

In the first part of *If You Know not Me*, scene xviii, Queen Mary consents to give an audience to Princess

Elizabeth, but first instructs her husband to remain (unseen) to overhear the conversation:

Queen. Our fauor shalbe farre boue her desert,
And she that hath been banisht from the light,
Shall once againe behold our cheerfull sight.
You my Lord shall step behind the arras,
And heare our conference, weele shew her Grace,
For there shines too much mercy in your face.
Phill. We beare this mind, we errors would not feed,
Nor cherish wrongs, nor yet see *Innocents* bleed.
Queen. Call the Princesse.   *Exeunt for the Princesse,*
                                Phillip behind the arras.
                Enter all with Elizabeth.
All forbeare this place except our sister now?
                                Exeunt omnes.

Thirty-two lines later:

Phill. [aside]. Myrror of vertue and bright natures   *behind*
     pride,   *the arras.*
     Pitty it had been, such beauty should haue dy'd.

And fifteen lines still later Phillip emerges to take part in the conversation.

This business of hiding behind an arras is encountered again and again. In *The Noble Gentleman*, III. i, Shattillion refuses to talk to the Duke in the presence of others.

Duke. Depart the room, for none shall stay,
     No, not my dearest Duchess.
Wife [aside]. We'll stand behind the Arras and hear all. *Exeunt.*
Duke [supposing that he is now alone with Shattillion]. In that chair
     take your place, I in this,
     Discourse your Title now.

Some forty lines later the Duke becomes alarmed at Shattillion's mad claims and calls out, "Treason, help!" whereupon the Wife comes forward from the arras and others rush into the room from the antechamber.

Stealthy movements are called for in a scene of spying and counter-spying in *The Jew's Tragedy*, V:

Eleazer.   I'le hear him all;
Mean while. I'le hide me here . . .
                    Behinde the orras; exit Zareck.
Stand close. stand close. hah. whats that.
Attendant. A ratt behinde the hangings.
Elea. A comes, a comes, a comes.
                    Enter Zareck. coms out soft.

Similar movements are recorded in *Orgula*, V. ii. The
scene opens with the direction, "*A Banquet set with a soft
kind of Musick.*" Mundello, present as the scene opens,
leaves the room for a brief interval, re-entering "*Unbut-
ton'd in a loose posture.*" Not long after his return he is
aware of approaching footsteps; the direction reads:

Noise. Mu[ndello] *slinks behinde the hanging, while Org*[ula] *enters in
a night Robe, and dressing amorously accosting Fidelius.*

On the next page of the old quarto:

Mundello appears from behind the hanging.

In *Cupid's Whirligig*, sig. H1, two separate places are
used for concealment. During an inner-stage scene a
servant advises Nan and "Lady":

Wages. I would have ye hide your selves here behinde the hangings.

No sooner have they disappeared when "*Enter Knight.*"
Unaware that there are others present, he also talks with
Wages, but in the end he steps behind an arras (on the
other side of the room?) and the ladies emerge.

Since there was always the danger of an eavesdropper
lurking behind the arras, conspirators often search the
room before discussing their plans. In *The Turk*, for example, at line 1077:

Lady Fulsome. Phego doe you espie no motions behind the arras, no
squals, mufflings, or pages standing sentinell? . . .
Phego. Surely I see no body stirring Lady.

But in *Andromena* (written in 1641?), IV. viii, a council of state sits down to a secret conference without taking the necessary precautions against spies. Their deliberations concluded, "*They begin to rise*" from the council table. Just then, "*Plangus stirs behind the hangings . . . Rinatus draws and runs at him.*"

Rin.   The devil hath
 Armour on!
Ephorbas. Drag him to torture.
          They fetch him out.
 My son!

Additional examples of eavesdropping behind the hanging at the rear of the study (or in the corresponding place behind the upper-stage hangings) are listed in the notes.[21] From a study of the group as a whole one observes an interesting principle of acting, namely that concealment behind the rear hangings took place only after the actor intent on eavesdropping already had entered on the rear stage.

Other Shakespearean plays illustrate a related but more elaborate use of hangings at the rear of the study. In Act II of *The Merchant of Venice*, for example, scene vii, following an outer-stage scene in Venice, opens in Portia's house at Belmont (represented by the study):

> *Enter Portia with Morrocho, and*
> *both their traines.*
>
> *Por.* Goe, draw aside the curtaines and discover
> The severall Caskets to this noble Prince:
> Now make your choyce.

Once Morocco has chosen the golden casket, read his fate, and departed, Portia remarks:

---

[21] *Andromena*, IV. vii-viii; *Anything for a Quiet Life*, V. i; *Bussy D'Ambois*, V. i; *The City Madam*, I. iii; *The English Traveller* (Heywood's *Dramatic Works*, ed. Pearson, iv. 79); *The Fatal Union*, II. v; *The Honest Man's Fortune*, III. i; *Northward Ho*, E4; *Philaster*, II. i; *The Rebellion*, B2; *The Spanish Tragedy*, IV. iii; *The Swisser*, IV. ii.

A gentle riddance: draw [i.e. close] the curtaines, go:
Let all of his complexion choose me so.   *Exeunt.*

The next scene is on an unidentified Venetian street (the outer stage), but scene ix returns to Belmont:

Enter Nerrissa and a Serviture.

Ner. Quick, quick I pray thee, draw [i.e. open] the curtain strait.
The Prince of Arragon hath tane his oath,
And comes to his election presently.

When Aragon, likewise disappointed, has gone, the curtains concealing the caskets are again closed, and scene ix ends shortly after. Then follows Act III, with scene i in a Venetian street and scene ii in Portia's house. In details of curtain business the latter scene is identical with its Belmont forerunners.[22]

Now the nature of these three casket scenes, the turn of the dialogue, and the interposed street scenes in Venice show beyond a doubt that they were enacted on the inner stage. From this fact it follows (1) that the "curtains" in question are not the front-stage curtains, for the inner stage has each time been discovered before the caskets were displayed, and (2) that they are not the side hangings, for caskets placed behind such hangings would be visible to only a fraction of the audience, and (3) that they must be either the rear hangings *or* temporary curtains — called "traverses" by certain Elizabethan dramatists — strung across some part of the study in front of the rear hangings. The first alternative would mean placing the three caskets in the passageway immediately behind the study. This method of staging doubtless was earlier than the use of a traverse, and had the advantages of simplicity, of unexpectedness (for there was no visible hint in advance of a coming display), and of leaving the study unencumbered. The second method had the advantages of leaving the passageway unobstructed, of permitting variations in the

[22] For other examples of similar displays, see *The Fatal Dowry*, II. ii; *Old Fortunatus*, II. i; *Valentinian*, II. iv.

height, type, and location of the traverse to suit the needs of different plays, and of bringing the objects to be revealed closer to the audience. (I shall return to the subject of traverses in a few pages.)

In the final scene of *The Winter's Tale* (acted on the combined outer and rear stages) the statue of Hermione is revealed by Paulina's drawing a curtain ("Do not draw the curtain" . . . "I'll draw the curtain" . . . "Shall I draw the curtain?"). It could have been staged in either of the two ways outlined above. The audience knew in advance that the statue was to be exhibited to Leontes and the Court; there was ample room for such a statue either behind or before the rear hangings; and the passageway was not needed for back-stage circulation once that point in the play had been reached. Today it must be a matter of opinion whether the statue, so minutely particularized in the dialogue, could in Shakespeare's time have been displayed to better advantage in one place rather than the other.

In certain scenes, however, the success of the discovery depended in no small degree upon its unexpectedness, and in such scenes concealment *behind* the normal hangings was preferable. *Albovine*, V. ii, furnishes a good example. The scene opens in the study.

> *A canopy is drawn, the King is discovered sleeping over papers; enter Paradine with his sword drawn.*

Paradine advances stealthily to the king and stabs him. Just then someone knocks at the study door.

Par. Hah . . . he must
  Be hid. I'm sure this noise can never wake him.
> *He puts him behind the arras, opens the door.*
> *Enter Rhodolinda.*

After he kills Rhodolinda, he disposes of her body similarly (the direction reads, "*Carries her in*"). Not long after he adds a third corpse to his "full Sepulcher." Later in the same scene "*He draws the Arras and discovers Albovine, Rhodolinda, Valdura, dead in chairs.*" The final display of Paradine's grim triumph is completely unexpected; moreover it must be fully visible to the audience. Obviously the hangings at the rear of the study were drawn aside and the bodies were revealed seated in a recess devised for the occasion in the passageway. Stage business of the same type is to be found in other plays.[23]

We are now in a position to understand how Shakespeare staged the "Shew of eight Kings" in *Macbeth*, IV. i, heretofore a puzzle to scholars. This very elaborate scene requires (1) a mechanized trap for raising and lowering the cauldron, (2) a trapdoor for the three "Apparations," [24] and (3) some spectacular means of exhibiting the eight Kings to Macbeth's and also to the audience's unobstructed view. The text reads as follows:

Macb.   Yet my Hart
    Throbs to know one thing: Tell me, if your Art
    Can tell so much: Shall Banquo's issue ever
    Reigne in this Kingdome?
All. Seeke to know no more.
Macb. I will be satisfied. Deny me this,
    And an eternall Curse fall on you: Let me know.
    Why sinkes that Caldron? & what noise is this?
                              Hoboyes.
1. Shew.
2. Shew.
3. Shew.
All. Shew his Eyes, and greeve his Hart,
    Come like shadowes, so depart.
        A shew of eight Kings, and Banquo last,
            with a glasse in his hand.
Macb. Thou art too like the Spirit of *Banquo*: Down:
    Thy Crowne do's seare mine Eye-bals. And thy haire
    Thou other Gold-bound-brow, is like the first:

---

[23] Similar alcove scenes occur in *The City Match*, III. ii; *The Distresses*, IV. v; and *The Unfortunate Lovers*, V. iv.
[24] See below, pp. 211.

A third, is like the former. Filthy Hagges,
Why do you shew me this? — A fourth? Start eyes!
What will the Line stretch out to'th cracke of Doome?
Another yet? A seaventh? Ile see no more:
And yet the eight appeares, who beares a glasse,
Which shewes me many more: and some I see,
That two-fold Balles, and trebble Scepters carry.
Horrible sight: Now I see 'tis true,
For the Blood-bolter'd *Banquo* smiles upon me,
And points at them [i.e. those seen in the "glasse"] for his. What?
   is this so?
1. I Sir, all this is so. But why
Stands *Macbeth* thus amazedly?
Come Sisters.

It will be observed that the Kings appear one at a time, each following closely on the heels of the one before. This matter of timing is important. Macbeth's commentary is skillfully varied, but at no point during the passage of the first seven Kings does he have time for more than one or two lines before the particular King he is describing passes the focal center of the stage, or wholly disappears, and the next comes into view. The first seven come and go in the time that it takes him to utter seven lines. Now it is well established that Elizabethan actors spoke their lines at an average rate of twenty to the minute,[25] a fact which means that — allow as one will for dramatic pauses in Macbeth's nerve-racked commentary — the eighth King was in view not much more than half a minute after the first appeared. These conditions cannot be met by the use of any Elizabethan trap on record. And certainly the Globe's one mechanized trap could not move fast enough to produce such a rapid "line" of Kings, nor silently enough to be disguised by the music of "hoboyes." Moreover, this mechanized trap was down stage, whereas Macbeth and the Witches were at this time, one supposes, up stage, and nearer the scene of the "Apparitions." Incidentally, the

[25] A. Hart, "The Time Allotted for Representation of Elizabethan and Jacobean Plays." *R.E.S.*, VIII (Oct., 1932).

normal use of the study floor-trap is well illustrated by the coming and going of the three "Apparations." I call attention to the timing of their appearances, and the direction "*Descend*" after each. These are normal indications of study trap-work, as we shall later see.

Every condition of the display of eight Kings can be met, however, by having them walk in single file through the passageway behind the study, coming successively into view as each moves at a dignified pace past an opening in the middle of the rear wall of the study made by drawing aside the rear hangings. The words "Shew! Shew! Shew!" marked, I believe, the drawing apart of the hangings by the witches. Such an action would give those words a startling accompaniment.

This method of staging the Shew of Kings would have several advantages. So far as I can learn, it was new, and hence unexpected and dramatic. It would suit the nature of the exhibition — "Come like Shadowes, so depart" — as would no commonplace walking across the inner stage (a matter of some 20 feet) *in front* of the rear hangings. It would frame each King in the aperture, focusing the attention of the audience upon him at just the moment that Macbeth himself descried him. Finally, it would avoid filling the study with many figures at one time — Macbeth, three Witches, and eight Kings — to the distraction of focused attention.

In the light of other scenes by Shakespeare — in *The Merchant of Venice*, *1 Henry IV*, and *The Winter's Tale*, which have already been studied in this chapter, and in *Timon of Athens*, *Troilus and Cressida*, *Cymbeline*, and perhaps also *The Tempest* — which draw the passageway behind the study into the sphere of dramatic action, it must seem not only possible, but probable, that the "Shew of Eight Kings" in *Macbeth* was staged in the manner suggested above.

6. The Study Door and Window

While reviewing the number and location of outer-stage doors I cited examples establishing the presence of a "middle door" in the rear wall of the inner stage. Play texts refer specifically to this "door" as early as 1578,[26] hence from 1576, the date of Burbage's Theater, onwards it probably constituted the normal means of entering the study from the passageway beyond. In pre-Globe playhouses, with inner stages not more than 15 feet wide, the "door" would have to be placed near the middle of the rear wall if action involving its use was to be visible to the audience. But in the much wider inner stages of the Globe it was possible to place a practicable door several feet to one side of the mid-line and, if desired, to balance it on the other side with a window.

In the majority of inner-stage scenes after 1600 a rear door and window could be used to advantage, and at such times we may suppose that hangings in the middle of the rear wall extended merely to the casings which framed these appurtenances and were perhaps lightly fastened there. In those scenes representing a tomb, a cave, a tent, or a forest, however, visible house doors and windows would have been highly inappropriate. At such times, because of the flexibility of the inner-stage "walls," hangings could readily be drawn in front of the door and the window, wholly concealing them.

The distance between the door and the window was great enough (a matter of 6 or 7 feet?) to permit large properties (such as a raised and canopied throne, or an elaborately furnished altar) used in combined-stage scenes to be centered without blocking the door.[27]

The study door appears to have been of normal domestic size and to have opened into the room. It was equipped, as shown earlier, with a practicable lock and key visible on

[26] *1 Promos and Cassandra*, V. v.

[27] See *The Bondman*, III. iii, for a throne-room scene requiring a rear door.

the inside. Despite a situation in a Whitefriars play [28] which seems to require a peep-hole, I believe that the "middle" door was not provided with a wicket of any sort, for in Globe plays actors talk through the keyhole,[29] and, if they wish to see who is knocking on the other side, they peer out of the rear window.[30]

As often as not the rear door was supposed to lead merely to other parts of a house. At other times, when treated as a back door leading to a garden [31] or as a street door on the far side of the house, the dialogue and the action make the fact clear. For example, in *The Coxcomb*, II. i, a study scene at midnight:

Antonio. Who's that, that knocks there? i'st not at the street door?
Servant. Yes, Sir.
Ant. Who's there, cannot you speak?
Within Viola. A poor distressed Maid, for gods sake let me in.
Mercury. Let her in and me out together, 'tis but one labor, 'tis pity she should stand i' th' street, it seems she knows you.

Additional illustrations are cited below and in the notes.[32]

The window in the rear wall of the study was obviously of less dramatic use than the door. Even so, situations created for it are discoverable with some regularity in plays after 1600. So far as I am aware the earliest Globe play implying a rear window is *The Alchemist*, IV, vii [33] (an interior in Love-Wit's house):

[28] *Cupid's Whirligig*, H4.
[29] *The Alchemist*, III. iv; *The Puritan*, IV. ii.
[30] *The Alchemist*, I. i. For other examples see below, pp. 194–195.
[31] *King John and Matilda*, V. ii; *The Humorous Lieutenant*, II. iii.
[32] *Barnavelt*, IV. iii; *Covent Garden Weeded*, II. i; *The Coxcomb*, III. i; *Every Man out of his Humour*, V. iv; *The Island Princess*, II. i; *Measure for Measure*, I. v; *The New Academy*, III. i; *Sir John Oldcastle*, line 2086; *The Strange Discovery*, III. v, and IV. ii.
[33] Lawrence (*Elizabethan Playhouse*, ii. 51–52) bases his case for the study window on four examples: (1) *The Massacre at Paris*, scene ix; (2) *The Merry Wives of Windsor* (1623), I. iv; (3) *The Alchemist*, IV. iv; and (4) *The Spanish Gipsy*, I. iii. The window did indeed exist, but Lawrence's examples are uncon-

Face. How now, Dol? Hast' told her,
The *Spanish Count* will come? *Dol.* Yes, but another is come,
You little look'd for! *Fac.* Who's that? *Dol.* Your master:
The master of the house. *Svbtle.* How, Dol! *Fac.* Shee lies.
This is some trick. Come, leave your quiblins, Dorothee.
Dol. Looke out, and see. *Svb.* Art thou in earnest?
Dol. 'Slight, Fortie of the neighbours are about him, talking.
Fac. 'Tis he, by this good day. *Dol.* 'Twill proue ill day,
For some on vs. *Fac.* We are vndone, and taken.

A more ambitious situation is developed by Jonson in
Catiline, I. i. The play opens on the rear stage (Sylla's
Ghost *"Discouers Catiline in his study"*), and at line 305:

Cat. Boy, see all the doores be shut, that none approach vs,
On this part of the house . . .

A fiery light appeares.

Vargvnteivs. What light is this?
Cvrivs. Looke forth. *Lentvevs.* It still growes greater! *Lecca.* From
whence comes it?
Longinvs. A bloudy arme it is, that holds a pine,
Lighted, aboue the *Capitoll*! and, now,
It waues vnto vs!

It is, of course, conceivable that a property arm holding a
lighted torch was lowered through the stage heavens and
that Longinus looked out on the side next to the audience,
but, taking all the facts into account, I think it far more
probable that the "fiery light" held "aboue the Capitoll"
was an imaginary spectacle "visible" only to the actors
peering through the study window at a rapidly increasing
fiery glow created in the passageway beyond.

The Maid in the Mill, I. iii, illustrates the normal use of
the window, that is, to enable those inside the study to
recognize others approaching the house from the rear.
Ismena and Aminta, in a room on the ground floor of their
house at night, await the coming of Antonio.

---

vincing. In (1) the window was a bay-window on the second level of the tiring-
house over one of the stage doors; in (2) it is mentioned but may well have been
off stage; and in (4) it appears to be at the rear of the upper stage.

Ism. Look out, 'tis darkish.
Am. I see nothing yet: assure yourself, *Ismena*,
  If he be a man, he will not miss. . .
                    Men of this age
  Are rather prone to come before they are sent for.
  Hark, I hear something: up to th' Chamber, Cosin,
  You may spoil all else.

Ismena first runs to the window and looks out: "Let me
see!" But it is dark outside, and she can only decide that
"they are Gentlemen; It may be they." The two girls then
leave the lower room for the bay-window of their chamber above (facing the audience), and the lower stage curtains close. Antonio and his friend Martine then enter
the outer stage and feel their way in the "dark" across the
scenic wall until they come to Ismena's house. There they
pause, look up, and see her, lighted by a candle, in the bay-
window over their heads.

    Again, from *The Ghost*, III. i. Erotia, a bawd, and
Cunicula, a whore, are in their house, but near a street
door awaiting the arrival of customers.

Ero. One knocks, a Booty I hope, look out Cunicula
Cu. O Patroness, silk Cloaks and silver Lace,
  A Coach-ful on um.
Er. In and prepare yourself . . .   *Knocks again.*
  Why what's the matter there?   *Knocks still.*
  Will you knock down my doors you saucy Jacks?
Pinnario. Erotia, sweet Erotia let us in.   *Within.*

    Other examples of study-window scenes are listed in the
notes.[34]
    One or two minor features of the rear-stage window may
be worth noting. Because it "opened" merely into the
passageway beyond the study, the window could con-
tribute nothing towards illuminating the rear stage. This

   [34] *Andromena*, II. vi; *Captain Underwit*, V. ii; *The Cunning Lovers*, V;
I Honest Whore, scene x; *The New Academy*, IV. ii; *The Novella*, III. i; *The
Parson's Wedding*, IV. vi; *The Spanish Curate*, II. iv.

fact is perhaps corroborated by the woodcut appearing on the title-page of the 1630 quarto of *Friar Bacon and Friar Bungay*, representing the rear stage. A window with small panes cut in a conventional pattern and set in lead is shown in the rear wall to one side. The panes are pictured as dark. In the playhouse such darkness of the panes is hardly to be wondered at, for without semi-opaque glass the back-stage movements of actors, musicians, and property-men through the passageway would have been observed by the audience. Further, the absence of any situation requiring an actor in the passageway to look through the window into the rear stage (reversing the normal situation of an actor in the rear stage peering through the window as if into a street or garden) implies the impossibility of so doing.

In no play, so far as I am aware, is the study window ever opened.[35] In *The Puritan*, IV. ii, Edmund believes that the Devil has been in the room during his absence and suggests opening the study window to air the room and lessen the stench of brimstone. But he is ridiculed and dissuaded — "'Tis but your conceit" — and, leaving the window closed, he turns to see if the hangings have been singed.

7. THE HANGINGS AT THE ENDS OF THE STUDY

In the Globe, and in playhouses modeled upon it, the hangings at the "ends" of the study formed a wide angle with the rear wall in a manner analogous to the flanking sections of the scenic wall. The reasons for this oblique disposition are, first, that a right angle would have created a corner invisible to those spectators who sat in a side gallery in the same half of the house, and secondly, that almost innumerable situations (some of which are examined below) require that the study's side exits — more specifically the

---

[35] The upper-stage window could be opened. See the discussion in Chapter VIII.

openings between the pairs of curtains forming the end walls of the study — be in full view of the audience.

Although less conspicuous in that they were not squarely faced by the majority of spectators, the side hangings were quite as useful in eavesdropping scenes as the rear hangings because they were actually known to give access to adjoining "rooms" and corridors off stage. An actor's exit from the rear stage to hide in a near-by room, or his entrance from some other part of the house to take a position immediately behind the side hangings, was often more in accord with normal behavior or with the dramatist's requirements than an actor's slipping behind the rear hangings and having (at least in theory) to remain there until some later moment in the scene. The quarto version of *The Merry Wives of Windsor*, I. iv, a study scene, illustrates the usual procedure in such cases:

Mistress Quickly [to *Simple*]. Lord blesse me, who knocks there?
  For Gods sake step into the Counting-house,
  While I goe see whose at doore.
        He steps into the Counting-house.

The Counting-house, which is never revealed to the audience, is, of course, merely off stage at one side. A more explicit example is found in a study scene in Brome's *New Academy*, V. ii:

Cash. Pray obscure
  Your selves in that by-room there, where you may
  See and hear all that passes, nor can any
  Passe out o' th' house without your notice.

The implication that Cash's hidden associates will find themselves between the inner room and the front or street door of the house (that is, between the study and the main stage door) follows precisely the actual ground plan of the tiring-house and hence would seem logical to the audience.

Again, in the quarto version of *The Merry Wives of Windsor*, IV. ii (a study scene), Falstaff, on hearing Mrs. Page enter Ford's house, looks about for a place to hide.

Mrs. Ford suggests, "Step behind the arras, good Sir John." The same situation in the folio version reads, "Step into th' Chamber, Sir John," and thirty-odd lines later Falstaff re-enters, protesting to Mrs. Ford that he will not again submit to leaving the house packed in the laundry basket. Here, one observes, the "chamber" is on the side of the study opposite from the street door through which Mrs. Page enters. By "arras" the quarto could have referred to either the rear or the side hangings.

Other examples of action at one of the side hangings are listed in the notes.[36]

A situation demanding an entrance to the study from one side (or possibly through the door at the rear) together with an exit into a "room" at the other side is found in *1 Henry IV*, II. iv. Prince Hal, it will be recalled, directs Poins to stand "in some by-room while I question my puny drawer to what end he gave [me] the sugar; and do thou never leave off calling 'Francis' that his tale to me may be nothing but 'Anon!'" Poins then retires behind the hangings at one side; little Francis enters the study and is bewildered by a cross-fire of questions and calls, until at last the Vintner rushes in to scold Francis and to announce Falstaff's arrival at the outer door.

Other plays make clear use of entrance to the study from both sides. For example, *Women Beware Women*, III. iii, line 1:

Enter Guardiano and Isabella at one door, and the Ward and Sordido at another.

(A number of clues, including the line "her father and her friends are i' the next room," show that this direction inaugurates an inner-stage scene.)

In reporting the ludicrous behavior of two amateur

[36] *Albovine*, IV. i; *Andromena*, IV. viii; *The Ball*, III. iii; *Blurt Master Constable*, III. ii; *The Devil's Law Case*, IV. ii; *The Laws of Candy*, IV. i; *The Noble Gentleman*, III. i; *The Wise-Woman of Hogsdon*, III. i; *The Wits*, II. i; *The Wizard*, I. iii.

actors playing the part of ghosts, Gayton wrote: [37] "At
their entrance, just as they put their heads through the
hangings of the Scene, comming out at two severall sides
of the Stage, they shook [with fright]."

When an actor already in the study concealed himself
behind the *rear* hangings, the audience saw him disappear
and was prepared for his later re-entry, for normally it was
assumed that those hangings fronted a solid wall. When,
on the other hand, an actor left the study by way of the
rear door or through one of the side exits, and later returned to listen at the *side* hangings, it was necessary to
direct the audience's attention to his return, for otherwise
his presence there would go unsuspected. The way Elizabethan dramatists managed this is illustrated by the following passage from *The Honest Man's Fortune*, III. iii.
Lady Orleance, Lamira, and others leave the room for a
walk "in the orchard." Montague, Laverdine, La Poop,
and Malicorn remain, and are soon quarreling:

Mont.   I would take off
This proud film from your eyes, that will not let you
Know I am *Montague.*
                    Enter Lamira behind the Arras.
Lam. I will observe this better.
Lav. And art thou he? I will do thee grace.

Thirty lines later:
                    Lamira [advances] *from the Arras.*
Lam. Indeed you act a part
Doth ill become you my servant; is this your duty?
Mont. I crave your pardon.

One observes first that Lamira's position *"behind the
Arras"* shields her from view of those on the inner stage;
and secondly that her line, "I will observe this better,"
is not noticed by them (this second observation suggests
that she stood at one end of the stage and not at the rear).

[37] *Pleasant Notes on Don Quixot,* 1654, p. 95.

The audience, on the other hand, must be able to see Lamira clearly, if only for a few seconds, and also to hear her aside, for the force of what follows depends on every spectator's knowing that she is in a position to overhear what passes between Montague and the others. I suggest, therefore, that Lamira entered to the opening in one pair of side hangings, peered into the room, spoke her aside, and then remained between the overlapping flaps of the arras. This action on her part would be observed by all alert spectators but would pass unseen by actors in the inner stage unless facing her side of the room. Once she had announced to the audience her presence at the side hangings, Lamira could afford to remain inconspicuous until time to advance *"from the Arras."*

Similar stage business is found in *The Lady of Pleasure*, III. ii. Bornwell leaves the room with two others on some pretext and returns 32 lines later to overhear the conversation of his love, Celia, and others left behind:

Celia.   Do you possess
  Your wits, or know me, gentlemen?
        [Re-]*enter Bornwell*
Born. [aside]. How's this?
Kickshaw. Know you? yes: we do know you to an atom.
Littleworth. Madam, we know what stuff your soul is made on.
Cel. But do not bark so like a mastiff, pray. —
  Sure they are mad. — Let your brains stand awhile,
  And settle, gentlemen; you know not me.

Fifty-odd lines later Bornwell mutters an exasperated aside, and after twenty more lines he breaks into the conversation:

Born. [aside]. Brave soul! [advancing into the room] You brace of
    horse-leeches! I have heard
  Their barbarous language, madam; you are too merciful.

Other examples of eavesdropping at the side hangings are listed in the notes.[38]

[38] *The Bondman*, III. iii; *The City Wit*, III. iv; *The Country Girl*, V. i; *A New Way to Pay old Debts*, III. ii; *Volpone*, III. vii; *The Walks of Islington*, I. ii.

An understanding of these two ways of staging eavesdropping scenes makes it possible to reconstruct the management of more complex scenes where actors move freely
on and off the stage or where both the lower and upper
inner stages are simultaneously in use. In *The Little French
Lawyer*, III. iii, for example, the husband Champernel, reported to be asleep in his off-stage chamber above, has in
fact arisen to observe in the study below the efforts of
Dinant, aided by Cleremont, to seduce his wife, Lamira.
Lamira, intent on making fools of the two gallants, insists
that Cleremont get into bed with her husband (whose
place has been taken for the occasion by Champernel's
pretty young niece) in order to allay suspicion of her being
elsewhere.

Din. But for his Beard —
Lam. To cover that you shall have my night Linnen,
  And you dispos'd of, my *Dinant* and I
  Will have some private conference.
                    Enter Champernel, privately.
Cler. Private doing,
  Or I 'll not venture.
Lam. That's as we agree.   *Exeunt.*
        *Enter Nurse, and Charlotte, pass over the Stage with Pillows,
        Night cloaths, and such things.*
Cham. What can this Woman do, preserving her honour?
  I have given her all the liberty that may be,
  I will not be far off though, nor I will not be jealous . . .
                          Stands private.
  She may be, and she may not, now to my observation.
              Enter Dinant, and Lamira.

The scene continues with Dinant and Lamira sitting down
in the study to drink wine together, all the time spied upon
by Champernel, who in asides to the audience comments
delightedly upon his wife's faithfulness and her skill in out-
maneuvering Dinant. Just as the latter supposes his desires are about to be gratified, off-stage musicians begin to
play so loudly that Cleremont, shaking with fright, appears
above, as if having crept out of Champernel's bed, and

calls down the stairs for silence lest the old husband be
awakened. Lamira, below, calls up to him:

> Lie you down,
> 'Tis but an hours endurance now.
>
> *Cler.* I dare not, softly sweet Lady — heart?
>
> *Lam.* 'Tis nothing but your fear, he sleeps still soundly,
> Lie gently down.
>
> *Cler.* 'Pray make an end.
>
> *Din.* Come, Madam.
>
> *Lam.* These Chambers are too near. *Ex*[eunt] *Din. Lam.*
>
> *Cham.* I shall be nearer;
> Well, go thy wayes, I'le trust thee through the world
> Deal how thou wilt.

Here both the lower and the upper inner stages are in use,
but the action spied upon by the husband takes place below. Champernel "stands private" behind one of the side
hangings, leaving the rear door and the opposite side-exit
free for the comings and goings of the servants, of Lamira
and her would-be lover and the calling up the stairs to
Cleremont. For his long speeches when alone Champernel
probably emerged from behind the hangings; the rest of
the time he was hidden from Dinant and Lamira (but not
from spectators) by his ability to stand, partially concealed, between the side hangings.

The evidence relating to inner-stage "walls" so far presented would seem to establish for the Globe Playhouse:
(1) that the side walls were formed by woven, figured, or
painted cloth hangings;
(2) that the middle portion of the rear wall was formed by
hangings;
(3) that different sets of hangings could be used, and that,
subject to the limitations of the playhouse supply, sets
appropriate to each play and scene might be used;
(4) that eavesdropping and the concealment of inanimate
objects for discovery during the course of an inner-stage

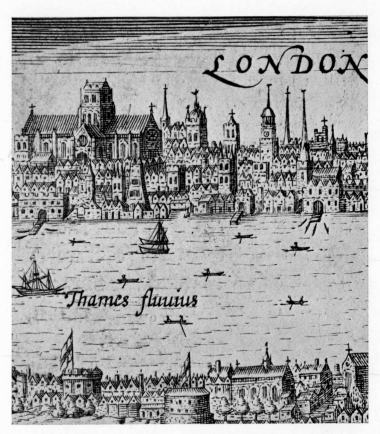

THE BEAR GARDEN AND THE ROSE, *circa* 1593

A view of London by Hondius set in a large map of "The Kingdome of Great Britaine and Ireland" included in John Speed's *Theatre of the Empire of Great Britaine,* 1611. From the original in the Folger Shakespeare Library

scene could be managed behind the rear hangings, where the action was in full view of the audience;

(5) that stage business at the middle of the rear wall shows that there were hangings instead of a solid partition just there; but, none the less, entrances from the rear passageway had to be accomplished through the visible door and not through the hangings;

(6) that a door and a window, opening onto the rear passageway and flanking the hangings referred to in (5), were appurtenances normally visible in the rear wall of the study;

(7) that each side hanging was suspended in such a way as to form an oblique angle with the rear wall, thus bringing the side hanging into view of the audience and eliminating blind corners;

(8) that eavesdropping took place at the side as well as at the rear hangings (but not concealment of inanimate objects), and, if the actor had earlier left the stage, his return to the side hangings usually was announced by some signal to the audience; and

(9) that the passageways and "rooms" which in fact did exist beyond the side hangings were referred to and made dramatic use of, but never revealed to the audience during the course of a play.

8. SUPPLEMENTARY INNER-STAGE HANGINGS

In addition to the hangings normally employed to form a substantial portion of the inner-stage walls, supplementary hangings — sometimes called "traverses" by a few Elizabethan dramatists — were occasionally strung up in front of the rear hangings to create a recess at the back of the study, or were strung up at right angles to the rear hangings to divide the study into two or more compartments. As the latter use appears to have been the earlier, I shall discuss it first.

By 1590 dramatists had already used the cloth-walled

rear stage as a tent in which a king or a general near some battlefield held council, wrote dispatches, spent a ghost-haunted night, and so forth.[39] It was only a question of time before a dramatist undertook to provide the leaders of two factions with tents; this was done by dividing the study into two rooms. *Richard III* (1592–1593?), V. iii, not only requires a tent for Richard and another for Richmond,[40] but its detailed stage-directions and elaborate action show that the two tents (though presumably some distance apart) were in fact adjoining,[41] and that they could be revealed to the audience separately or simultaneously.[42]

Tent scenes are of course less frequently employed after the heyday of the historical play,[43] but the ability to divide the inner stage into compartments was useful in scenes representing a row of madmen's cells [44] or (more frequently) a row of shops facing a street.[45] In view of the origin and nature of the inner-stage walls, one assumes that when two or more tents, cells, or shops were called for, the dividing walls were formed by cloth traverses strung up from front to back.

[39] Examples: *Edward I*, lines 1675 and 1867; *Julius Caesar*, IV. iii; *A Looking Glass for London*, line 533; and *The Trial of Chivalry*, C4 verso.

[40] Cf. lines 6 and 46.

[41] Cf. lines 118–178.

[42] Cf. lines 47–79, 80–117, and 118–178.

[43] Later examples, however, are to be found; for example, *The Amorous War*, IV. iv; *The Devil's Charter*, A2 verso, H4, and I1 verso; *1 Iron Age*, IV. iii; *King Lear*, IV. vii.

[44] *1 Honest Whore*, V. ii.

[45] Scenes with one shop: *Anything for a Quiet Life*, II. ii; *Every Man out of his Humour*, IV. iii–v; *Greene's Tu Quoque*, B1; *1 Honest Whore*, E2; *2 Honest Whore*, F2; *A Mad Couple Well Matched*, II. i and ii; *The New Exchange*, II. i; etc. Scenes with two shops: *The Merry Devil of Edmonton*, V. i and iii; *The Shoemaker's Holiday*, 1600, F3 and G1 verso; *Two Lamentable Tragedies*, I. i–iii. Scenes with three shops: *Bartholomew Fair*, II–V, requires booths for the pig-woman, the ginger-bread woman, and the hobby-horse man; *The Roaring Girl*, I: "*The three shops open in a ranke: the first a Poticaries shop, the next a Fether shop; the third a Sempsters shop.*"

In Jonson's *Volpone*, V. ii, the traverse specified is of another sort. The situation is as follows: Volpone, wishing to observe the true characters of his acquaintances, sends out word that he is dead and orders Mosca to make ready for a part in the business.

> Hold, here's my will.
> Get thee a cap, a count-booke, pen and inke,
> Papers afore thee; sit, as thou wert taking
> An inuentory of parcels: I'le get vp,
> Behind the cortine, on a stoole, and harken;
> Sometime, peepe ouer; see, how they doe looke;
> With what degrees, their bloud doth leaue their faces!
> O, 'twill afford me a rare meale of laughter.

In the next scene, when his would-be heirs have come and are watching Mosca draw up the inventory —

> *Volpone peepes from behinde a trauerse*
> *Volp.* I, now they muster . . . Rare!
> Be busie still. Now they begin to flutter:
> They neuer thinke of me. Looke, see, see, see!
> How their swift eies runne ouer the long deed,
> Vnto the Name, and to the legacies,
> What is bequeath'd them, there — *Mosc.* Ten sutes of hangings —
> *Volp.* I, i'their garters.

One observes that the traverse or "cortine" cannot have been higher than 6 or 7 feet above the floor, for with the aid of a stool Volpone can "peepe ouer" long enough to speak a good many lines in asides to the audience. Furthermore, if strung across some part of the study near the rear wall, it could not be higher than 6 feet if Volpone's head was to be visible to spectators in the top gallery.

For another study scene requiring a low traverse — "*Medlay appeares above the Curtain . . . He draws the Curtain and discovers the top of the Tub*" — see Jonson's *Tale of a Tub*, V. x.

This is not the place for an exhaustive discussion of inner-stage traverses, but I believe that the following tentative conclusions are now evident:

(1) As early as 1593 the rear stage could be divided into two compartments by a traverse strung up from front to back, and in the wider studies of later playhouses three small compartments were feasible.

(2) As early as 1595 the rear stage could provide a small recess screened off by a traverse either behind or in front of the rear hangings. The usual clue to such a traverse consists of the word "*draw* . . ." in stage-directions occurring during the progress of an inner-stage scene. This traverse device, subsequently employed for larger and more elaborate revelations [46] and occurring with increasing frequency in plays written after 1615, is in direct line with the Restoration stage practice of making ready a series of two or three scenes, one behind the other at increasing depth up stage, and successively exposing them by drawing aside the requisite number of traverses [47] (or their later theatrical equivalent, "flats" [48]).

9. ENTERING THE STUDY FROM THE OUTER STAGE

Examples of actors passing through an outer-stage door into the study as if from the street into a house have been given in the quotations from *The Puritan*, *The Golden Age*, and *Amends for Ladies* cited on pages 160–161. Those scenes show, either by dialogue or by stage-directions, the movement from one stage to the other; ordinarily, however, such movement leaves little or no trace in the text, for it was both logical and normal. In most scenes one must be guided by the situation and mentally supply part or all of the direction. For example, in *Romeo and Juliet*, V. iii, Romeo, while engaged in forcing the locked door of the Capulet tomb (one of the two outer-stage doors) — "thus I enforce thy rotten jaws to open" — is halted

---

[46] See, for example, *The Distresses*, IV. i and v; *The Lover's Progress*, III. i; *The Unfortunate Lovers*, V. iv; *The White Devil*, V. iv; and *The Woman-Hater*, V. i.

[47] See *The Duke of Guise* (1682), V. iii.

[48] For discussion see Summers, *The Restoration Theatre*, pp. 97 ff.

by Paris who has been hiding near by (probably behind the doorposts). They fight. Paris falls. Paris's dying request is for burial in the tomb with Juliet. Romeo accedes, picks up the body, and carries it to the now unfastened vault door, saying,

> O give me thy hand,
> One writ with me in sowre misfortunes booke.
> Ile burie thee in a triumphant grave.

(At this point he enters the door, the stage curtains open, and Romeo at once appears inside the study, carrying Paris. Romeo continues his speech, but makes a significant change in his metaphor on seeing Juliet:)

> A Grave; O no, a Lanthorne, slaughtred Youth:
> For here lies *Juliet*, and her beautie makes
> This Vault a feasting presence full of light.

A second example, from the Globe and Blackfriars play *The Queen of Corinth*, II. iv, is more typical, for there is no mention of the door by which one enters. Conon and Crates have just met on some street (the outer stage).

Con. What's this a Tavern?

Cra. It seems so by the outside.

Con. Step in here then,
  And since it offers it self so freely to us,
  A place made only for liberal entertainment,
  Let's seek no further, but make use of this,
  And after the Greek fashion, to our friends
  Crown a round cup or two.
          Enter Vintner and Drawer.

Cra. Your pleasure, Sir.
  Drawers, who waits within?

Draw. Anon, anon Sir.

Vint. Look into the *Lilly-pot*: why *Mark* there;
  You are welcome Gentlemen; heartily welcome
  My noble friend.

Cra. Let's have a good Wine mine Host,
  And a fine private room.

Vint. Will ye be there Sir?
  What is't you'll drink? —

and so on, with the scene continuing thereafter to its close in the tavern (i.e. the study). Now at some point in the passage quoted the two friends left the platform through the stage door and entered the inner stage, which was immediately discovered. A survey of other examples, some of which contain a less laconic stage-direction, suggests that in this scene the curtains were opened at " *Enter* [i.e. "discover"] *Vintner and Drawer*," and that Conon and Crates left the outer stage after Crates's line, "Your pleasure, Sir." His "Drawers, who waits within?" probably was called out while passing into the tavern. That the two friends are almost at once visible inside the study is shown by the salutation of the Vintner ten words later.

The timing in the following similar situation is more obvious. In *Two Noble Ladies*, at line 82, Barebones, running from pursuers, crosses the outer stage:

> Alas, more yet? Ile runne into my masters studdy, and hide mee in his inckehorne. O Mr. Mr. Mr.
>
> *Ciprian discovered at his booke.*
>
> *Cyp.* How now? What's the buisnes?
> *Bare.* O absurditie to a scholler!

Again, from *The Novella*, II. i. Nicolo, on the outer stage, has brought his master to a gentleman's house and seen him enter there; turning away from the door, he encounters Fabritio.

> *Fab. Nicolo* well met, I saw you house my Father,
> And waited for you. Come, you shall draw neare.
> This is a neare friends Lodging.
>
> *Piso, Francisco, Hora*[tio discovered] *at a Table, Wine &c.*
>
>   Gentlemen
> My fathers speciall man I told you of;
> Pray bid him welcome.
> *Hor.*   Most intirely,
> Please you to sit sir.

Further examples are listed in the notes.[49]

[49] See *The Amorous War*, IV. iii, and *The Goblins*, I. ii.

10. THE STUDY FLOOR TRAP

The Globe study was provided with two traps of the hinged-door type, one in the floor and the other directly overhead in the ceiling. The floor trap, though smaller and less centrally placed with respect to the audience than the outer-stage trap, was the most often-used trap in the entire playhouse. Because of its position in a curtained stage, and because of the fact that properties could be set up over the trap, and apparatus of various sorts placed below it in the cellar, it was also the most versatile. It lent itself to three basic types of trap scenes: open graves and pits, river banks and wells, and subterranean vaults and passageways. A representative example of the first type occurs in *Hamlet*, V. i. That scene, using the combined stage, opens with two "Clowns" discovered in the rear stage digging Ophelia's grave. They stand in the almost completed grave and from time to time shovel out earth and bones. The scene closes soon after the fight between Hamlet and Laertes in the grave itself. Other open-grave scenes are listed in the notes,[50] together with related scenes in which the trap is used as a pit,[51] ditch,[52] or nondescript hole in the ground.[53]

A representative example of the second type occurs in *Pericles*, II. i. Pericles, entering to the outer stage after the waves have cast him, "wet," upon the shore, meets fishermen and subsequently watches two of them at work in the study portion [54] of a combined-stage scene.

> *Enter* [i.e. discover] *the two Fisher-men, drawing up a Net.*
> 2. Helpe Maister helpe; heere's a Fish hanges in the Net,
> Like a poore mans right in the law: t'will hardly come out.
> Ha bots on't, tis come at last; & tis turned to a rusty Armour.
> *Per.* An Armour friends; I pray you let me see it?

[50] *The Bloody Banquet*, D1 verso; *The Queen of Corsica*, MS. *Lansdowne*; and *The Turk*, line 603.

[51] *The Atheist's Tragedy*, E1 verso; *Look About You*, line 2043; *The Old Wives Tale*, line 1148; *The Strange Discovery*, III. v; *Titus Andronicus*, II. iii.

[52] *Arden of Feversham*, G2 verso; *Edward II*, line 2469.

[53] *The Princess*, V. ii; *Timon of Athens*, IV. ii; *Two Noble Ladies*, line 1900.

[54] Cf. Lawrence, *Pre-Restoration Stage Studies*, p. 159.

Again, from a Globe play of 1606, *The Devil's Charter*, sig. F4. Caesar Borgia and Frescobaldi have waylaid the Duke of Candie on a dark street and have stabbed him to death. They then look about for a means of disposing of the body.

Caes. Helpe *Frescobaldi* let vs heaue him ouer,
  That he may fall into the riuer *Tiber*,
  Come to the bridge with him.

Fres. Be what he will the villaine's ponderous,
  Hath he some gould about him shall I take it?

Caes. Take it were there a million of duckets,
  Thou hast done brauely *Frescobaldi*,
  Stretch thee, stret[c]h out thine armes feare that he
  Fall not vpon the arches.

Fres. Ile wash him doubt you not of a new fashion.

Caes. I thinke thou neuer hadst thy Christendome,
  Follow for Company prenitious villaine.

Fres. Hold hold, Coxwounds my Lord hold,

Caes. The diuell goe with you both for company.
                Caesar casteth Frescobaldi after.

As I reconstruct this scene, the outer stage represented the street where the Duke was murdered; the study represented the "bridge" to which the body was carried; and the study trap, perhaps fronted by a property parapet, furnished the means by which the dead Duke was lowered out of sight "into the river" and the live Frescobaldi sent tumbling after. Manifestly such stage business required a trap opened and made ready before the scene began, hence in this scene the study trap, not the outer-stage trap, was used. Additional beach [55] and river-bank [56] scenes are listed in the notes, together with related scenes in which the trap is used as a spring or well.[57]

The third type, in which the trap opens to a subter-

[55] *The Prisoner*, IV, ii; *The Two Maids of More-clacke*, F4.
[56] *The Aphrodisial*, I. iii; *Locrine*, IV. iv, and V. iv.
[57] *The Duchess of Suffolk*, E3; *The Old Wives Tale*, line 743; *Tiberius Nero*, lines 3285 and 3303.

ranean passage or vault, is more frequently encountered than all others combined. A striking example occurs in *Richard III*, V. iii, where, it will be recalled, eleven ghosts "*enter*" in succession to threaten Richard and to encourage Richmond as the two men sleep in their respective tents near Bosworth Field. Similar scenes in other plays suggest that when referring to such visits from ghosts the direction "enter ——" meant rising through the floor trap. A second example, from *Macbeth*, IV. i, merits closer examination than was given it a few pages back.

All [Witches]. Come high or low:
  Thy Selfe and Office deaftly show. *Thunder.*
        1. Apparition, an Armed Head.
Macb. Tell me, thou unknowne power.
1. He knowes thy thought:
  Heare his speech, but say thou nought.
1. Appar. Macbeth, Macbeth, Macbeth:
  Beware *Macduffe*,
  Beware the Thane of Fife: dismisse me. Enough.
                He Descends.
Macb. What ere thou art, for thy good caution, thanks
  Thou hast harp'd my feare aright. But one word more.
1. He will not be commanded: heere's another
  More potent then the first.   *Thunder.*
        2. Apparition, a Bloody Childe.
2. Appar. Macbeth, Macbeth, Macbeth. . .

Five lines later the second apparition "descends"; then, soon after, following more "*Thunder,*" the third apparition appears, speaks, and "*descends.*"

Still another example, from *The Roman Actor*, V. i, occurs during a study scene representing the private room where Caesar kept his magic statue of Minerva.

Caes. Bring my couch there   *Enter with couch.*
  A sudaine but a secure drousinesse
  Inuites me to repose my selfe. Let Musicke
  With some choyse dittie second it. I the meane time
  Rest there deare booke, which open'd when I wake
                Layes the booke under his Pillow

Shall make some sleepe for ever.
        The Musicke and song.
                                        Caesar sleepes.
        Enter Parthenius and Domitia.

The two silently cross the room, withdraw the book from under Caesar's pillow, and leave; then:

A dreadfull Musicke sounding, enter [the Ghosts of] *Junius Rusticus, and Palphurius Sura, with bloudie swords, they waue them ouer his head. Caesar in his sleepe troubled, seemes to pray to the Image, they scornefully take it away.*

(Junius Rusticus and Palphurius were executed at Caesar's orders earlier in the play.) It is to be assumed, I believe, that the two Ghosts rose through the trap in the study floor and left, carrying the statue, by the same means.

Related examples, in which the trap is used as the entrance to an underground vault or passage (not connected with Hell), differ in one vital respect from those just given. No thunder or music accompanies the opening of the trap. In *A Larum for London*, a Globe play of 1600, following line 1300, Van End has entered an Antwerp burgher's house and threatened the Wife with death if she does not reveal where her money is hidden. Reluctantly she opens the trap-cover in the floor:

Wife. Within that vault lyes all my wretched wealth,
    My golde, my plate, my Iewels all are there.
Van. Then, there that heape of glorie lyes for me,
        Which is the way?
                                She pushes him downe.
Wife. That is the cursed way.

Three lines later a fellow townsman enters to ask what her outcry signifies. Told who is in the vault, he throws down stone after stone until Van End is dead.

In *The Fatal Contract*, IV. iii (a study scene), during a conference between Landry and the Queen, the text reads:

Enter Clovis from under the Stage with his Fathers Gown and Robes on.
Qu. What noise is this? guard me divinitie . . .

A few lines later:

> *Enter Lamont at* [i.e. through] *the trapdoor.*

And in a Blackfriars play of 1634, *Love and Honour*, III. iv, the "cave" under the floor is used twice, and is "locked" after each descent.

> [Alvaro] *Descends the cave.*
>
> *Evandra.* Lock safe the door, Melora, with this Key.
> *Prospero.* What's your design? mean you t'imprison him?

Later in the same scene:

> *Prospero takes from behind the arras a bottle and bag.*
> *They open the cave...* [He] *Descends the cave.*
>
> *Evan.* Once more, Melora, lock the door. Now they
> Are both secure.

Additional scenes in which ghosts rise from below [58] or in which the floor trap is used as the mouth of an underground vault [59] or as a passage leading to some subterranean part of a castle or city [60] are listed in the notes.

Additional facts about the nature and operation of the study floor trap emerge from an examination of other scenes.

(1) No signal was needed when the trap could be made ready (as in *Hamlet*, V. i) before a study scene was dis-

---

[58] *Adrasta*, G1; *Alphonsus of Aragon*, lines 951 and 1027; *Antonio's Revenge*, line 1009; *The Atheist's Tragedy*, II. vi; *Bussy D'Ambois*, V. iii and iv; *Caesar's Revenge, passim*; *The Devil is an Ass*, V. iv; *Dr. Faustus, passim*; *Four Plays in One*, III; *Lady Alimony*, III. vi; *Locrine*, lines 1620 and 1990; *The Lost Lady*, IV. i; *Macbeth*, III. iv; *Mercurius Britanicus*, II. i; *1 Richard II* (*Thomas of Woodstock*), line 2439; *The Valiant Scot*, V; *The Vow-Breaker*, IV. ii; *The White Devil*, IV. i; *The Witch of Edmonton*, IV. ii.

[59] Used as a vault: *The Arcadia*, E4; *Bussy D'Ambois*, V. i; *The Hog hath lost his Pearl*, IV; *The Martyr'd Souldier*, V. i; *The Pilgrim*, V. iii; *The Revenge of Bussy D'Ambois*, V. iii. Used as a dungeon: *Antonio's Revenge*, line 844; *Lust's Dominion*, I. i.

[60] *Aglaura*, III. ii; *Bussy D'Ambois*, V. iv.

closed. During the course of a study scene an actor opening the trap-cover from above (examples: *Sophonisba*, V. i;
Lust's Dominion, I. i; *Love and Honour*, III. iv) took his
cue from the dialogue. An actor opening it from below
(examples: *Bussy D'Ambois*, V. iv; *The Bloody Banquet*,
sig. F4; *The Fatal Contract*, IV. iii) perhaps took his cue
similarly (see *The Martyr'd Souldier*, V. i) or followed a
signal given off stage by the prompter.

(2) The absence of disguise sounds accompanying the
normal use of the study trap points to the absence of an
operating mechanism. Action involving persons falling
into a pit (examples: *Titus Andronicus*, II. iii; *The Hog
Hath Lost His Pearl*, V. i) or ghosts rising into a room or
tent (examples: *Richard III*, V. iii; *The White Devil*, IV. i;
Macbeth, III. iv) was therefore unexpected and sometimes
startling. Sounds incidental to the trap entry of an apparition are so slight as not to rouse a sleeper (examples:
1 Richard II, lines 2439 ff.; *Cymbeline*, V. iv; *The Vow-
Breaker*, IV. ii; *The Arcadia*, sig. E4) or even to attract the
attention of some person having his back turned (examples:
Julius Caesar, IV. iii; *Adrasta*, sig. G2 verso). It follows,
therefore, that the study trap could be used silently.

(3) Scale drawings and section plans of the Globe show
that the down-stage position of the platform trap made it
impossible to screen the lowering of the trap from spectators in the upper galleries. Customarily, therefore, the
trap was closed (that is, returned to stage level) as soon as
possible. In no scene, so far as I am aware, does it remain
open as long as a minute. The up-stage position of the
study floor trap, on the other hand, prevented spectators
from seeing more than a negligible distance into the opening when the cover was opened. Because of this fact, the
study trap could, if desired, remain open indefinitely, and
hence allow a wider range of stage business. Furthermore,
its position in a curtained stage meant that well-heads,
windlasses, altars, magic rocks, gratings, and other proper-

ties could be set up over the trap opening in advance of "discovered" scenes, thus adding still further to the range of trap scenes.

(4) When two or more actors emerge or descend through the study trap, they pass, as a rule, in single file (examples: *Bussy D'Ambois*, V. i; *The Revenge of Bussy D'Ambois*, V. iii; *The Pilgrim*, V. iii) or else one at a time with an interval between (examples: *Sophonisba*, III. i; *Richard III*, V. iii; *Macbeth*, IV. i; *The Devil's Charter*, sig. F4; *The Valiant Scot*, V). For such scenes a ladder or a removable flight of steps leading up from the cellar to the stage level was doubtless available. In other types of scenes, where actors fall or are dropped into a pit, the steps must have been removed and some means provided to break the actor's fall. In still other types of scenes, where actors stand waist-deep in the trap, as to dig a grave or to fight in it, a platform as large at least as the trap opening and raised to within 2 or 3 feet of the floor level probably was used.

Still other conclusions can be drawn from the examples cited.

The trapdoor could be opened either from above (*A Larum for London*, line 1307) or from below (*Richard III*, V. iii). Probably it was hinged, and swung upwards [61] to rest flat on the floor (a "false trap," i.e. one swinging downwards, would have been highly dangerous [62] and would have been hard to close from above [63]). The opening must have measured at least 2 by 6 feet, for large objects of rather inflexible nature, such as a coffin, or a trunk containing a live girl, were lowered through it. And it may have been possible to open merely a section of the trap-

[61] For a contemporary illustration of a hinged trap-cover with steps leading down see "The Suckling Faction," 1641, reproduced by Hotson, *Commonwealth and Restoration Stage*, facing p. 10.

[62] Cf. *The Witch*, V. iii.

[63] For explicit directions for closing the trap from above see *Sophonisba*, III. i.

door (a few scenes appear to require a hole merely large enough for a bag of gold or a dipper of water).

It is now evident that study trap-work conforms to a pattern of operation quite unlike platform trap-work. The chief differences are set out below.

The Platform Trap	*The Study Trap*
1. Normally required an audible signal given by some actor.	1. Usually functioned without a signal.
2. Normally (perhaps invariably?) was accompanied by loud music or thunder to drown out the noise of the trap mechanism.	2. Often was unaccompanied by sounds of any sort.
3. Normally was closed directly after opening. (Action at this trap was limited to the raising or lowering of actors and properties.)	3. Could remain open indefinitely. (Action at this trap was greatly varied, and was enhanced by a number of properties placed over the trap. Evidently considerable apparatus also was available in the cellar below for use in conjunction with the trap.)
4. Could lift or lower by sub-stage machinery as many as eight actors or a combination of actors and properties.	4. Normally entered by one actor at a time. Objects are tossed into or lowered through the trap by actors in the study. Inanimate objects seldom, if ever, rise through the trap.

For convenience and visibility, the study trap must have been constructed near the middle of the study floor and with its long axis running from side to side; but whether precisely in the middle or a foot or two forward of the middle, the plays do not make clear. If the trapdoor were placed somewhat forward near the front curtains, trap scenes would gain in visibility and at the same time would interfere less with the normal position of study properties.

11. Rushes on the Study Floor

Although, as noted in an earlier chapter, the floor of the outer stage was not everywhere covered with rushes, the floors of both the lower and upper inner stages normally were. The practical reasons for this imitation of the then standard domestic practice may have been to safeguard actors and their costumes and to minimize sounds incidental to changing rear-stage settings. Study scenes from every playhouse and from almost every year contain references to a carpet of rushes. Representative quotations follow. From *1 Henry IV*, III. i:

Glendower. She bids you on the wanton rushes lay you down.

From *Every Man out of his Humour*, line 2529:

Fastidious. Fore God (sweet Ladie) beleeue it,
   I doe honour the meanest rush in this chamber for your loue.

In *The White Devil*, II. ii, a dumb show (in the study) enacts the murder of Camillo, who, during a supposedly friendly game of "vaulting," is overpowered and has his neck broken. Later (III. ii) we read:

Francisco.   What a prodigy was't
   That from some two yardes height a slender man
   Should break his necke!
Monticelso. I' th' rushes.

From *The Duchess of Malfi*, V. v:

Cardinall. Looke to my brother:
   He gave us these large wounds, as we were strugling
   Here i' th' rushes.

In *The Cunning Lovers*, IV, Mantua pretends that he has lost a ring while at the banquet:

Prospero. Lights for the Lords, t'was dropt sure by the way.
   Helpe him to seeke it.
Julio. Look well there in the Rushes.

References to rush matting in place of strewn rushes appear at intervals after 1607, much as they do with respect to the platform, but never, it appears, did the braided completely supplant the loose form, even in plays written in the second decade of Charles's reign. On the other hand, a few references to cloth carpets spread out on the rear-stage floor begin to appear after 1601. These carpets, probably small, were usually laid down to honor a special guest. Typical references follow. From Heywood's *Royal King*: [64]

Bawd. If my rugges be rub'd out with your toes, can they be repair'd without money?

From *The Tragedy of Hoffman*, sig. H1 verso:

Martha. Spread me a Carpet on the humble earth:
My hand shall be the pillow to my head.

From *The Gentleman Usher*, II. i, an inner-stage scene:

Enter Bassiolo with Servants, with rushes and a carpet...
Bas. Come, strew this room afresh; spread here this carpet;
Nay, quickly, man, I pray thee; this way, fool;
Lay me it smooth, and even; look if he will!
This way a little more; a little there...
Look, how he strows here, too . . . lay me 'em thus;
In fine smooth threaves; look you, sir, thus, in threaves,
Perhaps some tender lady will squat here,
And if some standing rush should chance to prick her,
She'd squeak.

From *Byron's Conspiracy*, I. ii:

Enter Picoté, with two others, spreading a carpet.
Pic. Spread here this history of Catiline,
That earth may seem to bring forth Roman spirits
Even to his genial feet . . .
Byron. They hide the earth from me with coverings rich.

And from Nabbes's *Hannibal and Scipio*, II. iv:

Syphax. Cover the pavement which her steps must hallow
With Persian Tapestry.

[64] *Dramatic Works*, ed. Pearson, vi. 48.

Additional references to rushes, rush matting, and carpets are listed in the notes.[65]

12. The Study Ceiling Trap

On the basis of the final scene in Marlowe's *Jew of Malta*, a Rose play of 1594, Victor E. Albright in 1909 postulated a trapdoor in the "gallery" at the rear of the outer stage.[66] His conjecture, though hitting close to the mark, has been dismissed by subsequent writers on the Elizabethan stage for the reason that they have been unable to find similar instances in other plays. There are, however, at least thirty plays written between 1599 and 1639 which make use of a trapdoor in the study ceiling, and these plays are drawn from every playhouse, public and private, of that period. *The Jew of Malta* happens merely to be an early example. There the stage business runs as follows: "*Enter* [Barabas] *with a Hammar aboue very busie.*" Barabas is arranging a death-trap for Calymath, and describes his handiwork as "a dainty gallery, the floore whereof, this Cable being cut, Doth fall asunder." Owing to a deliberately arranged premature cutting of the cable, Barabas falls a victim of his own ingenuity:

A charge, the cable cut, a Cauldon [in the study] *discovered* [into which Barabas has fallen].

Obviously it was not feasible to show Barabas's actual fall from the upper stage into the supposedly boiling water of

[65] (The examples listed in this note are drawn from both inner stages.) For loose rushes see *Arden of Feversham*, V. i; *Blurt Master Constable*, V. ii; *The Chaste Maid in Cheapside*, III. i; *Cymbeline*, II. ii; *An Humourous Day's Mirth*, viii; *The Just Italian*, II. i; *The Martyr'd Souldier*, III. iv; *The Merry Devil of Edmonton*, I. i; *The New Inn*, III. ii; *Valentinian*, II. iii; *The Widow's Tears*, III. ii; *Women Beware Women*, III. iii; etc. For braided rush matting see *The Atheist's Tragedy*, I. iv, and IV. v; *The Broken Heart*, III. ii; *The Fair Favorite*, III. ii; *Love's Sacrifice*, line 2305; *A Mad World, my Masters*, IV. iii; *No Wit, no Help*, III. i; *Orestes*, IV. vi; *The Scornful Lady*, II. i; *The Siege*, II. i; etc. For carpets see *The Bondman*, II. ii; *The White Devil*, III. ii; etc.

[66] *Shaksperean Stage*, p. 74.

the cauldron in the study, but the stage curtains could be opened directly following a commotion above to "discover" Barabas in the cauldron and shouting for help.

A comic parallel to this scene occurs in Middleton's *Blurt Master Constable*, a Paul's play of 1601-2. Imperia, long importuned by Lazarillo for a clandestine meeting, seemingly yields (III. iii) and gives him the key to her apartments (on the upper stage). But in an aside to her attendant, Simperina, she asks:

Is the Trap-doore readie?
Simp. Tis set sure.
Imp. So, so, so, I will bee rid of this broilde red Sprat.

Later (IV. ii):

Enter Lazarillo [above] *bareheaded in his shirt* . . .
Laz. Sweet beautie; Shee'll not come, Ile fall to sleepe,
And dreame of her, loue-dreames are nere too deepe.
Falles downe [i.e. lies down and falls through a trapdoor.
Enter], *Frisco aboue laughing.*
Fris. Ha, ha, ha! . . .
Enter Imperia aboue.
Imp. Is he downe *Frisco?*
Fris. Hee's downe, he cryes out he's in hell, it's heauen to me to haue him say so.

In this scene, it will be noticed, no attempt is made to show Lazarillo in the study after his fall.

In another Paul's play of the same period, *Antonio's Revenge*, the ceiling trap was used in a different way. Antonio is shown, at midnight, in St. Mark's Church before the tomb of his father, Andrugio. Following an enlightening talk with his father's ghost, he contemplates revenge upon Piero, the man who had murdered his father, his friend Feliche, and his father's page. The quarto, beginning at line 1104, reads as follows:

Ant. All hell-straid iuyce is powred to his vaines,
Making him drunke with fuming surquedries,

Contempt of heauen, vntam'd arrogance,
Lust, state, pride, murder.

And. Murder.
Fel. Murder.   } *From aboue and beneath.*
Pa. Murder.

Ant. I, I will murder: graues and ghosts
Fright me no more, Ile suck red vengeance
Out of *Pieros* wounds.   *Piero's* wounds.

The repeated words "Piero's wounds," I take it, were echoed by the same three ghosts who, placed "aboue and beneath" the study, had echoed the word "Murder." Be that as it may, the presence of a trapdoor in the ceiling suggests how the particular ghost stationed "aboue" could most effectively have projected his voice into the stage below.

A third example from a play written for Paul's occurs in *The Faery Pastoral,* IV. v. Fancia lies down on the ground and pillows her head upon a "bank" of flowers. She recites a charm. The stage-direction then reads:

She had no sooner executed the whole praecept many tymes as might suffice, but a Scrolle fell into her lap from above.

The presence of a standard property, the familiar "moss-bank" of other plays, indicates a discovered scene. The scroll, therefore, probably fell through the ceiling trap.

Additional examples from plays written for private theatres by Middleton, Chapman, and Heywood are listed in the notes.[67]

Stage business in Heywood's spectacular Red Bull play, *The Brazen Age,* appears to require a ceiling trap. At the close of Act I occurs a lavish dumb show interpreted by the play's presenter, Homer. After relating undramatized episodes in the life of Hercules, Homer concludes:

[67] *The Family of Love,* III. vi, Whitefriars; *Michaelmas Term,* II. iii, Paul's; *The Revenge of Bussy D'Ambois,* V. v, Whitefriars; and *Your Five Gallants,* V. i, Blackfriars.

Now we the Ægyptian tyrant must present,
Bloudy Busiris, a king fell and rude,
One that in murder plac't his sole content,
With whose sad death our first Act we conclude.

He then opens the stage curtains and discloses an Egyptian temple:

Enter Busyris with his Guard and Priests to sacrifice; to them two strangers, Busyris takes them and kils them vpon the Altar; enter Hercules disguis'd, Busyris sends his Guard to apprehend him, Hercules discouering himselfe beates the Guard, kils Busyris, and sacrificeth him vpon the Altar, at which there fals a shower of raine, the Priests offer Hercules the Crowne of Ægypt which he refuseth.

It is hard to see how the shower of rain could be managed without the use of the ceiling trap. Similar stage business — with a variant in the stage-direction that may throw light on the Heywood scene — occurs in a later play, *The Royal Slave*, V. iii: "*The Temple again discover'd, an Altar, and one busie placing fire thereon . . . a Showre of raine dashing out the fire.*" [68]

The following scenes show how the ceiling trap was used in plays produced by the King's Men both before and after the fire which destroyed the first Globe.

From *The Captain* (first acted 1609–1612), IV. iv. Angelo has come to the home of Lelia ("a cunning wanton Widow"), bribed the Maid, and been admitted secretly to an upper room ("*Enter Angelo above*") from which he is able "undiscerned" to hear and observe Lelia in the room below. Meanwhile Lelia's father, disguised so as to be unrecognized by her, has arrived at the house door, which he found open, and entered. He finds servants laying out a supper for two in a lower room (the study). Lelia enters the room and at once offers herself to him —

    My treasure, body, and my soul
Are your's to be dispos'd of.

[68] For yet another example, see Heywood's *Wise-Woman of Hogsdon*, V, acted at the Red Bull.

Fa. Umh, umh. —   *Makes signs of his white head & [b]eard.*

Lel. You are old,
  Is that your meaning? why, you are to me
  The greater novelty . . . this day I did refuse
  A paire of 'em, *Julio* and *Angelo*,
  And told them they were as they were
  Raw fools and whelps.   *Ang. makes discontented signs.*

Maid. Pray God he [i.e. Angelo] speak not.
                    Maid laies her finger cross her mouth to him.

Lel. Why speak you not sweet sir?

Fath. Umh. —   *Stops his ears, shews he is troubled with the Musick.*

Lel. Peace there, that musique, now Sir speak
  To me.

Fath. Umh. —   *Points at the Maid.*

Lel. Why? would you have her gone? . . .

Fath. Umh. —   *Points at her again.*

Lel. Be gone then, since he needs will have it so,
  'Tis all one.
          Exit Maid [to upper stage]. *Fath. locks the* [study] *door.*

Once they are alone (except for Angelo watching them
from the room above) the Father reveals himself, spurns
her advances, and threatens to kill her.

Fath. The doors are fast, thou shalt not say a Prayer,
  'Tis not Heavens will thou shouldst; when this is done
  I'll kill my self, that never man may tell me
  I got thee.
          Father draws his sword, Angelo [above] *discovers himself.*

Lel. [an error for "Nell," the Maid, now above at the trap with Angelo].
  I pray you, Sir, help her, for Heavens sake, Sir.

Ang. Hold, Reverend Sir, for honour of your Age.

Fath. Who's that?

Ang. For safety of your Soul, and of the Soul
  Of that too-wicked woman yet to dye.

Fath. What art thou? and how cam'st thou to that place?

Ang. I am a man so strangely hither come,
  That I have broke an Oath in speaking this . . .
  And I desire your patience: let me in,
  And I protest I will not hinder you

In any act you wish, more than by word,
If so I can perswade you, that I will not
Use violence, I'll throw my Sword down to you;
This house holds none but I, only a Maid
Whom I will lock fast in as I come down.

Fath. I do not know thee, but thy tongue doth seem
To be acquainted with the truth so well,
That I will let thee in; throw down thy Sword.

Ang. There 'tis.   [Exit Angelo above.]

Lel. [aside]. How came he there? I am betray'd to shame,
The fear of sudden death struck me all over
So violently, that I scarce have breath

                             He lets in Angelo, and locks the Door.
To speak yet.

In elaboration of detail this scene is the most remarkable
of its kind in the Elizabethan drama. I call attention (1)
to the Maid's ability to signal through the ceiling aperture
to Angelo above, (2) to the locking of the study door after
she has been dismissed, (3) to Angelo's "discovering" his
presence above to those in the locked room below, (4) to
his dropping his sword through the trap as evidence of
his good faith — for corroboration, see the rest of the
scene, and (5) to the three-line aside spoken by Lelia while
Angelo descends from the room above and is let in by the
Father, who then relocks the study door.[69]

[69] It will perhaps be urged that to stage this scene from *The Captain* it was
only necessary for the action in the study to flow forward to the platform and
for Angelo, "above," to station himself on the tarras or in a window-stage. In
either of these places he could observe the business below, catch the maid's
signal, and later throw down his sword. But such an interpretation is open to a
number of objections, among them:

(1) If Angelo was on the tarras or in a window-stage, then the scene below
with all its business — business which specifies a table, chairs, and a banquet
and which involves sitting down, filling glasses with wine, toasting, etc. — must
have taken place on the platform well forward of the scenic wall. But this
hypothesis must be rejected, for when the scene opened the platform represented
not a private room but the street fronting Lelia's house upon which first Angelo
and later the Father entered on their way to her door.

(2) If Angelo looked down from the tarras or from a window-stage to observe
the business below on the platform, he would have been very conspicuous

The majority of ceiling-trap scenes follow a simpler routine. During the course of a study scene one of the characters present draws another aside and suggests spying on the scene from above. Their departure from the study is then marked by a brief stage-direction. A few lines later they "*enter above.*" From time to time thereafter they comment from above on events or dialogue below (as a rule their words are treated as if inaudible in the study). Usually those above descend and "*enter below*" before the scene closes. The following Globe and Blackfriars plays illustrate this procedure. In *Bonduca* (acted in 1613), II. iii, five captured starving Roman soldiers have been brought to General Caratach's headquarters. Instead of executing them as they all expect him to do, he orders food brought for them. Queen Bonduca's two daughters, also present, wish to see the starving men eat without themselves being seen:

2. Daugh. Let's up and view his entertainment of ['em].
I am glad they are shifted anyway, their tongues else
Would have murdred us.

1. Daugh. Let's up and see it.   *Exeunt*
         Enter Hengo [to the study].

(recall that he "discovers" himself after being joined there by the Maid). On the tarras, indeed, he would have been quite as visible to Lelia and her Father as they were to him. But this conclusion clearly violates the implications of the text.

(3) Had Angelo stood farther back from the tarras railing, that is, in the upper inner stage behind the curtain line, then he could not have seen those below until they had moved forward to the outer half of the platform. But this is simply an illustration of a principle observed in hundreds of Elizabethan plays, namely, that action in the chamber is rarely if ever related to action on the platform.

(4) After the Maid has been dismissed below, Lelia's father "locks the door" to keep his daughter in the room and to keep all other persons out. In a study scene this business would be familiar to the audience and theatrically convincing. But in an outer-stage, or a combined-stage (the platform and the study) scene, locking only one of the three conspicuous doors would be thoroughly unconvincing.

Car. Sit down poor knaves: why where's this Wine and Victuals?
   Who waits there?
Swet. within. Sir, 'tis coming. . .

Forty-odd lines later the princesses appear on the upper
stage.

                                          Daughters above.

Car. Well said.
1. Daugh. Here's a strange entertainment, how the thieves drink.
2. Daugh. Danger is dry, they look'd for colder liquor.
Car. Fill 'em more wine, give 'em full bowls . . .
Judas [the Roman corporal]. By this Wine,
   Which I will drink to Captain *Junius*,
   Who loves the Queens most excellent Majesties little daughter
   Most sweetly . . .

During the ensuing talk between Judas and Caratach the
princesses (above) hear that Junius, a Roman captain,
loves the younger of them. She writes a note to him, descends to the lower room, and gets a servant to slip it and
a coin into Judas's hand as he is leaving for the Roman
camp.

Again, in Massinger's *Bashful Lover* (acted in 1636),
V. iii. This scene opens in the study where Hortensio and
Beatrice are awaiting the arrival of Matilda. As Matilda
appears, Beatrice leaves:

Beat. She's come; there are others I must place to hear
   The conference.   *Aside and exit.*

Shortly after,

             Enter above Beatrice with Lorenzo, Gonzaga,
                    Uberti, and Farneze.

They listen attentively to the parley between Matilda and
Hortensio below, commenting once or twice in lowered
voices. Following a turn in the affairs below they break
off, leave the upper stage, and re-enter the study below ten
lines later.

Other scenes in which the ceiling trap is used are listed in the notes.[70]

From a study of these scenes as a whole little can be deduced as to the size or location of the ceiling trap. In no public playhouse after 1599, so far as I am aware, are objects larger than Angelo's sword dropped through the trap. On the other hand as many as six persons are able to stand about the trap and watch what takes place below, which suggests an opening of some size. That no actor undertakes to fall through the trap in sight of the audience is not surprising, for the drop to the floor below was 12 feet. Unlike platform and study floor traps connected with the cellar, the ceiling trap had no machinery regularly available below it. In short, the ways in which it could be turned to dramatic account were limited, and having, it would seem, no equivalent in the normal home, its use in the theatre was, in the sense of holding a mirror up to life, illogical. The late W. J. Lawrence was possibly correct in his conjecture that the ceiling trap was primarily intended for moving heavy properties from one level of the playhouse to another during the morning hours of preparation for the day's play.[71] This would imply that the ceiling trap was directly over the floor trap (which may still further help to explain why actors and heavy objects could not with impunity be required to fall through the trap) and that a trap in the ceiling of the upper stage, in line with the other two, opened to a windlass or a block and tackle in the stage superstructure.

Except for trap openings, the ceilings of the Globe inner

[70] The following plays are arranged in approximate order of production: *The Gentleman Usher*, V. i; *The Woman-Hater*, V. iii; *Four Plays in One*, III; *The Brazen Age*, IV; *The Second Maiden's Tragedy*, V. i; *The Duchess of Malfi*, V. v; *The Custom of the Country*, IV. i; *The Heir*, V. i; *The Virgin Martyr*, II. iii; *Love's Cure*, IV. ii; *The Renegado*, III. v; *The Roman Actor*, IV. ii; *The Great Duke of Florence*, II. iii; *The Picture*, IV. iv; *A Very Woman*, IV. ii; *Love's Sacrifice*, lines 675 ff. and 2345 ff.; *A New Trick to Cheat the Devil*, III, i and iii; *The Emperor of the East*, I. ii; *The Novella*, IV. ii; *The Rebellion*, V. iii.

[71] *Pre-Restoration Stage Studies*, p. 147.

stages were probably plastered. The builder's contract for the Fortune reads:

The said Peeter Streete shall not be chardged with ani manner of pay[ntin]ge in or aboute the saide fframe howse or Stadge . . . Nor seeling anie more or other roomes then the gentlemens roomes Twoe pennie roomes and Stadge before remembred.

Plaster ceilings, often ornate, were a feature of Elizabethan domestic architecture, as even the plays of the period bear witness. In Middleton's *Trick to Catch the Old One*, II. i, Lucre calls attention to the value of the house which his nephew will inherit as a marriage portion:

You see this house here, widow; this house and all comes to him; goodly rooms, ready furnished, ceiled with plaster of Paris, and all hung about with cloth of arras.

There is a more specific reference to the study ceiling in *The Puritan*, sig. G2:

Sir Godfrey. Oh, how if the divill should prove a knave and teare the hangings.
Captain. Fuh, I warrant you Sir Godfrey:
Edmond. I, Nuncle, or spit fire upp 'oth seeling!
Sir Godf. Very true too, for tis but thin playsterd, and twill quickly take hold a the laths . . . My Sister is very curious & dainty ore this Roome.

The Revenger's Tragedy, III. v, possibly alludes to the plaster ceiling in the Globe. During a rear-stage scene Hippolito asks,

Why what's the matter brother?
Vindicie. O tis able to make a man spring up & knock his for-head Against yon silvar seeling.

Where fact leaves off and poetic license begins in Iachimo's minute description of Imogen's bedroom (*Cymbeline*, II. iv) which he so pointedly examined only two scenes earlier —

The Roof o' th' Chamber
With golden Cherubins is fretted —

I leave to the reader's judgment.

Chapter VII

THE TIRING-HOUSE: STAIRS

A MULTIPLE stage on five levels requires stairs. The questions: How many stairways were there in the Globe? and Where were they placed? can be answered only by a systematic study of the plays of the period, for all other records disregard the topic.

As to the number of stairways leading from the ground level to the second level of the tiring-house, it is surely significant that no situation in any play written between 1560 and 1660 requires more than one flight.[1] Even in those scenes where a row of two-story houses is represented by the multiple stage — scenes in which two sets of stairs

---

[1] Dialogue in *The Lover's Melancholy* (acted in 1628), III. ii, and in *The Walks of Islington* (acted in 1641), I. i, seems to imply a back, as well as a front, stairway; but action in neither scene requires two stairways. Compare *The Wits*, IV:

Elder Palatine. Is he coming hither?

Engine. He's at the door! . . .

El. Pal. Then I'll be gone.

Eng. No, sir; he needs must meet you in
    Your passage down.

Again, from *Love's Cruelty*, III. iv. Bellamente learns that his wife's lover is with her in the bedroom above. He orders his servant:

> Come draw, take my sword, I will be double arm'd,
> I charge thee by thy duty, or thy life
> If that be more, stay you at the bottome of
> The staires, while I ascend their sinful chamber
> And if my Pistoll misse his treacherous heart
> He has no way to passe but on thy sword.

See also *Necromantes*, fol. 171, where Galanthis and Melanthis ascend to "*either end of the stage* [the tarras] *from within.*" The last two words of this stage-direction dispose of the implication of two stairways.

from one level to the other would be employed if available
— I can discover no evidence pointing to more than one
stairway. A highly complex scene of this type occurs in
the undivided *Two Lamentable Tragedies*, printed in 1601.
At least three houses, each with a street door, a shop below, and a room above, are called for; but only in the
middle house, Merry's dwelling, does action take place
which requires the use of stairs. Again, in the Globe play,
The Devil is an Ass, II. ii, two two-story houses are required, but in only one of them do actors move up and
down the stairs. In the other house actors remain during
the course of the scene on the level where they first appeared. This curious limitation can hardly be a coinci-
dence; it occurs time and again; and it is never evaded
(except, of course, by means of property scaling ladders
set against the tiring-house "walls," or of rope ladders let
down from a window). On two grounds, then, — the one
that if two sets of actors' stairs had existed, scenes in considerable number would have been devised to take advantage of that fact; and the other that during the course of
all house-row scenes, where two or more separate stairways
might logically be expected, dramatists consistently re-
strict to one house and to one stairway the visible circulation of actors from one level to the other — we are justified
in assuming that the tiring-house contained only one stairway connecting the first with the second floor.

Where was this stairway? It certainly was not, as some
have suggested, in front of or incorporated in the tiring-
house façade. The normal direction marking all but a very
few transfers from one level to the other is "Exit A," followed, a few lines later, by "Enter A" (or expanded equiv-
alents, such as "Exit A . . . Enter above A," or "A and B
descend . . . Re-enter A and B"[2]). The well-nigh count-

[2] These, with other interesting variants, occur in *The Distresses*, II. iii; *The
Family of Love*, I. i; *The Goblins*, V. v; *1 Henry VI*, V. iii; *The Island Princess*, V;
Lady Alimony, IV. vi; *The Novella*, IV. i; *The Obstinate Lady*, IV. iv; *The
Revenge of Bussy D'Ambois*, V. v; *The Royal Slave*, II. iv; *Sforza*, IV. v; *Titus*

less instances of these paired directions indicate a procedure so consistently followed and so stàndardized that
the exceedingly rare exceptions which omit the word "exit"
may reasonably be taken as mere variants in the phrasing
and treated accordingly. (But inasmuch as W. J. Lawrence based his theory of a staircase on the tiring-house
façade upon these exceptions, I list and discuss them in Appendix D.) The point I wish to stress here is that the
"Exit A . . . Enter A" formula denotes a complete disappearance from the stage and from the sight of the audience.[3] In other words, the actors' stairs were somewhere
off stage, behind the scenic wall.

A second fact emerges from an examination of all scenes
involving stairs, namely that *occasionally*, and *under certain circumstances*, a part of the actors' stairway was visible
to on-stage actors and to the audience. Scrutiny of the
dialogue of such scenes reveals that every time the stairs
are indicated by the phrase "those stairs," "yonder stairs,"
and the like, the speaker is at that moment in the study.
Examples follow (in each the use of properties, the context,
or the dialogue establishes beyond doubt that the scene is
a "discovery"). From *Look About You*, line 1577 (a tavern
scene):

John. Where is he?
Skink. Vp them stayres, take heede of him.
  He's in the Crowne. . .   *Exeunt.*

From *The Second Maiden's Tragedy*, line 953:

Andronicus, I. i; *The Twins*, V. ii; *The Unnatural Combat*, II. i; *The Woman-
Hater*, V.

  [3] It is hardly necessary to labor this point. The use of scaling-ladders and
rope-ladders to mount to the second level of the tiring-house façade would be
unconvincing if permanent stairs were available there. And in an outer-stage
scene in *The Maid in the Mill*, IV. ii, we are expressly informed that "here are
no stairs to rise by." No stairs appear in the four contemporary representations of the stage. The theory of visible stairs is rejected by Adams, Albright,
Chambers, and others.

Votarius. you should ha seene a fellow
A common bawdy howse ferrit one *Bellarius*
steale throughe this roome, his whoorish barren face
three quarters mufled, he is somewher hidd
about the howse sir

Anselmus. which waie tooke the villaine . . .
speake which waie took hee?

Vot. Marry my lord I thinck
let me see which waie wast now? vp yo'n staires

An. the waye to chambringe . . . harke?

Vo. tis his footinge certaine

An. are you chamberd?
ile fetch you from aloft.   *Exit Anselmus.*

From *Two Lamentable Tragedies*, sig. B4, a scene in Merry's
shop and the room above it:

Merry. Goe up those staires, your friends do stay above.
          [Beech goes up as directed; Merry lingers
              for a moment, picking up a hammer.]
Here is that friend shall shake you by the head,
And make you stagger ere he speake to you.
          *Then being in the upper Rome Merry strickes
              him in the head fifteene times.*
Now you are safe . . .
          Enter [to the shop] *Rachell and Harry Williams.*

Wil. Who was it *Rachell* that went up the staires?

Rach. It was my brother, and a little man
Of black complexion, but I know him not.

Wil. Why do you not then carry up a light,
But suffer them to tarry in the darke.

Rach. I had forgot, but I will beare one up.   *Exit up.*

Wil. Do so I prethee, he will chide anon.   *Exit.*

          Rachell [above] *speaketh to her brother.*

Further examples of dialogue implying a visible flight of
stairs are listed in the notes.[4]

4 *Brennoralt*, IV. i; *The Devil is an Ass*, II. iv; *The Dumb Knight*, V. i; *The
Lover's Melancholy*, III. ii; *A Trick to Catch the Old One*, III. iii; *The Walks of
Islington*, G1.

These well-defined interior scenes show that the stairs were near by and even visible upon occasion to actors in the study. The stairs were indicated by phrasing and perhaps an accompanying gesture which directed the attention of spectators to what they themselves as well as the actors could probably see, namely some part — perhaps the foot and a bit of hand-rail — of the stairway. Now as earlier chapters have shown, it was the habit of Elizabethan dramatists to accept the equipment of their stage rather literally and to refer to that equipment in dialogue. It was not the habit, I believe, to indicate some prosaic stage fixture which either did not exist or which lay outside the range of vision. Doors, door posts, wickets, stage posts, windows, "penthouses" (projections from the second level of the scenic wall) — all were actual parts of the visible scene, and all were made a part of the sphere of dramatic action and were referred to realistically. It seems reasonable, therefore, to suppose that allusions to "those stairs" had a foundation equally realistic.

But though some part of the stairway may have been visible both to actors on the inner stage and to the audience, it does not follow that the staircase was constructed inside the study, or that it opened directly into the study with merely the foot of the stairs showing.[5] Were it constructed in either of these ways, the direction "exit . . . enter" marking the movement of an actor from the study to the chamber directly above would be inappropriate inasmuch as he would be in view of some part of the audience all — or almost all — the time (note that no "exit . . . enter" is required when an actor passes from the platform through a stage door into the study). And there are other objections. Stairs constructed inside the study or even opening from the study would make all scenes in which privacy and security are obtained by locking the study door unconvincing. Furthermore, stairs visibly connecting an upper and a lower room would rule out

[5] Cf. Chambers, iii. 95.

scenes wherein the two rooms are treated as having no
means of communication. And finally, so long as the study
was discovered, all back-stage movement between floors by
actors, musicians, and stage-hands would have to cease;
only those legitimately in the study could use the stairs.
Such a limitation is inadmissible.

But if the stairs were not constructed inside the study
nor even based there (with the remainder of the flight off
stage behind a study wall), they were close at hand, as the
citations given above and those to follow make clear. In
The Devil is an Ass, II. i, Pug and Mrs. Fitzdottrel are in
a room on the ground floor of her house. He has been
urging upon her the suit of young Wittipol; but she will
not commit herself, if only because she suspects that her
husband is eavesdropping. To test her suspicions she suddenly calls out for Fitzdottrel. The husband enters at
once, causing her to remark ironically:

> You were not planted i' your hole to heare him,
> Upo' the stayrs? or here, behind the hangings?

Her remark implies that all three places were close at hand.
In *Valentinian* (a Globe play), II. iv, upper and lower
rooms connected by stairs are required. Lucina, accompanied by her waiting-women Claudia and Marcellina, has
come to the emperor's palace in search of her husband.
Upon entering the "great Chamber" (the combined platform and study), she is met by Chilax, who, forcing his
services as guide upon her, leads her towards the stairs
which mount to the rooms of the emperor's panders.

Luc. Will ye goe forward, since I must be man'd,
  Pray take your place.
Claud. Cannot ye man us too Sir? . . .
  If ye do Sir,
  Take heed ye stand to't.
Chil. Wondrous merry Ladies.
    Enter [in chamber above] *Licinius, and Proculus, Balbus.*
Luci. The wenches are dispos'd, pray keep your way Sir.
    Ex[eunt Lucina and her women led by Chilax].

Lici. She is coming up the stairs; Now the Musick;
 And as that stirs her, let's set on: perfumes there.
Pro. Discover all the Jewels.
Lici. Peace. *Musick.*
  [At this point the text offers a choice of two songs
      each of twenty lines.]
    Enter [above] *Chilax, Lucina, Claudia, and Marcellina.*
Luci. Pray Heaven my Lord be here, for now I fear it.

For all that a song was sung while Lucina is mounting the
stairs, the close connection of the lower room, the stairs
(on which she is seen or heard mounting by Licinius the
moment after she quits the lower room), and the upper
room is clear.

In the following citations we can discover, I believe, the
exact location of the stairs. From *Brennoralt* (a Globe and
Blackfriars play), III. iv, a study scene:

Bren. This was the entry, these the stairs.

This statement connects the stairs with an "entry," a term
yet current in England for a passageway containing stairs.
From *The Queen's Exchange*, III. i (the scene is an ante-
room of the palace):

Jeffrey. I hope you will further my suit to the King and so I'l wait
 his coming in at the back Stairs. *Exit.*

This remark, like many others,[6] seems to show that the
stairs were at the back of the tiring-house. Several scenes
establish a close connection between the stairway and the
rear doors of the lower and upper inner stages. From *The
Woman's Prize* (a Globe play), II, ii: Maria, in an upper
window facing the audience, is directing Livia, on the
street below (the outer stage) how to enter the house and
mount to the second floor.

  [6] See, for example, *Brennoralt*, III. iii; *The Distracted State*, IV; *Elvira*, I;
The Humorous Courtier, V. iii; *The Lover's Melancholy*, line 1348; and *The Lovers'
Progress*, III. i (in which the stairs are called the "garden stairs").

Maria. Meet at the low parlour door [i.e. the study door?] there lies a close way.

An association of the stairhead and the chamber door is found in scenes involving the upper stage. From *The Lover's Melancholy*, III. ii:

Kala. O speake little.
Walke vp these staires, and take this key, it opens
A Chamber doore.

From the belatedly printed first quarto of *Money is an Ass* (1668), page 30: Clutch, on the upper stage, wishes to descend to his sons below, but he finds that Calumny has locked him in:

Clutch. Open the door Calumny.

Cal. I cannot find the key sir.

Clutch. Not find the key, dainty fine tricks . . . break open the door, you Hell-hound.

Cal. I have found it now. . .   *Exit Clutch and Calumny.*

And eight lines later (the usual interval) Clutch enters below. From *2 Henry IV*, II. iv (an upper-stage scene):

Enter Drawer.

Draw. Sir, Ancient Pistoll is below, and would speake with you. . .

Hostesse. If hee swagger, let him not come here . . . shut the doore, I pray you. . .

Falstaffe. Do'st thou heare? it is mine Ancient. . .
Call him up (Drawer.)

In *The Princess*, IV. iii, friends who have been visiting Tullius in his bedroom upstairs decide to leave:

Captain. Come leave him, he is drunk.

Lieutenant. How now, what would'st you have?

Tullius. You'll give me leave to wait on my Captain down?

Capt. No Ceremony, good Tullius, no Ceremony.

Tull. It shall be yours Captain, indeed it shall be yours. . .

As they go away he rises out of his bed and reels after them to the door.

Exit Captain.

Further examples are listed in the notes.[7]

This intimate association of the stairs and the rear doors of both the lower and the upper inner stages is the clue to the exact position of the actors' stairs.

To sum up. Only one stairway to the upper stage existed in the tiring-house. Every time an actor goes from one floor to another his leaving the stage is noted as an "exit" and he disappears from the view of the audience. The stairs, therefore, were not on the front of the tiring-house façade but somewhere behind. Every time an actor points to the stairs he is found to be in the study or in the chamber above; hence the stairs were associated with the lower and upper inner stages and not with the outer stage. Yet the staircase was not constructed inside the study, nor did its foot rest within the study, for both inner stages could be isolated and made "secure" by shutting and bolting the door at the rear. On the other hand, the stairs are pointed at (which implies that they lay at the rear center and not at the sides of the study where the audience could not see them); they are described as "at the back" of the house, and as in or near "an entry"; and finally they are intimately associated with the rear doors of both the lower and the upper inner stages. Now as we have already seen, behind each of these inner stages lay a passageway approximately 5 feet wide. And the relationship of rear doors, passage, and stairway is so close that only one conclusion can be drawn, namely that a portion of the stairway was visible once an inner-stage door was fully opened, and that the stairway itself was constructed in the passageway at the rear of the study.[8]

[7] *The Captain*, IV. iv; *Four Plays in One* (*Beaumont and Fletcher*, ed. Glover and Waller, x. 347 ff.); *The Hector of Germany*, II. ii; *The Scornful Lady*, I; *The Walks of Islington*, I. i; *A Wife for a Month*, I. i.

[8] The conjectural designs of the Globe Playhouse made by Mr. G. T. Forrest (and reprinted in *The Site of the Globe Playhouse Southwark*, 1921, Appendix I, facing p. 40) show the tiring-house stairway enclosed in a shaft outside the rear wall of the playhouse, directly behind the passage at the back of the inner stage. Several objections appear to stand in the way of this interesting suggestion,

In addition to the evidence of the plays, there are other considerations which support the location here set forth. Placed in the passageway behind the study, a stairway would be more accessible from all points of the tiring-house than in any other available position. The two outer-stage doors would be approximately 15 feet from the foot of the stairs if an actor crossed the study, and some 25 feet away if he had to go round the study. Now experiments with a stop watch show that to cover such distances, climb a full flight of stairs, and then advance a few steps further demands between 12 and 15 seconds if taken at a normal walking pace. This is roughly the time required to recite some five or six lines of blank verse. Again, to leave the center of an assumed "study," pass through an open doorway, and mount stairs to a room overhead takes a little more than half that period, or approximately the time for speaking three or four lines of verse. These experiments corroborate the oft-repeated evidence of the plays.

Moreover, by being placed against an outside wall of the building, the stairs could be readily lighted: note the "convenient windowes and light[es] glazed to the . . . tyreing howse" mentioned in the Fortune contract.[9]

An allusion in *The Tragedy of Claudius Tiberius Nero* (line 1984) to "winding stayres" prompts a consideration as to whether the staircase was circular in shape. In this particular instance, however, the character Germanicus is describing an assault upon the "Keepe" of a castle, and one must therefore bear in mind that the playwright is using images appropriate to such an edifice; and that for structural and military reasons in stone construction "winding" (i.e. circular) stairs are the rule. From the

---

among them: (1) the contemporary views of London do not show a stairway shaft on the fully depicted *south* side of the building, (2) the clauses of the playhouse builder's contracts relating to stairs on the outside of the building occur in the paragraphs concerned with the auditorium, and not in the paragraphs concerned with the tiring-house.

9 *Henslowe Papers*, p. 6.

already demonstrated location and function of the tiring-house stairs we may assume that the flight was straight. When so placed against one of the passage walls (unquestionably the outer wall, that (1) the study doorway might be unobstructed, that (2) the first few steps could be seen through the doorway, and that (3) the study window and rear-curtained opening would not be blocked), the stairs had to mount, inside the passageway, from a point opposite the study door to a point opposite the upper-stage door 12 feet above. Only a straight flight would meet these conditions. Furthermore, such a stairway would be the most practical, inexpensive, and economical of space. Since the passage was approximately 5 feet wide,[10] the stairs must have been rather narrow. But, if space was at a premium, the stairs need not have been wider than a man's shoulders. I am aware of no situation in the Elizabethan drama (and I am not forgetting Falstaff's fondness for the upper room of the Boar's Head Tavern) which demands a stairway more than 2 feet wide. Other provision, as I have already suggested,[11] was probably made for moving bulky properties from one level of the tiring-house to another. And when several actors were called upon to pass from one floor to another, they could go rapidly enough in single file.

Inasmuch as the upper landing of a straight flight cannot be directly over the lower landing, the door opposite that landing in the upper stage could not have been directly over the door of the study below. It follows, therefore, that the door on the one level was to the left (balanced by a window on the right) and the door on the other level was to the right (balanced by a window on the left).[12]

[10] See above, p. 171.

[11] See above, p. 227.

[12] There is no sure way, so far as I know, to determine which level possessed the doorway on the right side and which the doorway on the left. The engraving on the title-page of the 1630 quarto of *Friar Bacon and Friar Bungay*, however, represents a study arranged for the famous brazen-head scene. The head stands upon a shelf of books, below which is placed a table covered with an overhanging cover. The collection of properties thus conceals the study doorway in which

The business of going to the door and calling up (or down) the stairway to someone on the other stage would appear entirely logical to the audience. Of this calling up there are several instances.[13] Other "business" involving the stairs occurs in many scenes, but is important to us more as showing how variously the stairs were brought into the range of dramatic interest than as adding to what we now know about the nature and location of the stairway.[14]

A second flight of stairs, wholly and invariably concealed from the audience, connected the second level of the tiring-house with the third-gallery music and property rooms, and still a third flight rose 9 feet more to the superstructure above. The location of these two stairways can only be guessed at, for inasmuch as actors, musicians, and stage-hands used them without being seen by the audience, the plays and other records furnish us with no data upon which to base a conclusion.

Two other short flights of stairs were needed in the tiring-house. One led from the stage door to the ground outside, a matter of some 2½ feet. (Perhaps the Globe, like the Rose Playhouse, had a little roofed porch sheltering these steps and the stage door.[15]) Another flight gave access to "hell" and served the unobtrusive going down of actors and stage-hands to make ready some trap scene or other subterranean activity.

---

stood the actor who uttered the brazen head's prophecies. This engraving, which probably reflects a period subsequent to 1600, shows the window on the left side. For hints in the plays themselves, see *Arden of Feversham*, II. ii, and *The Distracted State*, IV.

[13] See, for example, *The Coxcomb*, II. i; *The Little French Lawyer*, III. i; *The Merry Wives of Windsor*, IV. ii; and *Rule a Wife*, I. i.

[14] See, for example, *Albumazar*, III. ix; *Epicoene*, II. i; *A Mad World, my Masters*, IV. iii; *The Woman's Prize*, V. i; and *A Yorkshire Tragedy*, C3.

[15] *Henslowe's Diary*, i. 10.

Chapter VIII

THE TIRING-HOUSE: SECOND LEVEL

1. THE TARRAS

THE second level of the Globe tiring-house contained
four stages: a long narrow balcony stage in the middle,
projecting forward over the study opening; a curtained
inner stage behind the balcony and directly over the study;
and a flanking pair of window-stages over the outer-stage
doors. Of these four stages the balcony had been most
often used throughout the years 1576–1599. Its size and
disposition in the Globe will be more readily understood if
I summarize its history.

A useful and distinctive adjunct of the inn-yard stage
had been that section of railed gallery (galleries in Elizabethan inns encircled the yard as a means of access to upper rooms) which projected over the stage. Upon it actors
appeared as if upon the battlements of a castle or walled
city, or in the upper story of a house. When, therefore, in
1576 James Burbage designed the first permanent playhouse, he reproduced in the second level of his tiring-house
a section of open gallery. This gallery was fronted by a
balustrade or solid parapet; it probably was enclosed at
the back by curtains, for actors needed ready, unobtrusive
access to it from the rear (furthermore the dressing room
which lay behind it had to be screened from view). The
depth of this actors' gallery may have been as much as 5
or 6 feet; its width was probably that of the study opening
immediately below (a matter of 14–15 feet), for the gallery
was flanked at both ends by stage windows — all constructed in the flat scenic wall between corner posts of the
frame — precisely as the study was flanked by stage doors.

The actors' gallery in the earliest playhouses evidently
did not project noticeably beyond the scenic wall. Its
prototype in the inn-yard had not done so, and, before 1590,

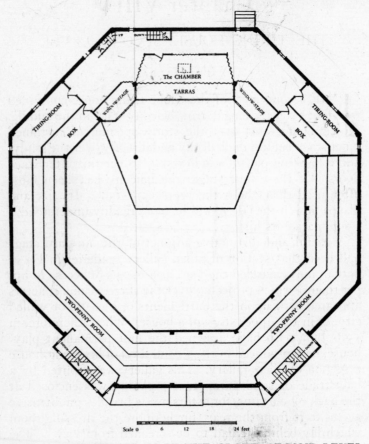

RECONSTRUCTED PLAN OF THE GLOBE: SECOND LEVEL

there was no curtained inner stage in the second floor of
the tiring-house which required the space occupied by the
gallery. (Many plays of the period 1576–1595 made no
demands upon the gallery, and on those occasions it was

available to privileged spectators—compare the figures seen over the stage in the De Witt drawing of the Swan.) After 1590, however, changes were gradually introduced in the second level; one observes, for example, that actors on the platform begin soon after that date to speak of hiding or taking shelter "beneath this tarras," or "under this penthouse," a fact which implies some fairly radical change in the originally flat scenic wall.

In the last decade of the sixteenth century the development of an upper curtained stage, inspired we may suspect by the success of the study, brought about several readjustments in the second-level arrangement of the tiring-house. In the Theater this second level probably had always been 10 inches deeper (as at the Fortune, according to its builder's contract) than the first, but even a depth of 13 feet 4 inches was not adequate for (1) a gallery at the front, (2) an inner stage in the middle, and (3) a passage-way at the rear having stairs leading up to it. In order to create a practicable inner stage and to bring that stage out towards the audience and the light, the permanent hangings formerly suspended as a rear wall to the gallery had to be moved a few feet back and a set of stage curtains, suspended on a rod, installed in the plane of the scenic wall.

This creation of an upper curtained stage meant that if the gallery was to be retained as a stage which could be used independently as in the past, it in turn had to be moved forward as an extension of the upper stage *in front* of the upper-stage curtains. In the wooden playhouses of the period such alterations were not difficult. (In the Rose Playhouse the addition of a projecting gallery may have been a detail in the extensive remodeling undertaken by Henslowe in the spring of 1592. The date and the materials paid for — notably the two dozen "turned ballyesters" [1]

---

[1] *Henslowe's Diary*, i. 8. It may be worth noting that Henslowe's entry affords an example of the word "baluster" earlier by several years than the first example given in the *N.E.D.*

— point in that direction.) There is reason to believe that a light balustrade was installed to guard the outer edge of the projecting gallery in place of the former heavy balustrade or solid parapet. (I shall return to this topic.)

Not yet familiar with the term "balcony" later to be introduced by travelers returning from Italy,[2] sixteenth- and early seventeenth-century dramatists referred to the projecting gallery as the "tarras."[3]

The scenes enacted on the tarras and the names by which it is called indicate that it must have extended for a considerable distance across the mid-section of the tiring-house façade, and have projected at least 3 feet from the scenic wall. The traditional and most frequent use of the tarras throughout the era was as a battlemented wall or tower upon which kings, knights, and warriors to the number of twelve or more appeared to parley with those on the outer stage below or to defend their stronghold from assault.[4] No doubt action there was essentially two-di-

[2] The first recorded instance in English print is dated 1618 (in the *N.E.D.*). Notice of the bearing of this fact upon the terminology of playhouse design was first taken by B. S. Allen, *PMLA*, XLVIII (Sept., 1933), 947.

[3] "*Tarras*." This is the spelling normally given in playhouse texts (the variants "tarrass," "tarrasse," "tarres," and "terrase" are in comparison rare). I shall adopt it in order to avoid the modern connotations of "terrace," namely "a raised walk in a garden, a level surface formed in front of a house on naturally sloping ground, &c." (The *N.E.D.*, giving 1703 as the first instance of "terrace" designating a "raised platform or balcony in a theatre," is thus a century out.) In Florio's *World of Words* (1598, p. 417) "*Terraccia*" is translated as meaning any one of the following: "a terrace, a leades, an open walke, a gallerie, a flat roofe, &c." Observe that the notion of a *projecting* balcony is not conveyed by any of the terms given.

[4] Representative scenes involving "walls" in plays before 1599: *David and Bethsabe*, line 222; *Edmund Ironside*, line 872; *Edward I*, line 900; *Edward III*, I. ii; *1, 2,* and *3 Henry VI, passim*; *King John*, IV. ii; *Selimus, passim*; in plays after 1599: *The Devil's Charter, passim*; *The Faithful Friends*, II. iii; *The False Favourite Disgraced*, V; *1 and 2 Iron Age, passim*; *The Jew's Tragedy*, lines 797 and 2732; *King John and Matilda*, I. iii, and V. i; *The Maid's Tragedy*, V; *The Seven Champions*, line 2758; *Timon of Athens*, V. iv; *The Turk*, line 1792; *The Vow-Breaker*, II. i.

mensional (the directions guiding some attacks tell of scaling ladders placed "at this end ... at that end ... and in the middle"), but even so, to provide for essential freedom of movement and to make possible a spirited struggle on the walls, the tarras had to have a depth of at least 3 feet. It cannot be that this depth was obtained by opening the curtains and extending the action to the forward portion of the inner stage. Long study of these problems has convinced me that once the curtains were opened the entire complexion of the upper stage changed and a very different set of principles governed the scene. Action on the tarras, for example, usually was directly related to action on the outer stage; action on the upper rear stage almost never. In no battlement scene of the entire era, so far as I am aware, is there a reference to the stage curtains or to any part of the inner stage behind the curtains. Rarely, if ever, does a scene begin on the tarras and continue, after the curtains are opened, as an upper-stage scene. In other words, there is no discernible difference between "on the walls" scenes written for a projecting tarras backed by a curtained inner stage above and those written for the earlier gallery backed by off-stage dressing rooms.

Length was desirable in the tarras in order to make room for a large group of actors. In many plays, notably the three parts of *Henry VI*, three or four leaders together with common soldiers enter on the tarras and do battle there with an attacking force below of similar size. No doubt the full resources of the company were engaged in such martial scenes, but it is impossible to be absolute about the numbers involved. In *Richard II*, III. iii, five principals are named:

Parle without, and answere within: then a Flourish. Enter on the Walls, Richard, Carlile, Aumerle, Scroop, Salisbury.

In Heywood's *Brazen Age*, IV. i, a clash on the walls involves nine principals and a number of mutes:

After an alarme, enter [below] *Hercules, Iason, Theseus, Telamon, and all the other Argonauts.*

They summon "th' ingrate *Laomedon* to parlee"; where-upon —

Enter vpon the wals, Laomedon, Anchises, Æneas, Priam, &c.

The parley is brief and fruitless:

Alarme. Telamon first mounts the walles, the rest after, Priam flyes, Laomedon is slaine by Hercules, Hesione taken.

Other types of scenes also suggest a tarras of some length. In the anonymous play *Claudius Tiberius Nero* (1607) four characters go off separately for meditation. Shortly after (sig. C4 verso) appears a direction relating to them:

Enter Caligula at one end of the stage, and Sejanus at the other end below. Julia at one end aloft, and Tiberius Nero at the other.

And all four, as if in complete isolation, speak in turn. Two or three observations are pertinent. Julia had announced her intention of seeking solitude in her "walking Gallerie." Here, as in other scenes referring to the tarras as a "walking gallery," [5] at least moderate length is implied. Again, the phrasing of the direction "at one end . . . at the other end" suggests that the two on the tarras above were approximately as far apart as the two on the lower stage, and normally the term "ends" was applied to the widely separated areas of the outer stage near the doors. Lastly, a tarras only 10 or 12 feet long would hardly convey the effect of wide separation — of actors out of earshot of each other — implied by the situation.

A minimum of 3 feet between the upper curtains and the tarras railing appears to be required not only in the

---

[5] See *Alphonsus of Germany*, IV. iii; *2 Henry VI*, IV. v; *Richard III*, III. viii; *Tiberius*, C3 verso. It is used as a "hill" in *Bonduca*, III. v; *The Hector of Germany*, D1; *Julius Caesar*, V. iii; *The Sea Voyage*, II. i. It is used as a "palace balcony" in *2 Henry VI*, IV. ix; *The White Devil*, IV. iii; etc.

types of scenes already discussed but also in yet another type wherein the tarras was used as a point of vantage from which to watch a lists, a masque, or a play-in-a-play.[6] Early instances, designed originally for the old-style gallery, are found in *Soliman and Perseda*, I. iii, in *The Spanish Tragedy*, IV. iii, and in *The Taming of the Shrew*, Induction. In the second of these plays "a chaire and a cushion" for the king are placed "in the gallerie" before his entrance there; in the third play the upper stage is for a time discovered, but as the play proper begins, Sly draws his "wife" forward to the tarras, and "The Presenters above . . . sit and marke" what follows.[7] Examples relating to the Globe tarras are readily found (the following are from plays in the Beaumont and Fletcher folios). In *The Maid's Tragedy*, I. i, the members of the Court assemble to see a masque; Melantius seeks a place for his Lady.

Enter Melantius and a Lady.

Diagoras. I hope your Lordship brings no troop with you, for if you do, I must return them.

Mel. None but this Lady Sir.

Diag. The Ladies are all plac'd above, save those that come in the Kings Troop, the best of *Rhodes* sit there [i.e. "above"], and there's room.

From *The Knight of Malta*, I. ii:

Zanthia. Hist, wenches: my Lady calls, she's entring
The Tarrase, to see the show. . .

Enter (above) Oriana, Zanthia, two Gentlewomen . . .

In the first of these two plays the number of spectators on the tarras is not given, though many are implied; in the second, four are listed and others suggested. In *The False One*, III. iv, ten are listed. (Ptolomy has arranged for a display of treasure, a masque, and a banquet with a view

[6] A dramatic device probably arising in the custom of renting the space to spectators when not required for the play.

[7] For further discussion see Chambers, iii. 93–94.

to diverting Caesar's attention from Cleopatra.) The scene opens with the direction:

Enter Caesar, Antony, Dolabella, Sceva, above.

At line 7 Cleopatra joins them:

Enter Cleopatra.
Ant. The young Queen comes: give room.
Caesar. Welcom (my dearest)
    Come bless my side.

At line 17, after all arrangements have been completed, Ptolomy, Achoreus, Achillas, Photinus, and Apollodorus enter to the tarras. The group "above" now numbers ten. Whether or not seats were used one cannot determine. Then at line 21 the first of the three spectacles, marked "*Treasure brought in*," is displayed in a procession crossing the outer stage below. The sight of such "matchless wealth" completely absorbs Caesar's attention. Cleopatra finds herself neglected; her efforts to draw Caesar's attention to herself meet with coolness. At line 42 the second spectacle appears:

Enter Isis, and three Labourers [below].

The masque, watched by all save an inattentive Caesar whose avaricious mind continues to dwell upon the treasure he has just seen, ends at line 112. Refusing the banquet, Caesar unceremoniously leaves the group, bringing the scene to an abrupt close.

Space for ten characters of exalted station implies a tarras of considerable length.

Other examples from Globe plays are listed in the notes.[8]

---

[8] *Love's Cure*, V. iii; *Pericles*, II. ii. Cf. the following from the Seventh Book of *Godfrey of Bulloigne*:

> The castell seem'd a stage with lights adorned
> On which men play some pompous tragedie;
>   Within a tarras sat on high the Queene,
>   And heard and saw, and kept herself vnseene.

As seen from the outer stage the projecting tarras resembled a feature common to many London housefronts, namely the "penthouse," a sloping, tiled ledge extending over shop fronts to protect the counters from the rain.[9] Several plays take this resemblance into account. In *The Merchant of Venice*, II. vi, Gratiano enters with Salarino, remarking:

> This is the penthouse under which *Lorenzo*
> Desired us to make a stand.[10]

From *Much Ado About Nothing*, III. iii:

Borachio. Stand thee close then under this penthouse, for it drissles raine, and I will, like a true drunkard, utter all to thee.

The tarras projected far enough to conceal actors standing under it on the lower stage from those on the upper stage (or at least to give the effect of such concealment). In *Every Man out of his Humour*, at line 1002, Sogliardo and others, in the street outside Puntarvolo's house, hear Puntarvolo approaching:

Sogliardo. List, list, they are coming from hunting: stand by, close vnder this Tarras, & you shall see it done better then I can shew it.   *A crie of hounds within.*

The bystanders are thereupon rewarded by a ludicrous scene first between Puntarvolo and a female servant and later between Puntarvolo and his wife — he stands in the street and the two women appear successively above in a window. The dialogue makes clear that Sogliardo and his companions are not visible to the women above.

From Chapman's *May Day*, III. iii, written in 1601 and acted at the Blackfriars:

---

[9] For details see the article by J. A. Gotch in *Shakespeare's England*, ii. 63. Penthouses appear in several plates of this work illustrating the London scene in the sixteenth century. Lawrence (*Physical Conditions*, p. 73) cites Cotgrave's *French-English Dictionary*: "*Soupendue*, a penthouse; iuttie or part of a building that iutteth beyond or leaneth over the rest."

[10] For a later but similar scene, see *Aglaura*, fol. 18a.

Enter Lodouico with a ladder of ropes,
[and] *Aurelio, (Æmilia aboue).*

Lod. Here's thy ladder, and ther's thy gallowes; thy Mistres is thy
hangman, and must take thee downe: This is the Tarrasse where thy
sweet heart tarries; what wouldst thou call it in Rime? . . . Stand
vp close, for she must not see you yet, though she know you are here.

Davenant's *Distresses* (acted in 1639[11]), II. ii, refers to a
common theme:

Enter Musicians.

1. Mu. This is the place. . . Stand all close beneath
The penthouse; there's a certain chamber-maid
From yond' casement, will dash us else. She was
Ever free of her wine.[12]

Such scenes as these imply that the tarras projected well
out from the scenic wall. On the other hand, London
penthouses of the period rarely are shown projecting more
than 2 or 3 feet, hence one is probably justified in assuming that the tarras did not much exceed 3 feet in depth.

Although the scenes reviewed in recent pages demonstrate that the tarras was of considerable length, they do
not furnish data that can be translated into terms of feet
and inches. The scenes now to be reviewed — scenes
which are from plays written after 1600 and which reveal
a means of entering the tarras through a side-casement in
one of the stage windows over the stage doors — make it
possible to determine the length of the Globe tarras with
some precision. In *May Day*, II, i, a preliminary dialogue
on the outer stage prepares the audience for a later tarras
scene.

Lodouico. Well Dame, leaue your superfluous nicety in earnest, and
within this houre I will bring him to this Tarrasse.

Æmilia. But good Cuze if you chance to see my chamber window open,
that is vpon the Tarrasse, doe not let him come in at it in any case.

Lod. Sblood how can he? can he come ouer the wall think'st?

[11] A. Harbage, *Annals of English Drama*, p. 112.
[12] See also *Greene's Tu Quoque*, F1 verso; *The Woman-Hater*, IV. ii.

Æm. O Sir, you men haue not deuices with ladders of ropes to scale such walles at your pleasure, and abuse vs poore wenches.

Lod. Now a plague of your simplicity, would you discourage him with prompting him? well Dame, Ile prouide for you.

After these broad hints it is easy for Lodovico to instruct Æmilia's lover how to gain access to her room. Act III, scene iii, opens with the direction: "*Enter* [below] *Lodouico with a ladder of ropes, Aurelio, (Æmilia aboue)*." At line 46 Lodovico tosses up one end of the ladder, bidding Æmilia "make the ladder as fast to the Tarrasse as thou wouldst be to *Aurelio.*" At line 103 Aurelio is coaxed up the ladder to the tarras, where, to Lodovico's dismay, he stands sputtering verses to his love. He is eventually persuaded to go with Æmilia from the exposed tarras through the casement into her private room.

In Jonson's *Devil is an Ass,* "Presented in the yeare 1616" at the Globe and Blackfriars, II. ii, Mrs. Fitzdottrel, interested in a gallant named Wittipol, sends Pug, her husband's new servant, to the young man with a message. She frames the message with care, for she suspects Pug of being hired solely to spy upon her.

Mrs. Fi. Bid him put off his hopes . . . I am no such foule,
Nor faire one, tell him, will be had with stalking.
And wish him to for-beare his acting to mee,
At the Gentlemans chamber-window in *Lincolnes Inne* there,
That opens to my gallery.

Wittipol, she imagines, will grasp the import of these words, and she is not mistaken. Act II, scene vi, opens with Wittipol and his friend Manly in the latter's "chamber-window." After a song by Manly, Wittipol, standing at the window "that opens to [Mrs. Fitzdottrel's] gallery," catches sight of her.

Wit. [to Manly]. Away, fall backe, she comes.
Man. I'll leaue you, Sir,
The Master of my chamber. I haue businesse.

Manly leaves. Mrs. Fitzdottrel enters the tarras ("gallery") and approaches Wittipol, who remains in Manly's room. The sense of certain lines in the dialogue which follows —

Wit. That since *Loue* hath the honour to approach
  These sister-swelling brests; and touch this soft
  And rosie hand . . .

together with a marginal note added by Jonson opposite these lines when, many years later, he prepared the text for the press, "He . . . playes with her paps, kisseth her hands, &c.," [13] shows conclusively that the ends of the Globe tarras extended as far as the window-stages in the flanking walls of the tiring-house.

A third illustration bears out this same relationship of tarras and stage window. It is found in the first act of Davenant's early Restoration play, *The Rivals*, written in 1663 for an Elizabethan-type stage and printed in 1668.

  *Enter Philander and Theocles, walking on the
  tarras in the citadel.*
Phil. The Provost does oblige us by permitting
  The freedom of this walk upon the tarras . . .
  Enter Celania and Leucippe as at a window.
Leu. This window, madam, looks into the tarras
  Where they are walking, you may overhear
  All their discourse, the [window] curtains being clos'd,
  Without discovery.[14]

Now a detailed discussion of the Globe window-stages will come later, but at this point I must anticipate a little.

---

[13] Two marginal notes appear in the 1631 Jonson folio opposite the passages quoted. The first, at line 38, reads: "This Scene is acted at two windo's, as out of two contiguous buildings." The second, at line 71: "He growes more familiar in his Courtship, playes with her paps, kisseth her hands, &c." These notes are literary (rather than stage-directions) and are designed to aid the reader who has not seen the play. Inasmuch as the first is contradicted by the text, which speaks of a "window . . . That opens to my gallery," not of "two windows," it must be disregarded in reconstructing the scene. The second note merely elaborates the text.

[14] See also *The Partial Law*, IV. iii; and *The Spanish Curate*, II. i.

In the early playhouses the upper-stage windows in the flat scenic wall appear to have been ordinary casements placed on either side of the actors' gallery and directly over the stage doors. In the Globe, however, the windows were moved, along with the stage doors, to the flanking walls. At the same time they were considerably enlarged and constructed in the form of bay-windows projecting well over the stage doors (and supported by the "door posts" discussed in an earlier chapter).

With these facts in mind we can now reconstruct the relationship of the projecting tarras and the projecting window-stages in a late playhouse of the Globe type. The tarras, which, from its accommodation of large numbers of actors, we know to have been long, evidently extended across the entire span between the corner posts, a distance of 24 feet, and the ends of the tarras were formed by the sides of the projecting bay-windows.

So far as I am aware there are no scenes other than the three just cited which unmistakably show that a casement in one of the bay-windows "opened" directly on the tarras. I emphasize the point here, for I shall refer to it when in the section on window-stages I undertake to show that the Globe bay-windows had casements facing three ways: towards the tarras, towards the middle of the yard, and towards the side galleries.

The plate on page 254 shows the evolution of the tarras and its relationship to other parts of the second level of the tiring-house as traced in the preceding pages.

One more detail before closing this section. Mention has already been made of a balustrade across the forward edge of the tarras. A guard-rail was imperative there to remind actors of the 12-foot drop to the platform below and to prevent their accidentally falling off. In the days of inn-yard performances when actors began to make use of a section of gallery over the stage to suggest a castle or a city wall, a balustraded railing across the outer edge — so contemporary inn-yard prints testify — was the

customary design. In early playhouses before the days
of inner stages on the second level of the tiring-house,

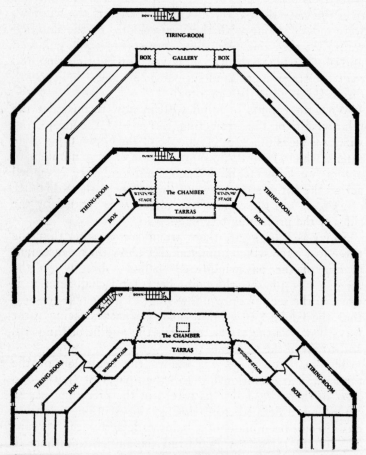

EVOLUTION OF THE TIRING–HOUSE: SECOND LEVEL
Theater (1576), Rose (1592–1595), and Globe (1599) plans compared

balustrades may have been replaced with a rail supported
by solid paling (such as that shown in the De Witt view
of the Swan in 1596, or that specified in the Fortune con-

tract as a "fence" for the first spectator-gallery). Solid paling across the front of the actors' gallery could be styled "yonder battlement" or "those walls" with more appropriateness than an open balustrade. It was also better fitted to withstand the rough and tumble assaults of mimic warfare.

But once the tarras became the forefront of a curtained inner stage the solid parapet had to be replaced by some other type of railing which would offer as little hindrance as possible to a view of the rear stage. We get a clue to this substitute, I believe, in the payment by Henslowe for "ij dozen turned ballysters" recorded in 1592 during the remodeling of the Rose playhouse.

The first appearance in English print of the word "balcony," according to the *Oxford English Dictionary*, occurred in 1618.[15] Within a few years playwrights took it up and applied it, reasonably enough, to the tarras. In Nabbe's *Covent Garden*,[16] I. iii, Mrs. Tongwell remarks:

How do you like the Belconee's? They set off a Ladies person well when she presents herselfe to the view of gazing passengers.

The word was still new a year or two later when Richard Brome wrote *Covent Garden Weeded* (Act I, scene i):

> *Enter Dorcas above upon a Bellconie. Gabriel* [below] *gazes at her. Dorcas is habited like a Curtizan of Venice.*

Croswill. Come Sir, what do you gape and shake the head at there? . . .

Gab. But truly I was looking at that Image; that painted idolatrous image yonder, as I take it.

Cockbrayne. O heresie! It is some Lady or Gentlewoman standing upon her Bellconey.

Belt. Her Bellconey? Where is it? I can spy from her foot to her face, yet I can see no Bellconey she has.

Cock. What a Knave's this: That's the Bellconey she stands on, that which jets out so on the forepart of the house; every house here has one of 'hem.

[15] See above, note 2.
[16] Written in 1632 (according to Harbage, *Annals of English Drama*, p. 104).

Belt. 'Tis very good; I like the jetting out of the forepart very well; it is a gallant fashion indeed.

This dialogue makes it abundantly clear that a tarras railing presented no obstacle to vision.[17] (Additional "balcony" allusions are listed in the notes.[18])

To sum up. The Globe tarras projected between 3 and 4 feet out from the scenic wall in front of the upper-stage curtains. It extended completely across the mid-section of the tiring-house, a distance of 24 feet, with its ends terminating in the side walls of the flanking bay-window stages. Casements in those side-walls opened to the tarras, so that an actor could pass through the casement from one stage to the other. Seen from below, the tarras was not unlike the "penthouse" of the normal sixteenth-century London shop. Actors standing under it were hidden (at least in theory) from the view of actors in the window-stages. Finally, a light railing supported by slender turned balusters marked its outer edge.

2. The Window-Stages

Second in the list of upper-level stage-units carried over to Burbage's Theater from the inn-yard stages of earlier years was a pair of stage "windows." These were apertures some 4 feet square (the width was that of the stage

---

[17] The notion of a heavy, closely-set balustrade in front of the upper stage has interfered with the perception of one or two modern scholars who have remained skeptical of the visibility of upper inner-stage scenes. But as the reader who has followed the quotations cited in chapters thus far can readily observe, such an opinion is untenable. The ability of Elizabethan carpenters to devise a waist-high guard-rail with balusters spaced 5 to 6 feet apart is illustrated by an engraving on the title-page of *Maroccus Extaticus or Bankes Bay Horse in a Trance*, 1595. Such a railing as that depicted would serve the needs of the playhouse and would cause no hindrance to a full view of the upper stage. For another illustration see *Shakespeare's England*, ii. 341, where an engraving from Turbervile's *Noble Arte of Venerie*, 1575, is reproduced.

[18] *Covent Garden*, I. v; and *Covent Garden Weeded*, III. i. For later scenes, see *Elvira* (1667), II; and *The Man's the Master* (1667), I. ii.

door below and its casing [19]) placed in the front of small stage boxes.

Directions and dialogue in plays written between 1576 and 1580 indicate that Burbage had from the outset placed his "windows" in the second level and had made the boxes behind them large enough to contain at least four actors.[20] These early boxes with their "windows" did not project (compare the De Witt view of the Swan) but were constructed inside the tiring-house with their openings forming part of the flat scenic wall.[21] I assume that they were no deeper than the adjoining gallery stage, for actors could be seen in them and spectators could view the play from them only if standing well forward.

Plays of the period 1580 to 1599 indicate a tendency to screen the window openings with lattice "casements" that could be opened and closed.[22] The casements were probably unglazed,[23] for glass would interfere with a view of the acting therein; moreover to Elizabethans the usual meaning of "window" was still what it had been to their forebears, namely a "wind-eye," that is "an opening in the wall or side of a building . . . to admit light or air, or both, and to afford a view of what is outside or inside." [24] Coincidental with the introduction of latticed and hinged

[19] See above, pp. 147, 170.

[20] *1 Promos and Cassandra*, II. ii.

[21] It may be doubted if Juliet's window, from which Romeo descended, was a bay-window projecting from the scenic wall. As originally staged the only projection was that shared by the entire second level, i.e. the "juttey forwards" of the playhouse frame.

[22] See, for example, *Fidele and Fortunio*, line 192; *1 Henry VI*, I. iv; and the following note.

[23] No early plays call attention to the presence of glass in the casements. On the other hand, references to grated stage boxes occur in Dekker's *Belman of London* (*Works*, ed. Grosart, iii. 80); Sir John Davies, *Epigrammes*, 1598 ("Rufus the Courtier"); *The Careless Shepherdess*, Induction; *Covent Garden*, I. i; etc. Other citations will be discussed later.

[24] *N.E.D.* Cf. "Your loop'd and windowed raggedness" (*King Lear*, III. iv); also Genesis 7: 11 and Judges 5: 28 (in the Authorized Version, 1611).

casements, the number of actors present at any one time in a window appears to shrink to one or two.[25]

The window-stages of the Globe differed in three important respects from the window-stages of the earlier theatres: they were "opposite" each other in the flanking side bays of the enlarged tiring-house; they were bay-windows, projecting some 3 feet out from the scenic wall; and they were considerably larger than their forerunners. These differences were radical, but possibly more radical in appearance than in effect upon the technique of staging window scenes. Many scenes written after 1599 could not, by reason of the large number of actors or of dependence upon some detail of construction, have been acted in the old-type window, but the majority are essentially indistinguishable from window scenes written for playhouses earlier than the Globe.

Stage-directions relating to window scenes in Globe plays often specify as well as imply that the windows were "above." The first three of the following quotations are representative of plays written before 1599; the remaining are from Globe plays written after. From *The Taming of the Shrew*, V. i:

Pedant lookes out of the window [and talks with Vincentio in the street below].

From the first quarto of *Romeo and Juliet*, III. v:

Enter Romeo and Juliet at the window [from which he later descends by the rope ladder].

From *Englishmen for my Money*, line 1998:

Anthony. I hear him at the Window, there he is.

                                                    Enter Pisaro above.

From *Othello*, I. i:

---

[25] I recall only one instance (*viz.* the brief appearance of the Nurse to warn Juliet in III. v), in plays of 1585–1599 in which more than two actors are shown in a window stage. For a general discussion of the use of windows in sixteenth-century plays see Chambers, iii. 58 ff.

[Enter] *Brabantio above, at a window.*

From *Catiline*, III. v:

Cicero appears at the window above.

From *Henry VIII*, V. ii:

Enter the King, and Buts, at a Windowe above.

From *The Duke of Milan*, II. i:

Marcelia appears at a Window above, in black.

Scholars who have studied the Elizabethan drama with a view to reconstructing the design of an Elizabethan stage have assumed that the windows were located directly over the stage doors.[26] I entirely agree with them, but would point out that, although many scenes imply a door surmounted by a window,[27] it is not easy to find texts or directions explicitly illustrating that relationship. However, there are a number of cogent reasons — the lack of space unaccounted for elsewhere in the second level of the scenic wall, the tendency of stage design to imitate contemporary London houses, the presence of windowed or latticed boxes over the proscenium doors of Restoration theatres, traditional stage design on the Continent before, during, and after the English era in question, and so forth — which corroborate the implications of Elizabethan plays. The cumulative force of the evidence establishes the location of the windows over the stage doors beyond a reasonable doubt. And since they were over the stage doors, the bay-windows were "opposite" each other in the flanking walls of the tiring-house.

Proof that the windows in the Globe were constructed

[26] E.g. Albright, *Shaksperean Stage* (1909), frontispiece; Lawrence, *Elizabethan Playhouse* (1913), ii. 37–38; Thorndike, *Shakespeare's Theater* (1916), pp. 133 ff.; Adams, *Life of William Shakespeare* (1923), plate facing p. 284; Chambers, *Elizabethan Stage* (1923), iii. 119.

[27] See, for example, *Catiline*, III. v; *The Chances*, IV and V; *Every Man out of his Humour*, lines 1010 ff.; *The Knave in Grain*, I. ii; *Monsieur Thomas*, III; and *The Wild Goose Chase*, V.

as bay-windows is to be found in a number of plays. In *Twelfth Night* (one of the first plays written by Shakespeare for his company's new playhouse) Malvolio is locked up while the madness is upon him (IV. ii):

Malvolio within.

Mal. Who cals there?

Clown. Sir *Topas* the Curate, who comes to visit *Malvolio* the Luna-
ticke. . . .

Mal. Sir *Topas*, never was man thus wronged, good sir Topas do not
thinke I am mad: they have layde mee heere in hideous darknesse.

Clo. Fye, thou dishonest sathan: . . . sayst thou that house is darke?

Mal. As hell sir *Topas*.

Clo. Why it hath bay Windowes transparant as baricadoes, . . . and
yet complainest thou of obstruction?

One would hesitate to build a case upon the Clown's jests were it not (1) that several other Globe plays refer by name to "bay-windows," and (2) that prison-cell scenes were as a rule represented on the upper level, either in one of the bay-windows or in the rear stage.

In *The Merry Devil of Edmonton* (a Globe play first pro-duced *circa* 1602), V. ii, Blague, host of the George Inn, de-fies a man who has come to his inn door:

D'yee see yon bay window? I serue the good duke of Norfolk, & tis
his lodging.

In *The Miseries of Enforced Marriage* (acted at the Globe in 1607), sig. G4, Ilford is above in a window overlooking the street hurriedly courting Scarborrow's sister:

Enter Wentloe, and Bartley beneath.

Bart. Here about is the house sure.

Wentlo. We cannot mistake it, for heres the signe of the Wolfe and the
Bay-window.

Enter Butler aboue.

But. Who so close? Tis well, I ha shifted away your Vncles Mistris,
but see the spight Sir Francis, if yon same couple of Smel-smockes,
Wentloe and Bartley, ha not sented after vs.[28]

[28] This and the preceding reference were first noted by Lawrence, ii. pp.
36–37. He was mistaken, however, in supposing that these two constitute "the

From Davenant's Globe and Blackfriars play, *Love and Honour*, IV. i:

Enter Frivolo, Tristan, Musitians and Boy.

Altesto. Come boy, lift up your voyce to yon bay window,
Sing the Song I gave you last night, and firke
Your fidles bravely too.

Now since there were bay-windows at the Globe, it follows according to the terms of the Fortune contract that there were bay-windows at the Fortune also. Moreover, one must assume that after 1609 there were bay-windows in the Globe Company's winter playhouse, the Blackfriars (see the citation last given and the stage history of the earlier Globe plays cited immediately before). In short, bay-windows became a standard feature of stage design after 1599 (and possibly earlier, but if so they left no trace), and it is to be expected that references and allusions to them can be found in the plays written for theatres other than the Globe. The following citations, therefore, are of interest. In Heywood's Cockpit play, *The English Traveller*, IV. i, Old Lionell has come to look at a house with a view to purchase:

Reignald [speaking of the owner]. Poore man, I pittie him;
H'ath not the heart to stay and see you come,
As 'twere, to take Possession; Looke that way Sir,
What goodly faire Baye windowes?

Old Lio. Wondrous stately.

From *The Antiquary*, II. i:

Aurelio. This is the window . . .   *Song above.*
                Enter Lucretia [in the window].

Luc. Cease your fool's note there! I am not in tune
To dance after your fiddle . . .   *Exit Lucretia.*
                Enter [below] *Lorenzo, Moccinigo, and Angelia.*

Lor. What are you, friend, and what's your business?

---

only evidence of the employment of bay-windows on the Pre-Restoration stage."

Aur. Whate'er it be, now 'tis dispatch'd.

Lor. This is rudeness.

Aur. The fitter for the place and persons then.

Lor. How's that?

Aur. You are a nest of savages, the house
  Is more inhospitable than the quick sands.
  Your daughter sits on that enchanted bay,
  A Siren like, to entice passengers,
  Who, viewing her through a false perspective,
  Neglect the better traffic of their life.

The presence of a bay-window with sides converging toward the front helps to explain the terms "enchanted bay" and "viewing her through a false perspective" employed by Aurelio. Again, from *The Parson's Wedding* (belatedly printed in 1663), I. iii:

> *Widow and Pleasant looking out at a window . . .*

Pleas. Your nephew, and his Governour, and his Friend! here will be a Scene, sit close, and we may know the secret of their hearts.

Wid. They have not met since they return'd; I shall love this bay window.

Four allusions which would seem to lack point on a stage unprovided with bay-windows are listed in the notes.[29]

Study of the Globe framework and of the history of the lords' rooms [30] leads one to suspect that each bay-window filled the entire 12-foot width of the bay from which it projected. While it is too much to assume that dramatic dialogues give us stage dimensions in feet and inches, it is as true for the bay-windows as for other constantly-used parts of the stage that a fairly clear notion of size is revealed by certain quotations. Reviewing these, I believe that modern writers on the Elizabethan playhouse have proposed stage windows of inadequate size. In the majority of scenes (and in all scenes between 1580 and 1599)

---

[29] *The Captives*, I. iii; *The Chaste Maid in Cheapside*, V. i; *Cupid's Whirligig*, D3; *Women Beware Women*, III. i; and perhaps also *The Doubtful Heir*, III; *Troilus and Cressida*, I. ii; and *1 Thomaso*, III. i.

[30] See above, pp. 21, 70–81.

only one or two actors appear in a window; and, of course, for them an aperture 3 or 4 feet wide would suffice. But for scenes in which a larger group appears at the casement so small an aperture would not serve. In plays written after 1599 the scenes which place four or more actors in a window-stage are relatively numerous. The following instances relate to the Globe windows. In *The Woman's Prize* (of 1604–06), II. vi, appears the direction:

> *All the Women above. Citizens and Country women.*

The context shows that they enter to a window. The implication of more than four persons is sustained in a contemporary MS. copy of the play [31] where the corresponding direction reads:

> *Enter above Maria, Bianca, a Citty Wife, a Country Wife, and 3 Women.*

Act IV, scene xv, of *Antony and Cleopatra*, it will be recalled, opens in the Monument with the direction:

> *Enter Cleopatra, and her Maides aloft, with Charmian & Iras.*

Almost at once Diomed enters below with news:

Diom. His death's upon him, but not dead.
  Looke out o' th other side your Monument,
  His Guard have brought him thither.
      Enter Anthony, and the Guard.
Cleo. O Sunne, . . . O *Antony, Antony, Antony*
  Helpe *Charmian*, helpe *Iras* helpe: helpe Friends
  Below, let's draw him hither. . . . come *Anthony*,
  Helpe me my women, we must draw thee up:
  Assist good Friends. . . . Yet come a little,
  Wishers were ever Fooles. Oh come, come, come,
          They heave Anthony aloft to Cleopatra.
  And welcome, welcome.

Now the text here reproduced tells us that Cleopatra's Monument "aloft" had two "sides" and indicates that

[31] Folger MS. 1478.2.

both "sides" faced the audience. In view of the fact that there were only three stages on the second level of the tiring-house that could be used in conjunction with the outer stage below, we must conclude that one "side" was represented by a bay-window and that the other "side" was represented either by the opposite bay-window or by the tarras. It suffices for our present purpose to point out that at least five persons were assembled — either in the first or in the second part of the scene as quoted — in a bay-window.[32]

From another Globe play of the same period, *Catiline*, III. v:

> *Cicero appears at the window above with Cato,*
> *Catulus, and Crassus.*[33]

The following are representative of scenes in plays written for other theatres. From *The Fawn*, V. i:

> *Whilst the Act is a-playing, Hercules and Tiberio enters; Tiberio climbs the tree, and is received above* [in the window] *by Dulcimel, Philocalia, and a Priest: Hercules stays beneath.*

From *The Partial Law*, I. iv:

> *Trumpets sound, the challenger passeth by, his Page bearing his Shield and his Squire his Lance. The King and Ladyes are above in the window. The Page passing by presents ye King with his Maister's Scutchion.*

As it stands, this direction may not appear to demand more than three actors in the window; later in the same scene, however, a citizen, in reply to a neighbor's questions, points to the royal box and tells who the personages are:

> 2. *Man.* The King, his daughter, with diverse Lords and Ladyes of the Court.

This enumeration implies a party of at least six and probably more. In *The Ordinary*, IV. v, four men "in a window" sing a series of songs; in *Love's Sacrifice*, beginning at line 691, four named persons with attendants assemble

---

[32] See Chapter X, pp. 346–349, for further discussion.
[33] The direction is supplied by Gifford; it is implicit in the text.

"above" in a window to watch the behavior of others below; and in *The Parson's Wedding*, II. viii, nine actors, disposed in two windows, are named in a long direction.[34]

These scenes and the stage business taking place in them warrant the conclusion that the bay-windows were at least 8 or 10 feet wide.

In the preceding chapter I stated that the tarras extended to the sides of the flanking bay-windows. Now a plan of the second level of the tiring-house drawn to scale shows that the side of the window facing the tarras must originate at the corner post of the frame if an awkward, structurally illogical, and unbridgeable gap is to be avoided between the window and the tarras (the citations reviewed show that no such gap existed). It follows, therefore, that in order (1) to connect with the tarras, (2) to be squarely over the stage doors, and (3) to be "centered" symmetrically in the sections of scenic wall from which they projected, the bay-windows must have been 12 feet wide and they must have projected almost as far from the flanking walls of the tiring-house as the tarras projected from the middle wall (i. e. a distance of approximately $2\frac{1}{2}$ feet).

The following observations and extracts tend to confirm these conclusions. Contemporary views of London streets show that bay-windows across the entire front of narrow dwellings were by no means uncommon.[35] This architectural fashion is referred to by Heywood in *The Captives*, I. iii:

Godfrey.   All our howses
Are nothinge nowe but windowes, broad bay windowes
So spatious that carts laded may drive throughe
And neather loush oth' topp or eather syde.
Lights every where, we shall have lightnes inoughe:
Heares stupid woork for daubers.

[34] Noted by Lawrence, ii. 45.
[35] For contemporary views of Elizabethan bay-windows see W. Besant, *London North of the Thames*, pp. 433 and 481; also his *London South of the Thames*, p. 110; *The Roxburghe Ballads*, ed. Cappell, 1881, i. 151; J. P. Malcolm, *Anecdotes of the Manners and Customs of London*, 1808, p. 454.

Here, as in other details, playhouse stage design doubtless reflected the contemporary London scene.

Again, the *Oxford English Dictionary* quotes the Clown in *Measure for Measure*, II. ii, "Ile rent the fairest house in it after three pence a bay," to illustrate its definition of "bay" as "the space lying under one gable, or included between two party walls." Thus the term "bay-window" in itself connoted a spanning of the entire façade from which it projected.[36] Edward Alleyn, part owner of the Fortune Playhouse, drew up the following specifications for a bay-window added in 1606 to his Paris Garden dwelling (the work was carried out by Peter Streete, builder of the Globe and Fortune):

And over the foresaid gate [i.e. street door] shall make one greete square windowe, to be in length ten foot of assize and to jetty over from the said frame three foote of assize, standing upon twoe carved Satyres, the same windowe to be in wheight [i.e. height] according to the depth of the story, and the same windowe to be framed with twoe endes with mullions convenient; and over the same windowe one piramen with three piramides.[37]

So much for the major problems of location, size, and design. Now for a brief discussion of certain distinctive details.

The apertures of the Globe bay-windows were no doubt made as large as possible in order to ensure good visibility and to permit a wide range of stage business. The following quotations indicate that the head, shoulders, and indeed the whole trunk down to the waist, were visible when an actor appeared "above" in a window. From *Antonio's Revenge*, line 359:

Antonio [below]. See, looke, the [window] curtaine stirs, shine natures pride,
    Loues vitall spirit, deare *Antonio's* bride.

[36] A clear distinction exists between "bay-window" and "bow-window." The latter denotes a round-fronted sash, often one of a tier, developed in the eighteenth century. The first recorded instance of the term occurs in *Sir Charles Grandison*.

[37] *Memoires of Edward Alleyn*, ed. Collier, 1841, p. 80.

The [window] *Curtain's drawne, and the bodie of Feliche,*
stabd thick with wounds, appeares hung vp.

What villaine bloods the window of my loue?

From *The Puritan*, sig. H2:

> *Eneter* [i.e. enter below] *Sir John Penidub, and Moll aboue*
> *lacing of her clothes.*

From *Lady Alimony*, IV. vi:

The Favourites appear to their half bodies [i.e. waists] *in their shirts, in*
rooms above . . . They attire themselves . . . They come down buttoning
themselves.

From *The Two Noble Kinsmen*, II. i:

> *Enter Palamon, and Arcite, above* [in a window].

Jailor [below]. Looke yonder they are; that's *Arcite* looks out.

Daughter. No Sir, no that's *Palamon: Arcite* is the lower of the twaine;
you may perceive a part of him.[38]

These scenes, representative of many others, require
openings of considerable size. An unimpaired view of
actors and action taking place in the window-stages was
imperative.

Other types of scenes confirm these dimensions in a
different way. Romeo's departure at dawn from the Capulet Palace (III. v) by means of a rope ladder lowered from
Juliet's window — the first in a long series of similar
episodes [39] — suggests that the casement through which
he clambered must have measured fully 18 inches in width
and 2 or 3 feet in height; and greater width would have

---

[38] Lawrence (*Elizabethan Playhouse*, ii. 27) cites a passage from Middleton's
Black Book, 1604: "And marching forward to the third garden-house, there we
knocked up the ghost of mistress Silverpin, who suddenly risse out of two white
sheets, and acted out of her tiring-house window," to show that Londoners were
familiar with acting in a window-stage.

[39] See, for example, *Blurt Master Constable*, IV. iii; *The Christian Turned
Turk*, F4; *The Insatiate Countess*, III. i; *The Partial Law*, II. v; and *The Wizard*,
V. ii. The rope ladder was provided with hooks at one end. See *Adrasta*, D3;
and *The Two Gentlemen of Verona*, III. i.

made the business easier. Anthony's entrance to Cleopatra's Monument bespeaks an even larger opening, for it is difficult to imagine how a helpless, mortally wounded man of his (and Burbage's) large proportions could have been drawn through a window much less than 3 feet wide. In the bay-window I have essayed to reconstruct in the foregoing pages space was available for a casement 6 feet wide facing front, and for openings in the sides for casements of half this size. In a bay-window with sills waist high, these openings could if desired have extended upwards as much as 6 feet. Following the standard Elizabethan design, the upper sections of leaded panes would have been affixed to rigid sashes or mullions, and the lower panes, those opposite the head and chest of a person inside, would have been attached to hinged sashes.

With regard to the nature of the window casements I cannot do better than to quote from a valuable article on the subject by W. J. Lawrence: [40]

I desire to iterate the statement that the casement was the normal stage window of that epoch, and . . . the kind of "window" most commonly employed. "Casement" in this connexion must be interpreted to mean a light iron or wooden sash for small panes of glass, as constituting a window or part of a window, and made to open outwards by swinging on hinges attached to a vertical side of the aperture into which it is fitted. When opened, the casement was generally held in position by a long hook. It is noteworthy that on the stage of today doors in room scenes are invariably made to open outwards because of the better stage effect (especially in the matter of striking exits) thereby attained. One desires to lay emphasis on the fact that the old English casement always opened outwards, because the French casement (of two hinged leaves), so well known on the Continent, opens inwards. The latter would have proved very clumsy and ineffective on the old platform stage. The supreme gracefulness of the casement as a permanent stage adjunct lay in the degree of illusion its employment lent to scenes of gallantry and intrigue. This is evidenced by the remarkable number of upper-window scenes in the Elizabethan drama.

[40] Lawrence, ii. pp. 32–33. Much of my present discussion has been made easier by his pioneer work and several of my citations were first advanced by him.

To these details a few others may be added. The bay-windows were provided with thin but opaque curtains [41] installed primarily with a view to making the window-stages available for musicians to play or sing unseen during the progress of some inner-stage scene.[42] (In private playhouses lacking a three-story tiring-house the window-stages normally were the music rooms.[43])

The usual window casement of Elizabethan and Jacobean houses was glazed with diamond-shaped panes of glass [44] — an improvement over the windy lattice or the inserts of translucent horn familiar to an earlier generation [45] — set in lead strips or "frets" which in turn were reinforced by iron bars let into the mullion or into the casement sash.[46] The presence of these iron bars in the unglazed (?) stage window is often referred to in the dialogue of prison scenes.[47] In *A Woman Never Vexed*, IV. iii, for example, the Jailor advises a new-comer:

Keeper. Sir being the youngest prisoner in the house
  You must beg at the iron grate above
  As others do, for your relief and theirs.

[41] See, for example, *Henry VIII*, V. ii; *The Jew's Tragedy*, lines 2212 ff.; *The Maid in the Mill*, I. ii; and *Monsieur D'Olive*, I. i.

[42] See, for example, *The Bondman*, III. iii; *The Fatal Dowry*, IV. ii; and *2 Promos and Cassandra*, I. ix.

[43] See, for example, the Paul's play, *Antonio's Revenge* (1602), line 2022: *"Whilst the measure is dauncing Andrugio's ghost is placed* [above] *betwixt the musick houses."* For brief discussion, see Chambers, iii. 119 and 137.

[44] Works on English architectural history record that diamond-shaped panes measuring approximately 4 inches on each side were standard. Square and round panes were less commonly used.

[45] *Shakespeare's England*, ii. 65.

[46] Cf. *Henslowe's Diary*, i. 197: "Item pd unto the smyth for iorne [iron] bares for the window vs." Window bars are illustrated by C. Holme, *Village Homes of England*, pp. 132–133; H. K. Morse, *Elizabethan Pageantry*, pp. 36, 62, and 82.

[47] A grated window was proverbial for a prison. Cf. *A Warning for Fair Women*, K1; *Eastward Ho*, V. ii; *The Puritan*, E3; *The Roaring Girl*, Prologue and G2 verso.

A subsequent direction bears this passage out:

> *Old Foster appears above at the grate, a box hanging down.*

The grating is evidently so closely made that Old Foster cannot put his head through, for he fails to recognize his son on the lower stage who drops a coin in the lowered box.

In a Globe play, *The Picture*, IV. ii, Ubaldo is seen "above" examining the cell in which he finds himself locked:

> Slight tis a prison, or a pigstie, ha!
> The windows grated with Iron I cannot force 'em
> And if I leap downe heere I breake my necke.

This passage tends to crystallize an impression I have de-rived from other scenes, namely that the aperture facing the side spectator-galleries was fitted with a heavy grate of lattice or of iron bars fixed solidly in place in contrast to the hinged casements used in the other two openings. (Two types of fittings in one window was not uncommon in houses of the period.[48]) We know from other scenes that the aperture facing the tarras could be opened; but there seems to be no means of telling whether it was a casement or a grate.

It is not easy to determine to what extent glass was used in Elizabethan and Jacobean stage windows. In support of his opinion that the casements were glazed, W. J. Law-rence wrote: [49]

> In *Greene's Tu Quoque, or The City Gallant*, as acted at the Red Bull circa 1611, we have pointed allusion to the realism of the stage case-ment. Apostrophising the sun, Geraldine says:
>
> > I call thee up, and task thee for thy slowness.
> > Point all thy beams through yonder flaring glass,
> > And raise a beauty brighter than thyself.

Then "enter Gertrude aloft". She speaks down to Geraldine, thanks him for his music, and makes reference to the fact that she is standing at a window.

[48] For contemporary illustration see Hotson, *Commonwealth and Restoration Stage*, plate facing p. 10.
[49] *Elizabethan Playhouse*, ii. 35.

In my opinion the phrase "yonder flaring glass" is used imaginatively rather than realistically; furthermore there is a passage in Beaumont's *Woman-Hater* (a Paul's play of 1606), IV. iii, which implies that the casements were partially or perhaps wholly unglazed:

> *Enter* [below] *Lazarello and his Boy.*
>
> *Laz.* Boy whereabouts are we?
>
> *Boy.* Sir, by all tokens this is the house, bawdy I am sure, by the broken windows.

Nor can this difference of evidence be explained merely by the fact that two different playhouses are involved. If glass was extensively used, then we must assume that the casements were opened at the beginning of every window-stage scene and before every occasion when musicians played there. This may well have been the case, for there is much ado about opening and closing the stage casements. Some scenes begin with a direction for opening the window; [50] others refer in the dialogue to opening the window; [51] and still others point to a closing of the windows when the scene has come to an end. [52] There probably were dozens of scenes in which the same procedure was followed without permanent notice having found its way into the text.

But against this procedure there may be set evidence which points to the windows remaining closed during part or all of several window-stage scenes. It is conceivable that Juliet opened the window while saying "Then window let Day in and let life out" (III. v). In *The Widow*, I. i, during a scene in which Martino and Francisco are conversing in the "garden" below:

> *Philippa and Violetta appear above at a window.*

[50] See, for example, *The Death of Robert, Earl of Huntington*, V. ii; *Fidele and Fortunio*, I. ii; and *Jack Drum's Entertainment*, C2 verso.

[51] *Doctor Faustus* (the 1616 quarto), scene ix; *The Woman's Prize*, I. iii.

[52] *Blurt Master Constable*, IV. i; *The Captain*, II. ii; *Greene's Tu Quoque*, F1; *The Maid in the Mill*, I. iii; *The Death of Robert, Earl of Huntington*, V. ii.

Philippa addresses a bashful greeting to Francisco below and then withdraws, returning to the window shortly after to watch him unobserved.

Phil. He cannot see me now; I'll mark him better
   Before I be too rash . . .
Vio. Mistress?
Phil. Yonder's the gentleman again.
Vio. O sweet mistress,
   Pray give me leave to see him!
Phil. Nay, take heed,
   Open not the window, and you love me.
Vio. No, I've the view of [his] whole body here mistress,
   At this little slit: . . .

Glass had become relatively inexpensive in Elizabethan England, but it was not yet entirely colorless or transparent; the grades normally used for windows gave rise to serious distortion, with the result that to see out of a window it was generally necessary to open a casement or peer through some hole in it.[53] This means that the audience's ability to see actors in the window-stages or to hear dialogue and music originating there would depend upon the casements being opened upon all occasions. But in addition to being contrary to the evidence, this solution obviates one difficulty only by creating another. If opening outwards, English fashion (as we are justified in assuming), the hinged casements probably would have screened the window openings from spectators in the side galleries; if opening inwards, French fashion, the casements would have been a nuisance to actors and would have hampered the use of curtains inside the window-stages.

I incline to believe, therefore, that glass was used sparingly if at all in Elizabethan stage windows. It would not have impeded sight or sound if inserted in the fixed casements at the top of the tall mullioned windows, but it probably was not feasible in the lower hinged casements.

[53] Cf. *All's Well that Ends Well,* II. iii, and Kirkman's *English Rogue* (reprinted by George Routledge & Sons, 1928), pp. 305–306.

I know of no way to determine precisely the location of the rear walls of the window-stages. Acting there made small demands upon depth, for, to be visible, actors had to stand at the casement line or not far behind. A partition or curtain placed 6 or 7 feet back from the front casements would have allowed ample space; actors rarely needed so much, and musicians probably no more. The entrances to the window-stages were probably near the corner posts flanking the upper stage, for actors pass from one stage to the other without an "exit" or an "enter" being marked. The entrance was not visible to the audience, witness the direction in *The Picture*, IV. ii:

> *The noyse of clapping a doore, Ubaldo* [appears] *aboue*
> *in his shirt.*

Ubaldo, the text makes clear, found himself locked into an upper room fitted with casements and grates overlooking the street. I suspect that a curtain hung across the entrance to each window-stage; the noise referred to could have been made by a stage-hand.

Ease and rapidity of movement from a window-stage to the upper rear stage are illustrated in many plays. *Romeo and Juliet*, III. v, for example, opens with the direction *"Enter Romeo and Juliet aloft."* The two are standing in one of the window-stages (compare the first quarto reading: *"Enter Romeo and Juliet at the window"*), but the adjoining rear stage, Juliet's bedroom, presumably is opened as the scene begins, for lines 69 to 215 take place there. The Nurse appears at line 36 to warn them that Lady Capulet is on her way to Juliet's "chamber"; Romeo thereupon descends the rope ladder and goes away, leaving Juliet at the casement above. Four lines later Lady Capulet appears in the bedroom (the "chamber"), entering by the rear door (she had mounted from the study). She finds the room empty. "Ho Daughter, are you up?" (Compare the first quarto: "Where are you Daughter?") Juliet's reply is evasive and prolonged:

Who ist that calls? Is it my Lady Mother.
Is she not downe so late, or up so early?
What unaccustom'd cause procures her hither?

The reason for this curious speech is not far to seek: Juliet,
still in the window-stage, is occupied with pulling up and
concealing the rope ladder (compare the first quarto:

Nurse. Madame beware, take heed the day is broke,
  Your Mother's comming to your Chamber, make all sure),

and until that is done she cannot leave the window-stage.
Once all is "sure" she joins her mother, who, startled by
her tearful appearance, exclaims:

Lad. Why how now *Juliet?*
Jul. Madam I am not well.

Now the point at issue is the relationship of the two
stages. Underlying this dialogue — indeed heightening it
with suspense — is the fact that the two rooms adjoined.
Lady Capulet came within an ace of discovering her
daughter's secret. Observe that no such direction as
"*Exit Juliet* [from the window-stage] ... *Enter Juliet* [in
the upper rear stage]" appears in any text. Her movement from window to bedroom is so swift and so logical
that no direction is needed. She was in view of the audience all the time.
Again, in the much later Globe and Blackfriars play,
Brome's *Novella*, IV. i, Flavia locks the half-dressed
Francisco into a "Presse" (a wardrobe standing in her
room) to hide him from her father, Guadagni, who un-
expectedly returns home. Guadagni comes to her room,
searching for a lost document and believing it to be in the
press. Flavia swoons with fright, but her clever maid
Astutto comes to the rescue. Affirming that the paper and
the key to the press are together locked up in a small
cabinet, she runs to get the cabinet, and, pretending haste
and carelessness in opening it —

Shee lets the Cabinet fall out of the Window.

Ast. Ay me the fruits of rashnes? See, tis fallen
  With all her Jewells and your writing too
  Into the street. O my unlucky hand!
Gua. Peace giddy headed harlot, watch that none
  Take it away, while I runne to recover't.

But before he can reach the street (his servant is slow in unlocking the front door), "*Enter a Zaffie, taking up the Cabinet.*" Now the window faces the audience, which means that Astutto must have darted from the upper curtained stage into a window-stage. The whole business is done swiftly and naturally, implying that the one stage opened directly into the other.

3. THE "CHAMBER"

As previously recorded in this chapter, an upper stage similar to the study below first made its appearance early in the last decade of the sixteenth century. This was the last major unit to be added to the Elizabethan multiple stage. Prior to its introduction all interior scenes had to be laid in the study, despite the fact that most London citizens utilized the ground floor of their houses for shops and had their living quarters above. The development, therefore, on the second level of the tiring-house of a sizable curtained stage which could be prepared in advance as a living room, a bed- or dressing room, a private room in a tavern, and so forth, enabled dramatists to reflect London life with greater fidelity. In general after 1595 such scenes as would in reality have taken place in some room on the second level of an Elizabethan dwelling, tavern, prison, or palace were presented above.

More important advantages than mere verisimilitude resulted from the addition of the new upper stage. Whereas previously dramatists had been forced to interpolate an exterior between a pair of interior scenes, particularly when the second interior differed in locality and setting from the first, they were now able to devise an action involving two adjacent interiors (for example, *Romeo and Juliet*, IV, in which scene iii represents Juliet's room above, scene iv a hall in the Capulet house below, and scene v Juliet's room again); or an action involving two separated interiors in sharp dramatic contrast (for example, *King Lear*, III, in which scene v represents a room in Gloucester's castle, scene vi a room in a farmhouse on the edge of the Heath, and scene vii a room in the castle again); or an action which flows logically from one interior to another in the same building (for example, *Hamlet*, III, in which scene iii uses the study to represent a hall in the castle where Claudius plans Hamlet's death and then kneels down to pray, and scene iv uses the upper stage as Gertrude's room to which Hamlet goes directly after passing through the lower hall where Claudius was kneeling). The importance of these contributions to dramatic pace, flexibility, and effect is at once apparent.

For convenience in distinguishing the upper curtained stage from the lower curtained stage (the "study") I shall call it the "chamber". (In a test made of a hundred apposite passages that designation for it occurs more often than any other.[54]) A word of caution, however: one occasionally encounters an unmistakable study scene in which some actor speaks of "this chamber"; or, though less frequently, a chamber scene referred to as "this study." Accordingly, more evidence than merely the occurrence of the term "chamber" or "study" is needed before one can determine which of the two curtained stages is being used.

The existence of the chamber, though not always so called, is now generally accepted by modern students of

[54] See, for example, *The Antipodes*, III. viii; *The Coxcomb*, IV. i; *The Cunning Lovers*, 1654 (Q1), p. 34; *The Custom of the Country*, III. ii and iii; *The Game at Chess*, IV. iii; *The Great Duke of Florence*, V. i; *The Jew's Tragedy*, line 2212; *The Match at Midnight*, line 1210; *The Miseries of Enforced Marriage*, G2 verso; *The Parson's Wedding*, V. ii; and *The Sparagus Garden*, III. i.

the Elizabethan theatre,[55] but there is considerable disagreement as to its size and appointments, and even more as to the extent to which it was employed by Shakespeare and his fellow dramatists. ——

Most of the following facts relating to the chamber in the Globe have emerged during the course of my investigation of other units of the multiple stage. Let me bring them together and illustrate where necessary with quotations not hitherto cited.

(1) The chamber was 11 feet high (see Chapter II).

(2) It was approximately 11 feet deep (if we include the tarras which formed its forward extension), and 8 feet deep behind its curtain.[56]

(3) It was 23 feet wide at the front. Beginning at the curtain (or scenic wall), it probably narrowed, like the study below, to a width of some 20 feet at the back. Since the evidence for the chamber-opening of 23 feet is the same as or similar to that for the study-opening, I refer the reader to Chapter VI, and merely add here the following observations. The properties commonly employed above — a bed (or a pair of beds), wardrobes, chests, tables, chairs, and so forth — are hardly less bulky than the properties employed below. The number of actors brought on above and the stage business conducted there show that the room was large. Jonson specifically refers

---

[55] Cf. Adams, *Life of William Shakespeare*, plate facing p. 286; Albright, *Shaksperean Stage*, frontispiece and pp. 76–78; Chambers, *Elizabethan Stage*, iii. 90–98, 115–120; Lawrence, *Physical Conditions*, pp. 75 ff.; Thorndike, *Shakespeare's Theater*, pp. 133 ff. G. F. Reynolds (*The Staging of Elizabethan Plays*, pp. 92–106) brings together references from Red Bull plays to the upper stage or "balcony" at that playhouse, but appears to conclude that the use of a curtained stage above was abnormal.

[56] The second level of the playhouse frame was 10 inches deeper than the first, i.e. 13 feet 4 inches (see Chapter II above). The tarras, an extension of the chamber in front of the curtains, was at least 3 feet wide (see Chapter VIII, section 1 above). From the sum of these two must be subtracted 5 feet 6 inches to allow for the rear passage and the exterior wall of the playhouse.

to it in his Globe play *The Alchemist*, IV. i, as a "great chamber" —

Face. Sir, you are too loud. I heare you, euery word.
    Into the laboratory. Some fitter place.
    The garden, or great chamber aboue.[57]

So far as size is concerned, the chamber and the study were substantially identical. Except by carefully examining the play as a whole the reader often has difficulty in determining whether a given inner-stage scene was originally acted above or below. A direction in Killigrew's *Parson's Wedding* (written in exile *circa* 1641), IV. vi, reading —

The Tyring-Room, curtains drawn, and they discourse, his Chamber, two Beds, two Tables, Looking glasses, Night-Cloathes, Waste-coats, Sweet-bags, Sweet-meats, and Wine, Wanton dressed like a Chamber-maid all above if the Scene can be so ordered —

implies that the two stages might be used interchangeably.

(4) The chamber was equipped with a pair of stage curtains suspended and operated in the same manner as the study curtains (see Chapter VI). The following quotations may be cited.[58] From the Globe and Blackfriars play, *The Emperor of the East*, I. ii:

The Curtains drawn above: Theo[doseus] and his eunuchs discovered.

From *The Goblins*, V:

A curtain drawn, Prince Philatell, with others, appear above.

From *The Game at Chess*, V. i:

Loud music. Black Bishops Pawn discovered above: enter Black Knight in his litter, as passing in haste over the stage.

To mark the close of the scene in *The Parson's Wedding* referred to above, the direction reads, "*The Curtains are Closed.*"

[57] In *Valentinian*, II. iv, it again is called "the great Chamber."
[58] The first two are cited by Lawrence, ii. 30.

(5) The chamber was enclosed on the two ends by hangings and at the back by rigid partitions together with flexible hangings disposed as in the study and used in precisely the same ways. In *Cymbeline*, II, ii, one recalls, Iachimo emerges from the trunk in Imogen's bedroom as she lies asleep. He makes a careful survey of the furnishings and appointments, entering the particulars in his note-book:

> But my designe.
> To note the Chamber, I will write all downe,
> Such, and such pictures: There the window, such
> Th' adornement of her Bed; the Arras, Figures,
> Why such, and such: and the Contents o' th' Story.

(The "story," one learns in II. iv, was that of

> Proud *Cleopatra*, when she met her Roman,
> And *Sidnus* swell'd above the Bankes.)

The following quotations (from Globe and Blackfriars plays) illustrate concealment behind the rear hangings. In *Hamlet*, III. iv, Polonius slips behind the arras when he hears Hamlet approaching the Queen's room (compare Q1: "I'le shrowde my selfe behinde the Arras. *Exit Cor*[ambis]"). The theatrical reason for having Polonius hide behind the rear hangings rather than behind one of the side hangings is that Hamlet's killing of Polonius and his subsequent identification of the body must be in full view of the audience. The Folio text, at line 21, reads:

Qu. What wilt thou do? thou wilt not murther me?
  Helpe, helpe, hoa.
Pol. What hoa, helpe, helpe, helpe.
Ham. How now? a Rat? Dead for a Ducate, dead.
                              Killes Polonius.
Pol. Oh I am slaine.
Qu. Oh me, what hast thou done?
Ham. Nay I know not, is it the King? . . .
  Thou wretched, rash, intruding foole farewell,
  I took thee for thy Betters, take thy Fortune.

The closing lines and the final stage-direction of the scene indicate once more that Polonius's body, perhaps partially exposed, lay at some distance from one of the exits, in other words, at the foot of the rear hangings. At line 200:

Ham. I must to England, you know that?
Qu. Alacke I had forgot: 'Tis so concluded on.
Ham. This man [i.e. Polonius] shall set me packing:
Ile lugge the Guts into the Neighbor roome,
Mother goodnight . . .
Come sir, to draw toward an end with you.
Good night Mother. *Exit Hamlet tugging in Polonius.*

The stage business in *The Duke's Mistress*, V. i, is in some details similar to that in *Hamlet*, III. iv. Valerio has entered Ardelia's room, closed the door, and threatened to ravish her. She defends herself with a pistol and warns him that the Duke is about to arrive. Just then —

One knocks.
Val. The Duke is come already, I am undone
Mercy, and some concealment.
Goes behinde the hangings.
Bentivolio opens the doer [i.e. door].

Ardelia tells Bentivolio that the Duke is concealed behind the hangings, whereupon:

He [Bentivolio] *wounds Valerio behind the hangings.*
Val. Oh
I am murder'd.

Ardelia and Bentivolio then leave together, and "*Valerio falls into the Stage.*" From *Women Pleased*, II. vi:

Claudio. What would you have me do?
Isabella. But for a while Sir,
Step here behind this hanging, presently
I'll answer him, and then —
Claudio. I will obey ye.

The following quotations illustrate the use of an alcove exposed by drawing the rear hangings aside. From *The Lover's Progress*, III. i:

Enter [to the chamber] *Clarinda with a Taper, and Lisander*
with a Pistol, two Chairs set out.

Clar. Come near.   *Calista sitting behind a Curtain.*
  I'll leave ye now, draw but that Curtain
  And have your wish . . .   *Exit.*

Lisander draws the curtain, discovers Calista asleep in her
chair, and extolls her beauty. She rouses and comes forward; they talk and exchange kisses until disturbed by the
approach of her husband. A similar alcove scene occurs
in *The Distresses*, IV. v:

> *He steps to the Arras softly, draws it. Claramante is discovered*
> *sleeping on her Book, her Glass by.*

Now the precise similarity of the directions governing
these alcove scenes and the directions governing certain
types of bed scenes leads to the conclusion that a bed (of
the four-poster, curtained, and canopied variety typical
of the period) was sometimes placed in the rear passage
and exposed by opening the rear hangings which thus
constituted the bed-curtains on the side facing the audience. Let me digress long enough to illustrate this important and often misunderstood detail of Elizabethan
stage practice. In *Antonio's Revenge* (at line 1273), Maria
orders her room cleared and prepares for bed:

Mar. Go[o]d night *Nutriche*. Pages, leaue the roome.
  The life of night growes short, tis almost dead.
> *Exeunt Pages and Nutriche.*
O thou cold widdowe bed, sometime thrice blest,
By the warme pressure of my sleeping Lord:
Open thy leaues, and whilst on thee I treade,
Groane out. Alas, my deare *Andrugio's* deade.
> *Maria draweth the courtaine: and the ghost of Andrugio*
> *is displayed, sitting on the bed.*
Amazing terror, what portent is this?

The Ghost comes down from the bed, rebukes her and
then comforts her; before leaving he assists her into it:

Sleepe thou in rest, loe here I close thy couch.

> *Exit Maria to her bed, Andrugio drawing*
> [i.e. closing] *the Curtaines.*

Love's Mistress, III. i, opens with the direction:

> *Enter Psiche in night-attire, with a Lampe and a Raysor.*

She invokes the aid of "Times eldest daughter Night" in the execution of her project:

> Psiche intreats thee
> No Iarre nor sound betray her bold attempt:
> *Cup*[id] *discovered sleeping on a Bed.*
> Soft silken vaile that curtaines in my doubt,
> Give way to these white hands . . .

There follows a long description of the beautiful sleeping boy, who is at last roused by the drops of scalding oil which fall from the lamp. He gets out of bed, reproves her, and leaves the room in anger. Finally, from *Love's Sacrifice*, at line 1268:

> *Enter* [to the chamber] *Biancha her haire about her eares, in her night mantle; she drawes a Curtaine where Fernando is discovered in bed, sleeping; she sets downe the Candle before the Bed, and goes to the Bed side.*

Occasionally these rear hangings are spoken of as "the canopy," a term more properly used to designate the tester, or cover of the bedstead (compare *The Wits*, IV. ii: "The canopy, the hangings, and the bed, are worth more than your rent"). In *The Platonic Lovers*, II. ii, Amadine, a servant, leads Theander to her mistress's room, supposing her to be there (a few minutes before Amadine had heard the sounds of a lute). The room appears to be empty, and Amadine suggests that her mistress must be in bed asleep.

Thea. Tread easie then! . . .

> *Draws a Canopie; Eurithea is found sleeping on a Couch, a vaile on, with her Lute.*

Give mee the light; now leave us, and retire.

Again, from *Sophonisba*, IV. i: "*Syphax hasteneth within the canopy as to Sophonisba's bed.*" Obviously the bed-curtains and not the tester are meant in these two passages.

Now in these bed scenes (there are others of the same type) the basic conditions are the same as in the alcove scenes cited above and in the chapter on the study: (1) The curtain or curtains mentioned are opened during the course of an inner-stage scene, which means that they are not the stage curtains. (2) The person to be revealed is not seen — his presence, or even the presence of a bed, usually is unsuspected — before the curtains in question are opened, which means that strictly speaking he is not on stage but sits or lies in a bed placed off stage in some immediately adjoining area. (3) The entire audience must be able to see the person revealed by the opening of the curtains, which means that the recess lies behind the hangings suspended in the middle of the rear wall.

The mechanics of staging bed scenes in this manner were elementary (but let me repeat that there were other standard ways of staging bed scenes). The rear passageway, 5 feet wide, led directly to property rooms on either side. To carry a bed (supplied with bed-curtains on three sides) into the passage and place it against the rear hangings was as easy as to carry it into the stage itself. The rear hangings then served as bed-curtains on the fourth side — the side towards the audience. So placed the bed was out of the way in scenes requiring a number of actors or much freedom of movement. When a full-sized Elizabethan four-poster bed was placed inside the room it must have occupied no inconsiderable part of an 11 by 23-foot stage.

A Juliet collapsing into her bed behind the rear hangings — "*She fals upon her bed within the Curtaines*" (first quarto reading, IV. iii) — would be free to make ready (as by a change of make-up?) for the Nurse's coming in the morning to find her apparently dead body. Her bed would be relatively remote during the period of inspection and grief which followed. And when at last the mourners depart and the bed-curtains are again closed —

> *They all but the Nurse goe foorth, casting Rosemary on her and shutting the Curtens —*

there is no cause for objection when the stage fills once again with clowns and their jokes.[59]

I am inclined to believe that Desdemona's bed was back there, and that the act of smothering her was to that extent shrouded. Her bed, too, had curtains:

Othello. I had forgot thee: oh come in *Æmilia.*
  Soft, by and by, let me the Curtaines draw.
  Where art thou?   *Enter Æmilia.*

From what takes place subsequently, it seems unlikely that the room itself was encumbered with a large bed.

In *Valentinian,* II. iv, the alcove is perhaps used for the display of jewels arranged to tempt the chaste Lucina during her tour of the upper halls of the palace (compare the casket scenes in *The Merchant of Venice*). It fails.

Luc. Nay ye may draw [i.e. close] the Curtain, I have
    seen 'em   ⎰ *Jewels*
  But none worth half my honesty.   ⎱ *shew'd*

The following quotation illustrates the presence of side hangings, together with the practice of entering through them. From *The Lovers' Progress,* III. i (continuing the scene quoted earlier):

Calisto [to Lisander]. Retire behind the hangings [at the side or the rear], and there stand close — my husband, close, *Lisander.*
      Enter Cleander [the husband] *with a Taper.*

---

[59] Occasionally the rear hangings fronting the alcove are referred to as "the canopy" even when no bed is involved, as in Heminge's *Fatal Contract,* V. ii:

> *Enter the Eunuch, whilst the waits play softly and solemnly drawes the Canopie, where the Queen sits at one end* [of the alcove] *bound with Landry at the other, both as asleep.*

Later in the same scene comes the direction, "*draws the Curtain again.*" I take it that "canopie" and "curtain" are here the same.

Clean. Dearest, are you well? . . .
Methought there came a Dragon to your Chamber, . . .
And methought he came
As if he had risen thus out of his Den
As I do from these Hangings.

(6) The chamber had a door at the rear and hence a passageway beyond. (Into the passageway, as shown in the preceding chapter, the stairs mounted from behind the study below.) The following quotations supplement those presented in earlier discussions of these various points. From *2 Henry IV*, II. iv, a private room in the Boar's Head Tavern:

Enter Drawer.

Drawer. Sir, Ancient *Pistoll* is below, and would speake with you.
Dol. Hang him, swaggering Rascall, let him not come hither . . . shut the doore, there comes no Swaggerers heere. . .
Falstaffe. Hee's no Swaggerer (Hostesse:) . . . Call him up (Drawer.)

In *Alphonsus, Emperor of Germany*, I. i, Alphonsus, wishing to confer with the learned Lorenzo, secures the master-key of all palace doors. Armed with this key he leaves the study:

Alph. Now on a sudden will I try his wit,
I know my coming is unlook'd for

He opens the [chamber] *door and finds Lorenzo*
asleep aloft.

Nay, sleep, Lorenzo, I will walk awhile.

From *The Inconstant Lady*, IV:

Pantarbo appeares above. . . .

He encounters Busiro and two women already in the room and talks with them. Then —

Knock within.

Busi. Who's that knocks?
Rom. Keep fast the dore.
Ser't. [within]. It is one from the Duke would speak with the Lord Busiro.

In *The Chances* (acted at the Globe and Blackfriars), II. i
and iii, Frederick, having conducted Constantia to his
chamber, descends to the street, finds his friend Don John,
and tells him what he has done with Constantia. Don
John begs to be allowed to see her.

John.   I am answer'd:
  But let me see her though: leave the door open
  As ye go in.
Fred. I dare not.
John. Not wide open,
  But just so, as a jealous husband
  Would level at his wanton wife through.

Scene iii shows us Constantia above. After she has spoken
seven lines:

             Enter Frederick, and Don John peeping.
Fred. [to Constantia]. Peace to your meditations.
John. Pox upon ye.
  Stand out o' th' light.

Tourneur's *Atheist's Tragedy* (a Globe play?), II. v, has
an amusing action involving the chamber door and rear
hangings:

Enter Leuidulcia [Belforest's wife] *into her chamber man'd by Fresco.*
Leu. Th' art welcome into my chamber, Fresco. Prethee shut the dore.
  —Nay thou mistakest me. Come in and shut it. . . .

In the midst of her talk with him —

             Sebastian knockes within.
Leu. Vds body; my Husband! . . . you must suffer for the treason you
  neuer committed. Goe hide thy selfe behind yound' arras, instantly.
       Fresco hides himselfe, Enter Sebastian.

Leuidulcia and Sebastian are no sooner in each other's
arms than —

             Belforest knockes within.
Leu. I thinke I am accurs'd! . . .

But thinking quickly, she instructs Sebastian to draw his sword and rush out of the house as soon as her husband enters the room:

> *Enter Belforest.*
>
> *Seba.* Now by the hand of *Mercurie.*   *Exit Sebastian.*

Leuidulcia then explains to her amazed husband that one unknown man had chased another into the house, and that she had saved the life of the first by hiding him. She then calls to Fresco.

> *Fresco peepes fearefully forth from behinde the Arras.*

Fresco, of course, has heard everything and has wits enough to take his cue from her explanation and slip away.

In *The Maid's Tragedy*, IV. i, Melantius, wishing to talk privately with Evadne, his brother's wife, finds her, attended by her ladies, in an upper room of the palace.

> *Mel.* I would not have your women hear me
> Break into commendation of you, 'tis not seemly.
> *Evad.* [to her Ladies]. Go wait me in the Gallery — now speak.
> *Mel.* I'le lock the door first.   *Exeunt Ladies.*
> *Evad.* Why?
> *Mel.* I will not have your guilded things that dance in visitation with
> their Millan skins choke up my business.

The only "Gallery" into which the Ladies could pass through an upper-stage door capable of being locked is the passage behind the chamber.

A similar reference to the rear passage occurs in *The Scornful Lady*, III. i:

> *Lady.* A parting kiss, and good Sir, let me pray you
> To wait me in the Gallerie.
> *Welford.* I am in another world, Madam where you please.
>   *Exit Welford.*

Again, from *Wit Without Money*, III:

> *Isabella.* I have a tongue can talk too: and a Green Chamber *Luce*, a
> back door opens to a long Gallerie.

This practice (limited to Beaumont and Fletcher?) of referring to the upper passageway as the "gallery" (i.e. a long narrow hall) corresponds to the more widespread practice of referring to the lower passageway as "the way to the back gate." Both allusions take the facts of play-house design into account. I do not wish to convey the impression, however, that the term "gallery" was reserved for the passageway; as a rule the term was used with reference to one of the inner curtained stages.

A close relationship between chamber, passageway, and stairs down to the floor below is implied in the following quotations. From *The Lovers' Progress*, III. i (continuing the misadventures of Lisander and Calisto). Once Calisto has persuaded her husband to return to his bedroom, she calls to Lisander:

Cal. Come out again, and as you love, *Lisander*,
　　Make haste away, you see his mind is troubled;
　　Do you know the door ye came in at?
Lis. Well, sweet Lady.

But parting is such sweet sorrow that in a little while the husband's footsteps are again heard approaching.

Cal. Once more, farewel;　　　　　　　　　　*Noise within.*
　　O that my modesty cou'd hold you still, Sir — he comes again.
Lis. Heaven keep my hand from murther,
　　Murther of him I love.
Cal. Away, dear friend,
　　Down to the Garden stairs, that way, *Lisander*,
　　We are betray'd else.
　　　　　　　　　Enter Cleander.
Lis. Honour guard the innocent.　　　　　*Exit Lisander.*
Clean. Still up? ·I fear'd your health.

As Cleander leads her off to bed a pistol shot rouses the entire household. There are various explanations offered by the servants, but the true one is whispered in her mistress's ear by the faithful Clarinda:

> *Lisander* stumbled, Madam,
> At the Stairs-head, and in the fall the shot went off;
> [He] Was gone before they rose.

In *The Yorkshire Tragedy*, a Globe play of 1605, sig. C3, a maddened husband mounts to his wife's bedroom where he finds her asleep and his infant son in the arms of a maid-servant:

Hu. Whore, giue me that boy,   *Striues with her for the child.*
M. O help, help, out alas, murder murder,
Hus. Are you gossiping, prating sturdy queane, Ile breake your clamor
  with your neck down staires:
  Tumble, tumble, headlong,   *Throws her down.*
  So, the surest waie to charme a womans tongue.
  Is break hir neck, a pollitician did it.

Again, from Heywood's *Royal King and the Loyal Subject*, II. iii. The guests dining at an ordinary object to the presence of a decayed Captain and ask the Host to send him away.

4 Gent. If he will not leave the roome, kicke him downe staires. . . .
Host. Nay, if you prate, I shall use you somewhat extraordinary.
Gent. Downe with the Rogue.
Captain. Since you hate calmes, and will move stormy weather,
  Now Host and guest shall all downe staires together.
Clown. Ah well done Master, tickle them noble Captaine.

Some part of the stair head may have been visible to persons in the chamber (see Chapter VII). Be that as it may, the location of the stairs was well known to the audience. For example, in *The Walks of Islington*, I. i, written in 1641, Mrs. Trimwell and her friends learn with dismay that her husband is on the way up to the tavern room where they are gathered.

Mrs. Trim. What will become on's.
Pimpwell. There's but one way, and that's this, here is a door goes
  down another pair of stayrs, whilst he comes up, do you run down,
  you may easily escape unseene by the back-side of *Islington*. Let me
  alone here.

Flylove. I, I, come let's go . . .   *Exeunt* [through rear door].
          Enter Trimwell [through hangings at one side].

He asks the whereabouts of his wife.

Drowsy. Was the woman in the black Guown yawr woife Sir?
Trim. Yes, which way went they?
Drow. Marry 3 Gentlemen carried her down them stayrs,
     You were best make haste after 'um.

It was sometimes convenient, on the other hand, to regard the door opening to the passage and the stairs as the
door of a closet; in such cases, of course, those mounting
the stairs from below had to enter the chamber through the
hangings at one side. *Love's Cruelty*, III. iv, and IV. i,
provides an illustration. In the earlier scene Bellamente
returns home late at night and asks the servant where his
wife is. He is told that she is upstairs with Hippolito.
The servant is sent to fetch her, but, a moment later, he
returns to Bellamente in the study and reports that he
found the bedroom door locked.

Bel. Come draw, take my sword, I will be double arm'd,
     I charge thee by thy duty, or thy life
     If that be more, stay you at bottome of
     The staires, while I ascend their sinfull chamber
     And if my Pistoll misse his treacherous heart
     He has no way to passe but on thy sword, . . .   *Exeunt.*

The action then continues above (IV. i):

     Enter [i.e. discover] *Hippolito and Clariana upon a bed.*

Confident that her husband is far away, Clariana talks
scornfully about him, when "*Enter Bellamente.*" Bellamente at once locks Hippolito in the closet — "get into
that closet . . . So, you are fast" (i.e. thrusts him through
the chamber door and locks it) — and calls out to the
Servant below:

Bel. You sirra at the bottome of the staires, come up.
          Enter Servant.

The Servant is ordered to find Hippolito, but, although searching everywhere inside the room, he is unsuccessful. Bellamente then reprimands him for telling tales about his mistress and sends him off to bed. I call attention to the fact that in this scene, as in others which to a similar extent depart from normal procedure or from the normal names for units of the stage, the dramatist takes particular pains to help the audience follow the action. Bellamente's emphatic orders — when in the study with his servant: "Stay you at bottome of The staires, while I ascend their sinfull chamber . . . He has no way to passe but on thy sword"; when above in the chamber with Hippolito: "get into that closet"; and then, while still above, to the Servant below: "You sirra at the bottome of the staires, come up" — ought to enable all spectators to regard the door at the rear of the chamber as the door to a closet, and the entrance at one side of the chamber as the entrance from the stairs leading up from the study below.

Let me cite three or four more "closet" scenes. From *The Scots Figaries*, sig. G4, a tavern scene above:

Enter Drawer

Draw. Gentlemen your noise has drawn Souldiers into the house, th'are comming up; as many as can, get into that little Closet.

[Four go in and hide.]

From *The Costly Whore*, I. i, a study scene:

Euphrata. Therefore within my closet hide thyselfe;
  Your friend shall Julia guide into the garden,
  Where through a private doore, but seldom us'd,
  He may at pleasure leave us and returne.

In *The Maid in the Mill*, V. ii, Otrante learns that the King is coming to his house. Hoping to conceal Florimell, a young girl who loves him, he locks her in the "Closet" of his room. Don Philippo enters, accompanied by courtiers, and at once begins to examine the room.

Phil. Me-thinks 'tis handsome, and the rooms along
  Are neat, and well contriv'd: the Gallery
  Stands pleasantly and sweet: what rooms are these?
Otr. They are sluttish ones.
Phil. Nay, I must see.
Otr. Pray ye do Sir, . . .
Phil. Fit still, and handsome; very well: and those?
Otr. Those lead to the other side o'th'house, and't like ye.
Phil. Let me see those.
Otr. Ye may, the dores are open. . . .
Phil. This little Room? [The King points to the door.]
Otr. 'Tis mean: a place for trash Sir,
  For rubbish of the house.
Phil. I would see this too:
  I will see all.

Otrante tries to divert the King from looking into the
closet, but to no avail. His various excuses are swept
aside.

Phil. But I will see it: force the lock (my Lords)
  There be smiths enough to mend it: I perceive
  You keep some rare things here, you would not show Sir.
              Florimel discover'd.

Observe that the "Closet" door was locked before the
King arrived, hence he and his train (looking attentively
for Florimell as they came) must have entered from one
side.[60] The King then looked into the room which Otrante
described as "sluttish," that is, probably, between the
alcove hangings. Next he looked into the rooms which
"lead to the other side o'th'house," that is, he peered
through the hangings on the far side of the room. Last he

---

[60] These closet scenes raise the question: Were there perhaps two doors in
the rear wall of the study and also of the chamber? For if so, one could serve as
the door of the closet and the other as the usual exit to the rear passageway and
stairs. A number of objections — for example, the common stage practice of
securing the privacy of either inner stage by locking *one* door — are immediately apparent, however, showing that the hypothesis is untenable.

came to the rear door, with the success outlined above. The scene appears to take place in the study, but so far as stage design is concerned it could equally well have taken place in the chamber, witness the searching party which ransacks Sabrina's house in *The Goblins*, II. i and ii. There, when at last Philatel enters, "dragging out his Sister" from some side room into the chamber and threatening her:

Orsabrin (within the closet) bounces thrice at the door: it flies open.

(7) The chamber had a window facing into the rear passage. Iachimo, in the lines from *Cymbeline* cited on page 279, observed the window and made a note of it. In Fletcher's Globe play, *The Captain* (1609–1612), V. ii, the housemaid is instructed by her master and his friends to empty a urinal out of the window upon the head of the fiery Jacomo, said to be standing below in the street, as a means of inciting him to enter the house. (It is clear that Jacomo is off stage.) When all is ready —

Fabricio. What, is the Wench come up?
Enter Wench.

Clora. Art thou there, Wench?

Wench. I.

Fab. Look out then if thou canst see him.

Wench. Yes, I see him, and by my troth he stands so fair I could not hold were he my Father, his hat's off too, and he's scratching his head.

Fab. O, wash that hand I prithee.

Wench. 'Send thee good luck, this is the second time I have thrown thee out today, ha, ha, ha, just on's head.

Frank. Alas!

Fab. What does he now?

Wench. He gathers stones, God's light, he breaks all the Street windows.

Jacomo [within]. Whores, Bawds, your windows, your windows.

Wench. Now he is breaking all the low windows with his sword. Excellent sport, now he's beating a fellow that laugh'd at him. Truly the man takes it patiently; now he goes down the street gravely.

The nature of the jest (as well as the dialogue) requires that the housemaid stand at a second-story window; inasmuch as Jacomo never "enters" the stage during any part of the episode, and his wild behavior is made known to the audience only by way of the maid's commentary, we must assume that he, and the window in question, were at the back of the stage.[61]

There is one other upper-stage scene which suggests that the chamber window could be opened. In *The Walks of Islington and Hogsdon* (acted in 1641), IV. i, it is used as a serving hatch by the drawer waiting on debtors incarcerated in the Debtors' Prison.

> *Enter as in the Compter Wildblood, Rivers, Flylove, Mrs. Trimwel and Keeper.*

Refreshments are sent for.

Keeper. Hugh, Hugh.
> *Enter Drawer at the window.*
Hugh. What a Hugh and cry you make . . .
Wild. Prethee honest *Hugh* . . . fill us one pottle of Canary, let's have clean pipes and Tobacco.

It may be nothing but chance that two examples of opening the chamber window and none of opening the study window occur in extant play texts, but I suspect that there was some practical reason behind the distinction. Perhaps the greater use of the lower passageway (for lower-stage scenes outnumber upper-stage scenes by at least three to one), or the location of the stairs or of an exterior window to the tiring-house, made feasible above what was not feasible below.

A more usual situation turning upon the upper-stage rear window occurs in Middleton's *Spanish Gipsy*. Early

---

[61] Cited by Lawrence, ii. 47–48. Lawrence also found references to a rear window in the upper stage in *The Great Duke of Florence*, V. i; *If You Know not Me*, scene v; and *The Devil's Law Case*, V. v. I interpret the last-named example quite differently.

in the play (I. iii) Clara, daughter of the noble Don Pedro, is abducted by a stranger and ravished in some house unknown to her. Left alone for a few minutes, she tries, despite the darkness, to fix the house in mind.

Clara. It is a Chamber sure, the guilty Bed,
   Sad evidence against my losse of honour
   Assures so much, what's here, a window curtaine?
   Oh Heaven! the stars appeare too, ha! a chamber,
   A goodly one, dwells Rape in such a paradice!
   Help me my quickned senses, 'tis a garden
   To which this window guides the covetous prospect,
   A large one and a faire one, in the midst
   A curious Alablaster Fountaine stands.

Later in the play (III. iii) an accident in the street leads to her being carried into a private room upstairs in the house of Fernando, Corregidor of Madrid. Her father observes her close scrutiny of the room:

Pedro. Soule of my comfort, . . . why dost thou speede
   Thine Eye in such a progresse 'bout these Walls?
Clara. Yon large Window
   Yields some faire prospect, good my Lord looke out,
   And tell mee what you see there.
Ped. Easie suite,
   Clara it over viewes a spacious Garden,
   Amidst which stands an Alablaster Fountaine.

Manifestly the garden and the fountain are unseen by the audience and lie, supposedly, at the back of the house, hence the window discovered by Clara was in the rear wall of the chamber. The subsequent dialogue of the scene indicates that the room was on the upper stage.

(8) The floor of the chamber was strewn with rushes and contained a simple trapdoor in the middle. The ceiling was plastered and may have contained a trap directly over the floor trap. The evidence bearing upon these four points was presented in Chapter VI.

To sum up. It is apparent from the evidence of the plays that the Globe chamber on the second level of the

tiring-house closely corresponded to the study in position, size, and appurtenances. It was approximately 11
feet high, 23 feet wide, and 11 feet deep (including the
tarras, which, with its guard-rail, merged with the chamber whenever the curtains were opened). It was provided
with stage curtains operated in the same way as the study
curtains. It had a rear door (fitted with a lock) and a rear
window, both opening on the passage behind. It had
hangings at the rear (which could be opened to expose an
alcove), hangings on both sides, rushes on the floor, a floor
trap (perhaps also a ceiling trap), and a plastered ceiling.

In Chapter VI the evidence bearing upon the visibility of
study scenes was reviewed. During the discussion it was
pointed out that spectators in the yard and the first gallery commanded a view of all parts of the study — its
floor, its three inner walls, and its ceiling; spectators in the
middle gallery commanded all but the study ceiling; and
spectators in the top gallery all but the study ceiling and
the upper third of its rear wall. From a consideration of
these facts one might well expect the typical stage business
of study scenes to involve the floor trap and side walls (up
to the height of a man's head) and to stress action on or
near the floor. This hypothesis is borne out by the plays,
which abound with scenes involving graves, vaults, pits,
river-banks, beaches, wells and springs, and so forth,
enacted in the study.

A similar examination (working as in Chapter VI from
a Globe section plan drawn to scale) of the sight lines entering the chamber shows that spectators in the yard could
not see the chamber floor, nor, if standing forward near
the platform stage, the lower third of the rear hangings.
Spectators in the first gallery saw substantially all but the
floor; those in the second gallery had a complete view; and
those in the third gallery saw all but the ceiling. Chamber scenes, therefore, could be expected to minimize stage
business conducted near the floor or in the lower portion
of the rear alcove — a conclusion supported by the facts.

The instances of sitting or reclining upon the chamber floor (a commonplace of study scenes) are rare indeed. The chamber floor trap is used chiefly as a means of eaves-dropping on a study scene below — a business which may require those above to group themselves about the aperture but which does not require them to lie down. No Falstaff is found sleeping on the floor behind the rear hangings. On the contrary, when actors are discovered in the alcove, they are found to be standing, sleeping in a four-poster bed, or sitting in a chair. The upper stage, in fact, was so placed relative to the auditorium that scenes enacted there were more completely visible to the triple-tiered gallery audience — to the majority of spectators, that is to say — than scenes enacted in the study. (I am not forgetting the forward railing: see pages 253-256.) The only spectators placed disadvantageously for chamber scenes were the groundlings — those paying the lowest admission price — but even their rights were respected. Chamber scenes, unlike study scenes, are as a rule lacking in stage business taking place at floor level.

Now in all theatres charging admission, the best seats and the highest prices must in the main correspond. In the Globe and other public playhouses the audience was distributed in such a way that the cheapest places were at the bottom and at the top of the auditorium. The more expensive places lay midway between, in the first and second galleries. Such a plan might conceivably have arisen through some peculiarity of inn-yard or animal-arena design, but it could hardly have persisted from 1576 to 1642 in a succession of specially designed playhouses had it run counter to logic and common sense. This traditional seating plan, however, accorded precisely with a tradition of acting on two levels — the distinguishing characteristic of the Elizabethan drama from its inception.[62]

[62] The different disposition of the private theatre audience — with the best seats in the pit, following Court practice — in time forced dramatists to minimize chamber scenes and eventually to abandon the upper stage entirely.

Chapter IX

THE TIRING-HOUSE: THIRD LEVEL

1. THE MUSIC GALLERY

EARLY in the chapter on the Globe tiring-house I spoke of the music gallery in the third level directly over the upper curtained stage. I turn now to the evidence relating to this part of the multiple stage.

No one denies the existence of a third story in the tiring-house, but considerable disagreement arises with regard to its function.[1] The question turns on the location of the stage superstructure. (The superstructure, technically known as the 'heavens,' consisted of a "hut," the under side of which was provided with trapdoors used for lowering and raising gods between Heaven and Earth, and a forward extension, the "stage-cover.") Now if the under side of the superstructure was on a plane with the ceiling of the second-level stage and of the middle spectator-gallery, then the scenic wall was only two stories high (23 feet from the platform to the floor of the hut) and the third level of the tiring-house lay outside the sphere of dramatic activity. Basing their contention in part upon the extant views of Elizabethan and Carolinian playhouse interiors, the majority of scholars regard this position of the superstructure and this disposition of the third level of the tiring-house as probably correct.

If, on the other hand, the under side of the superstructure was on a plane with the ceiling of the *third* level of the tiring-house and of the top spectator-gallery, then the scenic wall was three stories high (32 feet), and the third

---

[1] Cf. Lawrence, *Physical Conditions*, p. 94: "The disposition and offices of [this] story of the tiring-house form, I fear, an unsolvable mystery."

level of the tiring-house thus included in the visible scene was capable of development as a unit of the multiple stage. The evidence of the plays points to this more elevated position of the superstructure as correct — in the Globe, that is to say, and in other playhouses of its type and period.

First let us consider the extant pictorial representations of Elizabethan playhouse interiors. Two of the three views, the *Roxana* and *Messallina* title-page vignettes, are so very small that the engravers had no choice but to cut into the sides and to omit altogether the top features of the stage (i.e. the superstructure and, if it existed, the third story of the tiring-house). It does not follow, therefore, that because no third story is shown in either of these vignettes, none existed. Some sort of "heavens" over head and a pair of stage doors at the sides were normal features of every permanent stage from 1585 onwards, and yet they too are missing, presumably because the engraver lacked sufficient space to show them.

The third interior view, the De Witt sketch of the Swan in 1596, is considerably larger than the other two. It depicts the stage half of the playhouse containing the deep platform, the tiring-house with spectator-galleries converging upon it from both sides, the stage-cover, the hut, and the playhouse flag. Unfortunately for the present discussion, however, it is drawn as if the artist looked down into the yard from a position well above the roof-line, so that the third level of the tiring-house is wholly concealed by the large projecting stage-cover. The sketch, moreover, is so crudely executed and its perspective so distorted, particularly in those areas where the stage-cover joins the hut, and the hut joins the tiring-house, that one cannot determine at which point the hidden under side of the superstructure met the scenic wall — whether at the floor or at the ceiling level of the third story of the tiring-house.

The first, rather than the second, of these interpretations appears on first inspection to reflect the intention of the artist. (It is the interpretation generally accepted; [2] it leads to the conclusions outlined in the second paragraph of this chapter.) But closer study shows incontestably that the second interpretation only is practicable.

Four factors governing the location of the Swan stage-cover must be taken into account in considering the problem: (1) The third spectator-gallery extended to the sides of the tiring-house (see the De Witt sketch). (2) The third spectator-gallery was popular (see Chapter III) and hence well filled. (3) The stage-cover projected over slightly more than half the platform, and the platform extended to the middle of the playhouse yard (see the De Witt sketch). (4) The stage-cover was a useful but by no means essential unit of the stage. It played no part in descents to the outer stage from above; it was merely a roof projecting forward from the hut to shield the scenic wall and the rear half of the platform from rain and too much light (recall that in the Fortune contract the stage-cover is called "the shadow"). It could not have been tolerated had it intervened between any considerable number of spectators and a major unit of the multiple stage.

Now as experiments with a ruler applied to the Swan drawing (or to modern reconstructions based upon it) conclusively show, had the under side of the stage-cover

[2] In 1907 Mr. W. H. Godfrey, assisted by the late W. J. Lawrence and William Archer, undertook to reconstruct plans for the Fortune Playhouse. Inasmuch as the Fortune builder's contract merely specified "a shadowe or cover over the Saide stadge" modeled upon the cover at the Globe, Mr. Godfrey apparently turned to the Swan sketch for guidance in reconstructing this detail. Assuming that the under side of the Swan cover was level with the ceiling of the upper stage (and the middle spectator-gallery), Mr. Godfrey drew his plans accordingly. The wide reproduction of these plans in texts having to do with the Elizabethan drama has tended to establish this location of the stage-cover as correct. Not all scholars have accepted Mr. Godfrey's plans, however. Dr. J. Q. Adams, for example, represented the Globe with a third-level stage (*A Life of William Shakespeare*, 1923, p. 284).

been level with the floor of the third spectator-gallery, patrons throughout that gallery would have been unable to see upper-stage scenes. Patrons in the side bays of the top gallery would furthermore have been unable to see the stage door opening from the platform on the side of the theatre opposite to them.

Had the stage-cover been constructed 5 feet higher (midway, that is to say, between the floor and the ceiling of the third level of the frame),[3] top-gallery spectators opposite the tiring-house would have fared somewhat better, but those in the side bays would still have been unable to see the sides of the tarras and chamber opposite to them, or any part of the window-stage beyond — elements not included in the De Witt drawing but known, notwithstanding, to have existed at the Swan.

These experiments with a ruler demonstrate that the stage-cover cannot be lower than the head of the highest-placed spectator in the top gallery if he is to see all parts of the first and second levels of the stage. This interpretation of the Swan drawing, we must conclude, correctly reflects the intention of the artist.

Now the Globe stage-cover projected fully as far over the outer stage as did the Swan stage-cover (see Chapters IV and X), and hence what applies to the position of the one applies with equal force to the position of the other. If, therefore, my conclusion about the Swan is correct, the under side of the Globe stage-cover also was level with the ceiling of the third spectator-gallery, and the façade of the third story of the tiring-house was an integral, visible part of the scenic wall. Inasmuch as the third story of the Globe frame was everywhere 9 feet high, the total height of the scenic wall was 32 feet.

Portions of this third-story façade consisted of solid wall pierced by windows lighting the storage lofts within; but the middle portion, over the chamber, opened to form

---

[3] For illustration see the reconstruction by S. A. Tannenbaum, reproduced by Lawrence, *Those Nut-Cracking Elizabethans* (1935), frontispiece.

a small gallery. This gallery was guarded by a railing and was screened by a curtain behind which the playhouse orchestra performed except at such times as the "book" called for occasional music elsewhere. I turn now to the evidence substantiating these statements.

In plays written after 1592 there are a number of scenes which clearly require some sort of acting space in the scenic wall higher than the tarras. The earliest of these occurs in *1 Henry VI*, a play produced for many years by Shakespeare's company and eventually printed for the first time in the First Folio. Act III, scene ii, illustrates the capture of Rouen.

> *Enter* [on the outer stage] *Charles, Bastard, Alanson* [and Reignier].
> *Charles.* Saint *Dennis* blesse this happy Stratageme,
>   And once againe wee'le sleepe secure in Roan.
> *Bastard.* Here entred *Pucell*, and her Practisants:
>   Now she is there, how will she specifie?
>   Here [i.e. Where] is the best and safest passage in.
> *Reig.* By thrusting out a Torch from yonder Tower,
>   Which once discern'd, shewes that her meaning is,
>   No way to that (for weaknesse) which she entred.
>   *Enter Pucell on the top, thrusting out a Torch burning.*
> *Pucell.* Behold, this is the happy Wedding Torch,
>   That joyneth Roan unto her Countreymen,
>   But burning fatall to the *Talbonites*.
> *Bastard.* See Noble *Charles* the Beacon of our friend,
>   The burning Torch in yonder Turret stands.

After suitable alarums and excursions:

> *Enter Talbot and Burgonie without* [i.e. on the outer stage]: *within*,
> *Pucell, Charles, Bastard, and Reignier on the Walls* [i.e. on the tarras].

Sir Edmund Chambers comments upon this passage as follows: [4]

There is an interesting bit of staging in the use of 'top' in [*1 Henry VI*] I. iv and III. ii, but I do not accept Gaw's elaborate argument to

[4] *William Shakespeare* (1930), i. 293.

show that this was a new structural feature first invented at the Rose in 1592, or think with him that it was the loft from which the theatre's flag waved and its trumpet was blown. Nothing here could come into the action of a play, in view of the intervention of the projecting 'heavens'. The 'top' must have been over the stage balcony, on a level with the upper row of galleries, as the balcony itself was on a level with the middle row.

With this interpretation I wholly agree.

A second example occurs in *Claudius Tiberius Nero* (printed in 1607, author, company, and theatre unknown), scene xiv. Instead of a Turret overlooking city walls, this scene demands a Keep overlooking the outer defenses of a castle. Germanicus and his Roman legions are besieging the castle of Vonones, King of Armenia. Beaten in the first engagement outside the castle, Vonones and his son retreat into the castle and appear upon the walls where they exchange taunts with Germanicus below. Then, at line 1880:

Germanicus and Piso scale the walles, Germanicus is repulst the first assault, Piso winneth the wall first, but is in danger by Vonones and his sonne: Germanicus rescueth Piso, Vonones and his sonne flie.

Germ. *Che sara, sara,* maugre all their force,
  Tigranocerta, is subdued to vs.
  Romanes assault the Keepe, let them not breath,
  Till with the cinders of the fired Tower,
  Your dreadfull furie cleane dissolued be.
          Sound a parley within.
Piso. But harke, th' Armenians doe a parly craue.
  I thinke thei'l yeeld, and so our labour saue.
Ger. Then sound terror to their melting hearts.
      They resound a parley, and [enter] *Vonones on the Keepe.*

Vonones does not offer to surrender, however, but demands a chance to meet Germanicus in single combat. At line 1917:

Germ. Discend Vonones, on my honours pawne
  For to performe this resolution.
      Germanicus comes downe to the Stage [i.e. the platform].

Romaines, on your alleagiance be gone,
Perswasion is the sight of present death:
I see the Garlands dangling in the skies,
Of Coruin and Torquates victories.

Vonones commeth downe [i.e. to the platform], *they fight and breath,
Vonones being wounded.*

In the second bout Vonones is slain; then (at line 1944):

*Piso and all the Romaines come downe from the wall to Germanicus,
and Germanicus speaks to them.*

Observe that from line 1880 to line 1944 the tarras is occupied by Romans. The "Keepe," therefore, is represented by some other stage, presumably higher than the
tarras, for it was the nature of a keep to dominate all other
defenses. Observe also that while on the walls himself
(that is, on the tarras), Germanicus calls to Vonones "on
the Keepe" to "Discend." And finally, observe that it
takes Vonones four lines longer to descend from the Keep
(by the actors' stairs) than it takes Germanicus to climb
down a scaling ladder from the tarras to the ground and
to dismiss the Roman soldiers standing by on the outer
stage. Every fact and implication of this scene points to
a stage in the third story of the tiring-house.

A third example is one of a series of ship scenes in which
the platform stage serves as the main deck, the tarras as
the raised quarter deck, and the music gallery as the main-
top or crow's nest. From *The Double Marriage* (a play
by Fletcher and Massinger, produced at the Globe and
Blackfriars in 1620 by the King's Men), II. i:

Enter Boateswain and Gunner [to the platform] —

Boats. The ship runs merrily, my Captain's melancholly,
And nothing cures that in him but a Sea-fight:
I hope to meet a sail boy, and a right one.

Gun. That's my hope too; I am ready for the pastime.

Boats. I' th' mean time let's bestow a Song upon him,
To shake him from his dumps, and bid good day to him.
Ho, in the hold.

Enter a Boy.

Boy. Here, here.

Boats. To th' Main top, Boy.
And thou kenst a ship that dares defie us,
Here's Gold.

Boy. I am gone.   *Exit Boy.*

Boats. Come sirs, a quaint *Levet.*   *Trump. a Levet.*
To waken our brave General. Then to our labor.

      Enter the Duke of Sesse above [on the tarras], *and his*
          daughter Martia, like an Amazon.

Ses. I thank you loving mates; I thank you all,
There's to prolong your mirth, and good morrow to you.

Nineteen lines later the Boatswain calls up the Master of
the Ship; and "*Enter below* [i.e. on the platform] *the Master
and Sailors.*" The Duke and his daughter above talk with
the Master and Gunner below for approximately one
hundred lines. Resuming:

Mast. We have liv'd all with you,   *Boy a top.*
And will die with you General.

Ses. I thank you Gentlemen.

Boy above. A Sail, a Sail.

Mast. A cheerful sound.

Boy. A Sail.

Boats. Of whence? of whence boy?

Boy. A lusty Sail.

Daugh. Look right, and look again.

Boy. She plows the Sea before her,
And fomes i' th' mouth.

Boats. Of whence?

Boy. I ken not yet sir. . . . I think of *Naples* Master,
Methinks I see the Arms.

Mast. Up, up another,
And give more certain signs.   *Exit Sailor.*

Twelve lines later (decasyllabic lines for the most part) the
Sailor joins the Boy on the Main top:

Sayl. above. Ho.

Ses. [on the tarras]. Of whence now?

Sail. Of *Naples, Naples, Naples.*
  I see her top-Flag, how she quarters *Naples.*
  I hear her Trumpets.
Ses. Down, she's welcome to us.

Inasmuch as this scene employs a "top" stage located with reference to the tarras and outer stage in such a way as to suggest a masthead high above the quarter deck and main deck of a ship, we are justified in believing that the Globe had a stage in the third level of the tiring-house. Observe that an interval represented by twelve lines of dialogue is provided to enable the sailor to leave the outer stage and reach this top gallery. This is double the allowance normally provided for mounting to the tarras.

Another ship scene making demands upon the music gallery is found in Heywood and Rowley's *Fortune by Land and Sea,* first produced between 1607 and 1609 at the Red Bull Playhouse. With considerable daring the authors, in Act IV, introduce two ships. Scene i presents the main deck of the pirate ship (an outer-stage scene); scene ii presents the "upper deck" of the English ship searching the seas for a worthy prize (a tarras scene). In scene ii, at line 48:

Young Fortune [on the tarras]. Would we in the mid sea encounter them!
  Climb to the main-top, boy, see what you kenne there.
Boy. I shall, I shall Sir.   [Exit boy.]
Young For. We seek for purchase, but we tak't from foes,
  And such is held amongst us lawful spoyl;
  But such as are our friends & countrymen
  We succour with the best supply we have
  Of victuals or munition being distrest.
Above, Boy. Ho there.
1. Mariner. Ha boy.
Boy. A sayl.
1. Mar. Whence is she?

The pirate ship is at last identified and overtaken; amid alarums and gun fire the two engage; the English ship

THE INTERIOR OF THE SWAN PLAYHOUSE

The sketch is based upon the "observations" of Johannes De Witt, who visited London in 1596

triumphs. Observe that an interval of five lines is provided to enable the Boy to leave the tarras and reach the music gallery.

Other scenes making use of a mast-head or of a similarly elevated point of observation are listed in the notes.[5]

In still another type of scene the top gallery is used by a privileged spectator intent on viewing the action below. In *Lady Alimony* (printed in 1659; author and company unknown), Trillo announces his intention of watching the action (which subsequently takes place on both levels of the stage) from aloft, and to applaud only when genuinely pleased. In III. iv, comes the first interruption:

Trillo from the high gallery. I cannot, gentlemen contain myself.
Timon. Thy genius has surpass'd itself;
   Thy scene is richly various; prease on still;
   These galleries applaud thy comic skill.
He takes his seat again.[6]

Again, IV. vii:

     Trillo from the gallery.
Bravely continued, Timon, as I live;
Each subtle strain deserves a laurel sprig.

Now the "high gallery" could, of course, be the top spectator-gallery, but in view of the scenes reviewed in this chapter we may reasonably assume that the music gallery, facing the audience, was used.[7]

  [5] *Dick of Devonshire,* I. iii; *The Fair Maid of the West,* Part 1, IV; *ibid.,* Part 2, III; *The Hector of Germany,* IV. vi. Later in this chapter I shall have occasion to show that *The Tempest,* III. iii, and *The Roman Actor,* II. i, are related scenes.

  [6] The text appears to be corrupt. The speech here assigned to Timon should be a continuation of Trillo's praise of Timon, the supposed author.

  [7] For similar stage business see *Fuimus Troes* (an academic play, *ca.* 1625), Induction; and *The Silver Age,* III. The playhouse custom of placing a deity in the music gallery where he surveys the stage below is perhaps glanced at in Heywood's *Apology for Actors,* 1612:

      If then the world a theater present
      As by the roundness it appears most fit,
      Built with starre galleries of high ascent
      In which Jehove doth as spectator sit, . . .

To sum up. The under side of the Globe stage-cover (and hut) was level with the ceiling of the top spectator-gallery. The scenic wall therefore included the façade of the third story of the tiring-house and was 32 feet high. The first extant play containing an action which involves this third story dates from the last decade of the sixteenth century. Dramatists thereafter occasionally made use of some opening at this level to create scenes in which a turret, tower, keep, masthead, or high gallery overlooks the tarras and the outer stage below.

It is probably worth noting that eight of the eleven scenes quoted (or listed in note 5) were produced at public playhouses, specifically the Globe, Red Bull, Curtain, and (in the case of *1 Henry VI*) perhaps also the Rose and the Theater. We may conclude, therefore, that every public playhouse, certainly after 1599, had a stage of some sort on the third level of the tiring-house. The fact that *The Double Marriage*, *The Tempest*, and *The Roman Actor* were owned and produced by the King's Men suggests that the Blackfriars Playhouse had a stage similarly located.

It is hardly necessary to point out that no scene yet cited gives any indication of the nature of this third-level stage. No revealing stage business takes place there; as a rule only one actor at a time appears there, and then for a brief period. Except that Trillo "takes his seat again," one might be justified in supposing that a window in the façade above the tarras served the purpose.

But by pursuing a different line of enquiry we come upon details which establish a curtained gallery, distinct from the chamber, located aloft in the tiring-house. And this gallery, though primarily the domain of the playhouse orchestra, furnished the stage "on the top" which we have been investigating.

It is well known that by 1600 the Elizabethan drama had entered upon a period in which music played an ever increasing part. Companies of boy actors originally

trained as choristers ushered in the new style. For a few
seasons, indeed, they were so much the fashion that their

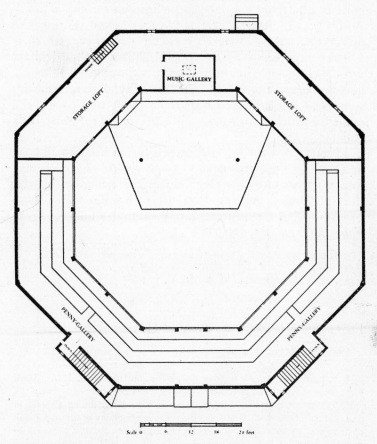

RECONSTRUCTED PLAN OF THE GLOBE: THIRD LEVEL

older rivals had lean audiences and were even reduced to
touring the provinces. To meet this competition the adult
companies recruited expert singers and instrumentalists,
and encouraged playwrights to introduce songs and music

of every type on every suitable occasion.[8] Music became one of the chief attractions of the theatre. Gamaliel Ratsey comments in *Ratseis Ghost*, 1605: "I have often gone to plaies more for the musicke then for the action." And Coryat, that sagacious voyager, after visiting the finest theatres of Venice, reports: "Neither can their actors compare with us, for apparel, shows, and musicke." [9]

W. J. Lawrence has traced with admirable skill the origins and growth of the Elizabethan playhouse orchestra.[10] At this time, therefore, I need review only that part of the evidence which throws light on the nature of the musician's gallery.

Except when the "book" called for an accompaniment or a song on the visible stage, the playhouse musicians performed in some gallery high up in the tiring-house, and they performed unseen. Play after play illustrates these conditions. A few representative examples follow. From *Four Plays in One*, Part IV:

> *Jupiter and Mercury descend severally. Trumpets small above.*

From *The Unfortunate Lovers*, V. iv:

> *Strange music is heard above.*

From *Love's Changelings Change*, II. i:

> *Still Music from above with shrill voice naming Philoclea.*

[8] Cf. E. W. Naylor, *Shakespeare and Music*, pp. 162–163: "*Music, Music plays, Music within*. This direction is found forty-one times in twenty-two plays, half of which are comedies. In eight cases we have *Music* during a speech or dream of one of the characters; seven times as the symphony or the accompaniment to a song; seven times in wedding processions or pageants; six times for dancing; and five times during a banquet. To give a just idea of the amount of stage music considered necessary in or near Shakespeare's time, there must be added to the above, all the stage directions in other terms, e.g. *Hautboys*, which is found about fourteen times . . . *Trumpets* . . . some fifty-one times in twenty-two plays, either alone, or in connection with sennet, discharge of cannon, etc."

[9] *Crudities*, 1611, p. 247.

[10] "The English Theatre Orchestra, Its Rise and Early Characteristics," *Musical Quarterly*, III (January, 1917), No. 1.

From *The Cruel Brother*, V. i. Foreste enters Corsa's room (a chamber scene), accuses her of adultery, and after tying her into a chair, opens a vein in her arm so that she bleeds to death.

Corsa. Mercy heaven!
>   *She dies. Still music aboue.*
Fores. Hark!
>   As she ascends, the spheres do welcome her
>   With their own music. . .   *Cease Recorders.*

As any number of illustrations make clear, the music coming from the upper regions of the tiring-house lacked, seemingly, a point of origin. Let me cite a few examples. From *Sun's Darling*, II, immediately before a passage of music:

Delight. Hover, you wing'd Musicians, in the air;
>   Clouds leave your dancing, no windes stir but fair.

From *The Spanish Gipsy*, IV. iii:

Soto. I have sought him, my lord . . . in air, wheresoever I heard noise
>   of fiddlers.

From *A New Trick to Cheat the Devil*, IV. i:

Slightall.   What musicke's this
>   *Musicke.*
>   Descends it from the Spheares? Hangs it in the Aire?
>   Or issues it from Hell?

Glendower's turn of phrase when calling for music in his Welsh castle illustrates this fact (*1 Henry IV*, III. i):

>   And those Musitians that shall play to you,
>   Hang in the Ayre a thousand Leagues from thence;
>   And straight they shall be here: sit and attend. . . .
>   *The Musicke playes.*

On the basis of these examples and the many others like them, we may conclude that the music gallery was located at the top of the tiring-house. A definition by Robert

Cawdrey appearing in his *Table Alphabeticall of English Words*, 1604, is worth repeating here:

Poulpitre: m. A lecterne, (high) Deske, or Pulpit; also a Presse for bookes to stand in; also a Stage, or part of a Theater wherein Players act; also, a roome for Musicians in th' upper part of a Stage, &c.

(In one or two private theatres the tiring-house may have been only two stories high; [11] there the musicians probably performed either in the chamber or in one of the window-stages, preferably the latter, because the sash-curtains were of lighter material than the stage curtains and because the projecting windows permitted a better view of the stage below.)

Implicit in the dialogue and stage-directions I have quoted is the fact that the playhouse musicians were unseen by the audience. This concealment was essential. When "trumpets small above" herald the descent of celestial beings, when a soul ascends into Heaven to "still music aboue," or when the "drummers make thunder in the tyring-house," [12] the sight of those producing the sounds would be distracting and inartistic. A second and more compelling reason for screening the music room was that the musicians were constantly being called upon to descend singly or in groups to some other part of the stage for songs, accompaniments, and incidental music, some-

---

[11] The Blackfriars tiring-house, as noted earlier, appears to have had three levels. A detailed stage description in Percy's *Faery Pastoral*, written in 1602 for Paul's, seems to indicate a third level in that theatre: "*Highest, aloft, and on the Top of the Musick Tree the Title The Faery Pastorall, Beneath him pind on Post of the Tree The Scene Eluida Forrest. Lowest of all over the Canopie* ΝΑΠΑΙΤ-ΒΟΔΑΙΟΝ *or Faery Chappell.*"

[12] Cf. Melton's *Astrologaster*, 1620, p. 31: "Another will fore-tell of Lightning and Thunder that shall happen such a day, when there are no such Inflamations seene, except men goe to the Fortune in Golding-Lane, to see the Tragedie of Doctor Faustus. There, indeede, a man may behold shagge-hayred Deuills runne roaring ouer the Stage with squibs in their mouthes, while drummers make thunder in the tyring-house." Cf. also *Every Man in his Humour*, Prologue; and *The Birth of Hercules*, line 2319.

times performed visibly (as in *Much Ado About Nothing*, II. iii; *Othello*, III. i; *The Lady Mother*, II; and *The Knave in Grain*, III) and sometimes off stage. The following quotations from Globe and Blackfriars plays will suggest a few of these back-stage shifts. The first quarto of Massinger's *City Madam* preserves in its margins certain notes entered in the prompt-copy. In IV. ii, at line 131:

Whilst the Act Plays, the Footstep, little Table and Arras hung up [in the study] *for the Musicians.*

The Act closes at line 160. In V. i, at line 7:

Musicians come down to make ready for the song at Arras.

And in V. ii (the final scene), at line 43 comes the direction for which the others were preparing:

Musick. At one door Cerberus, at the other Charon, Orpheus, Chorus.

In *The Bondman*, III. iii, Poliphron has been responsible for the preparations for a dance (an outer-stage scene):

Gracculo. Where's the Musicke.
Poliphron. I have plac'd it in yon Window.
Grac. Begin then sprightly.
                    The dance at the end, Enter Pisander.

In this scene, evidently, as in others where the dance must go off creditably, the musicians are brought down to a position nearer the dancers. Poliphron's explanation is characteristic of the pains most dramatists took to account smoothly for the placing of musicians in a stage commonly associated with acting. When a dance is given on the platform or in one of the inner stages and the music must be heard clearly by both actors and audience, the musicians usually play in a window-stage with the sash-curtains closed. A tavern scene (in the chamber) in *Covent Garden Weeded*, IV. ii, illustrates this procedure and the steps taken to account for the musicians being unseen.

Mihil. I'le stop your mouth, you said you came to be merry.

Nick. Yes, I vow, and brought Fidlers along, but they must play i'th next room, for here's one breaks all the Fiddles that come in his reach. Come sir, will you drink, dance, and do as we do?

Gabriel. I'le drink, I'le dance, I'le kisse, or do any thing, any living thing with any of you, that is Brother or Sister. Sweet-heart let me feel thy Coney.

Mih. I now he's in. Play Fidlers. Dance [i.e. *They Dance*].

The following quotation from *The Fatal Dowry,* **IV.** ii (an inner-stage scene), suggests that Jacobean audiences became wholly accustomed to music rendered by unseen performers:

Beaumont [to musicians within]. Begin the new ayre.

Charalois. Shall we not see them?

Aymiero. A little distance from the instruments
    Will to your eares convey the harmony
    With more delight.   *Song above.*

But it was often desirable not to bring the musicians down from their gallery aloft to play for a dance or to provide an accompaniment for a singer. At such times signals were employed to co-ordinate the music produced above and the action or the song below. Apart from direct commands given in the course of dialogue, these signals took various forms. Let me illustrate three used commonly. From *The Faery Pastoral,* V. v: "*Musick to the song her*[e] *knock't up.*" A similar prompter's note, reduced to the one word "Strike," precedes an accompanied song in *The Beggar's Bush,* II. i: [13]

All. O gracious Prince, 'save, 'save the good King *Clause.*

Higgen. A Song to crown him.

Ferret. Set a Centinel out first.

Snap. The word?

[13] See also *The Aphrodisial,* III. i; *Arabia Sitiens, passim; The Cuck-Queanes and Cuckolds Errants, passim; Cupid's Sacrifice, passim; The Knave in Grain,* II. i, and III. i; *Necromantes, passim; The Valiant Welshman,* C2; *What You Will,* II. ii; *A Wife for a Month,* II. v; and *The Witches of Lancashire,* IV. i and v.

Hig. A cove comes, and fumbumbis to it. *Strike.*
The SONG.
"Cast our Caps and cares away: . . ."

This standard signaling procedure is followed in *The Fair Maid of the Inn*, IV. ii, during a little entertainment prepared by Forobosco for the Host and his family. Acting the part of the book-holder or prompter, Forobosco waits until all the guests are seated. Then:

Foro. lookes in a booke, strikes with his wand, Musick playes.
Enter 4 Boyes shap't like Frogs, and dance.

The similarity between this type of music signal and a normal trap signal (see Chapter IV) is apparent.

A second standard type of music signal was visual rather than audible. From *The Cruelty of the Spaniards in Peru*, I:

The Chief Priest of Peru wav'd his verge toward the Room where the Musick are plac'd behind a Curtain.

Although this example is drawn from an entertainment presented at the Cockpit in Drury Lane in 1658, I have cited it first because it illuminates earlier instances of the same type of signal, as, for example, the two found in Shakespeare's *Tempest*. The one occurs during the scene (II. i) in which Alonso, Gonzalo, and Adrian lie sleeping (on the outer stage), and Antonio and Sebastian offer to stand guard. Instead of protecting the king, however, the two treacherous nobles agree to kill him and Gonzalo. At line 290:

Seb. Thy case, deere Friend
   Shall be my pre[ce]dent: As thou got'st Millaine,
   I'le come by *Naples*: Draw thy sword, one stroke
   Shall free thee from the tribute which thou paiest,
   And I the King shall love thee.
Ant. Draw together:
   And when I reare my hand, do you the like
   To fall it on *Gonzalo*.

At this point, all modern editors agree, the two men draw their swords and raise them in unison. But just as they are about to drive the blades into Alonso and Gonzalo, Sebastian calls, "O, but one word." Then follows the direction:

Enter Ariell with Musicke and Song.

In this episode the pointedly unified raising of the two swords constitutes the signal awaited in the music room.

The other example occurs in the final scene of *The Tempest* during the noble passage in which Prospero puts away his magic powers (an outer-stage scene):

But this rough Magicke
I heere abjure: and when I have requir'd
Some heavenly Musicke (which even now I do)
To worke mine end upon their Sences, that
This Ayrie-charme is for, I'le breake my staffe,
Bury it certaine fadomes in the earth,
And deeper than did ever Plummet sound
Ile drowne my booke.   *Solemne musicke.*

Heere enters Ariel before: Then Alonso with a frantic gesture,
attended by Gonzalo.

I assume that Prospero raised his staff as a signal to the playhouse orchestra while speaking the words "which even now I do." The succeeding lines probably were accompanied by the opening bars of the *Solemne musicke.*

Still another type of signal passed through an intermediary. In Jonson's Whitefriar's play *Epicoene*, IV. ii, Otter remarks at line 12:

Gentlemen, I haue plac'd the drum and the trumpets, and one to giue 'hem the signe when you are ready.

Then at line 69 he adds, "Sound Tritons of the Thames," whereupon follows the direction:

Morose speakes from aboue: the trumpets sounding.

I have had a double purpose in mind in setting out this review of music signals. In addition to showing how music and action were co-ordinated on the Elizabethan stage, the signals supply final proof of the location of the music gallery in the third level of the tiring-house. This fact will appear yet more clearly in the two scenes I am about to cite, both of which are found in plays acted at the Globe and Blackfriars theatres.

In Act II, scene i, of *The Roman Actor*, Caesar, on the outer stage, sends Aretinus into the palace with a message to Domitia (see line 171):

> And say I doe entreate (for she rules him
> Whom all men else obey) she would vouchsafe
> The musicke of her voice, at yonder window,
> When I aduaunce my hand thus.   *Exit Aretinus.*

Later in the same scene (at line 214), to torture Domitia's husband, Caesar continues:

>   I sing her praise?
> 'Tis farre from my ambition to hope it.   *Musicke aboue*
> It being a debt she onely can lay downe,   *and a song.*
> And no tongue else discharge. Harke. I thinke promp[t]ed
> With my consent that you once more should heare her,
> She does begin. An vniversall silence
> Dwell on this place. 'Tis death with lingring torments
> To all that dare disturbe her. Who can heare this *The song*
> And falls not downe and worships? in my fancie,   *ended*
> *Apollo* being iudge on Latinos hill,   *Caesar goe[s] on.*
> Fair hayr'd *Calliope* on her iuorie Lute, . . .

The scene is thus printed in the only seventeenth-century edition of the play (dated 1629). It is obvious that the directions in the quarto are crowded out of their proper places by the long lines and are placed as near as may be in the spaces left by the short lines. Accordingly, modern editions, following Gifford, print this scene (lines 214–222) as follows:

> *Domitia appears at the window.*
> Caesar. I sing her praise?
>   'Tis far from my ambition to hope it;

It being a debt she only can lay down,
And no tongue else discharge.
            He raises his hand. Music above.
                        Hark! I think, prompted
With my consent that you once more should hear her,
She does begin. An universal silence
Dwell on this place. 'Tis death with lingering torments,
To all that dare disturb her. —
                        A song by Domitia.
                        Who can hear this
And falls not down and worships?

Try as one may, one cannot reject any one of these modern-ized stage-directions nor dispute their placement in the text. Thoroughly understood, then, this scene in *The Roman Actor* shows clearly how a song in the window-stage and its unseen accompaniment by the playhouse orchestra in the music gallery were co-ordinated by a signal from an actor on the outer stage.

In the necessity for Caesar's signal lies proof that the music gallery was located in the third level of the tiring-house. Consider the alternative possibilities. They are limited to the second level of the tiring-house (compare "musicke above"); to a curtained stage (the musicians never "enter" the stage) which at the same time looks out on the lower stage (otherwise Caesar's signal could not have been seen). We are thus left with the two window-stages. Had the musicians shared the window-stage in which Domitia stood, she could have given the signal and Caesar's would have been wholly unnecessary. Had they occupied the opposite window-stage, they could have seen Domitia once she appeared in her window, and, more-over, they would have been close enough to the lower stage to follow every word of the dialogue. It is very doubtful, however, if instrumentalists in one window-stage could successfully have accompanied a singer in the other. There is no instance, so far as I know, of this procedure.

But placed in the music gallery in the third level of the

tiring-house, the musicians could not see Domitia in the window below, nor (as examples of music signals in other plays indicate) could they be sure of beginning on time without a signal either from the prompter off stage or from some actor. In the scene before us, therefore, Caesar gives the signal to them to begin playing because he (unlike the prompter) stands where he can see Domitia and at the same time be seen by the playhouse orchestra.

In *The Tempest*, III. iii (an outer-stage scene), three long directions are inserted in the Folio text to guide the spectacle which marks the routing of Prospero's enemies and the turning point of the play. The first occurs at line 19:

Solemne and strange Musicke: and Prosper on the top (inuisible:) Enter seuerall strange shapes, bringing in a Banket; and dance about it with gentle actions of salutations, and inuiting the King, &c. to eate, they depart.

The King and his companions recover from their amazement and (at line 50) approach the table. At line 52:

Thunder and Lightning. Enter Ariell (like a Harpey) claps his wings vpon the Table, and with a quient deuice the Banquet vanishes.

In the stunned silence which follows Ariel delivers his message from Prospero; when it is concluded (at line 82):

He vanishes in Thunder: then (to soft Musicke.) Enter the shapes againe, and daunce (with mockes and mowes) and carrying out the Table.

Prospero speaks in praise of Ariel and makes his exit at line 94.

Except for the nature of the "quaint device" and the manner of its operation (matters which I have already analyzed in another place [14]), no part of these three directions is more interesting than the reason underlying Prospero's appearance "on the top" (compare *1 Henry VI*, III. ii). His costume supposedly makes him visible

---

[14] *R.E.S.*, XIV (October, 1938).

only to the audience. He apparently takes no part in the action. His few lines are in the nature of an aside and throw no light on the real cause of his being present.

Our present insight into Elizabethan playhouse music signals, however, illuminates Shakespeare's purpose in placing Prospero in the forefront of the music gallery. Observe the sequence of events after Alonso and his companions have entered the outer stage. (1) *Music sounds*; while it continues Prospero takes his place "on the top"; and Shapes enter below (through one of the stage doors) bringing in a table set with food; they dance and depart. (2) Alonso and his companions draw near the table, intending to taste the food. (3) *Thunder sounds*; Ariel descends from the stage heavens through a trap and causes the banquet to disappear from the table. (4) Ariel delivers his message. (5) "Ariel vanishes in Thunder," i.e. *Thunder sounds* for the second time and while it rumbles Ariel ascends and disappears into the stage heavens. Finally (6) the thunder subsides and *music sounds* once more: the Shapes appear, dance a second time, and carry out the table.

Now it will be found that four parts of this action are associated with signals coming from the musicians and thunder-makers placed directly behind Prospero in the music gallery.[15] The signals follow a more logical and rou-

---

[15] The traditional English method of simulating thunder employed a battery of snare drums and kettledrums. A second method, probably of Italian origin, is described by Sabbatini, *Practica di fabricar Scene e Machine ne' Teatri*, 1638 (translated by Campbell, *Scenes and Machines*, p. 157): "A thirty-pound ball of iron or stone to be rolled down an uneven set of steps fixed in a channel constructed in the chamber above the heavens." Both methods were employed in the Elizabethan playhouse (in addition to the machine in the huts, the Globe may possibly have had a second machine in the Hell — see *A Woman Never Vext*, II. i). Jonson refers to both methods of producing thunder in the Prologue to *Every Man in his Humour*. The thunder drums were located in the tiring-house proper (see note 12 above), and specifically in the music loft. This last fact gives point to a passage in *The Woman's Prize*, IV. iv, where, speaking in the language of the playhouse, Jaques advises:

tine pattern than may at first glance appear. Two of them, the music signals, are designed as cues for the prompter standing behind the scenic wall two floors below. The other two, the thunder signals, are designed as cues for the stage-hands inside the stage superstructure immediately overhead. These unmistakably dissimilar pairs of cues, originating in the music gallery and spread by the sounding-board effect of the stage-cover, would penetrate to every corner of the playhouse. Each time the *music* sounds, the prompter knows that he must send the Shapes on stage for their round of duties. Each time the *thunder* sounds, the stage-hands above know that they must attend to Ariel, lowering him the first time and raising him the second. Both sets of signals — music for the dancing and thunder for the trap-work — are strictly in accord with normal Elizabethan stage usage.

Now if this display, one of the most complex ever written for an Elizabethan playhouse,[16] was to run off smoothly, the person directing it had to be placed where he could follow every move on the stage and at the same time be in close touch with the source of these all-important music and thunder cues. No position *inside* the tiring-house met these conditions. But "on the top" did. For that reason Shakespeare placed a responsible actor — none so suitable as Prospero — in front of the music-gallery curtains and had him unobtrusively transmit orders to the musicians concealed immediately behind him. By this arrangement

---

To laugh at all she do's, or when she railes,
To have a drum beaten o'th top o'th house,
To give the neighbors warning of her Larme
As I do when my Wife rebels.

[16] Observe that it actively involves (1) a group of six actors in the royal party; (2) a group of dancers probably numbering six or more; (3) Prospero; (4) Ariel; (5) stage-hands to operate the heavens windlasses; (6) musicians; and (7) the prompter. Moreover, three levels of the tiring-house are involved: the main stage, the music gallery (for Prospero as well as the musicians), and the "huts."

the appropriate sound-cues were evoked without a second's delay for all the company to hear.

A few words about the music-room curtains before which Prospero stood. They were wholly unlike the stage curtains below. The latter had to be heavy, opaque, and strong in order to shut off all sight of inner stages when not in use (and muffle any sounds made there during the alteration of settings), and to withstand the strains occasioned by being rapidly opened and closed many times a day. But the music curtains had to be just the opposite. In order not to muffle the music, which ranged all the way from the soft and delicate to the harsh and clamorous, they had to be thin. Translucency, moreover, was essential. The light by which the musicians worked was not produced artificially inside the gallery but came through the curtains from the unroofed yard. This last fact meant that a fabric of loose weave and the lightest texture could be used and still effectively screen the musicians from the audience (who faced the curtains from the same side as the source of light).

Because the musicians almost never opened their curtains [17] and because actors seldom had occasion to do so, it is not to be wondered at that references to music curtains are rare in the literature of the period.[18] Richard Brathwait

---

[17] In Heywood's *Witches of Lancashire*, F4 verso, occurs the following episode:

Arthur [on the outer stage]. Play fidlers any thing.

Doughty. I, and lets see your faces, that you play fairely with us.

   Musitians shew themselves above . . .

Shakston. Play out that we may heare you.

Fidler. So we do sir, as loud as we can possibly.

   Cf. also *The Knight of the Burning Pestle*, II. ii.

[18] The window-curtains were installed primarily to make those stages available for musicians, and were probably made of the same fabric. But because they were installed in a stage used frequently by actors who required the curtains opened (unlike the musicians who required them closed), they gave rise to not a little stage business and to frequent allusions in dialogue. For examples, see Chapter VIII.

mentions them in his *Whimzies, or a new cast of characters,* 1631, when describing a Gamester: [19]

Hee seldome ha's time to take Ayre, unlesse it be to a play; where if his pockets will give leave, you shall see him aspire to a box: or like the *Silent Woman,* sit demurely upon the stage. Where, at the end of every act, while the encurtain'd musique sounds, to give enter-breath to the actors, and more grace to their action, casting his cloake carelessly on his left shoulder, hee enters into some complementall discourse with one of his ordinarie gallants.

I have already quoted a direction from *The Cruelty of the Spaniards in Peru* (produced at the Cockpit in 1658) which mentions "the Room where the Musick are plac't behind a Curtain." A third reference is found in a contemporary account of Davenant's yet earlier play *The Siege of Rhodes* (produced at Rutland House in 1656): "The Musick was above in a loover hole railed about and covered with sarcenetts to conceal them." [20] The words "railed about" suggest that the "loover hole" was open to the floor but guarded against accidents by a railing perhaps similar to that fronting a tarras. (It is worth adding here that the frontispiece of *The Wits, or Sport upon Sport,* 1672, shows a railing behind the curtains of its second-level music gallery.) "Sarcenet," one discovers, was the name given to a very thin silk fabric originally manufactured by the Saracens and imported into England as early as the middle of the sixteenth century. A fourth reference occurs in the Revels Accounts for 1611, where mention is made of "a curtain of silk for the Music House at White-Hall." Diaphanous curtains appear in the music-loft openings of the Duke's Theatre, built in 1671, but I cannot discover what they were made of.

Even in 1670, when playhouse orchestras were larger

[19] Edited by J. O. Halliwell, 1860, p. 40.

[20] *State Papers Domestic,* 1656, CXXVIII, art. 108. A much earlier account (*State Papers Domestic, Ser. Elizabeth,* XXXVI, No. 22) dated Feb. 18, 1564/5, includes: "a rocke or hill for the ix Musses to sing uppone with a vayne of sarsnett drawen upp & downe before them."

than in Shakespeare's day, the music lofts of English and Continental theatres were relatively small. It seems reasonable, therefore, to assume that the Globe music gallery was perhaps half the width of the chamber and was placed midway in the façade directly overhead.

When in 1660 theatres threw open their doors again only four of the old-style public playhouses were still in existence. Two, the Curtain and the Fortune, were in the last stages of decay and were soon pulled down. A third, the Hope, was refurbished for animal baiting but not, as in days gone by, for plays as well. Only the Red Bull was serviceable, but after three years it too was abandoned by its company in favor of a new home. In the new theatres which sprang up (all of which were roofed and had auditoriums with the private-theatre seating plan), if much was changed, much remained the same. The musicians, for example, found themselves placed in a loft high above the stage, a loft constructed over the proscenium arch and level with the third spectator-galleries.[21] In most of the new theatres the loft continued there until different styles of entertainment required the transfer of the musicians to a section of the pit between the audience and the apron.[22] The first theatre to experiment with the new location was the Theatre Royal in Drury Lane, which Pepys visited on May 8, 1663. Let me close this section by quoting his comparison of the old and the new:

> Thence to my brother's, and there took up my wife and Ashwell to the Theatre Royall, being the second day of its being opened. The house is made with extraordinary good contrivance, and yet hath some faults, as the narrowness of the passages in and out of the pitt, and the distance from the stage to the boxes, which I am confident cannot hear; but for all other things it is well, only, above all, the musique being below, and most of it sounding under the very stage, there is no hearing of the bases at all, nor well of the trebles, which sure must be mended.[23]

[21] For illustration see the plates included in *The Empress of Morocco*, 4to, 1673 (two are reproduced by Summers, *Restoration Theatre*, facing pp. 104 and 206).

[22] See *The Tempest, or the Enchanted Island*, 1670, I. i.

[23] *Diary*, ed. Wheatley, iii. 108.

2. STORAGE ROOMS AND DRESSING ROOMS

Flanking the music gallery and extending into the wings of the tiring-house over the window-stages lay, it seems, two great lofts used by the company for the storage of costumes and properties. In Brome's *Antipodes*, III. v, Letoy, a madman, is reported as having broken into some storage place where properties were kept:

Byplay. He has got into our Tyring-house amongst us,
  And tane a strict survey of all our properties,
  Our statues and our images of Gods;
  Our Planets and our constellations,
  Our Giants, Monsters, Furies, Beasts and Bug-Beares,
  Our Helmets, Shields, and Vizors, Haires, and Beards,
  Our Pastbord March-paines, and our Wooden Pies . . .
  Spying at last the Crowne and royall Robes
  Ith upper wardrobe, next to which by chance
  The divells vizors hung, and their flame painted
  Skin coates.

This imaginary list is considerably less complete and fantastic than the sober inventories taken by Henslowe in March, 1598, of the properties and apparel belonging to the Admiral's Men.[24] His completed inventory contains 182 entries, many of which itemize a number of articles. Though I cannot here reproduce the whole, let me at least give selections suggesting the extraordinary extent and diversity of the collection. Entries 16–20, for example, list apparel:

Item, j senetores gowne, j hoode, and 5 senetores capes.
Item, j sewtte for Nepton; Fierdrackes sewtes for Dobe.
Item, iiij genesareyes gownes, and iiij torchberers sewtes.
Item, iij payer of red strasers [i.e. strossers, tight hose], and iij fares [i.e. fairies'] gowne of buckrome.
Item, iiij Herwodes [heralds' ?] cottes, and iij sogers cottes, and j green gown for Maryan.

---

[24] Reproduced in full in *Henslowe Papers*, pp. 113–121. I have drawn upon Mr. Greg's glosses for obscure terms.

Entries 39–43 itemize musical instruments, apparel, and properties:

> *Item*, iij trumpettes and a drum, and a trebel viall, a basse viall, a bandore, a sytteren, j anshente [i.e. ancient, an ensign or flag], j whitt hatte.
>
> *Item*, j hatte for Robin Hoode, i hobihorse.
>
> *Item*, v shertes, and j serpelowes, iiij ferdingalles.
>
> *Item*, vj head-tiers, j fane [i.e. fan], iiij rebatos, ij gyrketruses [i.e. a compound of jerkin and tight hose].
>
> *Item*, j longe sorde.

Entries 65–69 itemize miscellaneous properties:

> *Item*, j wooden canepie; owld Mahemetes head.
>
> *Item*, j lyone skin; i beares skyne; & Faetones lymes, & Faeton charete; & Argosse heade.
>
> *Item*, Nepun forcke & garland.
>
> *Item*, j crosers stafe; Kentes woden leage.
>
> *Item*, Ierosses head, & raynbowe; j littell alter.

Entries 95 to 182 itemize particular costumes. These were especially valuable. In a shorter list appended to his larger inventory of March, recording "all suche goodes as I have bought for the Companey of my Lord Admirals men, sence the 3 of Aprell, 1598," Henslowe includes:

	£	s.	d.
Bowght j black satten dublett...................			
Bowght j payer of rownd howsse paned of vellevett..	4	15	0
Bowght a robe for to goo invisibell...............			
Bowght a gown for Nembia.....................	3	10	0
Bowght a dublett of whitt satten layd thicke with gowld lace, and a payer of rowne pandes hosse of cloth of sylver, the panes layd with gowld lace......	7	0	0
Bowght of my sonne v sewtes....................	20	0	0
Bowght of my sonne iiij sewtes..................	17	0	0

In 1598 these sums represented very considerable outlays. The average cost of one of these costumes (which do not include hats, gloves, shoes, swords, jewels, and so forth) is somewhat greater than an entire week's rent for the use of the Rose Playhouse (in the same period) paid by the Admiral's Company to Henslowe, the owner of the building.[25]

Lofts of some size and security were required to store this wealth of costumes and properties. The King's Men, the leading London company, must have been put to it to find sufficient space in the Globe tiring-house for the even greater stocks accumulated by years of prosperity. With this in mind, I earlier advanced the theory that the bays of the third gallery directly over the gentlemen's rooms were probably closed off to spectators (who could not have seen well from seats that were both high up and close to the sides of the stage [26]) and incorporated in the tiring-house, thereby doubling the capacity of the storage lofts.

The Fortune builder's contract called for "convenient windowes and lightes glazed to the saide Tyreinge howse," a few of which no doubt lighted the lofts. In *The Walks of Islington and Hogsdon*, IV. iii, an actor is called upon to lower himself by means of a rope from some third-floor room (described earlier in the play as a prison cell "two stories higher [than] the street") to the outer stage.

Enter above with a long rope Sir Rev[erence] Lamard.

Sir Rev. 'Tis very light, begar me sall be discover; now if my string do slip, down goes *Sir Reverence* upon some Washmans head . . . I can see no candle, dere be no body up in de street, . . . So, so, vas very fast, and so fast as me can, me vill down; . . . Begar here comes sombody vith light, me sall be   *He slides down and resteth on* taken, dere be no vay to scape,   *the Feathers Tavern* [sign]. *Enter* and me canot clime up agen: *Pimpwell drunk with a Torch* Oh Diabolo vat sall become of   *in his hand.* me, de vindow be shut, me can no creep into de Tavern, and I sall not be taken for Zhorge a hors-back, as me saw once in de Play; begar dis man be drunk, I see by his stagger . . . but I have an invention he sall no spy me, begar me vill creep into dis Bush [i.e.

---

[25] *Henslowe's Diary*, ii. 132.
[26] See Chapter III. p. 64.

the bush which, placed over the door like an inn-sign, marked an ale-house], and ven he be gone me sall go down courageo. . . . Begar me have extream need to make vater, I sall pish my breesh, Oh Diabolo I sall be found, begar me can stay no longra, me sall burse.

Pimpw.   I will knock up this rogue *Hugh* at the Feathers . . . Nouns
what's that.   *Sir Rev. pisseth upon him.*

Sir Rev.   Begar now I be undon in a pissing vhile.

Pimpw.   You son of a Batchelor, do you throw your Pispots upon my head, if I could finde stones I'de break your windows, but since I cannot, I will even make bold to set fire to your Bush, . . .

Sir Rev.   Oh Mordieu, me sall be burn in de Bush . . .

Pimpw.   What's here, a Rope? some prisoner has   *Pimpw. spieth*
made an escape out of the Master's-side. . . .   *the rope.*

His cries arouse the Keepers. A noisy scene follows, and all rush off to find Sir Reverence. Once the stage is again clear:

Sir Rev. comes out of the Bush.

Sir Rev.   Oh the great pox run with you all . . . [He descends to the ground.] So, now me are down.

Now it is not yet known in what playhouse Jordan's play had its run of "19 days together" in 1641, but the tone, action, and stage-directions all point to a public playhouse. If this attribution is correct, then we must assume that the rope by which Sir Reverence descended the scenic wall from top to bottom dangled from a window in the third level and not from the music gallery. Had he descended from the music gallery he would have landed on the tarras and not near the locked windows and the capacious bush projecting over the stage door. Beneath its vulgarity, therefore, this scene points to a third-floor casement directly over one of the window-stages. Such a window on one side of the music gallery implies a similar window on the other side.

A few lines tracing the history of the tiring-rooms and other off-stage offices in the Globe will not be amiss.

Early in Elizabeth's reign actors donned their costumes in the curtained alcove set up behind the platform, or, if the stage was erected in an inn-yard, they perhaps passed through the alcove into some room behind. After 1576, with the alcove regularly employed as a stage, actors in public playhouses probably had to mount to the floor above in order to change a costume or repair a beard. And after 1590 the development of upper stages usurped nearly all the space in the second level. Until such time as the Globe set a new style with its enlarged tiring-house, back-stage quarters probably were cramped (we have already seen that the musicians were placed in the third floor). I cannot agree, however, with those who suggest that the curtained stage on the second level served as a dressing room. As often as not the chamber set had to be altered each time the curtains were closed. Moreover (with the stage curtains closed) the room was dark except when the side hangings were drawn back to facilitate the movement of properties and the work of setting the stage. Nor is it necessary to suppose that for lack of space in the Globe tiring-house an actor had to effect a change of costume amid the comings and goings of stage-hands moving properties. Off stage, against the exterior walls of the playhouse, were several rooms each better adapted to the needs of a dressing room than any inner stage.

The back-stage sections of the Globe had, in fact, a larger floor area than all the inner stages combined. On both the first and the second levels these sections formed a corridor, extending inside the tiring-house from the abutment of the two-penny spectator room on one side to the corresponding point on the other side, a distance of 112 feet. The depth of this corridor varied according to the depths of the several inner stages. On the first level the passageway (behind the study) was 5 feet deep; the sections behind the stage doors were a full 12 feet deep; and the sections at the ends, behind the gentlemen's rooms, were approximately 6 feet deep.

Now the sections immediately behind the stage doors could not well be used as dressing rooms, nor for storing any properties other than those brought down from the lofts for use in the day's play. Instead they served as lobbies (12 feet wide and approximately 18 feet long) into which members of the company could enter from all parts of the tiring-house and the stage. There the actors assembled before going on (during battle scenes large numbers charged in and out through the stage doors); there a triumphal procession, or a hearse followed by mourners, lined up and made ready; there also, not far behind his wicket in the stage door, stood the prompter, listening to the dialogue, guiding all back-stage routine, and whispering the first words of a speech to an actor about to enter. As lobbies, indeed, these sections of the tiring-house were indispensable.

On the second level the rooms corresponding to what I have called the lobbies below were slightly narrower (to allow depth to the window-stages). From them opened a pair of rooms some 22 feet long and 8 feet wide lying behind the upper boxes. Because these latter rooms could be well lighted by means of casements, because they were off the beaten track (no one could pass through them to some other part of the tiring-house), and because they lay near the stairs leading down to the lobbies, they were admirably adapted for use as dressing rooms. There the costumes, beards, hats, and hand-props required in a given play could be set out by the company's "tire-men," and there also, I assume, hung on its peg the "plot" or outline of the play, supplied to remind an actor of the order of events and his entrances and exits scene by scene.

These rooms, the forerunners of the Green-Room of a succeeding age, were relatively quiet and secluded amid the bustle of the tiring-house generally. Several writers of the period note this fact. Quarles, for example, in his *Divine Fancies*, 1632, writes:

> Our life's a tragedy; those secret rooms
> Wherein we tyre us, are our mothers' wombes.

Middleton conveys the same impression in a passage in *The Black Book*, 1604.[27] His main character, Lucifer, disguised as a constable, goes up the stairs of a brothel to a hidden room which, using the language of the theatre, he calls "the tiring-house," and there finds the lost Pierce Penniless. Returning to his own home Lucifer goes to his dressing room: "Into my tiring-house I went, where I . . . shifted myself into the apparel of my last will and testament"; then, advancing to "another room," he finds all his heirs assembled.

In Davenant's *Playhouse to be Let* (1662), I. i, written for the Red Bull shortly before his company's new theatre was ready for occupancy, is found a passage which implies that the old playhouse was able to provide two dressing rooms, one for the male members of the company and the other for the female.

Player. Be pleas'd, sir, to retire awhile, and tune
   Your instruments. . . .
Musician. I'll chuse the women's tiring-room for privacy.

There are many other passages in the literature of the age, early and late, which refer to the actors' dressing rooms, but one example must serve for all. On March 23, 1661, Pepys visited the Red Bull:

All the morning at home putting papers in order, dined at home, and then out to the Red Bull (where I had not been since plays come up again), but coming too soon I went out again and walked all up and down the Charterhouse yard and Aldersgate street. At last came back again and went in, where I was led by a seaman that knew me, but is here as a servant, up to the tireing-room, where strange the confusion and disorder that there is among them in fitting themselves, especially here, where the clothes are very poor, and the actors but common fellows. At last into the pitt, where I think there was not above ten more than myself, and not one hundred in the whole house. And the play, which is called "All's lost by Lust," poorly done; and with so much disorder, among others, that in the musique-room the boy that was to sing a song, not singing it right, his master fell about his ears and beat him so, that it put the whole house into an uprore.[28]

---

[27] *Works*, ed. Bullen, viii. 24–25, 33.   [28] *Diary*, ed. Wheatley, i. 338.

Chapter X

THE SUPERSTRUCTURE

1. The Huts

ONE final area of the Globe Playhouse — the super-structure or "heavens" constructed over the tiring-house and outer stage — remains to be considered. The Globe heavens was composed of three parts: an enclosed hut or loft corresponding to the "tower" of a modern theatre; a stage-cover or "shadow" (which entered our discussion of the music gallery); and the turret supporting the flagpole and the playhouse flag.

Contemporary views provide several illustrations of playhouse huts. The De Witt sketch of the Swan depicts a rectangular hut above the tiring-house, three-fourths as wide as the stage below, as deep apparently as the gallery frame, and one and one-half times as high as the man standing in its doorway. The hut is not placed directly over the frame, but is brought forward a few feet (its projection over the outer stage had to be great enough to allow for trapdoors in the overhanging portion of its floor). The hut is represented as having a gable roof of thatch, two windows facing the yard, a doorway in the visible end facing the "tectum" on the right, a flagpole and a flag with a large device of a swan upon it. If any part of the De Witt sketch is trustworthy, its representation of the hut should be, for, compared with the difficulty of depicting the curving galleries and the projecting stage with its forward columns, the drawing of the hut was a simple matter.

Panoramic views of the Bankside in the first half of the seventeenth century show a superstructure on top of every playhouse.[1] Inasmuch as the most trustworthy of these views is the original Visscher panorama drawn while the first Globe was in existence, I shall base my observations chiefly on it.[2] Visscher's representation of the Swan Playhouse includes a superstructure formed and placed precisely as in the De Witt sketch: the hut is rectangular with a gable roof; it rises above the inner slope of the main roof and extends part way over a portion of the yard, presumably the stage. The only difference worth remarking in the two representations is that in the Visscher view the flagpole is much taller and the flag larger and lacking the Swan insignia.

Visscher's Bear Garden has a superstructure of much the same size, but its position relative to the frame is altered. The long axis (marked by the ridge) of the hut runs at right angles to the section of the frame upon which it rests, instead of parallel to the frame. As a result, the gable end with its door (over which appear two small windows) faces the yard. The pole and flag are similar to those in Visscher's representation of the Swan.

Visscher's Globe has a differently shaped and much larger superstructure. Its design combines the Swan and Bear Garden huts in the form of a cross, and adds a turret above the intersection. The axis of one unit is parallel to the section of frame on which it partly rests (as at the Swan); the other bisects it at right angles, parallel to the main axis of the playhouse (as at the Bear Garden). The units appear to be of equal length, a length approximately

[1] The Hollar representation of the Globe includes a vague peak in the roof-line where the huts should be. For discussion see below and Chapter I. Flags but not huts appear in the Hondius View, 1610, and in the inset views found in Holland's *Herwologia Anglica*, 1620, and Baker's *Chronicle*, 1643. These last three views reflect the Bankside of 1587–1598 (see Appendix A). Neither flag nor hut appears over the two little amphitheatres of Norden's map of 1593.

[2] See the preceding note. Delaram, concerned primarily with the equestrian portrait of James I, has conventionalized his background, the London scene. The Visscher-Hondius, Merian, and Londinopolis views are derived from the Visscher original.

that of one section of the playhouse frame. Two windows are set in each of the visible gable ends, and also in the sides of the square tower rising some 8 feet above the intersection. The tower itself has a four-sided sloping roof rising to a peak out of which emerges a flagpole some 15 feet high flying a large white flag.[3]

If Visscher's representation is to be relied upon, the Globe huts measure some 24 feet from end to end of each of the two main units; but, though trustworthy in outline — see Chapters I and II, and recall that his representation of the Swan hut agrees closely with that of De Witt — Visscher's dimensions and proportions must be confirmed by other sources before they can be accepted. I shall return to this problem after a glance at Hollar's Long View.

In Hollar's panorama, the Globe superstructure is wholly conventionalized (the probability is that the artist had never visited that theatre, for it is hard to believe that a trained observer would draw so vaguely). On the other hand, his representation of the Hope superstructure is rich in detail and is drawn with an assurance quite lacking in his representation of the Globe. The Hope superstructure extends over half the yard (compare the Hope builder's contract: "And shall also builde the Heavens all over the saide stage." The Hope stage, however, was removable and probably smaller than the stages of the Globe and Fortune). It is formed of a large square hut with a twin-gable roof forming an "M" in cross section (presumably to avoid the needless height and waste of space and materials which one large A-shaped gable would have entailed). The turret, topped by an onion-shaped dome, rises between the two ridges at a point near the outer wall of the building. No doors or windows are included in the

---

[3] In the derivative representations of the Globe by Visscher-Hondius and Merian the same units are included but the draftsmanship is faulty, resulting in a hodgepodge in which the relationship of one unit to another and to the playhouse frame is obscured.

half-timbered gable end facing the yard. There is neither flagpole nor flag.

I turn next to the size and location of trap-openings in the floor of the superstructure, since a study of these openings will help us to determine the size and shape of the huts.

Early dramatists were content to lower a single actor seated upon a chair (perhaps nothing more than a "bosun's chair"?), as in Greene's *Alphonsus of Aragon*, acted in 1589. The play opens with the direction:

After you have sounded thrise, let Venus be let downe, from the top of the Stage, and when she is downe, say:

The play ends:

Exit Venus. Or if you can conueniently, let a chaire come downe from the top of the stage, and draw her vp.

For such scenes a heavens-trap measuring three feet square located medially in the "top of the stage" would probably suffice. But before many years had passed, trap-work from above became much more assured, flexible, and spectacular. The "chaire" became a "gilded throne," the "top of the stage" became the "painted heavens," and actors to the number of four or more were sometimes lowered in a single car, or in a pair of cars, through the traps. I shall begin with stage-directions that indicate the size of the car lowered through the opening. From a Red Bull play, *The Seven Champions of Christendom*, at line 2309:

[*Enter spirits with throne.*]
Argalio. Seest thou this Throne by sable spirits borne,
  In it wee'le mount, so unbeleev'd a height, . . .

And at line 2338, as the Champions enter to seize Argalio:

[*The throne ascends into the air.*]
Denis. O act of wonder, we in vaine pursue
  Looke how they raise themselves into the clouds.

From a late Blackfriars play, *The Variety*, IV:

> *Musick. Throne descends . . . A Song in the Throne.*
> As I singing now come down
> I do bring you *Bacchus* Crown.

The Globe and Blackfriars play, *A Wife for a Month* (acted in 1624), II. vi, contains a masque which opens:

> *Cupid descends, the Graces sitting by him, Cupid being bound the Graces unbind him, he speakes.*

Twenty lines later:

> *Cupid and the Graces ascend in the Chariot.*

A second play from the same company, *The Prophetess*, II. iii:

> *Enter* [i.e. descend] *Delphia and Drusilla, in a Throne drawn by dragons.*[4]

When it is time to leave, Delphia gives the command: "Mount up my birds," and the quarto enters the direction "*Ascend.*"

Yet another type of car is found in Shirley's Cockpit play, *The Ball.* Act V, scene i, contains the direction: "*A golden Ball descends, enter* [from it] *Venus and Cupid.*"

A spectacle in *Cymbeline*, V. iv, merits quoting at length (to make the original staging comprehensible I shall occasionally interpolate a comment). The previous action had ended with Captains presenting the captured Posthumus to Cymbeline, who in turn delivered him over to the care of Gaolers.

> *Scena Quarta.*
> *Enter Posthumus and* [two] *Gaoler*[s].

---

[4] An illustration of a cloud-chariot drawn by peacocks, from *L'Educatione d'Achille*, performed at Turin in 1650, is reproduced by A. Nicoll, *Stuart Masques and the Renaissance Stage*, p. 45. For the same property in a later print, see also *ibid.*, p. 132.

THE SUPERSTRUCTURE

They enter the outer stage and come forward to one of the stage posts; there Posthumus is chained.[5]

Gao. You shall not now be stolne,
You have lockes upon you:
So graze, as you finde Pasture.

2. Gao. I, or a stomacke.   [Exeunt Gaolers.]

Post. Most welcome bondage; for thou art a way
(I thinke) to liberty: yet am I better
Then one that's sicke o'th'Gowt, since he had rather
Groane so in perpetuity, then be cur'd
By'th'sure Physitian, Death; who is the key
T'umbarre these Lockes. . . . Oh *Imogen*,
Ile speake to thee in silence.

At this point Posthumus falls asleep.

Solemne Musicke. Enter (as in an Apparation) Sicillius Leonatus, Father to Posthumus, an old man, attyred like a warriour, leading in his hand an ancient Matron (his wife, & Mother to Posthumus) with Musicke before them. Then. after other Musicke, followes the two young Leonati (Brothers to Posthumus) with wounds as they died in the warrs. They circle Posthumus round as he lies sleeping.

Sicil. No more thou Thunder-Master
         shew thy spight, on Mortall Flies: . . .

Their chant to Jupiter continues for sixty lines, concluding (at line 91):

Brothers. Helpe (Jupiter) or we appeale,
            and from thy justice flye.

Jupiter descends in Thunder and Lightning, sitting uppon an Eagle: hee throwes a Thunder-bolt. The Ghostes fall on their knees.

Jupiter. No more you petty Spirits of Region low
Offend our hearing: hush. How dare you Ghostes
Accuse the Thunderer, . . . Rise, and fade,
He shall be Lord of Lady *Imogen*,
And happier much by his Affliction made.
This Tablet lay upon his Brest, wherein

---

[5] Modern editors, following Pope, mistakenly supply the scene-location *"Britain. A Prison."* If in fact a new scene does begin here (which may be doubted), the heading should read: *"Britain. An open place near the British Camp."* See note 11 below.

Our pleasure, his full Fortune, doth confine,
And so away: no farther with your dinne
Expresse Impatience least you stirre up mine:
Mount Eagle, to my Palace Christalline.   *Ascends.*

At this point the stage-hands in the heavens begin to draw
Jupiter upwards. While he rises Sicillius speaks:

Sicil. He came in Thunder, his Celestiall breath
Was sulphurous to smell: the holy Eagle
Stoop'd, as to foote us: his Ascension is
More sweet then our blest Fields: his Royall Bird
Prunes the immortall wing, and cloyes his Beake,
As when his God is pleas'd.
All. Thankes Jupiter.   [Jupiter disappears.]
Sic. The Marble Pavement clozes, he is enter'd
His radiant Roofe: Away, and to be blest
Let us with care performe his great behest.   *Vanish.*

The Apparitions having gone, Posthumus awakens.

Post. Sleepe, thou hast bin a Grandsire, and begot
A Father to me: and thou hast created
A Mother, and two Brothers. . . .
What Fayeries haunt this ground? A Book? Oh rare one,
Be not, as is our fangled world, a Garment
Nobler then that it covers. . . .

Posthumus reads the prediction aloud before the Gaoler
comes for him. He is still in chains when a Messenger
arrives with orders to release the prisoner and lead him to
the King.

Now this scene is notable for several reasons. Perhaps
the first is the use of an eagle in place of the chair, throne,
or chariot used in earlier descents. The use of the eagle
not only broke with the tradition of actors sitting in or
upon some more or less conventional car, but paved the
way for Ariel's descent "like a Harpey" in *The Tempest* a
year or two later. The eagle was apparently most successful (Heywood promptly borrowed it or had one made for
his own Red Bull play, *The Golden Age*, performed the
following year). But more important yet, Ariel's descent

in a harpy costume — a descent obviously hatched out of Shakespeare's experience with Jupiter's eagle — was the first "free" flight in the history of the English public stage. Thereafter actors can "fly" down from the heavens without any other apparatus than some sort of belt or harness (concealed beneath their costumes?) to which a wire was attached.

The scene is also remarkable for its details of stage business. Observe that Posthumus is led by his Gaolers to an open place (the platform) and there manacled to some object (probably one of the stage posts) much as if he were a cow led out and chained to a stake in a meadow — "So graze as you find pasture." The reason for this by-play is that Posthumus must be forward on the platform in the orbit of a descent from the heavens. Again, Jupiter descended only part way (the eagle's foot apparently came no lower than the heads of the Apparitions on the stage).[6] Jupiter's visit to the Earth lasted twenty lines, the average time for a visit from above (see the line-count given in scenes quoted earlier). And again, observe that six lines are spoken between Jupiter's command, "Mount Eagle, to my Palace Christalline," and Sicillius's illuminating comment, "The Marble Pavement clozes, he is enter'd his radiant Roofe." [7] Coming from Shakespeare,[8] who knew the theatre of his age as no one else did, this fact suggests that some six lines were required to cover the time of raising an adult actor from a point approximately 7 feet

[6] A descent which halted part way down was not unusual. For other examples see *The Courageous Turk*, I. iv; *The Rebellion*, III; *The Tempest*. III. iii; *The Widow's Tears*, III. ii; *Women Beware Women*, V. i; etc.

[7] These lines seem to dispose of the suggestion advanced by Albright (*Shaksperean Stage*, p. 71), namely that the heavens floor was formed of cloth "so arranged that bodies could ascend or descend through it without any apparent opening."

[8] For brief discussion of the authorship of this scene see Chambers, *William Shakespeare*, i. 486. Most critics agree that Shakespeare had a hand in at least part of the scene; the chant beginning at line 30 is the part most often assigned to another hand.

above the outer stage into the heavens (the total distance from the platform to the ceiling was 32 feet) and to close the trapdoor. Many other plays suggest (sometimes by the length of a song) the time taken to lower or raise the car; but in such scenes one cannot be sure that the car is not being deliberately retarded. In *Cymbeline*, however, I see no reason why Jupiter's ascent should not take place as rapidly as dignity allowed, and hence the timing indicated by the six lines is significant.

And finally, this scene is important because we possess an early seventeenth-century Italian theatre print illustrating Jupiter descending upon an eagle.[9] The eagle there appears to have a wing spread of some 8 or 9 feet. Its upraised head is turned to one side (to minimize length from beak to tail?), and its legs, ending in outstretched talons, are thrust out below its body. Jupiter sits astride the eagle, holding on by his left hand, which grasps the eagle's shoulder. The wires by which the eagle is lowered are four in number, two on either side (to keep the bird from rotating and from rocking). Jupiter descending on an Eagle also appears in a design by Inigo Jones for the masque *Tempe Restored* (1632).[10] Here the relative sizes of actor and property are the same as in the Italian print, but a great "cloud" obscures the wires by which they are lowered.[11]

[9] Ducharte, *Italian Comedy* (trans. by R. T. Weaver, London, 1929, facing p. 73).

[10] Reproduced by Nicoll, *Stuart Masques*, p. 94.

[11] Of four stage designs by Inigo Jones (now in the Chatsworth Collection) representing two chambers, a desert, and a dream Professor Nicoll writes (*Stuart Masques*, p. 150): "Presumably these were made for the performance of some play, but to determine which particular drama is now almost impossible. One suggestion might very tentatively be put forward — that these scenes fit rather well the localities of *Cymbeline*. A king's chamber would be required there, a princess's bedchamber, . . . two camps, and a dream scene where Posthumus has his vision." At this point a note is subjoined: "The locality in *Cymbeline* is a prison, whereas the design shows an open place with trees at the sides." Resuming: "Whether or not we indeed possess here the first recorded scenery prepared for the performance of a Shakespearian drama, at least in these designs we have a

Another example of the Court masque type of car is found in the last act of *The Tragedy of Messallina*, acted at Salisbury Court in 1637:

The Antimasque [having] *gone off: and solemne Musicke playing: Messallina and Silvius gloriously crown'd in an Arch-glitering Cloud aloft, Court each other . . .*

Sil. Descend my *Venus* all compos'd of love.

Empresse. Lockt in thy Armes my Mars.

Sil. Downe, downe we come
 Like glistring *Phoebus* mounted in his Car, . . .

While they descend, Valens, Proculus [and others] *meete them beneath.*

These large and spectacular descents of golden balls, of thrones "borne by spirits" or "drawn by dragons," of chariots, eagles, and arch-glittering clouds (all may have been framed by a "cloud" of very light cloth — I shall return to the topic later) demand an opening in the base of the heavens fully 8 feet long (10 feet seems not unreasonable) and 3 or probably 4 feet wide. For reasons of display as well as structure the opening was parallel with the tiring-house façade. Moreover, to ensure that descending cars would not strike the projecting tarras at the second level of the façade, the rear edge of the opening had to be at least 3 feet out from the façade at the third level. Sicillius's comment following Jupiter's disappearance, "The Marble Pavement clozes," informs us that the opening was provided with a cover which was replaced once the ascent was completed. For reasons of safety, if nothing else, this cover would be essential. I assume that it was hinged for convenience, with the hinges placed on the rear line (so that the raised cover would shield operations in the huts from the view of spectators). I further assume that the cover was constructed in sections, one or more of which could be opened as needed.

---

series of sketches which are among the most interesting the seventeenth century has to give us." The bearing of my interpretation of the "prison" or dream scene upon Professor Nicoll's tentative identification of these Inigo Jones designs is obvious.

In the scenes cited thus far it seems probable that the car descended from the middle of the heavens. That path of descent would ensure full vision and prominence for the spectacle.

I turn next to scenes which in departing from the usual pattern furnish an insight first into the total length of the heavens-opening and secondly into the distance of the opening forward of the scenic wall. In the extant manuscript of *The Governor*, presumably the play of that name performed at St. James's Palace on February 17, 1636, by the King's Men,[12] a stage-direction reads: "*They descend on th' one side of the stage.*" How far to the side is not made clear, but in other plays the distance can be approximated. In *Englishmen for my Money*, a play written for the Rose in 1598 but continuing its stage history at the Fortune before its publication in 1616, the trap-work from above relates to one of the window-stages. The situation is as follows. Pisaro has three daughters who are in love with three English youths. A corpulent, elderly Dutchman named Vandalle, however, has taken a fancy to one of the daughters, Laurentia. One evening he arrives at their house and knocks. Laurentia and her sisters appear at the window above, but refuse to descend and let him in, alleging that their father would be aroused. Determining among themselves to cool his unwelcome attentions, the girls hit on the idea of raising him in a basket as if to admit him through the window. They plan, of course, to leave him hanging in mid air. Marina and Mathea leave to make all ready; Laurentia remains in the window holding Vandalle in conversation. At line 1745:

> *Laur.* Then you dare goe into a Basket; for I know no other meanes to inioy your companie, then so: for my Father hath the Keyes of the Dore. . . .

At this point the basket is lowered to the street. Laurentia continues to Vandalle:

[12] B. M. *MS. Additional.* 10,419.

Put your selfe into that Basket, and I will draw you vp:
But no words I pray you, for feare my Sister heare you.

Once Vandalle is in the basket Laurentia calls to her sisters off stage to heave away — "Merily then my Wenches" — and they pull the Dutchman up to a point well above the ground and leave him "hanging twixt Heauen and Earth" and go away. Vandalle cannot get through the window, and since he dares not jump down he spends the night in the basket, shivering with cold and fright. The next morning he is discovered. At line 2090:

Anthony. Out alas, what's yonder?

Pisaro. Where?

Frisco. Hoyda, hoyda, a Basket: it turnes, hoe.

Pisa. Peace ye Villaine, and let's see who's there?
Goe looke about the House; where are our weapons?
What might this meane?

Frisc. Looke, looke, looke; there's one in it, he peeps out: Is there nere a Stone here to hurle at his Nose.

Pisa. What, wouldst thou breake my Windowes with a Stone? How now, who's there, who are you sir? . . .
Why how now Sonne, what haue your Adamants
Drawne you vp so farre, and there left you hanging
Twixt Heauen and Earth like *Mahomets* Sepulchre?

Antho. They did vnkindly, who so ere they were,
That plagu'd him here, like *Tantalus* in Hell,
To touch his Lippes like the desired Fruite,
And then to snatch it from his gaping Chappes.

Aluaro. A little farder signor *Vandalle*, and dan you may put v hed into de windo and cash de Wensh.

At line 2137 Pisaro orders Anthony to let Vandalle down. Anthony runs into the house, appears at the window ("*Enter Anthony aboue*") to unfasten the rope, and lowers the chastened Dutchman to the ground.[13]

Now while first studying this scene the reader may form the impression that the basket probably was lowered by

---

[13] The episode here analyzed appears to be glanced at in *The Widow's Tears*, I. i. 68.

Laurentia in the window-stage by means of a rope which passed over the window-sill and dropped to the platform below; and that after Vandalle was in the basket, Laurentia, aided by her sisters (or by stage-hands) off stage, hauled in the rope and thus drew Vandalle in the basket up to the window. But this hypothesis will not work. It would have been physically impossible to raise the basket higher than the under side of the projecting window-stage. There, perforce, it would have stopped, leaving Vandalle suspended only a few feet off the ground, underneath the window-stage, and in front of the stage door. Such a conclusion is inadmissible for a number of reasons arising out of the text, among them the fact that the door is used more than once during the time that Vandalle is in the basket, and yet no one — not even the alert and suspicious Pisaro who enters there carrying a light — appears to notice the presence of such an extraordinary object directly in his path.

The more one studies this scene with a view to discovering a *modus operandi* which will reconcile all that takes place with the physical conditions of an Elizabethan stage, the more one comes to realize that the business involved the machinery in the stage heavens. For observe: First, that the basket was lowered to the street, not by Laurentia standing in the window-stage, but by Marina or some other person off stage (instructing Laurentia to "holde [Vandalle] in talke," Marina left the window to "provide" the basket and rope; the basket makes its appearance half a minute later, and Marina returns to the window soon after). Secondly, that only by lowering the basket from the heavens was it possible to suspend Vandalle in the place and in the manner indicated by the text.[14] And

---

[14] Among the points to be noted are the following: the basket could hardly have escaped the notice of those passing through the door to Pisaro's house had it been drawn up in front of the doorway underneath the overhanging bay-window (see especially lines 1795–1814, 1959–1966, and 2041–2063). It was in fact fairly high in the air (lines 2111–2113; observe also that no one in the street

thirdly, that it would have been a simple, routine matter for stage-hands in charge of a windlass in the huts to have lifted the corpulent Vandalle into the air, to have supported him there for a considerable period of time, and to have lowered him to the ground the next morning, whereas any other method of accomplishing the same results would have been abnormal and, in my estimation, difficult.

According to my interpretation, the stage business of this scene in *Englishmen for my Money* is unusual in only two important respects. One is that the path of the ascending basket lay close to a window-stage. The other is that efforts were made to disguise the dramatist's reliance upon stage equipment normally reserved for scenes of a different character — I refer (1) to the use of a basket in place of a more conventional car, (2) to the return of the free end of the rope to Laurentia in the window-stage so that she and her sisters can appear to exercise the force which lifted Vandalle into the air, and (3) to the dispatching of Anthony to the window-stage the next morning to untie the rope which seemingly keeps Vandalle suspended.[15] One other point is worth noting here. Frisco's comment,

---

suggests the possibility of rescuing Vandalle from below). It hung in the air on a relatively long rope without touching any part of the scenic wall (line 2092). It was out fully an arm's length from the façade of the window-stage (lines 2118–2119) and perhaps slightly below the level of the window-sill (lines 1762–1765). It was suspended with relation to the bay-window and the door below in such a way that it bore an obvious resemblance to an inn-sign (lines 2108–2110). Vandalle's head appearing over the rim of the basket was approximately in front of the windows (lines 2096–2099).

That the basket was not visible at midnight to the three English youths in the street talking to the three girls in the window (lines 1833–1918) is not to be wondered at, for much is made of the fact that the girls recognize their lovers only by the sound of their voices. Again, when the girls come down to the street (at line 1924) it is so dark that only by calling out names can the young people pair off correctly (for discussion of this last point, see Appendix D, p. 398).

15 The stage business in this scene was possibly intended to reflect the age-old practice of raising objects to the upper floors of a house by means of a block and tackle secured to a beam projecting from the gable-end over the street.

"Hoyda, hoyda, a Basket: it turns," illustrates how essential it was to use a pair of ropes or wires when lowering a car in a dignified scene. Here the rotation of the basket heightens the merriment; elsewhere rotation might be highly undesirable and inartistic.

While pondering the stage business in *Englishmen for my Money*, readers perhaps will have recalled the related but very different scene in which the dying Antony is heaved aloft to Cleopatra in her Monument.[16] The basic procedure is the same, I believe, in both. The First Folio, our earliest text of *Antony and Cleopatra*, is sparing of its stage-directions, but the dialogue and inescapable inferences enable us to reconstruct what took place. Cleopatra, terrified by the turn of events, has secured herself and retinue in her stronghold, the Monument: "*Enter Cleopatra, and her Maides aloft, with Charmian & Iras.*" They appear in a window-stage [17] awaiting the return of Diomedes, who (at line 6) enters on the platform through the door below them:

Cleo. How now? is he dead?
Diom. His death's upon him, but not dead.
  Looke out o'th other side your Monument,
  His Guard have brought him thither.

---

[16] "An analogous effect" is noted by Lawrence, *Physical Conditions*, p. 119.

[17] There is insufficient evidence to warrant complete certainty about the stages used by Cleopatra in this scene, but there is enough, I believe, to justify the interpretation I have set forth. I call attention to the following facts: First, that three stages in the second level of the tiring-house were available for use in conjunction with the platform — the tarras (with the chamber curtains closed), and the two window-stages. Secondly, that Cleopatra and her women appear successively in two of these stages. Thirdly, that the second of the two stages used is supposed to face out of the Monument on the side opposite to the first. Now in my opinion the use of the two window-stages separated by the broad middle section of the scenic wall would have sustained the illusion of "opposite" sides, whereas the use (in whatever order) of a window-stage and the tarras abutting upon it — a combination of stages not infrequently used (as in *The Devil is an Ass*, II. ii, and in *May Day*, II. i) to represent a bay-window and the "walking gallery" opening from it — would have destroyed the illusion.

Cleopatra and her women immediately leave the window on that side of the tiring-house and cross to the window-stage on "the other side." Diomedes leaves the platform — his exit is not marked, but he takes no part in what follows — through the door by which he entered. As soon as the stage is clear, "*Enter Anthony, and the Guard.*" Antony is carried in through the door on the opposite side and deposited on the ground (or perhaps supported on his shield) below the window in which Cleopatra and her women appear for the second part of the scene.[18]

[18] In *Prefaces to Shakespeare, Second Series*, pp. 162–163, Mr. H. Granville-Barker writes of this scene as follows:

> *Enter Cleopatra and her Maides aloft, with Charmian and Iras.*
>
> They are in the Monument, to which, in a moment, the dying Antony has to be hoisted. There are two slight difficulties. The hoisting of a full-grown man ten or twelve feet in the air asks some strength. However, this could be provided ostensibly by the 'and her maides,' actually by stage hands helping from behind the curtains; and Shakespeare makes dramatic capital out of the apparent difficulty. But the upper stage of the public theatre must have had a balustrade at least three feet high. Swinging a dying man over it and lowering him again asks some care. Granted this done with skill and grace, what of the effect of the rest of the scene, of Antony's death and Cleopatra's lament over him, played behind the balustrade as behind bars? Clearly it would be a poor one. The balustrade must, one presumes, have been removed for the occasion or made to swing open, if the ordinary upper stage was used.

From the references to "stage hands helping from behind the [upper-stage] curtains" and to "swinging a dying man over [the balustrade] and lowering him again," I infer that Mr. Granville-Barker has in mind a rope lowered to the platform from some point above the balustrade. If so, his theory of the means employed in drawing Antony aloft and my theory are basically alike. On the other hand, my theory that Antony was heaved aloft into a window-stage is not open to the objection which Mr. Granville-Barker discovers as a consequence of assuming that Antony was heaved aloft to the tarras, namely that the effect of playing the rest of the scene "behind the balustrade as behind bars" would have been "poor." Had this part of the scene been played in a window-stage, and had Antony, lying upon his shield, been drawn feet first through the window to the point where his head and shoulders came within reach of Cleopatra's embrace, the audience's view of Antony's death and of Cleopatra's lament over him would have been unexcelled.

Cleo. [looking down from the window]. Oh Sunne,
  Burne the great Sphere thou mov'st in, darkling stand
  The varrying shore o'th'world. O *Antony, Antony, Antony*
  Helpe *Charmian*, helpe *Iras* helpe: helpe Friends
  Below, let's draw him hither.
Ant. Peace,
  Not *Caesar's* Valour hath o'rethrowne *Anthony*,
  But *Anthonie's* hath Triumpht on it selfe. . . .
  I am dying Egypt, dying; onely
  I heere importune death a-while, untill
  Of many thousand kisses, the poore last
  I lay upon thy lippes.

But Cleopatra dares not descend to him, nor permit her gates to be unbarred to let him in.

Cleo. I dare not Deere,
  Deere my Lord pardon: I dare not,
  Least I be taken: . . . but come, come *Anthony*,
  Helpe me my women, we must draw thee up:
  Assist good Friends.
Ant. Oh quicke, or I am gone.
Cleo. Heere's sport indeede:
  How heavy weighes my Lord?
  Our strength is all gone into heavinesse,
  That makes the waight. Had I great *Juno's* power,
  The strong wing'd Mercury should fetch thee up,
  And set thee by Joves side. Yet come a little,
  Wishers were ever Fooles. Oh come, come, come,
                        They heave Anthony aloft to Cleopatra.
  And welcome, welcome. Dye when thou hast liv'd,
  Quicken with kissing: had my lippes that power,
  Thus would I weare them out.

But her efforts are unavailing, and twenty-one lines later he dies in her arms. The scene closes (at line 91) with the direction: "*Exeunt*, [those above] *bearing of Anthonies body.*"

Now Antony was of large stature and his weight was not a trifling matter. In this scene he is absolutely helpless — "his death's upon him, but not dead" — and cannot lift a finger to help those who are raising him to Cleopatra's window (the window-sill was approximately 15 feet above the outer stage). His Guards probably carried him to the Monument on his great shield, and on it, I assume, he lay throughout the scene. How then was the helpless Antony "heaved aloft" into Cleopatra's window?

The Guards below can raise him 6 or 7 feet above the street, but the distance to go is 15; and, unless provided with some machine, those above can do nothing to help — to "draw him hither" — until Antony is lifted to within a foot or two of the window-sill. Clearly there is more to heaving Antony aloft than hands — however numerous or willing — can accomplish unassisted. Whatever the procedure, it had to be simple and unobtrusive, employing standard equipment, for the text takes the business in its stride. It had to be graceful, for the scene is deeply moving; it had to be sure, for a slip would have been disastrous. The assistance had to come from above, for there is no stage-direction nor mention in the dialogue of a ladder or scaffold set out below the window. Nor would such a property be suitable in light of the ever-present threat of surprise by Caesar's forces.

These conditions — which, from the point of view of the mechanical problem involved, duplicate those in the earlier Rose and Fortune play, *Englishmen for my Money* — point to a rope lowered from a windlass concealed in the huts, one end of the rope being made fast by the Guards to Antony's shield — "Helpe, Friends below . . . Assist good Friends" — and the other, the free end returning from above, being passed through the window into the hands of Cleopatra and her Maids: "Helpe me my women, we must draw [him] up." They can simulate heaving on the rope — "O come, come, come" — while the Guards below raise and steady the burden as long as it is within their reach, but the actor taking the part of Antony has the comfort of knowing that the business actually is in the hands of expert workers in the huts.[19]

[19] I hazard the guess that the Roman soldiers who slipped into the well-secured Monument while Cleopatra, in one bay-window, was held in conversa-

If my interpretation of the stage business in these scenes from *Englishmen for my Money* and *Antony and Cleopatra* is correct, we can now estimate the length of the trap-opening in the floor of the huts. Both scenes appear to show that an actor on the platform could be lifted by means of a rope passing over a windlass in the heavens and descending in a path some 3 or 4 feet out from the façade of a window-stage. And inasmuch as the heavens-trap would for obvious reasons have been located symmetrically in the stage ceiling, it therefore appears that in the Rose, Fortune, and Globe playhouses the trap-opening in the floor of the huts extended from a point approximately above one bay-window to the corresponding point above the other. Now the distance between bay-windows at the Fortune and the Globe can be determined: it was 28 feet; and hence in those playhouses the heavens-trap was fully 20 feet long.

Of the heavens opening at the Globe Playhouse we now know the approximate width (4 feet), length (20 feet), and location (across the floor of the heavens from side to side between points over the window-stages).

Normally, of course, the heavens car is lowered in the middle of the stage and descends without reference to any part of the scenic wall. A few scenes, however, demonstrate that actors could, if desired, be landed on the tarras. These scenes give us the location of the heavens opening relative to the scenic wall in much the same way that ascents close to the window-stages give us the approximate length of the opening. Two examples, one from a Globe play and one from a Fortune play, will have to stand for the series, inasmuch as they must be quoted at length in order to exhibit the point in question.[20]

---

tion by Proculeius on the outer stage (V. ii), clambered up by way of the rope inadvertently left dangling (in IV. xv) from the other bay-window.

[20] The analysis of these involved and highly spectacular scenes from the period of greatest theatrical brilliance will serve to illustrate the sort of work

In Fletcher and Massinger's *Prophetess* (written for the King's Men in 1622), II. i, Drusilla complains to Delphia that Diocles since his rise to prominence no longer loves her.

O dear Aunt, I languish
For want of *Diocles's* sight: . . .
O bear me then (but 'tis impossible,
I fear to be effected) where I may
See how my *Diocles* breaks thorow his dangers,
And in what heaps his honours flow upon him.

Devoted to her niece, Delphia (the Prophetess) replies:

This is an easie Boon, which at thy years,
I could have given to any; . . .
From *Ceres* I will force her winged Dragons,
And in the air hung over the Tribunal;
(The Musick of the Spheres attending on us.) . . .

the two will watch Diocles. They leave the stage to the sound of "Soft Musick." Scene ii, extending to 179 lines, follows. During its progress Delphia and Drusilla make ready off stage for their part in scene iii.

Scene iii opens with the direction:

Enter Delphia and Drusilla, in a Throne drawn by Dragons.

Del. Fix here, and rest a while your Sail-stretch'd wings
 That have out-stript the winds: . . .

Dru. Good Aunt, where are we?

Del. Look down, *Drusilla*, on these lofty Towers,
 These spacious streets, where every private house
 Appears a Palace to receive a King:
 The site, the wealth, the beauty of the place,
 Will soon inform thee 'tis imperious *Rome*,
 Rome, the great Mistris of the conquer'd world.

Dru. But without *Diocles*, it is to me
 Like any wilderness we have pass'd o're:
 Shall I not see him?

Del. Yes, and in full glory,
 And glut thy greedy eyes with looking on

that lies ahead if the distinctive contribution of the Elizabethan multiple stage to the drama of 1590–1642 is to be comprehended by modern readers.

His prosperous success: Contain thy self;
For though all things beneath us are transparent,
The sharpest sighted, were he Eagle-ey'd,
Cannot discover us: nor will we hang
Idle Spectators to behold his triumph:
  Enter Diocles, Maximinian, Guard, Aper, Senators, Geta, Officers,
                with Litter [on the outer stage].
But when occasion shall present it self,
Do something to add to it. See, he comes.
Dru. How god-like he appears! . . .

But Delphia briefly commands her niece to forbear, and
the two above watch the scene unfolding below. Diocles
opens the litter and shows that Aper, instead of guarding
the brother of Charinus, Emperor of Rome, has murdered
him:

Diocles. Look on this,
  And when with horrour thou hast view'd thy deed,
  (Thy most accursed deed) be thine own judge, . . .
Aper. I confess
  My life's a burden to me.
Dio. Thou art like thy name,
  A cruel Boar, whose snout hath rooted up
  The fruitfull Vineyard of the common-wealth: . . .
  Yet, since my future fate depends upon thee,
  Thus, to fulfill great *Delphia's* Prophecie,
  Aper (thou fatal Boar) receive the honour   *Kills Aper.*
  To fall by *Diocles* hand. Shine clear, my Stars,
  That usher'd me to taste this common air
  In my entrance to the world, and give applause
  To this great work.
Del. Strike Musick from the Spheres.   *Musick.*
Dru. O now you honour me.
Dio. Ha! in the Air!
All. Miraculous.

While the music conjured up by Delphia continues, Diocles
is hailed co-emperor with Charinus and the robes and
symbols of state are sent for. Geta, Diocles's servant, re-
joices at his master's fortune:

My Master is an Emperour, and I feel
A Senators Itch upon me: would I could hire
These fine invisible Fidlers to play to me
At my instalment.

But in the speeches of Diocles Drusilla discovers that no
thought of her crosses his mind. To her expressions of
dismay Delphia replies:

If he dares prove false,
These glories shall be to him as a dream,
Or an inchanted banquet.

Emperor Charinus enters at this point, leading in his
"beauteous Sister, fair Aurelia," to thank Diocles and to
reaffirm his promise of joint rule to the man avenging his
brother's murder. Aurelia offers herself in marriage, and
Diocles promptly accepts:

O you gods,
Teach me how to be thankful: you have pour'd
All blessings on me, that ambitious man
Could ever fancie: till this happy minute,
I ne're saw beauty, or believ'd there could be
Perfection in a woman. I shall live
To serve and honour you: upon my knees
I thus receive you; and, so you vouchsafe it,
This day I am doubly married; to the Empire,
And your best-self.

Del. False and perfidious villain. —

Dru. Let me fall headlong on him: O my stars!
This I foresaw and fear'd.

Cha. Call forth a *Flamen*,
This knot shall now be ti'd.

Del. But I will loose it,
If Art or Hell have any strength.

Enter a Flamen, Thunder, and Lightning.

Cha. Prodigious!

Max. How soon the day's orecast!

Fla. The Signs are fatal:
Juno smiles not upon this Match, and shews too
She has her thunder.

Dio. Can there be a stop
　　In my full fortune?
Cha. We are too violent,
　　And I repent the haste: we first should pay
　　Our latest duty to the dead, and then
　　Proceed discreetly. Let's take up the body,
　　And when we have plac'd his ashes in his Urn,
　　We'll try the gods again, for wise men say,
　　Marriage and Obsequies do not suit one day. *Senate Exit.*

(The outer stage below is wholly cleared at this point.)

Del. So, 'tis deferr'd yet, in despite of falshood:
　　Comfort *Drusilla*, for he shall be thine,
　　Or wish, in vain, he were not. I will punish　　　　　　*Ascend.*
　　His perjury to the height. Mount up, my birds;
　　Some Rites I am to perform to *Hecate*,
　　To perfect my designs; which once perform'd,
　　He shall be made obedient to thy Call,
　　Or in his ruine I will bury all.　　　　　　　　*Ascends throne.*

This last direction brings the Act to a close.

　　This highly spectacular scene owes much to the resources of the Globe and the Blackfriars stages. Let me call attention to certain details.[21] Normally, as we have seen, a return to the heavens follows a descent after an interval represented by approximately twenty lines of dialogue. Few plays depart more than five or six lines from this average. This scene, on the other hand, calls for an interval represented by 175 lines, prolonged by a procession, stage business of importance, and exits and entrances below. The departure from the normal is so marked as to suggest some difference in procedure. The clue to the special procedure developed for this scene is found in

　　[21] In this analysis, and in the analysis of *The Silver Age*, IV, next following, let it be understood that I advance what is necessarily a conjectural reconstruction of the stage business. My comments are offered not as statements of absolute fact, but as hypotheses which I expect to see debated and, where necessary, corrected. In the light of this declaration I shall omit the words "probably" and "perhaps" from some three or four sentences in which, without such an understanding, I would insert them.

Delphia's opening words, "Fix here, and rest a while your Sail-stretch'd wings." Her command to the dragons "drawing in" the car reveals not only that the car has reached its proper destination ("Fix here"), but also that its weight is now borne by some object upon which the dragons and the car have descended ("and rest your Sail-stretch'd wings"). For if the car is still in mid air, though motionless, the dragons cannot reasonably be ordered to "Fix here and rest." What is this object? It must be lower than the stage heavens inasmuch as the car descends upon it. It must be higher than the outer stage in light of Delphia's comment to Drusilla and all that follows. It must be at the back, near the scenic wall, in order not to intervene between the audience and the action on the lower stage. Now only the tarras meets these conditions. It was large enough to receive and support the car. It projected from the scenic wall at the back. It was the only projection between the stage heavens and the outer stage. We must conclude, therefore, that stage-hands in the huts were able to vary the path of a descending car and, if required, to cause it to descend upon the tarras. This fact suggests either that there was a special opening over the tarras, or that the normal path was only enough in front of the tarras to clear its outer edge, and that the stage-hands could swing the car 2 or 3 feet back toward the scenic wall once it had been lowered the requisite distance (the floor of the tarras was 20 feet below the under side of the stage heavens). In view of the rarity of such scenes (and taking other heavens trap-work into account) I strongly incline to this second alternative. Specifically, then, this scene suggests that the rear edge of the heavens-trap was almost directly over the forward edge of the tarras.

There are one or two other details worth noting before turning from this scene. As is not infrequently the case, the descent from the heavens-trap is simply marked "Enter ——" in the stage-direction. Observe that Delphia gives the signal for the "Musick from the Spheres," that the "fiddlers" are invisible, and that the music seems to come from the skies: "Ha! in the Air! — Miraculous." Observe also that Delphia's command, "Mount up, my birds," precedes by four full lines the end of her speech and the direction marking the disappearance of the throne into the heavens. And finally, observe that although their manner of reaching the tarras is unusual, Delphia's and Drusilla's sitting there to watch the action below conforms to the normal practice of actors entering upon the tarras to watch a masque or interlude performed on the outer stage.

A yet more detailed and spectacular scene of the same order occurs in Heywood's undivided *Silver Age*, performed at the Red Bull in 1610. I cite it to show that stage design was essentially uniform in different playhouses of the same type and to prove that the scene in *The Prophetess* did not spring from some peculiarity in the equipment of the Blackfriars and the second Globe.

Act IV (as *The Silver Age* would be divided in a modern text) dramatizes the story of Jupiter's love for Semele and Juno's efforts to destroy her. It begins with a dumb show in the study, followed by a commentary by the Presenter, old Homer. (I shall supplement the existing stage-directions where necessary to ensure a ready grasp of the course of action.)

> *Dumbe shew. Enter Semele like a huntresse, with her traine, Iupiter*
> *like a wood-man in greene: he wo[o]s her, and winnes her.*

[Homer.] What cannot Ioue, infus'd with power diuine?
  He woes and winnes, enioyes the beauteous dame;
  The iealous Iuno spyes their loue in fine, . . .
  And 'gainst this beauteous Lady armes her spleene,
  Quite to destroy the bright Cadmeian Queene.

The action opens on the outer stage. Iris comes to report to Juno the name and the homeland of Jupiter's latest paramour. The scene concludes:

Iuno.   In what shape
  Saw'st thou him court that strumpet?

Iris. Like a wood-man.

Iuno. I met him on the mountaine *Erecine*,
And tooke him for the yong *Hyppolitus.*
Iris I hau't; 'tis plotted in my braine,
To haue the strumpet by her louer slaine.
Of her nurse *Beroe* Il'e assume the shape,
And by that meanes auenge me on this rape. *Exeunt.*

The action is then transferred to the study. For twenty-two lines Semele dilates upon her lover and her good fortune. She dismisses her usual attendants as unworthy to wait on her:

Go call hither my Nurse *Beroe*,
Whom I will make free-partner in my ioyes.

Enter Iuno in the shape of old Beroe.

Seruant. Beroe attends your grace. [Exit servant.]

Sem. Oh my deere nurse! liues there on earth a Princesse
Equally lou'd and grac'd by *Ioue* himselfe?

But Juno, safe in her disguise, manages to insinuate that the lover is nothing but a mortal in borrowed plumes. Semele, disturbed, asks how she can test him. Juno suggests that Semele demand a boon:

Sem. Beroe, what boone?

Iuno. To hugge you in that state
In which faire *Iuno* he imbrac'd so late.
To descend armed with celestiall fire,
And in that maiesty glut his desire.
His right hand arm'd with lightning, on his head
Heauens massy crowne; and so to mount your bed. . . .

Sem. Thou hast fir'd me *Beroe.*

Iuno [aside]. Thou shalt be on flame,
So great, the Ocean shall not quench the same.

Sem. Beroe away, my chamber ready make,
Tosse downe on downe: for we this night must tumble
Within the armes of mighty *Iupiter.*
Of whom Il'e begge th'immortall sweets of loue,
Such as from *Ioue* Imperiall *Iuno* tastes.
Begone without reply, my loue's at hand.

Iuno [aside]. Thy death's vpon thy boone: this *Iuno* cheares,
    That my reuenge shall mount aboue the spheares.   *exit Iuno.*
Sem. I will not smile on him, lend him a looke,
    As the least grace, till he giue free ascent
    To fill me with celestiall wonderment.
                Enter Iupiter like a wood-man.

Semele begins at once to press Jupiter with questions designed to test his powers. At last he promises:

    Aske what thou wilt to proue my Deity,
    And take it as thine owne faire *Semele.*

Still doubtful, she hints that he may fail to carry out his promise faithfully.

Iup. By dreadfull Styx, an oath I cannot change,
    But aske and haue.
Sem. Then bed with me to night,
    Arm'd with the selfe-same God-hood, state and power
    You *Iuno* meet.
Iup. Blacke day, accursed houre,
    Thou hast ask't too much, thy weake mortality
    Cannot indure the scorching fires of heauen.

Semele taunts him with lacking the powers he has claimed. Jupiter regrets his oath, but cannot change it. He departs to robe himself according to his promise.

Iup. Aboue my thunders are,
    Thither I must, and beeing arm'd, descend
    To giue this beauty (in her rashnesse) end.
Sem. Remember by this kisse you keep your oath.
Iup. Neuer did *Ioue* to heauen ascend so loath;
    Expect me this sad night.   [Exit Jupiter.]

Semele is left to anticipate her happiness, and the study curtains close six lines later:

            Dance my hart,
    And swim in free delights, my pleasures crowne
    This *Iouiall* night shall *Semele* renowne.   *Exit Semele.*

The action continues without pause in another part of the stage:

Iuno and Iris plac'd in a cloud aboue.

(They enter the forefront of the music gallery before the curtains.[22])

Iuno. Come *Iris*, ore the loftiest pinnacles
Of this high pallace, let vs mount our selues,
To see this noble pastime: Is't not braue?
Iris. Hath her suit tooke effect? 'lasse *Semele*!
Iuno. Hang, burne her witch, be all such strumpets fir'd
With no lesse heat then wanton *Semele.* . . .
            Oh 'twould please me *Iris*
To see this wanton with her bastard, blowne
And hang'd vpon the high hornes of the moone.
The howre drawes on, we may from hence espy
Th' adultresse sprall, the pallace vpward fly.

Enter [in the chamber] *two maids of Semeles chamber.*

1. Maid. Questionlesse my Lady lookes for some great guests, that she makes all this preparation.
2. Maid. 'Tis not like she expects them at supper, because she herselfe is preparing to bed.
1. Maid. Did you note how she made vs tumble & tosse the bed before the making of it would please her? . . . Why do you thinke her with childe.
2. Maid. Tis past thinking, I dare sweare. But let's attend my Lady.

Enter Semele drawne out in her bed.

(For a reading public, this stage-direction would be expanded somewhat as follows: "The two Maids go to the alcove at the rear of the chamber and draw the bed forward to the middle of the room. They open the bed-cur-

[22] Cf. the position of Prospero in *The Tempest*, III. iii (discussed on p. 320). Although it may have been feasible with the equipment of a public playhouse to suspend the two goddesses over the stage in one car and also to lower Jupiter in another, such a procedure would not meet the requirements of the scene. For one thing, Jupiter obviously is unaware that his wife and Iris are here spying on him. But how could he have failed to see them had they been suspended in the air a few feet away from the path of his descending car?

tains on the side facing the audience. Semele, appearing in the bed, addresses them.")

Sem. Away, we will haue none partake our pleasures,
  Or be eye-witnesse of these prodigall sweets
  Which we this night shall in aboundance taste.   [Exeunt Maids.]
  This is the houre shall deifie my earth,
  And make this drosse immortall: . . .
  Descend great *Ioue* in thy full maiesty,
  And crowne my pleasures: here behold me spred,
  To taste the sweets of thy immortall bed.
    Thunder, lightnings, Iupiter descends [to the tarras] *in his maiesty,
      his Thunderbolt burning.*
Iup. Thus wrapt in stormes and black tempestuous clouds,
  Lightning and showers, we sit vpon the roofes
  And trembling Tarrasses of this high house
  That is not able to containe our power.
  Yet come we not with those sharpe thunders arm'd
  With which the sturdy giants we ore-threw,
  When we the mighty *Typhon* sunke beneath
  Foure populous kingdomes: these are not so fiery,
  The *Cyclopes* that vs'd to forge our bolts,
  Haue qualifi'd their feruour, yet their violence
  Is 'boue the strength of mortals. Beauteous *Semele*
  In steed of thee I shall imbrace thy smoake,
  And claspe a fumy vapour left in place
                                    Thunder and lightning.
  Of thy bright beauty. Stormy tempests cease,
  The more I frowne, the more their breathes increase.
Sem. What terror's this? oh thou immortall speake!
  My eyes are for thy maiesty too weake.
    *As he toucheth the bed it fires, and all flyes vp. Iupiter from thence
      takes an abortiue infant.*
Iup. Receiue thy boone, now take thy free desire
  In thunder, tempest, smoake, and heauenly fire.
Iuno. Ha, ha, ha.
  Faire *Semele's* consum'd, 'twas acted well:
  Come, next wee'l follow *Hercules* to hell.
        [Exeunt Juno and Iris from the music loft.]
    Iupiter taking vp the Infant speakes as he ascends in his cloud.
Iup. For *Semele* (thus slaine) the heauens shall mourne
  In pitchy clouds, the earth in barrennesse; . . .

Jupiter's speech continues for a total of fourteen lines before his disappearance into the stage heavens. Directly after Homer resumes his commentary, bridging from this chapter of the story to the next in which Hercules descends to Hell to rescue Proserpine.

It will be well to analyze step by step the staging of this remarkable Act. The dumb shows before and after take place in the study, and call as usual for elaborate settings (notably in the second of the two) to compensate for the lack of dialogue. After the first dumb show the setting must be cleared away before a scene using a different setting can be staged there, hence IV. i, is enacted on the outer stage. Scene i lasts twenty-four decasyllabic lines, which, together with the closing lines of Homer's commentary, furnishes time to make the study ready for scene ii.

Scene ii is a study scene representing a room in Semele's palace. It lasts almost 170 lines. During this scene Juno and Iris mount back stage to the third level of the tiring-house to be ready for their entrance, and stage-hands set out the bed and the "abortive infant" in the chamber.

Scene iii opens with Juno and Iris coming forward to a place in front of the music curtains ("*Iuno and Iris plac'd in a cloud aboue*"). Their sixteen-line exchange of comments explains why they have come to such a lofty place of observation. (And it is not improbable that one of them guided the thunder cues soon to follow.) The Maids of Semele's chamber then appear — "*Enter two maids . . .*" — just where it is impossible to say without reference to what follows. Their eighteen lines add nothing to the development of the action, but, like those of Juno and Iris, they are padded to give Semele and Jupiter time in which to change costumes and make ready for the scene to come. A total of thirty-four lines — less than two minutes — is none too much for Semele to change to night attire, ascend to the chamber, and get into bed. A total of fifty-one lines — two minutes and a half — means nimble work for Jupiter, who must exchange his green forester's suit for his celestial robes, climb to the huts, and mount his "cloud."

Then comes the thunder inaugurating the climax. Jupiter descends in full regalia, "his Thunderbolt burning." In the initial direction the cloud is not mentioned. One must supply it from the closing direction, "he ascends in his cloud." He lands not upon the lower stage but upon the tarras — "We sit vpon the roofes And trembling Tarrasses of this high house." Once there he calls for the thunder to cease. The terrified Semele, unable to gaze upon the god's fiery majesty, closes the bed-curtains as if to protect herself (and, slipping unseen out of the far side of the bed, leaves the stage). Jupiter touches the bed with his flaming Thunderbolt — "*As he toucheth the bed it fires, and all flyes vp* [i.e. the bed-curtains and canopy flare up?], *Iupiter from thence takes an abortiue infant.*" [23] Jupiter's closing speech, delivered from his slowly rising cloud, lasts fourteen lines. Once he has disappeared Homer resumes, speaking eight lines to prepare the audience for the dumb show introducing Act V.

Jupiter's description of the place to which he descends from the heavens (together with the fact that the study is discovered for a dumb show twenty-two lines after he leaves the bed-side) establishes beyond question that Semele's bed was discovered in the chamber and not in the study (the only alternative [24]). *The Silver Age*, then, provides an example contemporary with the first Globe showing that the rear edge of the heavens-trap was not far forward of the front edge of the tarras.

We are now in a position to estimate the size and location of one of the Globe huts. Similar in function to the tower enclosing the "grid" constructed over a modern

[23] Elizabethans were skilled in many branches of stage pyrotechnics. For comparable scenes see *The Fatal Contract*, III. i; *The Jew's Tragedy*, V; and *The Silver Age*, III. For the fate of other stage-delivered infants see *Titus Andronicus*, G2 verso; and *The Fair Quarrel*, III. ii.

[24] Cf. Chapter VIII, section 3.

stage, the hut was constructed over the heavens-trap to protect it from the weather, shield it from view, provide working space above and around the opening, and house the machines by which the clouds were lowered and raised. It follows, therefore, that the Globe hut we are now concerned with measured fully 24 feet in length and at least 8 feet in depth. Headroom throughout was essential, together with greater height directly over the trap-opening to accommodate the pulleys [25] carrying ropes from the windlasses to the cars. The hut had to extend over the platform stage at least 8 feet in order to provide a trap-opening 4 feet wide sufficiently forward from the scenic wall. An overhang of more than 8 feet, however, was structurally undesirable (the more that the hut was supported by the playhouse frame, and the less by the two stage posts, the better).

It is at once apparent that this reconstruction based upon a study of descents from the stage heavens coincides precisely with the transverse hut appearing in Visscher's representation of the Globe superstructure.

A few related details should be considered before leaving the subject of descents.

Inasmuch as two or more windlasses would be needed to lower and raise the large cloth-draped cars carrying a number of actors,[26] it is not surprising that scenes occasionally call for the separate lowering of actors. The width of the heavens opening made paired descents in small cars entirely feasible. A good example is found in *Four Plays in One*, part IV:

> *Jupiter and Mercury descend severally. Trumpets small above.*

[25] The Revels Accounts for 1575 contain the item: "Pulleys for the clowdes and curteynes." In the drawings by Inigo Jones for the stage at Whitehall prepared in 1640 for the masque *Salmacida Spolia* (reproduced by Reyher, *Masques Anglais*, facing p. 370) pulleys carry the cloud ropes from the stage cellar up the outer frame and over to points above the descent.

[26] Windlasses operating in pairs are indicated in the plans referred to in the preceding note.

Twenty-four lines later the two gods "ascend again." [27]

Dramatists went out of their way to avoid lowering or raising an empty car. Several devices, illustrated by the following examples, were resorted to. From *The Silver Age*, II: "*Iuno and Iris descend* [together] *from the heauens.*" Juno dismounts from the car, for she must stay for a time among mortals. She concludes her opening speech (twenty-three lines long) by sending Iris back to the heavens to secure a black "cloud" from which to fashion a beldame's habit.

Iuno.   *Iris* away.
Iris. I flye Madame.   *Exit Iris* [up].

Seven lines later Iris descends "*with a habit*," hands it to Juno, and returns to the heavens. This little by-play after the lowering of Juno succeeds (1) in providing an interlocutor for Juno, (2) in calling attention to the black costume soon to be used in a scene in which the costume alone will identify Juno, and (3) in avoiding the return of an empty car. Again, from the concluding episode of *The Golden Age*, which represents the dividing of the universe among the gods:

Sound a dumbe shew. Enter the three fatall sisters, with a rocke, a threed, and a paire of sheeres; bringing in a Gloabe, in which they put three lots. Iupiter drawes heauen: at which Iris descends and presents him with his Eagle, Crowne and Scepter, and his thunder-bolt. Iupiter first ascends vpon the Eagle, and after him Ganimed.

Here (if I interpret correctly) Iris, holding Jupiter's three symbols of majesty, descends in a car which also brings down Jupiter's Eagle — his particular "car." Jupiter mounts the eagle, dons his crown, and rises holding the scepter and the thunderbolt. Ganymede then follows Jupiter in the car which brought Iris down.

A third example comes from Middleton's *Witch*, III. iii:

[27] Trap-work in *The Tempest, or Enchanted Island* (1670), I. ii, elaborates this use of two machines: "*They both fly up and cross in the air.*"

Song above.

Hecate [on the outer stage]. I come, I come.

Voice above. Here.

Hec. Where's Puckle?

Voice above. Here. . . .

Hec. I will but 'noint and then I mount.

A Spirit like a cat descends.

Voice above. There's one comes down to fetch his dues, . . .

Hec. Now I go, now I fly . . .

[Hecate and Spirit ascend into the heavens.]

The operation of the heavens machinery was not entirely silent. In the prologue to *Every Man in his Humour*, Jonson boasts that his play is written —

> as other plays should be.
> Where neither *Chorus* wafts you ore the seas;
> Nor creaking throne comes downe, the boyes to please.

It is understandable, therefore, that disguise sounds should accompany the lowering and raising of cars much as they accompanied the operation of the main trap in the middle of the outer stage. The reader will have noted the calls for thunder and for music of many kinds appearing in the stage-directions cited earlier in this chapter.[28]

Almost as early as the first descents over the stage, billowing folds of light cloth simulating clouds were added to the car for the purposes of enhancing the effect and also, perhaps, of concealing the ropes by which the car was suspended.[29] These cloth clouds, I suspect, were invariably added to the cars even though infrequently referred to. Sometimes the stage-direction marking the descent

---

[28] See also *The Seven Champions*, line 150; *The Rebellion*, III. ii; and *The Widow's Tears*, III. ii. For further discussion see Lawrence, *Physical Conditions*, p. 121.

[29] See Palsgrave's *Acolastus*, 1540: "Of whyche the lyke thyng is used to be shewed now a days in stage-plaies, when some God or some Saynt is made to appere forth of a cloude, and succoureth the parties which seemed to be towardes some great danger, through the Soudan's crueltie." See also note 25 above.

will omit all mention of the cloud but the related direction will include it (as in Jupiter's descent to the tarras in *The Silver Age*). Illustrations of clouds are available in contemporary sources.[30]

2. THE HUTS (*continued*)

The raising and lowering of gods and goddesses from the heavens constituted only one of the many duties assigned to the stage crew stationed in the huts. There the trumpeter stood who "sounded" thrice before the play began; there the cannon were shot off during battle and coronation scenes (or when King Claudius drank deep at Elsinore); there hung the great alarum bell the dreadful midnight clamor of which roused the citizens of Cyprus; there the heavy "bullet" was rolled to make thunder; and there the triple moons, blazing suns, comets, and similar fearsome portents were exhibited through the stage ceiling.

Now to store and operate all the varied equipment needed for these activities and displays obviously required no little space — much more space than a single hut some 8 by 24 feet in size could supply if (as at the Globe and other playhouses of its type) the trap-opening took up half the floor of the hut and the windlasses and the working space took up the remainder. The Visscher representation of the Globe superstructure indicates how additional space was provided. It shows not only the transverse hut placed exactly as the operation of descensions and ascensions require, but also two wings and a square tower added to the transverse hut. The relative size and location of the parts forming the Globe superstructure have already been given; let us now see how far the evidence warrants our assigning to the wings and tower the equipment referred to in the preceding paragraph.

[30] See, for example, the Italian engraving dated 1644 reproduced by Nicoll, *Stuart Masques*, p. 95; cf. also *ibid.*, pp. 45, 74, 78, 106, 107, 119, 124, etc.

Elizabethans inherited a long tradition of stage pyro-technics and were evidently highly skilled in their produc-tion and management.[31] Our concern here, however, is not so much with the nature of their pyrotechnic properties as with the provision made in the heavens for exhibiting them — whether through the large trap-opening used for descents, or through some special opening located else-where.

In the early playhouses with a single hut (as the Swan) the probability is that the one trap served for all functions, much as the study (in the first years of Burbage's Theater) served for all inner-stage scenes. But experience brought about specialization of function in the huts as it did in the tiring-house. The transverse section of the Globe super-structure (corresponding to the entire Swan hut) must have been completely occupied with the complicated ap-paratus designed for lowering cars and clouds of a size and weight unheard of in 1595. And it may be doubted if a large windlass and a trap measuring 4 by 20 feet could be used successfully in a display of lightning, burning planets, flaming swords, and similar properties, or if it were feasible to set such things ablaze so near to the lightly fabricated cars (with their clouds of diaphanous cloth and painted canvas) suspended over or stored close by the heavens trap.

A bit of stage business in Heywood's *Brazen Age* appears to show that there was a second opening 6 or 8 feet forward of the main heavens-trap, thus confirming Visscher's repre-sentation of a wing projecting forward into the yard from the middle of the transverse hut. The business in question occurs in the final scene of the play. After assembling material for his funeral pyre, Hercules enthrones himself in the midst and delivers his dying oration, concluding, "Alcides dies by no hand but his own." Then follows the stage-direction:

[31] For discussion see Lawrence, ii. 17–22; and Campbell, *Scenes and Ma-chines*, Chapter IV.

Jupiter aboue strikes him with a thunder-bolt,[32] his body sinkes, and from the heauens discends a hand in a cloud, that from the place where Hercules was burnt, brings vp a starre, and fixeth it in the firmament.

Since the property "hand in a cloud," lowered on its cord or light wire and descending vertically from some opening overhead, can pass through the hole in the outer stage made when the main trap sinks with Hercules (and presumably the hand must pass *through* the hole into the Hell if the star is to be attached to it), then it follows that this opening in the heavens is directly over the main outer-stage trap. But this opening cannot be any part of the main heavens-trap, for its outer edge was only 8 feet forward of the scenic wall, whereas the middle of the outer-stage trap was fully 14 feet forward of the scenic wall.[33]

Little can be determined about this secondary opening beyond the fact that it was located forward of the heavens-trap and was directly over the main trap "in the midst" of the outer stage below. I assume, however, that it was relatively small, for had it been large enough to permit an actor to pass through, almost certainly there would be scenes exploiting that fact (perhaps a descent by one of Lucifer's minions out of Heaven clear down into Hell, or perhaps some equivalent of the Carolinian Court masque in which an actor lowered in a small down-stage cloud is seen against a background of actors in a large up-stage cloud). An opening some 18 inches across seems adequate for the "*hand in a cloud, that . . . brings vp a starre, and fixeth it in the firmament,*" and for all the comets, moons, and blazing stars on record. Obviously a small, slotted cover would have many advantages not possessed by the

[32] For similar business see *Cymbeline*, V. iv; *The Martyr'd Souldier*, V. i; *Messallina*, F1; *The Prophetess*, V. iii; *The Seven Champions*, lines 2087 ff.; and *The Unnatural Combat*, V.

[33] Cf. Chapter IV, section 5. The middle of the outer-stage trap was therefore some 8 feet forward of a point directly under the middle of the heavens-trap.

large hinged covers of the main heavens-trap in carrying out such business.[34]

If, then, the Globe provided a separate forward wing in the superstructure for pyrotechnic and allied displays, we may assume that the playhouse cannon also were located there. Shakespeare's use of cannon is typical. In *2 Henry VI*, IV. i, the opening direction reads: "*Alarum. Fight at Sea. Ordnance goes off.*" In *Henry V* the cannon are fired twice, once during the chorus describing the sailing of the English fleet towards France, and again at the close of III. i (the siege of Harfleur). In *Hamlet* the cannon are fired at least three times, first in I. iv (the second quarto reading):

> *A florish of trumpets and 2 peeces goes of.*[35]
> *Horatio.* What does this meane my Lord?
> *Hamlet.* The King doth wake to night and takes his rowse.
>   Keepes wassell and the swaggring vp-spring reeles:
>   And as he draines his drafts of Rennish downe,
>   The kettle drumme, and trumpet, thus bray out
>   The triumph of his pledge.

Again, in the last scene, at line 278 (Quarto 2):

> *King.* Set me the stoopes of wine vpon that table,
>   If *Hamlet* giue the first or second hit,
>   Or quit in answere of the third exchange,
>   Let all the battlements their ordnance fire. . . .
>   giue me the cups,
>   And let the kettle to the trumpet speake,
>   The trumpet to the Cannoneere without,
>   The Cannons to the heauens, the heauen to earth,
>   Now the King drinkes to *Hamlet*, come beginne. *Trumpets the while.*
>   And you the Iudges beare a wary eye.
> *Ham.* Come on sir.
> *Laer.* Come my Lord.

---

[34] Occasionally rain and snow are mentioned in stage-directions or in dialogue (see for example *If You Know not Me*, line 600; *The Duchess of Suffolk*, F2 verso) in such a way as to suggest that artifice helped out illusion. In this connection a marginal note in the MS. play *Necromantes*, II. ii, is interesting: "From above a dish of water."

[35] In Quarto 1 the direction is limited to "*Sound Trumpets.*"

Ham. One.
Laer. No.
Ham. Iudgement.
Ostrick. A hit, a very palpable hit.

> *Drum, trumpets and shot.*
> *Florish, a peece goes off.*

Finally, at line 406 (Folio 1), to bring this martial play to a fitting end:

Fortinbras. Let foure Captaines
  Beare *Hamlet* like a Soldier to the Stage,
  For he was likely, had he beene put on
  To haue prou'd most royally:
  And for his passage,
  The Souldiours Musicke, and the rites of Warre
  Speake lowdly for him.
  Take vp the body; Such a sight as this
  Becomes the Field, but heere shewes much amis.
  Go, bid the Souldiers shoote.
Exeunt Marching: after the which, a Peale of Ordenance are shot off.

The cannon used to announce the arrival of the King at the Cardinal's Palace in *Henry VIII*, I. iv — "*Drum and Trumpet, chambers dischargd*" — made woeful history, for their discharge on the afternoon of June 29, 1613, a day of "Sunnshine weather," brought about the complete destruction of the Globe by fire. Two of the many contemporary accounts [36] contain details bearing upon the present discussion. Sir Henry Wotton wrote on July 2 to his nephew, Sir Edward Bacon:

> Now, to let matters of state sleep, I will entertain you at the present with what has happened this week at the Bank's side. The King's players had a new play, called *All is True*, representing some principal pieces of the reign of Henry VIII, which was set forth with many extraordinary circumstances of pomp and majesty, even to the matting of the stage; the Knights of the Order with their Georges and garters, the Guards with their embroidered coats, and the like: sufficient in truth within a while to make greatness very familiar, if not ridiculous. Now, King Henry making a masque at the Cardinal Wolsey's house, and

---

[36] For citation and discussion see Adams, pp. 250–255; and Chambers, ii. 419–423. The two selections quoted in the text are reproduced from Chambers.

certain chambers being shot off at his entry, some of the paper, or other stuff, wherewith one of them was stopped, did light on the thatch, where being thought at first but an idle smoke, and their eyes more attentive to the show, it kindled inwardly, and ran round like a train, consuming within less than an hour the whole house to the very grounds.

Howes's continuation of Stowe's *Annales* records:

Upon S. Peters day last, the play-house or Theater, called the Globe, upon the Banck-side near London, by negligent discharging of a peal of ordinance, close to the south-side thereof, the thatch took fire, and the wind sodainly disperst the flame round about, and in a very short space the whole building was quite consumed, and no man hurt; the house being filled with people to behold the play, viz. of Henry the Eighth.

Additional references to the firing of a cannon from the huts are listed in the notes.[37]

Where stood the thunder-machine, which Shakespeare glances at in *Othello*, V. ii — "Are there no stones in heaven But what serves for thunder?" — and which Jonson described as the "roul'd bullet heard To say, it thunders"? [38] Was it located in the rear wing of the superstructure, directly over the music gallery? That seems as reasonable a guess as any, for it was used in conjunction with the music-gallery kettle drums when the prompt-book called for a tempest, a "fearfull storme," or a "Boisterous Hurricano."

The employment and the location of the great alarum bell have been studied by others. In a charming and scholarly article entitled "Bells in the Elizabethan Drama," [39] Lawrence wrote:

There can be little doubt that one of the main uses of the flag-surmounted tower in the view of the old Globe given in Visscher's pictorial map of London was to house the large bell which had such a variety of offices that it must have proved the most useful of theatrical

---

[37] *1 The Contention*, F1 verso; *Edward III*, E3; *Ieronimo*, II. i; *A Larum for London*, line 203; *Lust's Dominion*, III. v; *The Maid of Honor*, II. iii; *The Revenge of Bussy*, IV. i; and *The Travels of the Three English Brothers*, *passim*.

[38] See Chapter IX, note 15.

[39] Revised and reprinted in *Those Nut-Cracking Elizabethans*, 1935.

accessories. This was the bell which, after the firing of ordnance, gave the signal for the wholesale slaughter of the Huguenots in Marlowe's *The Massacre of Paris*; the bell, which, to Barabbas's great delight, tolled the knell of the poisoned nuns in his *Jew of Malta*; and it was likewise the bell which gave the alarm in *Macbeth* and *Othello*.

Lawrence went on to trace and illustrate other uses of the bell, for example, in announcing the hours (as in *King John*, III. iii; *Macbeth*, II. i; *The Atheist's Tragedie*, IV. i; and *The Changeling*, V). It probably was heard when Francisco first appeared upon the battlements in the northern winter night at Elsinore and waited for Barnardo to relieve him.[40] Its ominous tolling would have made an effective opening for *Hamlet* and seems called for by the dialogue. At line 7:

Fran. You come most carefully vpon your houre,
Bar. Tis now strooke twelfe, get thee to bed *Francisco*;
Fran. For this reliefe much thanks.

(I have listed in the notes a few other references to playhouse bells not mentioned by Lawrence.[41])

3. The Stage-Cover

In addition to the posts rising from the platform to support the overhanging stage superstructure, the Fortune builder's contract calls for "a shadowe or cover over the

[40] *Hamlet*, ed. J. Q. Adams, p. 176.

[41] Compare with *Hamlet*, I. i, the opening lines from *Antonio's Revenge* (1602; the play has many resemblances to *Hamlet*), III. i:

Antonio. The black jades of swart night trot foggy rings
  Bout heauens browe — (12) [i.e. twelve strokes of the bell] Tis now starke deade night.
Is this Saint *Markes* Church?

For use as an "alarum bell" see *Alphonsus, Emperor of Germany*, III. i; *The Cardinal*, V; *The Fatal Contract*, II. ii; *The Island Princess*, II. i; and *Two Maids of More-clacke*, B4 verso. For use as a clock see *Cymbeline*, II. ii; *Julius Caesar*, II. i; *A Looking Glass for London*, B3 verso; *Richard III*, V. iii; and *The Roaring Girl*, E3 verso. Further references to the peal of bells discussed by Lawrence occur in *If You Know not Me*, line 865; *The Isle of Guls*, II. v; and *A Warning for Fair Women*, D1.

saide Stadge . . . to be covered with Tyle and to haue a sufficient gutter of lead to Carrie & convey the water frome the Coveringe of the saide Stadge to fall backwardes [i.e. outside the playhouse]." This Fortune cover presumably corresponds to the Swan stage-cover (appearing in the De Witt sketch), which appears as a roofed extension of the hut projecting as far as the middle of the outer stage and supported at its forward edge by the two posts. It will be observed that the Swan cover is as wide as the platform and has a roof (of thatch?) rising in a sloping plane from its fore-edge over the posts to the front of the hut behind. The fore-edge, moreover, is as high above the platform as the eaves-line of the playhouse frame is above the floor of the first gallery. No stage-cover is to be seen in Visscher's representation of the Globe, for it extended from that side of the huts which was not visible to the artist. Now the superstructures of the Swan, Globe, and Fortune were evidently of the same type, for all three playhouses had stage posts and huts; furthermore, the stage-cover is shown in a view of the first, is implied in the contract for the second (see the Fortune contract), and is named in the builder's contract for the third.

Posts rising from the platform constituted the easiest and strongest means of supporting the overhanging super-structure (indeed in wooden amphitheatres as large as the Globe, Fortune, and Red Bull posts were the only feasible means [42]). The posts, of course, were in the way, but by

[42] When in 1613 the old Bear Garden was replaced by a new structure de-signed for both animal baiting and plays, a means of supporting the super-structure without posts had to be devised. The Hope platform was not to be permanent, but was designed "to stande vppon tressells good substanciall and sufficient for the carryinge and bearinge of suche a stage," hence stage posts could not rest upon the platform, nor could they be tolerated in the yard when "Beares and Bulls [were] bayted in the same." Henslowe and Meade, the joint owners, therefore stipulated that Katherens, the builder, "shall also builde the Heavens all over the saide stage to be borne or carryed without any postes or supporters to be fixed or sett vppon the saide stage, And all gutters of leade needfull for the carrying of all such Raine water as shall fall vppon the same."

adding a stage-cover, which enlarged the base of the heavens without much increasing the weight, designers were able to place the posts well forward and also well apart; so placed they interfered least with the actors and with a view of the stage. No complaint by actors or spectators about the posts is to be found; and playwrights were able to turn them to dramatic account (see Chapter IV).

The stage-cover was primarily a structural unit. Only secondarily was it a protecting roof. Its size and shape, therefore, were determined in the main by structural considerations, a fact which simplifies the problem of reconstructing it.

The plan on the opposite page, though highly conjectural, is based on miscellaneous evidence already presented.

The stage posts, 32 feet high, are spaced 24 feet apart (A and A') — the spacing of the corner posts of the frame (B and B').[43] They stand 17 feet forward of the scenic wall in line with the pair of corner posts marking the ends of the gentlemen's rooms. A beam (A–A') 24 feet long spans the stage posts. Beams 17 feet long, affixed at right angles, cross from the top of each post to the corresponding corner posts of the tiring-house (A–B, A'–B'). Into these principal beams framing the base of the stage heavens

---

Apart from the requirement to support the heavens without the use of stage posts, the specifications differ in two other important respects from the Fortune specifications. First, no stage-cover is mentioned, and secondly, the heavens are to cover the entire platform. We do not know how large that platform was, but we may assume that in such a hybrid amphitheatre the removable platform probably did not extend to the middle of the yard, and that descents and displays originating in the huts were more modest than those of the Globe, Fortune, and Red Bull companies. We know, moreover, that the Hope was smaller than its three great rivals. These differences greatly simplified the problem of supporting a heavens "all over" the stage: the huts were smaller and the distances to be spanned in bridging over the stage less great. There is good reason to believe, therefore, that in depicting huts which cover half the entire Hope yard, Hollar exaggerated their size.

[43] To avoid confusion I am disregarding the fact that the yard was slightly smaller at the eaves-line than at the base-line (as a result of the successive projections of both upper levels).

secondary beams are secured to serve as sills for the huts
(C–C′, D–D′, and E–E′). Supplementary beams (A–F

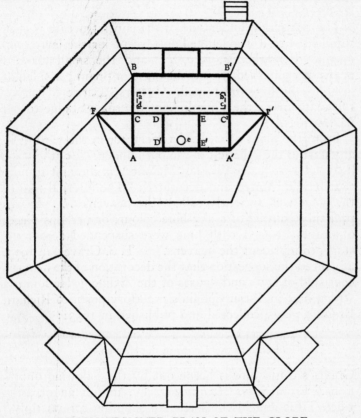

RECONSTRUCTED PLAN OF THE GLOBE
SUPERSTRUCTURE

and A′–F′) are required to ensure a rigid frame.[44] The
transverse hut used for descents rises over the rectangle
based on B, B′, C′, and C. The forward hut used for pyro-

[44] For a similar proposal see the design of the Globe included by Dr. J. Q.
Adams in his *Life of William Shakespeare*, p. 286.

technic displays rises over the rectangle based on D, E, E′, and D′. (The rear hut rises over corresponding beams supported by the playhouse frame on the other side of the transverse hut.)

The projecting under side of the superstructure is then supplied with a wooden ceiling (except for the large trap opening — marked *a*, *b*, *c*, *d* — and the small forward aperture — marked *e*), and the parts of the upper side not occupied by huts are roofed. Gutters "Carrie & convey the water frome the Coveringe of the saide Stadge to fall backwardes."

From the point of view of a spectator in the yard or in any part of the galleries, the smooth under side of the stage heavens was clearly visible. Malone was the first to note that it was painted and decorated: "The internal roof of the stage was anciently called 'the heavens' . . . It was probably painted of a sky-blue colour; or perhaps pieces of drapery tinged with blue were suspended across the stage, to represent the heavens." [45] T. S. Graves, in 1913, advanced the suggestion that the decoration of the heavens consisted of stars and figures of the Zodiac.[46] He found a strong hint in Aston Cokain's prefatory poem to Richard Brome's plays, collected and published in 1653: [47]

> The Bull take Courage from Applauses given,
> To Eccho to the *Taurus* in the Heaven.

Graves's conjecture is borne out by the following quotations. From *Titus Andronicus*, IV. iii (on an occasion when Titus and his kinsmen are shooting arrows tipped with messages for the gods):

Tit. Now Maisters draw, Oh well said *Lucius*:
Good Boy in *Virgoes* lap, give it *Pallas*.
Marcus. My Lord, I aime a Mile beyond the Moone,
Your letter is with *Jupiter* by this.

[45] *Variorum* (1821), iii. 108.
[46] *Court and London Theatres*, pp. 24–26.
[47] *Five New Playes*, 1653, A2 verso.

Tit. Ha, ha, *Publius, Publius,* what hast thou done?
See, see, thou hast shot off one of *Taurus* hornes.

From Dekker's undivided Fortune play, *The Whore of Babylon*: [48]

3 King. Can yonder roofe, thats naild so fast with starres,
Couer a head so impious, and not cracke?

From Heywood's undivided Red Bull play, *The Rape of Lucrece*: [49]

Horatius. Had I as many soules as drops of blood
In these brancht vaines, as many lives as starres
Stuck in yond' azure Rofe, and were to die . . .

The King's Men's pre-Globe play, *Edward III,* contains a triple allusion in the speech of the Countess of Salisbury (II. ii):

Co. O periurde beautie, more corrupted Iudge!
When to the great Starre-chamber ore our heads
The vniuersell Sessions cals to count
This packing euill, we both shall tremble for it.

From a later play by the same company, Massinger's *Very Woman,* II. iii:

Almira.   — But look yonder!
Amongst a million of glorious lights
That deck the heavenly canopy, I have
Descerned his soul, transform'd into a star.
Do you not see it?
Leonora. Lady!
Almi. Look with my eyes.
What splendour circles it! The heavenly archer
Not far off distant, appears dim with envy,
Viewing himself outshined.

"R. M." writes in *Micrologia,* 1629, of the character of a Player: "If his action prefigure passion, he raves, rages, and protests much by his painted heavens, and seems in

[48] Quarto I, 1607, A4 verso.   [49] *Works,* ed. Pearson, v. 192.

the height of this fit ready to pull Jove out of the garret where perchance he lies leaning on his elbows, or is employed to make squibs and crackers to grace the play." [50] Other references or allusions to the painted stage ceiling are listed in the notes.[51]

It goes without saying that the stage ceiling projecting well out into the yard served admirably as a sounding board for music, alarums, and thunder originating in the music gallery just beneath it. I suspect that Elizabethans knew all about sounding boards from long experience in and out of the theatre, but I find no specific record to that effect dating from Shakespeare's age. In October, 1675, however, artisans installed "a new Ceiling in the Theatre in Whitehall that ye Voyses may ye better be heard, & also to make the roome warmer." [52] In Elizabethan public playhouses with their yards open to the sky voices and instruments would be heard very much better if deflected and spread throughout the auditorium by the wooden ceiling of the heavens.

4. THE PLAYHOUSE FLAG

The Elizabethan custom of "sounding" a trumpet three times before the play began survived from the strolling players' device of gathering an audience by means of a parade, enlivened by costumes, drums, pipes, and a trumpet or two. The parade ended in the hall or inn-yard selected for the day's performance. By the middle of the sixteenth century the stronger troupes wintered in London

[50] *Elizabethan Stage*, ii. 546, note 2, quoting Morley, *Character Writing*, p. 285.

[51] Middleton's *Black Book*, Prologue; Dekker's *Raven's Almanacke*; *The Brazen Age* (see the direction quoted on p. 368; the implication, of course, is that the star shines not by itself, but in company with the stars of other heroes); *The Court Secret*, I; *The Fair Maid of the Exchange*, I; *Hamlet*, II. iii; *No Wit, no Help, like a Woman's*, V. i; *The Queen of Aragon*, III; *The Silver Age*, II; *The Wonder of a Kingdom*, III. i. See also the plate referred to in note 44 above.

[52] Cited by Boswell, *Restoration Court Stage*, p. 237.

and became identified with some suitable inn in which the balconied yard was reserved for their use and permanently equipped. Performing daily in the same place at a fixed hour, actors no longer needed to parade in order to attract patrons, but they continued to sound a short series of "flourishes" to warn stragglers that the play was about to begin. The response of Londoners to these soundings roused the ire of Puritan preachers: "Wyll not a fylthye playe, wyth the blast of a Trumpette, sooner call thyther a thousande, than an houres tolling of a Bell, bring to the Sermon a hundred?" [53] But plays, players, and the custom of sounding persisted. (De Witt shows the trumpeter sounding from the doorway of the Swan hut.)

When, following the edict of 1574, acting companies were forced out of the city to playhouses erected in Shoreditch and the Bankside, the need arose for a signal visible a mile or two away. Actors were ready, as in the past, to perform every afternoon, but no one could tell until the morning what the plague bill would decree, or what the skies might bring. The first of many references to the hoisting of a flag to announce that a play would be given that afternoon occurs not long after Burbage opened his Theater in 1576. "There is no Dicing house, Bowling alley, Cock pit, or Theater," writes John Field,[54] "that can be found empty [even on the Sabbath Day]. Those flagges of defiance against God, & trumpets that are blown to gather together such company, will sooner prevail to fill those places then the preaching of the holy worde of God . . . to fill Churches." A later comment in *The Curtain-Drawer of the World*, 1612, is to the same effect: "Each play-house advanceth his flagge in the aire, whither quickly at the waving thereof are summoned whole troops of men, women, and children." [55]

---

[53] John Stockwood, *A Sermon Preached at Paules Crosse*, 1578, p. 23.

[54] *A godly exhortation . . . giuen to all estates for their instruction, concerning the keeping of the Sabboth day*, 1583. Cited from Chambers, iv. 219.

[55] P. 55. Cf. *Variorum* (1821), iii. 65n.

Henslowe's entry concerning the refurbishing of the Rose in 1592 — "Jtm. pd for a maste . . . xijs." [56] — probably refers to his purchase of a flagpole for that playhouse. The cost seems appropriate in view of the 25 shillings he gave "in parte payment" for a stage post while erecting the Fortune in 1600. Henslowe's records also show that when the Worcester's Men came to the Rose in 1602 he bought for them a new flag: "Layd owt for the company the 4 of september 1602 to bye a flage of sylke the some of xxvjs. 8d." [57] In the seventeenth century silk appears to have been the usual material for playhouse flags.[58]

The flag in De Witt's sketch of the Swan displays a swan upon a white background. A St. George's cross appears on the flags represented in Hondius's Bear Garden and Rose, Delaram's Rose (the cross is distinguishable in an enlarged reproduction), and Hollar's Globe. None of these representations, however, has the authority of Visscher's panorama, which (together with the Visscher-Hondius, Merian, and other derivative views) shows a large and entirely unmarked white flag, visible, one would suppose, as far away as Westminster.

The following references and allusions to playhouse flags are typical of many more occurring in plays and pamphlets

[56] *Diary*, p. 7.

[57] *Papers*, p. 9. For discussion see above, Chapter IV, note 47.

[58] See "A Sonnet upon the Pitiful Burning of the Globe" (cited by Adams, p. 254), the third stanza:

> This fearful fire began above,
> A wonder strange and true,
> And to the stage-house did remove,
> As round as taylor's clew,
> And burnt down both beam and snagg,
> And did not spare the silken flagg.
> *Oh sorrow*, etc.

Cf. Heywood's translation of *De Arte Amandi*, i. 103; speaking of Roman theatres:

> In those days from the marble house did waive
> No sail, no silken flag, no ensign brave.

of the period. From the *Elegy on the Death of Richard Burbadge*: [59]

> And you his sad Compannions, to whome Lent
> Becomes more Lenton by this Accident,
> Hence forth your wauing flagg, no more hang out
> Play now no more att all, when round aboute
> Wee looke and miss the Atlas of your spheare.

From *A Mad World, my Masters*, I. i:

Follywit. Nay, faith, as for blushing, I thinke there's grace little enough amongst you all; 'tis Lent in your cheeks, the flag's down.

(These two passages allude to the closing of all playhouses during Lent.) Dekker, in *Work for Armourers*, 1609,[60] turns to the missing flag as a means of expressing how deserted all theatres seemed during a long idleness enforced by the plague: "Play-houses stand (like Tavernes that have cast out their masters) the dores locked up, the Flagges (like their Bushes) taken down." A similar observation occurs in *A New Book of Mistakes, or Bulls with Tales and Buls without Tales*, 1637: "The Red Bull in Saint Johns Streete . . . for the present (alack the while) is not suffred to carrie the flagge in the maine top." When in 1642 the Puritans closed all playhouses, the destitute actors sought authority to reopen, pleading, "Our boyes, ere wee shall have libertie to act againe, will be growne out of use, like crackt organ pipes, and have faces as old as our flags."[61]

But in happier days the hoisting of the flag brought crowds to the playhouses. From *A Mad World, my Masters*, III. iii:

Follywit. Well, say you have faire warning on't, the hayre about the hat is as good as a flag uppo' the pole, at a common Playhouse, to waft company.

[59] See Chapter III, note 6.
[60] *Works*, ed. Grosart, iv. 96.
[61] *The Actors Remonstrance, or Complaint for the Silencing of their Profession*, 1643, p. 6.

Observe the implication in the foregoing quotation that private theatres did not display flags. On the other hand, flags appear over the Bear Garden in most views between 1593 and 1647, and texts occasionally supply references to them, as in Turner's *Nosce Te*, 1607:

> Let heaven and earth with merry noise resound.
> The Flagge hanges out, to day thei'l baite the beares.

Or in Taylor's *Bull, Beare, and Horse*, 1638:

> And that we have obtain'd againe the Game
> Our Paris-Garden Flag proclaimes the same.

In short, the hoisted playhouse flag meant the actor's prosperity. When it waved above the huts all was well. For the time being the plague and the Puritans could be forgotten. Upon seeing the flag, London citizens of every degree would pause in the streets to scan the bills announcing the day's play at the Globe, or the Fortune, or the "tear-throat" Red Bull.

Atop the huts the flag continued to wave until the play was over. Then, as the audience streamed homeward, the halyards were loosened and the flag was taken in.

Plain-dealing. Shee takes downe the flagge, belike their play is done.[62]

[62] *The Whore of Babylon*, G3 verso.

APPENDICES

Appendix A

THE GLOBE PLAYHOUSE IN CONTEMPORARY MAPS AND VIEWS OF LONDON

TEN MAPS and views of London were published after 1592 and before 1658.[1] Nine of these were engraved between 1599, the year in which the first Globe was erected, and 1644, the year in which the second Globe was demolished, or were based upon views made within that period. Only six, however, have any bearing on the identity and shape of the Globe. Correctly to interpret the series as a whole one must start with Norden's map of 1593, the first map to illustrate the location of a Bankside playhouse.[2]

Norden shows two crudely drawn circular amphitheatres in the Liberty of the Clink. He labels the more westerly one "The Beare howse" and the more easterly one, farther back from the Thames, "The play howse." Not only are both structures named correctly,[3] but the location of each is indicated with considerable accuracy.[4] "The Beare Howse" (or Bear Garden) was erected in the spring of 1583 to replace the Paris Garden arena which collapsed in January of that year. The new building lay approximately 200 feet south of the Thames and to the west of Rose Alley.[5] "The play howse" (or Rose) was erected in 1587; and in 1593 it was still the only playhouse south of the Thames except for the seldom-used inn-theatre at Newington Butts (not included in any Bankside map) a mile distant from the southern end of London Bridge.[6] The Rose playhouse property consisted of a plot 94 feet square lying in the corner formed by Maiden Lane (later Maid Lane and now Park Street) on the south and Rose Alley, an alley some 400 feet long

[1] The maps are listed in full by Adams, pp. 457–459. For discussion see Chambers, ii. 353–354, 376–379, and 433.

[2] Cf. Adams, frontispiece and p. 147.

[3] The identity is accepted by all scholars. For discussion see Adams, p. 143; Chambers, ii. 377.

[4] See the reconstruction of Bankside lanes and properties superimposed upon the Ordnance Survey Plan of 1917 by W. W. Braines, *The Site of the Globe Playhouse*, 1924, p. 96.

[5] Distances are measured from the map drawn to scale by Braines, *Site of the Globe*, p. 91.

[6] Adams, pp. 136–141.

"leadinge [south] from the Ryver of thames into the saide parcell of grownde," [7] on the west.[8] Maiden Lane and some part of Rose Alley are both shown by Norden. The Rose Playhouse stood, therefore, approximately 120 feet east and *150 feet south* of its neighbor, the Bear Garden.[9] The proximity of the two amphitheatres is attested by Dekker's ironical comment in *Satiromastix* (1602):

Thou hadst a breath as sweet as the Rose that grows by the Beare-Garden, as sweet as the proud'st head of Garlicke in England.

The second view relating to the playhouse, Delaram's equestrian portrait of James I placed against a background consisting of the City of London, the Thames, and Southwark, is undated (it is ascribed to the period 1603–1620 [10]); but since it shows the Bankside in the coronation year 1603, and since it is the only map of the Bankside between 1599 (when the Globe was erected) and 1605 (when the Rose was torn down [11]), it alone is in a position to include the Bear Garden and both the Globe and the Rose playhouses. Delaram accordingly shows three flagged but unlabeled amphitheatres (the middle one circular, the other two octagonal), two of which are placed, with regard to each other and to the river, in precisely the same way as Norden's Bear Garden and Rose. Presumably, therefore, the third, and added, structure must be the Globe, erected six years after Norden's map was made. If so, the Globe was octagonal, stood well to the east of both its older neighbors, and was as close to the Thames as the Bear Garden. Its position *east* of the Rose Playhouse is confirmed by the names given to the alleys serving as approaches to these two playhouses. Later Bankside maps and records indicate a Globe Alley which ran west from Deadman's Place (the eastern boundary of the Liberty of the Clink) and turned at right angles north to Maiden Lane. The north-south extension of Globe Alley lay parallel to and approximately 300 feet *east* of Rose Alley.[12]

We come to the crux of the problem in turning to the third map, by Hondius, dated 1610, a small view of London set in a large map of "The Kingdome of Great Britaine and Ireland" printed in John Speed's *Theatre of the Empire of Great Britaine*, London, 1611. (This map may be taken as identical with two still later small inset views appearing on the title-pages of Henry Holland's *Herwologia Anglica*, 1620, and Sir Richard Baker's *Chronicle*, 1643, for, with respect to the Bankside playhouses, all three are substantially the same and probably derive from the same source.[13]) In Hondius, as might be expected from the date,

[7] *Henslowe Papers*, pp. 2–3.
[8] Adams, pp. 144 and 245.
[9] See note 5 above.
[10] Chambers, ii. 354, 377.

[11] Adams, p. 160.
[12] See note 5 above.
[13] Adams, p. 458; Chambers, ii. 354.

only two flagged amphitheatres (the western one octagonal, the eastern one circular) are shown, for the Rose was abandoned in 1605 and disappeared, leaving only the Bear Garden and the Globe in the Liberty of the Clink. The more westerly of Hondius's two structures is unquestionably the same Bear Garden that appears in Norden and Delaram; and if the date on the Hondius plate means that the view reflects the Bankside as it appeared between 1605 and 1610, one must assume that

THE BEAR GARDEN AND THE ROSE, *circa* 1593

Vignette from the title-page of Baker's *Chronicle*, 1643

Hondius intended his other flagged structure to represent the Globe. But if the date 1610 stands merely for the year in which the plate was engraved, then the view may well be taken to reflect the source from which Hondius worked, that is, some map of the Bankside executed between 1587, when two amphitheatres existed there, placed precisely as in Hondius, and 1599, when the Globe made a third in the Bankside group.

As they stand, Norden's and Hondius's maps lead to different and irreconcilable interpretations as to the identity of the middle (cylindrical) amphitheatre shown in Delaram's view. Norden, as we have seen, is supported in his placements and identifications by documentary evidence from other sources; and, according to Norden, Delaram's middle amphitheatre must be the Rose. But according to the date on the

Hondius plate, Delaram's middle amphitheatre must be the Globe. Both artists cannot be right unless the Rose was dismantled at some time between 1593 and 1599 to make its site available for the Globe — a supposition which is quite inadmissible. Moreover, if Delaram's middle structure is the Globe, then his easternmost structure, shown near the Thames and at a considerable distance from the Bear Garden, must be the Rose. But this supposition likewise is inadmissible, for in fact (1) the Rose Playhouse lay within a few yards of Maiden Lane at the point where the Lane was at its greatest distance (approximately 400 feet) from the Thames; (2) the Rose and the Bear Garden stood near to each other; and (3) the relative position of the Rose and the Globe — the Rose to the west and the Globe at some distance to the east — is established beyond question by the street names surviving for a century or more on the Bankside.

In light of these facts it is evident that despite the date on his plate, Hondius's cylindrical amphitheatre, standing precisely where the Rose should stand, is not the Globe. One may assume that his view (and also the later inset views in books by Holland and by Baker) was developed not from a first-hand study of the Bankside but from some earlier map made in the period 1587–1699. But whatever the source, the date on the Hondius view must be regarded as misleading. Instead of providing a key whereby one can determine the identity of the three flagged structures included in Delaram's view, it indicates nothing more than the year in which the plate was engraved; and hence we are justified in concluding that Hondius provides merely a belated picture of the Bear Garden and the Rose Playhouse as they existed prior to 1599.

So long as the Hondius view was accepted at its face value, scholars were unable to reconcile the seemingly conflicting evidence of the Bankside views.[14] It was argued, for example, (1) that only the Hondius view, dated 1610, could be ascribed with confidence to the period 1599–1613 when the first Globe was in existence; (2) that the derivative inset views appearing in Holland's *Herωologia Anglica*, 1620, and in Baker's *Chronicle*, 1643 — books contemporary with the second Globe — confirmed the Hondius representation of the Globe as a cylindrical structure; and (3) that Hollar's great "Long View" of 1647 (and its late derivative by de Wit, *ca.* 1690) gave authority to the series as a whole and to the representation of the Globe as circular in shape. The evidence for an octagonal Globe furnished by (1) the undated Delaram portrait of James I with its panoramic background of London, executed sometime between 1603 and 1620, (2) the large and detailed Visscher-Hondius panoramic view, dated 1616, and (3) its later derivatives by Merian, 1637, by "Ryther," 1636–1645, and others still later — this

[14] See, for example, Chambers, ii. 377–379.

evidence was held to be no more authoritative than that of the round-Globe series of Bankside views, and was regarded as less pertinent to a discussion of the first Globe because no member of the octagonal-Globe series could be ascribed with confidence to the period 1599–1613.

But once it is understood that the Hondius plate, though engraved in 1610, represents the Bankside as it appeared between 1587 and 1599, the entire case for a cylindrical Globe collapses. (1) The Hondius inset view can have no bearing upon the shape of the Globe. (2) The Holland and Baker inset views, developed from Hondius or from a source common to all three, also must reflect a period before the first Globe was erected. (3) Only the Long View, dated 1647 (together with one very late derivative) remains. But the Long View, dated three years after the Globe was demolished, four years after Hollar left England, and five years after the edict which closed all theatres, has nothing like the authority when standing alone that it had when forming one of a series. Compared to the Delaram, Visscher-Hondius, and Merian series executed between 1603 and 1638 (years in which the first and second Globes flourished), the Long View must be regarded as inaccurate in its representation of a cylindrical Globe. Add, moreover, to the series of contemporary views the superb Visscher original, 1606–1614 (unknown to the proponents of the cylindrical Globe theory), and the case for an octagonal Globe is established beyond question.

Appendix B

THE FORTUNE BUILDER'S CONTRACT

[The Fortune Playhouse builder's contract, dated January 8, 1599/
1600, by Peter Streete, master carpenter, with Philip Henslowe and Edward Alleyn, joint owners, for the erection of the Fortune at a cost of
£440. The contract exempts Streete from having to paint the woodwork
or to "render" the plastered interior walls, work subsequently undertaken by the owners at a cost of £80. Printed in type-facsimile from
Dulwich Muniments, No. 22, by W. W. Greg, *Henslowe Papers*, pp. 4–7,
from which this verbatim transcript is made.]

This Indenture made the Eighte daie of Januarye 1599 And in the
Twoe and ffortyth yeare of the Reigne of our sovereigne Ladie Elizabeth
by the grace of god Queene of Englande ffraunce and Jrelande defender
of the ffaythe &c Betwene Phillipp Henslowe and Edwarde Allen of the
p[ar]ishe of Ste Savio^rs in Southwark in the Countie of Surrey gentlemen
on thone p[ar]te And Peeter Streete Cittizen and Carpenter of London
on thother parte **witnesseth** That whereas the saide Phillipp Henslowe & Edward Allen the daie of the date hereof Haue bargayned com-
pounded & agreed wth the saide Peter Streete ffor the erectinge buildinge
& settinge upp of a newe howse and Stadge for a Plaiehouse in and
vppon a certeine plott or p[ar]cell of grounde appoynted oute for that
purpose Scytuate and beinge nere Goldinge lane in the p[ar]ishe of
Ste Giles w^thoute Cripplegate of London To be by him the saide Peeter
Streete or some other sufficyent woorkmen of his provideinge and
appoyntem^te and att his propper Costes & Chardges for the consid-
erac[i]on hereafter in theis p[rese]ntes expressed [/] Made erected,
builded and sett upp Jn manner & forme followinge (that is to saie) The
frame of the saide howse to be sett square and to conteine ffowerscore
foote of lawfull assize everye waie square w^thoutt and fiftie fiue foote of
like assize square everye waie w^thin wth a good suer ¹ and stronge foun-
dac[i]on of pyles brick lyme and sand bothe w^thout & w^thin ² to be
wroughte one foote of assize att the leiste aboue the grounde And the
saide fframe to conteine Three Stories in heighth The first or lower
Storie to Conteine Twelue foote of lawfull assize in heighth The second
Storie Eleauen foote of lawfull assize in heigth And the Third or vpper

---

¹ *suer*, i.e. sure.   ² I.e., for both outer and inner walls.

Storie to conteine Nyne foote of lawfull assize in height [/] **All which** Stories shall conteine Twelue foote and a halfe of lawfull assize in breadth througheoute besides a Juttey forwardes in either [3] of the saide Twoe vpper Stories of Tenne ynches of lawfull assize with ffower convenient divisions for gentlemens roomes and other sufficient and convenient divisions for Twoe pennie roomes wth necessarie Seates to be placed and sett Aswell in those roomes as througheoute all the rest of the galleries of the saide howse and wth suchelike steares Conveyances & divisions w^thoute & w^thin as are made & Contryved in and to the late erected Plaiehowse On the Banck in the saide p[ar]ishe of S^to Savio^rs Called the Globe W^th a Stadge and Tyreinge howse to be made erected & settupp w^thin the saide fframe wth a shadowe or cover over the saide Stadge wch Stadge shalbe placed & sett As alsoe the stearecases of the saide fframe in suche sorte as is p^r[e]figured in a Plott thereof drawen [4] And wch Stadge shall conteine in length ffortie and Three foote of lawfull assize and in breadth to extende to the middle of the yarde of the saide howse The same Stadge to be paled in belowe wth good stronge and sufficyent newe oken bourdes And likewise the lower Storie of the saide fframe w^thinside, and the same lower storie to be alsoe laide over and fenced wth stronge yron pykes And the saide Stadge to be in all other proporc[i]ons Contryved and fashioned like vnto the Stadge of the saide Plaie howse Called the Globe W^th convenient windowes and lightes glazed to the saide Tyreinge howse And the saide fframe Stadge and Stearecases to be covered wth Tyle and to haue a sufficient gutter of lead to Carrie & convey the water frome the Coveringe of the saide Stadge to fall backwardes And also all the saide fframe and the Stairecases thereof to be sufficyently enclosed w^thoute wth lathe lyme & haire and the gentlemens roomes and Twoe pennie roomes to be seeled wth lathe lyme & haire and all the fflowers [5] of the saide Galleries Stories and Stadge to be bourded wth good & sufficyent newe deale bourdes of the whole thicknes wheare need shalbe **And** the saide howse and other thinges beforemenc[i]o[n]ed to be made & doen To be in all other Contrivitions [6] Conveyances fashions thinge and thinges effected finished and doen accordinge to the manner and fashion of the saide howse Called the Globe Saveinge only that all the princypall and maine postes of the saide fframe and Stadge forwarde [7] shalbe square and wroughte palasterwise wth carved proporc[i]ons Called Satiers to be placed & sett on the Topp of every of the same postes And saveinge alsoe that the said Peeter Streete shall not be chardged wth anie manner of pay[ntin]ge in or aboute the saide fframe howse or Stadge or anie

---

[3] *either*, i.e. each.
[4] The "Plott" is no longer extant.
[5] *fflowers*, i.e. floors.

[6] *Contrivitions*, i.e. contrivances.
[7] *forwarde*, i.e. fronting the courtyard.

p[ar]te thereof nor Rendringe [8] the walls w[th]in Nor seeling anie more
or other roomes then the gentlemens roomes Twoe pennie roomes and
Stadge before remembred [/] **nowe theiruppon** the saide Peeter
Streete dothe conven[a]nt promise and graunte ffor himself his executo[rs] and admi[ni]strato[rs] to and w[th] the saide Phillipp Henslowe and
Edward Allen and either of them and thexecuto[rs] and admi[ni]strato[rs]
of them and either of them by theis p[rese]ntes Jn manner & forme followeinge (that is to saie) That he the saide Peeter Streete his executo[rs]
or assignes shall & will att his or their owne propper costes & Chardges
Well woorkmanlike & substancyallie make erect, sett upp and fully
finishe Jn and by all thinges accordinge to the true meaninge of theis
p[rese]ntes w[th] good stronge and substancyall newe Tymber and other
necessarie stuff All the saide fframe and other woorkes whatsoever Jn
and vppon the saide plott or p[ar]cell of grounde (beinge not by anie
aucthoretie Restrayned, and haveinge ingres egres & regres to doe the
same) before the ffyue & twentith daie of Julie next Comeinge after the
date hereof **And shall alsoe** at his or theire like costes and Chardges
Provide and finde All manner of woorkmen Tymber Joystes Rafters
boordes dores boltes hinges brick Tyle lathe lyme haire sande nailes
lade [9] Jron Glasse woorkmanshipp and other thinges whatsoever w[ch]
shalbe needefull Convenyent & necessarie for the saide fframe & woorkes
& eu[r]ie p[ar]te thereof **And** shall alsoe make all the saide fframe in
every poynte for Scantlinges [10] lardger and bigger in assize Then the
Scantlinges of the Timber of the saide newe erected howse Called the
Globe [/] **And alsoe** that he the saide Peeter Streete shall furthw[th]
aswell by himself As by suche other and soemanie woorkmen as shalbe
Convenient & necessarie enter into and vppon the saide buildinges and
woorkes And shall in reasonable manner proceede therein w[th]oute anie
wilfull detracc[i]on vntill the same shalbe fully effected and finished [/]
In consideracõn of all w[ch] buildinges and of all stuff & woorkeman-
shipp thereto belonginge The saide Phillipp Henslowe & Edward Allen
and either of them ffor themselues theire and either of theire executo[rs]
& admi[ni]strato[rs] doe Joynctlie & seu[r]allie Coven[a]nte & graunte to
& w[th] the saide Peeter Streete his executo[rs] & admi[ni]strato[rs] by theis
p[rese]ntes That they the saide Phillipp Henslowe & Edward Allen or
one of them Or the executo[rs] admi[ni]strato[rs] or assignes of them or
one of them Shall & will well & truelie paie or Cawse to be paide vnto

[8] *Rendringe.* 'Render, to give the finishing coat of plaster to a wall.' Halliwell, *Architectural Dictionary*, cited by Greg.

[9] *lade*, i.e. lead.

[10] *Scantlinges*, i.e. the measurement of timber in cross-section. (Cf. the Hope contract where such measurements are given.) The Fortune Playhouse was thus to be made sturdier than the Globe, but not, so far as this specification is concerned, larger.

the saide Peeter Streete his executo^{rs} or assignes Att the place aforesaid
appoynted for the erectinge of the saide fframe The full some of ffower
hundred & ffortie Poundes of lawfull money of Englande in manner &
forme followeinge (that is to saie) Att suche tyme And when as the
Tymberwoork of the saide fframe shalbe rayzed ^{11} & sett upp by the
saide Peeter Streete his executo^{rs} or assignes Or wthin Seaven daies then
next followeinge Twoe hundred & Twentie poundes And att suche time
and when as the saide fframe & woorkes shalbe fullie effected & ffyn-
ished as is aforesaide Or wthin Seaven daies then next followeinge,
thother Twoe hundred and Twentie poundes wthoute fraude or Coven
Prouided allwaies and it is agreed betwene the saide parties That
whatsoever some or somes of money the saide Phillipp Henslowe &
Edward Allen or either of them or thexecuto^{rs} or assignes of them or
either of them shall lend or deliver vnto the saide Peter Streete his exec-
uto^{rs} or assignes or anie other by his appoyntem^{te} or consent ffor or
concerninge the saide Woorkes or anie p[ar]te thereof or anie stuff
thereto belonginge before the raizeinge & setteinge upp of the saide
fframe, shalbe reputed accepted taken & accoumpted in p[ar]te of the
firste paym[en]^{te} aforesaid of the saide some of ffower hundred & ffortie
poundes And all suche some & somes of money as they or anie of them
shall as aforesaid lend or deliver betwene the razeinge of the saide
fframe & finishinge thereof and of all the rest of the saide woorkes
Shalbe reputed accepted taken & accoumpted in p[ar]te of the laste
pa[y]m[en]te aforesaid of the same some of ffower hundred & ffortie
poundes Anie thinge abouesaid to the contrary notwthstandinge [/]
In witnes whereof the p[ar]ties abouesaid to theis p[rese]nte Jnden-
tures Jnterchaungeably haue sett theire handes and seales [/] Yeoven
the daie and yeare ffirste abouewritten.

P S

Sealed and deliu^{r}ed by the saide Peter Streete in the p^r[e]sence of
me william Harris Pub[lic] Scr[ivener] And me Frauncis Smyth ap-
pr[entice] to the said Scr[ivener]

[seal wanting; endorsed:]
Peater Streat ffor The Building of the ffortune

^{11} *rayzed*, i.e. raised.

Appendix C

THE HOPE BUILDER'S CONTRACT

[The Hope Playhouse builder's contract, by Gilbert Katherens with Philip Henslowe and Jacob Meade, dated August 29, 1613, for the replacement of the Bear Garden at the cost of £360. Printed in type-facsimile from *Dulwich Muniments*, No. 49, by W. W. Greg, *Henslowe Papers*, pp. 19–22, from which this verbatim transcript is made.]

Articles Covenauntes grauntes and agreementes Concluded and agreed vppon this Nyne and Twenteithe daie of Auguste Anno Dñi 1613 [/] Betwene Phillipe Henslowe of the p[ar]ishe of St Savio^r in sowthworke wth in the coũtye of Surr· Esquire, and Jacobe Maide of the p[ar]ishe of St Olaves in sowthworke aforesaide waterman of thone p[ar]tie, And Gilbert Katherens of the saide p[ar]ishe of St Saviour in sowthworke Carpenter on theother p[ar]tie, As followeth That is to saie

Imprimis the saide Gilbert Katherens for him, his executo^rs administrato^rs and assignes dothe covenaunt p[ro]mise and graunt to and wth the saide Phillipe Henslowe and Jacobe Maide and either of them, thexecutors administrato^rs & assigns of them and either of them by theise p[rese]ntes in manner and forme followinge That he the saied Gilbert Katherens his executo^rs administrato^rs or assignes shall and will at his or theire owne proper costes and charges vppon or before the last daie of November next ensuinge the daie of the date of the date of theise p[rese]ntes above written, not onlie take downe or pull downe all that Same place or house wherin Beares and Bulls haue been heretofore vsuallie bayted, And also one other house or staple wherin Bulls and horsses did vsuallie stande, Sett lyinge and beinge vppon or neere the Banksyde in the saide p[ar]ishe of St Saviour in sowthworke Comonlie Called or knowne by the name of the Beare garden [/] But shall also at his or theire owne proper costes and Charges vppon or before the saide laste daie of November newly erect, builde and sett vpp one other Same place or Plaiehouse fitt & convenient in all thinges, bothe for players to playe Jn, And for the game of Beares and Bulls to be bayted in the same, And also A fitt and convenient Tyre house and a stage to be carryed or taken awaie, and to stande vppon tressells good substanciall and sufficient for the carryinge and bearinge of suche a stage, And shall new builde erect and sett vp againe the saide plaie house or game place neere or vppon the saide place, where the saide

game place did heretofore stande, And to builde the same of suche large
compasse, fforme, widenes, and height as the Plaie house Called the
Swan in the libertie of Parris garden in the saide p[ar]ishe of St Saviour,
now is [/] And shall also builde two stearecasses wthout and adioyninge
to the saide Playe house in suche convenient places as shalbe moste fitt
and convenient for the same to stande vppon, and of such largnes and
height as the stearecasses of the saide playehouse called the Swan, nowe
are or bee [/] And shall also builde the Heavens all over the saide stage
to be borne or carryed wthout any postes or supporters to be fixed or
sett vppon the saide stage, And all gutters of leade needfull for the
carryage of all suche Raine water as shall fall vppon the same, And
shall also make Two Boxes in the lowermost storie fitt and decent for
gentlemen to sitt in [/] And shall make the p[ar]ticōns betwne the
Rommes as they are at the saide Plaie house called the Swan [/] And to
make Turned Cullumes vppon and over the stage ^{1} [/] And shall make
the Principalls ^{2} and fore fronte of the saide Plaie house of good and
sufficient oken Tymber, And no furr tymber to be putt or vsed in
the lower most, or midell stories, excepte the vpright postes on the
backparte of the saide stories (all the Byndinge Joystes ^{3} to be of oken
tymber) The Jnner principall postes of the first storie to be Twelve
footes in height and Tenn ynches square The Jnner principall postes in
the midell storie to be Eight ynches square The Jnner most postes in the
vpper storie to be seaven ynches square [/] The Prick postes ^{4} in the
first storie to be eight ynches square, in the seconde storie seaven ynches
square, and in the vpper most storie six ynches square [/] Also the
Brest sommers ^{5} in the lower moste storie to be nyne ynches depe, and
seaven ynches in thicknes and in the midell storie to be eight ynches
depe and six ynches in thicknes [/] The Byndinge Jostes of the firste
storie to be nyne and Eight ynches in depthe and thicknes and in the
midell storie to be viij and vij ynches in depthe and thicknes [/] **Item**
to make a good, sure, and sufficient foundacōn of Brickes for the saide
Play house or game place and to make it xiij^{teene} ^{6} ynches at the leaste
above the grounde **Item** to new builde, erect, and sett vpp the saide

---

^{1} Implying that elsewhere the posts were square?

^{2} *Principalls*, i.e. main vertical posts of the frame.

^{3} *Byndinge Joystes*, i.e. main horizontal beams crossing between inner and outer walls.

^{4} *Prick postes*, i.e. vertical posts between the corner posts.

^{5} "*Breastsummer*. A 'summer' or beam extending horizontally over a large opening, and sustaining the whole superstructure of wall, etc." *N.E.D.*, cited by Greg.

^{6} The corresponding clause in the Fortune contract reads: "one foote of assize att the leiste aboue the grounde."

Bull house and stable wth good and sufficient scantlinge tymber plankes and bordes and p[ar]ticōns of that largnes and fittnes as shalbe sufficient to kepe and holde six bulls and Three horsses or geldinges, wth Rackes and mangers to the same, And also a lofte or storie over the saide house as nowe it is [/] **And** shall also at his & theire owne prop[er] costes and charges new tyle wth Englishe tyles all the vpper Rooffe of the saide Plaie house game place and Bull house or stable, And shall fynde and paie for at his like proper costes and charges for all the lyme, heare,[7] sande, Brickes, tyles, lathes nayles, workemanshipe and all other thinges needfull and necessarie for the full finishinge of the said Plaie house Bull house and stable [/] And the saide Plaiehouse or game place to be made in althinges and in suche forme and fashion, as the saide plaie house called the swan (the scantling of the tymbers, tyles, and foundacōn as ys aforesaide wthout fraude or coven) **And the saide** Phillipe Henslow and Jacobe maide and either of them for them, thexecutors administrato^{r}s and assignes of them and either of them doe covenant and graunt to and wth the saide Gilbert Katherens his executo^{r}s administrato^{r}s and assignes in mann^r and forme followinge (That is to saie) That he the saide Gilbert or his assignes shall or maie haue, and take to his or their vse and behoofe not onlie all the tymber benches seates, slates, tyles Brickes and all other thinges belonginge to the saide Game place & Bull house or stable, And also all suche olde tymber whiche the saide Phillipe Henslow hathe latelie bought beinge of an old house in Thames street, London, whereof moste parte is now lyinge in the Yarde or Backsyde of the saide Bearegarden **And** also to satisfie and paie vnto the saide Gilbert Katherens his executors administrato^{r}s or assignes for the doinge and finishinges of the Workes and buildinges aforesaid the somme of Three Hundered and three score poundes of good and lawffull monie of England in mann^r and forme followinge (That is to saie) Jn hande at thensealinge and deliuery hereof Three score pounds wch the saide Gilbert acknowlegeth him selfe by theise p[rese]ntes to haue Receaued, And more over to paie every Weeke weeklie duringe the firste Six weekes vnto the saide Gilbert or his assignes when he shall sett workemen to worke vppon or about the buildinge of the p^{r}misses the somme of Tennepoundes of lawffull monie of Englande to paie them there Wages (yf theire wages dothe amount vnto somuche monie,) And when the saide plaie house Bull house and stable are Reared then to make vpp the saide Wages one hundered poundes of lawffull monie of England, and to be paide to the saide Gilbert or his assignes, And when the saide Plaie house Bull house and stable are Reared tyled walled, then to paie vnto the saide Gilbert Katherens or his assignes, One other hundered poundes of lawffull monie of England [/] And when the saide Plaie house, Bull house and stable

[7] *heare*, i.e. hair.

are fullie finished builded and done in mann^r and forme aforesaide,
Then to paie vnto the saide Gilbert Katherens or his assignes, One
other hundred Poundes of lawffull monie of England in full satis-
facõn and payment of the saide somme of CCClx^ll And to all and
singuler the Covenantes grauntes Articles and agreementes above in
theise p[rese]ntes Contayned whiche on the parte and behalfe of the
saide Gilbert Katherens his executo^rs administrators or assignes are
ought to be observed p[er]formed fulfilled and done, the saide Gilbert
Katherens byndeth himselfe his executo^rs administrators and assignes,
vnto the saide Phillipe Henslowe and Jacob Maide and to either of
them, thexecuto^rs administrato^rs and assignes of them or either of them
by theise p[rese]ntes **In witnes** whereof the saide Gilbert Katherens
hath herevnto sett his hande and seale the daie and yere firste above
written

the mark   G K   of Gilbert Katherens

[no trace of seal; witnessed on back:]

Sealed and Deliuered in the p^rsence of
witnes Moyses Bowler

    Edwarde Griffin

[endorsed, last three words added by Alleyn:]

Gilbert Katherens articles & bond

Appendix D

STAIRS ON THE TIRING–HOUSE FAÇADE

IN THE one earlier attempt to determine the nature and location of the actors' stairs W. J. Lawrence (*Pre-Restoration Stage Studies*, pp. 16–23) brings together six citations implying movement from one level to another (but lacking the word "exit") in an effort to prove that "an outer visible staircase" (distinct from the actors' stairs inside) existed on the tiring-house façade. Relative to a passage of dialogue in *The Sea Voyage*, II. i, he writes: "Albert begins a speech on the lower level and finishes it on the upper," implying that during Albert's ascent there was no break in the speech caused by his leaving the stage. Both early editions of the play, however, read as follows:

Albert. Follow me, my *Aminta*: my good genius
　Shew me the way still; still we are directed;
　When we gain the top of this near rising hill,
　We shall know further.
Exit. And Enter above.

Albert.
　Courteous *Zephyrus*, . . .

Here Lawrence's reliance upon a sophisticated text has misled him.

Again, commenting upon a line in the Rose play *Englishmen for my Money*, he writes:

[Pisaro's] three daughters are on the upper stage and their three English lovers below. At line 1859 Mathea says, "Prepare your armes, for thus we flie to you." Evidently the girls all rush down the [outer] stairs, for we have at once the direction, "They embrace."

Now close reading of the dialogue of which this line forms a part reveals that the direction has been entered in the text at least five lines too soon (a type of error familiar to all students of Elizabethan bibliography). The Malone Society edition reads (at line 1918):

Matt. Prepare your Armes, for thus we flie to you. *they Embrace.*

Walg[rave]. This workes like waxe, now ere to morrow day,
　If you two ply it but as well as I,　　　　　　　　[line 1920]
　Weele worke our landes out of *Pisaros* Daughters:

And cansell all our bondes in their great Bellies,
When the slaue knowes it, how the Roge will curse.
Matt. Sweete hart.
Walg. Matt.   [line 1925]
Mathe. Where art thou.
Pisa[ro]. Here.
Mathe. Oh Jesus heres our father.
Walg. The Diuell he is.

The scene takes place at night, and no lights are carried. In the dark,
therefore, it takes a second or two before Mathea (or Matt) and her
sisters can find their respective swains. The dialogue as a whole makes
sense only if (1) we add *"Exeunt above"* after "we flie to you," (2) if we
add *"Re-enter below Mathea, Marina, and Laurentia"* after line 1923,
and (3) if we transfer *"they Embrace"* to a position *after* line 1926. So
edited, Walgrave's five-line comment to his companions is spoken while
the girls are coming down (the interval is of normal length for such a
descent) and not in their hearing; and the absurdity of Mathea's calling
out "Where art thou" to Walgrave while she is in his arms is avoided.

Again, of a passage in *Julius Caesar*, V. iii, Lawrence writes:

Cassius and Pindarus are supposed to be standing on a hill. Cassius bids the man
go higher up and tell him what he sees. No "exit" is marked, but five lines later
Pindarus utters an exclamation, showing that he had been watching, and proceeds to describe the capture of Titinius. Cassius orders him to come down, and
two lines later he is evidently again on the lower stage, since Cassius bids him
"come hither" and stab him.

Here also Lawrence's source is faulty. The basic text for *Julius Caesar*
is the First Folio, which reads:

Cassi. Go *Pindarus*, get higher on that hill,
  My sight was ever thicke: regard *Titinius,*
  And tell me what thou not'st about the Field.
  This day I breathed first, Time is come round,
  And where I did begin, there shall I end,
  My life is run his compasse. Sirra, what newes?
Pind. Above. O my Lord.
Cassi. What newes?
Pind. Titinius is enclosed round about
  With Horsemen, that make to him on the Spurre,
  Yet he spurres on. Now they are almost on him:
  Now *Titinius.* Now some light: O he lights too.
  Hee's tane.   *Showt.*
  And hearke, they shout for joy.

Cassi. Come downe, behold no more:
   O Coward that I am, to live so long,
   To see my best Friend tane before my face.

                        Enter Pindarus.

   Come hither sirrah: . . .

Now in the light of the First Folio reading, Lawrence's hypothesis fails, for, needless to say, Pindarus's "exit" from the stage, whether marked or not, is implied when, a few lines later, a stage-direction in the text calls upon him to "enter."

Lawrence also cites at some length a passage from Middleton's *Family of Love*, I. iii, in which the character Lipsalve tells of having once witnessed a remarkable feat ("I saw Sampson bear the town-gates on his neck from the lower to the upper stage") in another play, *Samson* (no longer extant), at another playhouse, the Fortune. I do not question the possibility of such a feat having been performed at the Fortune, but I do question the ability of Lawrence or of anyone else to make a convincing case for "visible stairs" out of Lipsalve's unparticularized account.

The two remaining examples cited by Lawrence are also questionable, but instead of reviewing them let me briefly outline certain larger objections to his theory of visible stairs constructed in the scenic wall.

(1) The evidence supporting such a theory is far from clear. The best that even Lawrence can say of it is that some half-dozen passages "seem to support the theory."

(2) Such a staircase would in one sense be unique: it would be the only major unit in the tiring-house façade *not* giving rise to repeated allusion in the dialogue and to stage business (compare the abundant textual references to doors, curtains, posts, and so forth, and the stage business and stage-directions relating to them).

(3) Such a staircase would be architecturally incongruous, for it could not rise in the middle of the stage because of the study opening. At one side it would make the stage unsymmetrical. Two staircases, one on either side, would inevitably have given rise to scenes exploiting the pageantry of paired ascents and descents, the excitement of stage chases, and so forth. But there are no such scenes.

(4) I doubt if there was room for a practicable staircase unless at the expense of the inner-stage opening or of the width of the stage doors. Lawrence, one observes, does not attempt to suggest precisely where his proposed staircase could be set.

(5) Scenes in which scaling ladders were employed in mounting to the "walls" or in which rope ladders were lowered from the window-stages would have been theatrically unconvincing had there been visible stairs leading to those upper stages from the platform below. An Eliza-

bethan audience was accustomed to accept the stage doors as "city gates," the balcony as "walls," and the scenic wall itself as a "cliff" or a "hill." Guided by emphatic dialogue, it could even disregard the presence of the tiring-house façade altogether. Similar demands are successfully made of a modern audience. But there are limits to what the imagination can accept or ignore. It is one thing to treat a wide balcony as battlements; it is quite another to set up scaling ladders to assault those battlements and ignore a permanent staircase palpably giving access to them.

INDEX

Index